DREAMING
WIDE AWAKE

"David Jay Brown's book is a brilliant synthesis of current research, ancient and indigenous wisdom, and extensive personal experience. Based on a wealth of hard data, historical research, and dream diaries, Brown deftly ties together not only lucid dreams but also similar events from other altered states. While the book centers on lucid dreams, it incorporates parallel experiences in psychedelic use and shamanism, giving us, perhaps, the first sophisticated synthesis for exploring difficult to access realms of consciousness. Filled with practical and doable suggestions on how to enhance lucid dreaming and how to maximize its healing effects, *Dreaming Wide Awake* is a splendid, well-written, revelatory, yet pragmatic look at the dreaming mind."

JAMES FADIMAN PH.D., MICRODOSE RESEARCHER AND
AUTHOR OF *THE PSYCHEDELIC EXPLORER'S GUIDE:*
SAFE, THERAPEUTIC, AND SACRED JOURNEYS

"Encyclopedic yet personal, rigorous yet highly accessible, Brown's book is enormously successful. The author covers every conceivable theoretical and practical aspect of lucid dreaming: from neuroscience to shamanism, anthropology to the occult, ethnobotany to telepathy, the electronic to the pharmacologic. In so doing, he brings clarity and relevance to this mysterious and potentially highly influential consciousness-altering tool."

RICK STRASSMAN, M.D., CLINICAL ASSOCIATE PROFESSOR OF
PSYCHIATRY AT THE UNIVERSITY OF NEW MEXICO
SCHOOL OF MEDICINE AND AUTHOR OF *DMT: THE SPIRIT*
MOLECULE AND *DMT AND THE SOUL OF PROPHECY*

"For millennia, many tribal shamans have used lucid dreaming and psychedelic plants to obtain information that they have used in helping and healing members of their community. In this groundbreaking book, David Jay Brown has brought together findings from contemporary science to demonstrate the similarity between these two types of altered consciousness and how the insights they provide can help alleviate nightmares, restore health, hasten recovery from injuries, and even yield creative insights. *Dreaming Wide Awake* may evoke a new field of research, both experimental and applied, that will enhance human potentials in ways that have been too long neglected."

STANLEY KRIPPNER, PH.D., COAUTHOR OF
EXTRAORDINARY DREAMS AND HOW TO WORK WITH THEM

"With his customary precision and style, David Jay Brown illuminates the dreamtime . . . and he tells you how you can work and play in that dream space. An important book for true dreamers."

R. U. SIRIUS, MUSICIAN, DIGITAL CULTURE ICONOCLAST,
AND AUTHOR OF *TRANSCENDENCE: THE DISINFORMATION
ENCYCLOPEDIA OF TRANSHUMANISM AND THE SINGULARITY*

"Kapow. Brown's *Dreaming Wide Awake* connects the multidimensional dots that are strewn throughout the tiered cosmos. He goes far and deep into the mysteries of the dreaming mind and, even more impressively, does this with his feet planted on the ground and armed with a skeptical but compassionate outlook."

RYAN HURD, COEDITOR OF *LUCID DREAMING:
NEW PERSPECTIVES ON CONSCIOUSNESS IN SLEEP*
AND AUTHOR OF *DREAM LIKE A BOSS*

"A fascinating read. With curiosity and heart, David Jay Brown invites the reader to explore a unique fusion of shamanism, psychedelics, and lucid dreaming. Watch the doors between the worlds swing open!"

CLARE JOHNSON, PH.D., AUTHOR OF
BREATHING IN COLOUR AND *DREAMRUNNER*

DREAMING
WIDE AWAKE

Lucid Dreaming, Shamanic Healing,
and Psychedelics

DAVID JAY BROWN

Park Street Press
Rochester, Vermont • Toronto, Canada

Park Street Press
One Park Street
Rochester, Vermont 05767
www.ParkStPress.com

SUSTAINABLE FORESTRY INITIATIVE — Certified Sourcing
www.sfiprogram.org
SFI-00854

Text stock is SFI certified

Park Street Press is a division of Inner Traditions International

Note to the Reader: *The information in this book is provided for informational and
educational purposes only. Nothing in this book should be considered medical advice,
and the author is not responsible for how the information in this book is used.*

Library of Congress Cataloging-in-Publication Data
Names: Brown, David Jay, author.
Title: Dreaming wide awake : lucid dreaming, shamanic healing, and
    psychedelics / David Jay Brown.
Description: Rochester, Vermont : Park Street Press, 2016. | Includes
    bibliographical references and index.
Identifiers: LCCN 2016004548 (print) | LCCN 2016022673 (e-book) |
ISBN 9781620554890 (pbk.) | ISBN 9781620554906 (e-book)
Subjects: LCSH: Lucid dreams.
Classification: LCC BF1099.L82 B76 2016 (print) | LCC BF1099.L82 (e-book) |
    DDC 154.6/3—dc23
LC record available at https://lccn.loc.gov/2016004548

Printed and bound in the United States by Lake Book Manufacturing, Inc.
The text stock is SFI certified. The Sustainable Forestry Initiative® program
promotes sustainable forest management.

10 9 8 7 6 5 4 3 2 1

Text design by Virginia Scott Bowman and layout by Priscilla Baker
This book was typeset in Garamond Premier Pro with Berliner Grotesk, Scala
Sans, Legacy Sans, and Avenir used as display typefaces

To send correspondence to the author of this book, mail a first-class letter to the
author c/o Inner Traditions • Bear & Company, One Park Street, Rochester, VT
05767, and we will forward the communication, or contact the author directly at
dajabr@well.com.

For Rebecca Ann Hill,
my lucid-dream girl come true

CONTENTS

ACKNOWLEDGMENTS

Though I have been fascinated by dreams my whole life and have had lucid dreams since I was a teenager, the genesis for this book was sparked during a sacred shamanic journey several years ago. During that particular voyage, like a bolt of lightning from the heavens, a detailed outline for this book was downloaded directly into my brain. I spent the next twelve hours writing down the outline, and then the next year researching and writing the book that you now hold in your hands.

First and foremost I extend my deepest gratitude to the spirit of the sacred mushroom, the voice of ayahuasca, the support of my ancestors, the extraterrestrial transmissions from other star systems, the divine communications of the cosmic deity, the independently function-ing parts of my own brain, the universal mind, the alien, the Other, or whatever it is that inspired me to write this book and guided me through the process. I don't know what it is, but there's an intelligence far superior to that of humans that appears to communicate with us in our dreams, in our shamanic visions, and in the events of our daily lives, if and when we pay attention.

In his seminal book *Communing with the Gods,* about conscious-ness, culture, and the dreaming brain, anthropologist Charles Laughlin writes about his own writing process. He says, "I have more than once had the sense that the book is 'writing itself.'" I know that feeling well! I was amazed at how this book developed, seemingly on its own, as fresh ideas and new directions just kept appearing in my head as I moved along with the project.

I would also like to thank the lucid-dream experts and researchers who have allowed me to interview them for this book: Stephen LaBerge, Robert Waggoner, Stanley Krippner, Charles Tart, Rick Strassman, Clare Johnson, Ryan Hurd, Daniel Siebert, Stanislav Grof, Jazz Mordant, and Ian Koslow. I am most grateful for your generous time and valuable energies.

Special thanks to the late psychiatric researcher Oscar Janiger, who introduced me to the scientific study of lucid dreaming; to my herbalist, Boa Cowee, for masterfully preparing many of the oneirogenic herbal tinctures that I tried for this book; and to Sherry Hall for her stellar help in transcribing the interviews I did.

Additionally, I would like to express my sincere appreciation to the following people for their generous contributions and valuable support: Carolyn Mary Kleefeld, Arleen Margulis, Becca Ann Hill, Serena Watman, Audreanne Rivka Sheehan, Patricia Holt, Sara Huntley, Maria Grusauskas, Mariateresa Gutierrezmacanilla, Kelly Matthews, Peter Maich, Hana Fiona Theobald, Jon Graham, Keelin, Meriana Dinkova, Momo Mercurious, Mike Alperin, Jacob Andrade, Ania Grycan, Jess Buckner, Danielle Bohmer, Deidra Henry, Danelle Benari, Amanda Rose Loveland, Lily Ross, Erin Dellinger, Jessi Daichman, Sara Mokhtari-Fox, Selina Reddan, Veronika King, Jesse Ray Houts, Linda Parker, Denis Berry, Zach Leary, Thomas Graves, Rebecca McClen Novick, Annie Sprinkle, Bruce Damer, Kelly Hollerbach, Heather Goldstein Greenberg, Brandi Goldstein, Geoffrey and Valerie Goldstein, Louise Reitman, Sammie and Tudie, Rick Doblin, Amy Barnes Excolere, Suzie Wouk, Sherri Paris, Robert Forte, Valerie Leveroni Corral, David Wayne Dunn, Robin Rae, Brummbaer, Deed DeBruno, Randy Baker, Steven Ray Brown, B'anna Federico, Anna Damoth, Alan E. Mason, Sandy Oppenheim, Lorey Capelli, Dana Peleg, Mimi Peleg, Bethan Carter, Al Brown, Cheryle and Gene Goldstein, Dina Meyer, Bernadette Wilson, Nick Herbert, Erin Jarvis, Jody Lombardo, Erica Ansberry, Jessica Ansberry-Gagnon, Goo Bear,

Maria Ramirez, Linda D'Amato, Nathan West, Paula Rae Mellard, Mike Kawizky, Linda Capetillo-Cunliffe, Ivy Summer Abshell, Alan Shoemaker, Massimiliano Geraci, Jeff Rosenbaum, Allisun Shine, Mark Van Thillo, Gaie Alling, Liza Gopika Lichtinger, Justin MacGregor, Lupita Uribe, Torrey Peacock, Robert J. Barnhart, Frank Allen Bella, Brittany Nicole, Susanne G. Seller, Teresa King, Ben Osen, Jim Steele, Patrice Villastrigo, Rupert Sheldrake, Tod Barnett, Dragonflower Lyoness, Arlene Istar Lev, Catherine McBride, Ralph Metzner, C. Michael Smith, Simon Posford, Massimiliano Geraci, and Dieter Hagenbach.

Finally, thanks to everyone in the lucid-dream community and my worldwide network of Internet friends who inform me about new scientific developments, support my work, share their creative talents, and challenge my ideas. I am most grateful for everyone's contributions and communications.

EXPLORING THE SECRET REALM OF THE WAKING DREAM

Dormiens vigila.*
While sleeping, watch.

As children, we're all taught to sing:

> *Row, row, row your boat,*
> *Gently down the stream,*
> *Merrily, merrily, merrily, merrily,*
> *Life is but a dream.*[1]

However, when we get older, we rarely reflect on the meaning of these powerfully succinct lines. What does it mean that "life is but a dream"?

According to Hindu philosophy, all that we perceive is *maya*, illusion, while modern neuroscience tells us that everything we ever experience is just a series of mental constructs, models, or simulations of reality created in our brains from a massive sea of electrical sensory signals. However, these insights do not mean that the world we see around

---

*This Latin inscription from European alchemy is found in a circle within the famous engraving titled "The First Stage of the Great Work," created in 1604 by the physician Hienrich Khunrath, in his book *Amphitheater of Eternal Wisdom*.

us isn't real. Rather, it just means that things are not what they initially appear to be.

One of the first lessons we learn from lucid dreaming is that the dream world appears to be every bit as real, or unreal, as the physical world we inhabit during our waking hours. This understanding has profound philosophical and spiritual implications that we'll be discussing in this book. But first let's take a look at what lucid dreaming is, how we can use it to improve our daily lives, and how it relates to shamanic healing.

WHAT IS LUCID DREAMING?

Having a lucid dream means that you become self-aware and "awake" within a dream, that you realize you are dreaming while it is happening. This means that during the dream you are in full or partial possession of your higher cognitive reasoning, critical faculties, rational mind, and intellectual abilities. With this extraordinary sense of awakening comes (1) a clear perception of the continuity of oneself between waking and sleeping; (2) access to one's waking-world memories while dreaming; and (3) the ability to significantly influence what happens within the dream.

There are degrees of lucidity; it's a continuum of awareness and memory across states of consciousness, from what has been described as "prelucidity" to "superlucidity."[2] One can be aware that one is dreaming, that his or her body is lying soundly in bed, but still be bound by unrealized psychological restraints in the dream realms. It takes practice to realize that you have the ability to influence and change the world around you in a dream, and discovering the limits of these superpowers is what all the fun is about.

Although reports of people experiencing lucid dreaming are found in religious texts that go back thousands of years, the phenomenon was not identified in a scientific publication until 1913, by Dutch psychiatrist Frederik van Eeden.[3] However, the first detailed reports of experiments in lucid dreaming come to us from the French sinologist Marquis d'Hervey de Saint-Denys—who also coined the term *lucid dream* in his native tongue as *rêve lucide*. In his 1867 book *Les rêves et les moyens de les diriger* (*Dreams and How to Guide Them*),[4] Saint-Denys describes his many adventures while lucid dreaming and shares the results of his experiments as well as his personal methods for navigating and controlling the dream environment.

The first signals ever scientifically recorded from a lucid-dream state occurred in 1975 at the University of Hull, in England, when lucid dreamer Alan Worsely signaled to dream researcher Keith Hearne by making prearranged Morse Code–like eye signals (now known as left-right-left-right, or LRLR, signals) from within the dream state to an eye-movement recording device, while hooked up to a brain-wave monitor.[5] EEG patterns verified that Worsley was asleep when he made these signals, yet there were clearly defined eye movements recorded that corresponded to the prearranged pattern. Then in 1978, Stanford University sleep-lab researcher and psychophysiologist Stephen LaBerge independently conducted virtually the same study using himself as a test subject, and also delivered LRLR signals from within a dream state to an eye-movement recording device while hooked up to a brain-wave monitor.[6] The scientific history of lucid dreaming will be discussed in detail in chapter 3.

The widespread publication of LaBerge's work helped to popularize the notion of lucid dreaming, and this was how I first heard about it. I interviewed LaBerge in 1992 for my book *Mavericks of the Mind* after meeting him at the home of our mutual friend, the psychiatric researcher Oscar Janiger, who conducted the LSD and creativity studies discussed in chapter 1 of this book. Before reading LaBerge's book *Lucid Dreaming,* I had been regularly having lucid dreams several times a month since I first began doing psychedelic drugs and plants as a teenager.

Lucid dreaming can be an unbelievably magical experience, every bit as solid, vivid, and real as anything in waking life (perhaps even more so), giving people the opportunity to genuinely experience whatever they please, without any physical or social consequences. When I interviewed LaBerge he told me that lucid dreaming is like "high-resolution virtual reality." The sense of freedom from physical and social constraints can feel exhilarating beyond words, and upon first encountering a lucid-dream state many people immediately rush off to do two things—fly high above the world, and then have sex with their ideal lover. Motivated people can spend years living out their wildest fantasies in lucid-dream adventures: soaring through outer space or exploring underwater oceans, flying through walls and passing through solid objects, materializing anything out of thin air, changing environments, shifting form, or making any living or dead, real or imaginary person instantly appear. Some of these many, seemingly unlimited possibilities will be discussed in chapter 4.

However, as we'll learn in this book, although fantasy-fulfillment dreams can certainly be great fun and may have important therapeutic value, this stage is just the beginning of one's adventures with lucid dreaming. If you stick with lucid dreaming, and discipline yourself to systematically explore this state, over time it can become a powerful path to greater awareness, heightened creativity, spiritual awakening, and communication with what is best described as simply "the Other." But one need not have these lofty goals in mind to enjoy lucid dreaming, and for it to have practical applications in our lives.

HOW CAN WE USE LUCID DREAMING TO IMPROVE OUR DAILY LIVES?

Although fun and worthwhile as an experience unto itself, lucid dreaming can also be so much more than mere entertainment. For example, lucid dreaming can help with healing from both physical and mental illness. Psychotherapeutically, it can be used to help us confront the fears in our personal nightmares and heal from emotional traumas. There is also compelling evidence that actions performed in lucid dreams can help us heal from bodily injury.

Some people also use lucid dreaming to learn new skills or to rehearse a particular professional activity such as athletic training, public speaking, or music performance. Lucid dreaming can dramatically enhance creativity and fuel the imagination by increasing our access to the vast unconscious (or "other conscious") regions of the mind. Many artists, writers, inventors, and scientists report using lucid dreaming as a way to be more innovative with their work and come up with new ideas. We'll be hearing from some of these creative people in chapter 2.

Dreaming with greater awareness can help us develop our natural psychic abilities, facilitate profound mystical experiences, and reveal hidden knowledge about ourselves and the world. Some of the people I've spoken with report experiences with lucid dreaming that appear to be every bit as life-transforming as a powerful psychedelic, mystical, or near-death experience. It seems that lucid dreaming may also be useful as a tool for exploring the Jungian collective unconscious, for developing genetic/DNA awareness, for retrieving archetypal-mythic racial memories, or for navigating the higher mind of the biosphere. Some dreams appear to transcend our personal lives and allow us to tap into a collective sense of something larger than ourselves. We'll be examining these ideas more in chapter 10.

Becoming lucid in dreams may help us explore the ever-looming questions that stem from our basic sense of philosophical ignorance, of not knowing who or what we truly are, how we arrived here, or what our lives are really about. Self-aware dreaming can also be used for healing psychological dissociation and for recovering and integrating lost fragments of our minds, our elemental or multiple personalities. This is an idea that we'll be taking a look at in chapter 7.

It appears that lucid dreaming may also allow us to connect with other people in previously unimagined ways, through a shared, Internet-like mental space or psychic virtual reality that transcends our physical bodies, and that in a quantum way connects everyone through the core of our minds. The notion of a collective dream space reported by oneironauts (dream travelers or dream explorers) is similar to what many psychonauts (those who explore psychedelic states of mind) describe as "hyperspace" after ingesting a strong dose of the psychedelic substance DMT, or after drinking ayahuasca, a subject we'll be discussing in chapter 1.

In chapter 6 we'll be exploring some mind-boggling new technologies that will enable us to dial in and tune our brains to the lucid-dream state, allowing us to send "text messages" from our lucid dreams to people in the waking world. We'll see why it won't be long before we can digitally record our dreams and share them with one another over the Internet, making our experiences in the dream realm ever more social and communicable.

But perhaps most importantly, as I mentioned, lucid dreaming offers us a golden path toward spiritual development; in fact, techniques for developing this as a learnable skill have been an important part of Tibetan Buddhist practice for more than a thousand years.

HOW DOES LUCID DREAMING RELATE TO SHAMANIC HEALING?

Lucid-dreaming skill development, or "dream yoga" practice, is an important part of Vajrayāna (Tantric) Buddhism, as well as in the Bön religion and other Eastern philosophical systems. Tibetan Buddhists have used lucid dreaming "as a means of experiencing the illusory nature of personal reality, and as one part of a set of practices said to lead to enlightenment and the discovery of the ultimate nature of self."[7]

Contemporary Buddhism in Tibet evolved out of earlier religious traditions, one of which was called "Bön." Bön predates Buddhism, and is the oldest known form of religion in Tibet. It appears to have developed from even earlier, more shamanic, or pagan-like spiritual traditions.

Shamanism is a term that refers to the ceremonial healing and spiritual guidance practices of indigenous people around the world. Like social insects that have genetic castes for various occupations, it appears that human tribes are similarly organized by DNA intelligence, and they will naturally produce a shaman within tribal societies.

A shaman is first and foremost a healer, a medicine man or woman who uses medicinal herbs (some with psychoactive properties) and rituals to treat physical, psychological, and social problems within the tribe.

The shaman generally combines these treatments with repeated drumming, chanting, singing, and/or dancing that produces a psychological trance state or enhances an altered state of consciousness. Shamans also provide personal and social guidance for the tribe. One can effectively argue that many of our highest cultural achievements as a species—in science, medicine, art, philosophy, and spirituality—evolved from the shamanistic instinct in early human societies.

The two primary states of consciousness that a shaman works with in healing practices are what have been commonly described as "channeling spirits" and "out-of-body journeying,"[8] which, as we shall see in later chapters, are both related to lucid dreaming in different ways, while lucid-dreaming practices themselves are incorporated into many shamanic traditions around the world. Native American healer Rolling Thunder has said that lucid dreaming can be a more reliable source of shamanic visions than psychedelic plants,[9] and intentional dreaming is an inherent part of many indigenous shamanic systems around the world.[10] Peruvian-American anthropologist Carlos Castaneda (1925–1998) wrote extensively about lucid dreaming as being an important component of his shamanic training in his popular books about the teachings of a Yaqui shaman-trickster named Don Juan Matus.[11] Russian psychiatrist Olga Kharitidi writes about how a secret brotherhood of shamans have long utilized lucid dreaming as a method to heal from traumas in Siberia.[12]

Ibn El-Arabi, a thirteenth-century Sufi master, spoke about the importance of "controlling one's thoughts in dreams." He said that this would produce "awareness of the intermediate dimension,"[13] which he considered to be of great benefit. Dream prophecy is woven into the ancient scriptures of the Hebrew Bible and the Koran, and the role of symbolic messages in dreams are crucial to many religions. Eckankar—a religious movement that began in 1965 and is based on the "light and sound of God"[14]—is devoted to gaining spiritual insight from dreaming, which it views as a form of "soul travel."

During ayahuasca healing ceremonies, shamans say that they call in the spirits of different plants and beings as well as offer protection to participants by singing and whistling sacred invocation songs called *icaros*. These icaros are often reported to come to the shamans in their dreams. I suspect that our experiences with shamanic states of consciousness are helping to bring the dream world closer to the waking realm, and that lucid-dreaming experiences are helping to bring greater waking awareness into the dream realm. Notably, the key to success in both realms appears to be the same: belief in oneself and in the power of one's imagination.

In the pages that follow I'll be explaining how these two different worlds are cross-fertilizing and merging with each other, and how this inter-realm unification of worlds may be part of our purpose as human beings in the larger scheme of things. In this book I'll be primarily referring to ayahuasca-based shamanism, which originated in the Amazon jungle of South America; I'll be discussing how my personal experiences doing ayahuasca in Peru essentially cured me of childhood post-traumatic stress disorder.

Ayahuasca is a powerful, mind-altering brew composed of plants that work synergistically to produce a state of consciousness that many people describe as a kind of waking dream, and it is during this experience that Amazonian shamans perform their healing ceremonies. As with Tibetan Buddhism, lucid dreaming is really a branch of shamanism; it is one pathway for the shaman to access knowledge or healing power from other realms of existence or higher forms of intelligence.

Shamans see themselves as travelers between worlds that are accessible in what psychiatrist Stanislav Grof would call "nonordinary states of consciousness." These states of consciousness can be reliably produced by shamanic plant brews, psychedelic drugs, drumming, dancing, chanting, fasting, meditation, and lucid dreaming. During these states of altered consciousness shamans say that they can telepathically communicate with plant and animal spirits, the ghosts of ancestors, disembodied beings, angels, demons, deities, extraterrestrials, the biosphere, and one's higher mind. Others use different explanations, like "untapped portions of our brains," or "God," in trying to better understand the mystery behind what appears to be independently operating intelligences that speak to us in dreams and on shamanic voyages and seem to understand us better than we understand ourselves.

As we'll be discussing more in chapter 1, recent brain-scanning research at Germany's Goethe University reveals that psilocybin, the psychedelic substance in magic mushrooms, activates a primitive network in the brain, one linked with emotion. Most interestingly, several parts of this primitive neural network, such as the hippocampus and the anterior cingulate cortex, become simultaneously activated by psilocybin in a way similar to the brain-activation pattern observed when people are dreaming. It seems that psychedelic experiences are like waking dreams, and it's noteworthy that many people report having lucid dreams in the nights that follow a shamanic or psychedelic experience. I suspect that there's a largely unexplored connection between lucid dreaming and psychedelic experiences, and it is this intuition that prompted me to write this book.

ONEIRONAUTS, PSYCHONAUTS, AND SHAMANS EXPLORE THE SAME REALM OF INNER SPACE

Many of the subjects who were given the psychedelic substance DMT in medical researcher Rick Strassman's 1990–1995 study at the University of New Mexico believed that they were communicating with intelligent nonhuman entities while under its influence.[15] DMT appears to be a hormone and neurotransmitter, or a chemical messenger, that is naturally found in the human body and reaches its highest levels in the bloodstream at around 3:00 a.m. No biochemist has been able to explain what DMT is doing in the human organism or in so many species of animals and plants, but some researchers suspect that the mysterious molecule might influence our dreaming.

DMT is also one of the primary components of ayahuasca, and it is largely responsible for the extraordinarily rich and meaningful visions that people generally see during the experience. Strassman and other researchers have wrestled with the notion of whether or not the beings that people encounter on DMT have an independent existence in some alternative dimension, or whether they are simply projections of our own minds.

Anyone who has personally experienced an encounter with these seemingly hyperdimensional beings knows that this is a very tricky philosophical question to answer. The same philosophical conundrum exists with lucid dreams. Not only can we meet characters in our lucid dreams who can convincingly claim to have independent minds and personalities, we eventually discover that the entire landscape of our dreams, like the shifting tapestry of an ayahuasca vision, is actually a living intelligence that we can communicate with. This living intelligence is what psychologists ironically call the *unconscious* or what Jung calls the *collective unconscious,* and it appears to be the same entity that, depending on one's cultural context, some people describe as their higher self, the Other, an alien, the dormant parts of the brain, divine intelligence, the mushroom spirit, the Mother, DNA, the Goddess, or God.

However, what's most intriguing is that over time, with both shamanic voyaging and lucid dreaming, one begins to develop a dialogue with this cosmic mind—what author and lucid-dreaming expert Robert Waggoner cleverly calls the "conscious unconscious."[16] From the perspective of our experiences with lucid dreaming and shamanic journeys it appears that the universe is an intelligent living organism, a conscious being that we can paradoxically both unify and dialogue with. It seems that this cosmic mind is always communicating with us, if only we'd listen. She speaks to us through a metalanguage of symbolic events and synchronicities in our lives, in our dreams, and in our psychedelic experiences. This same transcendent awareness orchestrates events behind the scenes of our waking lives, in our dreams, throughout all of reality, and is simultaneously the source of one's primal awareness that is entangled with one's basic sense of self. Most curiously, our tiny egos can dialogue with this grand intelligence through our lucid dreams and mystical experiences.

The primary source of illumination for understanding how lucid dreaming and psychedelic healing operate will come from our study of the brain. Further development of these powerful shamanic skills will arrive with the newly emerging electronic technologies that are merging with our nervous systems, and rapidly expanding the potential of our minds. Recent polls conducted by Swansea University psychologist and dream researcher Mark Blagrove indicate that more people are having lucid dreams now than ever before. The increase may be "between 10 and 40 percent since the 1980s," reports Blagrove.[17] This research suggests that around 80 percent of people will recall having a lucid dream at some point in their lives. But what is going on in all these dreaming brains?

WHAT HAPPENS IN OUR DREAMING BRAINS?

In chapter 2 we'll be exploring the physiology of sleep and dreaming, with a specific focus on lucid dreaming and how dreams relate to shamanic states of consciousness. Recent research demonstrates that the fastest brain-wave frequencies ever recorded by human beings occur during lucid dreaming. These ultrafast brain waves in the gamma range operate at frequencies as high as 50 Hz, or 50 cycles per second. This contrasts with waking consciousness, when our brains generally operate at frequencies between 14 and 40 Hz, and during sleep, when brain-wave frequencies tend to cycle between 4 and 14 Hz. So this research suggests that when we are lucid dreaming we may actually be more conscious or self-aware than we generally are in normal waking consciousness.

Using transcranial electrical stimulation to generate gamma waves in an area of the brain known as "the prefrontal cortex," researchers at J. W. Goethe University in Frankfurt, Germany, were able to induce lucid dreaming in their sleeping volunteers—so it appears that the technology to faithfully produce lucid dreams on command is really just around the corner. In chapter 6 we'll be exploring the possibilities of transcranial electrical brain stimulation, as well as the currently available electronic technologies like the REM-Dreamer, to help us lucid dream. We'll also be looking at ancient and recently developed psychological methods for inducing lucid dreaming in chapter 4, along with other new technologies for improving lucid dreams, and we'll explore how different herbs, drugs, and supplements can enhance dreaming. I have personally tried around three dozen herbs and supplements that can help with lucid dreaming, which I'll be reporting on in chapter 5.

Intriguingly, psilocybin and ayahuasca tend to slow down brain waves, not speed them up, and they appear to shut down areas of the left hemisphere of the brain. Also, acquired savant syndrome—extraordinary mathematical or other mental abilities that suddenly appear after traumatic brain injury—usually occurs after damage to the left hemisphere. The left hemisphere of the brain, which governs symbolic, linear thinking, may also have a dominating effect on the brain, suppressing the creative, psychic, or unknown abilities of the more intuitive, whole system–thinking right hemisphere of the brain. In other words, it may be that psychedelics shut down dominant parts of the left brain that suppress the hidden talents of the right brain, and perhaps dreaming is really a doorway into the unrevealed dimensions of the mind. We'll be discussing this possibility in chapter 1.

TELEPATHIC DREAMS, OUT-OF-BODY EXPERIENCES, PSYCHIC PHENOMENA, AND MUTUAL DREAMING

In chapter 8 we'll explore the mind-expanding possibilities of shared dreams, dream telepathy, and mutual lucid dreaming. Research by psychologist Stanley Krippner* and psychiatrist Montague Ullman has produced compelling evidence indicating that people can seemingly transfer thoughts or mental imagery to someone who is dreaming. Additionally, dream researcher Linda Lane Magallon has collected

---

*I interviewed Krippner for this book, and he has been a good friend and colleague for many years. He has a rare kind of genius, a lively spirit, and a golden heart. You'll find his influence throughout these pages.

many dozens of mutually verified reports from people who have shared dreams in some form or another. Some people report meeting in nonlucid dreams, others report having uncannily similar "meshing" dreams, while some advanced dreamers actually report meeting one another in mutual lucid dreams. As one example of the mainstreaming of this idea, the 2010 film *Inception* was inspired by the notion of being able to lucidly share dreams.

The flexibility of time and space will be explored in chapter 9, as time and space appear to operate very differently in the metaphysiological dream realm. Some people report living for days, weeks, or even years as another person, all within the span of a single Earth night! The relationship between out-of-body experiences and lucid dreaming will also be explored in chapter 9, where I'll share my personal experience with these mysterious states of consciousness.

RESEARCH, INTERVIEWS, AND PERSONAL EXPERIENCE

In this book I blend over thirty years of personal experimentation with altered states of consciousness with expert opinions gathered from numerous interviews and a comprehensive compilation of summarized scientific research about the relationship between lucid dreaming, out-of-body experiences, and shamanic healing. What this book offers to the community of established lucid dreamers that is missing from the other wonderful books on the subject is a deeper exploration of the relationship between psychedelics, herbs, drugs, nutritional supplements, and lucid dreaming. We'll be looking at the interface of shamanic experiences with visionary plants and psychedelic drugs, and guided, intentional, lucid, or interpreted dreaming, to see how both can be used for healing the mind and body. I include excerpts from some of the many interviews I've done with experts on consciousness, dreaming, psychology, unexplained phenomena, and physics, so my approach is interdisciplinary. Both formal and informal researchers on the cutting edge of lucid-dream knowledge were interviewed for this volume, including Stephen LaBerge, Charles Tart, Stanley Krippner, Robert Waggoner, Rupert Sheldrake, Ryan Hurd, Clare Johnson, Dean Radin, Rick Strassman, Daniel Siebert, Stanislav Grof, and the late Terence McKenna.

Along with covering the basic physiology of sleep and dreaming, I'll summarize the leading psychological theories about why we dream and review all of the major lucid-dream research to date. A map for exploring the mysterious territory of our minds will also be offered in this book, and in chapter 7 I'll provide some basic guidelines for interacting with the strange characters we meet in our dreams. Finally, we'll reflect on the philosophical and spiritual implications of lucid dreaming as a way of better understanding the true nature of reality.

Lucid dreaming is a potent psychedelic experience that no government can ever outlaw. No one can prevent you from lucid dreaming. People may try to belittle the experience by saying "it was just a dream," but anyone who has experienced lucid dreaming knows better. It is an open window into higher dimensions of reality, a space-twisting portal, a magic mirror that anyone can climb through and go into their own personal universe. Dreaming with an open third eye can lead to some of the happiest and most profound states of consciousness that a human being can experience, and this can help to improve our individual lives and the world. Waking up in our dreams can be more enchanting than any fairy tale, more liberating than any social or scientific revolution, and more fun than any earthly adventure.

And it can happen to you tonight . . .

1

SHAMANIC PLANTS, PSYCHEDELICS, AND MIND-BODY HEALING

> *All that we see or seem*
> *Is but a dream within a dream.*
>
> EDGAR ALLAN POE

It seems that there is a deeply intertwined yet largely unexplored relationship between psychedelic states of mind and lucid dreaming. In this opening chapter I will summarize the important scientific research into psychedelic drugs and plants and show how these valuable studies shed some light on the fascinating connection between lucid dreaming and other shamanic states of consciousness.

Strictly forbidden and severely criminalized by almost every world government, and long demonized, ridiculed, or ignored by the mainstream media, psychedelic drugs are now finally receiving the serious scientific attention they have long deserved. New research confirms the promising results of earlier studies, which suggested that these strange and controversial substances actually have a broad range of useful medical applications, and even the mainstream media has finally embraced the scientific truth about the potential benefits and considerable safety of these remarkable substances.

After eighteen years in which no clinical studies involving psyche-delic drugs appeared anywhere in the world, there is now an explosion of research occurring all over the globe, such that we're currently liv-ing in the midst of a psychedelic renaissance. Over the past decade a growing number of clinical studies have begun to explore the potential therapeutic benefits of mind-shifting drugs like LSD, MDMA, psilo-cybin, DMT, ayahuasca, ketamine, and ibogaine. Articles now appear regularly in mainstream publications like the *New York Times* ("LSD, Reconsidered for Therapy"[1]) and *Newsweek* magazine ("Psychedelic Drugs 'Safe as Riding a Bike or Playing Soccer'"[2]).

Much about the precise biological mechanisms governing how these unusual drugs produce their visionary effects, and their profound heal-ings, remains mysterious. Nevertheless, they often produce similar psycho-active and perceptual experiences, such as the suspension of conventional belief systems, immersive visual imagery with closed eyes, and ego and personal boundary dissolution, while engendering an openness to new ways of thinking. This makes these drugs potential therapeutic agents.

THE WEST AWAKENS AND THE JOURNEY BEGINS

Scientific research into the effects of psychedelic drugs began in 1897, when the German chemist Arthur Heffter first isolated mescaline, the primary psychoactive compound in the hallucinogenic peyote cactus. Half a century passed before the next milestone occurred when, in 1943, Swiss chemist Albert Hofmann discovered the psychedelic effects of LSD (lysergic acid diethylamide) at Sandoz Pharmaceuticals in Basel while studying ergot, a parasitic fungus that grows on rye. Initially, Sandoz Laboratories thought that the powerful psychedelic drug might have two possible applications: to enhance the healing potential of psy-chotherapy and to instruct medical professionals in what it might be like to be temporarily psychotic, although to their credit Hofmann and others quickly recognized LSD's valuable potential for fostering mysti-cal experiences and enhancing creativity.

In 1954, Aldous Huxley's book *The Doors of Perception* was published. It poetically described the author's spiritual awakening while using mescaline. This short, sixty-three-page gem of a book, written by one of the most respected literary figures of the twentieth century, brought greater public awareness of the knowledge that mescaline could sometimes produce visionary or mystical experiences. Then in 1958, Albert Hofmann became the first scientist to isolate psilocybin and psilocin, the psychoactive components of the Mexican "magic mushroom," *Psilocybe mexicana*.

Between 1943 and 1972, a significant amount of research was conducted with LSD, psilocybin, DMT, and mescaline. Before a global research ban was instituted in 1972, close to seven hundred studies with psychedelic drugs took place. This research suggested that psychedelics offer significant benefits: they help alcoholics stop drinking, ease the anxieties of terminal cancer patients, and alleviate the symptoms of many difficult-to-treat psychiatric illnesses such as post-traumatic stress disorder. For example, studies conducted between 1967 and 1972 with terminal cancer patients by psychiatrist Stanislav Grof and colleagues at the Spring Grove State Hospital in Baltimore showed that LSD combined with psychotherapy could alleviate symptoms of anxiety, depression, psychological withdrawal, tension, insomnia, and even extreme physical pain. Many researchers believed that they had stumbled on a safe and effective, near-miraculous treatment for a whole spectrum of medical disorders. During this era other investigators found that LSD and mescaline may have potential applications as a means of enhancing the imagination and facilitating creative problem-solving abilities. A small number of creativity studies with psychedelics were done by the late psychiatrist Oscar Janiger and psychologist James Fadiman, both of whom wrote books that summarized this important research.[3]

Then came the dark years, from 1972 until 1990, when there were no government-approved human studies conducted with psychedelic drugs taking place anywhere on planet Earth. Their complete disappearance from clinical research was the result of a political backlash that followed the promotion of these drugs by the 1960s counterculture. This political reaction not only made these substances illegal for personal use, it also made it extremely difficult for researchers to get government approval to study them scientifically.

Fortunately, things began to change during the last decade of the twentieth century, when "open-minded regulators at the FDA decided to put science before politics when it came to psychedelic and medical marijuana research," said public-policy expert Rick Doblin* when I interviewed him. It wasn't long after these changes in the FDA occurred that the doorway into new dimensions opened again.

DMT RESEARCH AND THE INTERDIMENSIONAL PORTAL

In 1990, a portal into new dimensions of the mind (and possibly reality) opened at the University of New Mexico when the FDA and the DEA granted approval for psychiatric researcher Rick Strassman to study the psychoactive effects of dimethyltryptamine (DMT) in healthy human volunteers. DMT is a mysterious psychedelic neurotransmitter, a chemical that's naturally found in the human body[4] and in many species of animals and plants, although no biochemist knows precisely what biological function it serves in any of these places. In fact, DMT is so commonly encountered in the natural world that the late American biochemist and psychopharmacologist Alexander Shulgin wrote, "DMT is, most simply, almost everywhere you choose to look. [It] is . . . in this flower here, in that tree over there, and in yonder animal."[5] Trace amounts of DMT are even found naturally in every glass of orange juice.[6]

However, when smoked, snorted, or injected in sufficient quantities, DMT becomes one of the most powerful psychedelic substances

---

*Doblin is the founder of the Multidisciplinary Association for Psychedelic Studies (MAPS), which helps to arrange and fund psychedelic-drug research for medical purposes. I worked as a guest editor at MAPS for several years, editing their special-edition bulletins, and the interview that I did with Doblin can be found in my book *Frontiers of Psychedelic Consciousness*. To learn more about MAPS, see www.maps.org.

known, on an order of magnitude more intense than a strong LSD experience. The experience completely overwhelms one's senses, separating awareness of the body from the physical world and transporting one to a magical realm beyond belief. This enchanted realm, described as "hyperspace" by DMT voyagers, appears to exist with the same consistency as waking reality or a lucid dream, and it is seemingly populated by swarms of spirits and noncorporeal beings. DMT has thus been called the "spirit molecule" and the "ultimate metaphysical reality pill."[7]

Why is this chemical naturally found in our bodies? No one knows for certain. Because our body's endogenous DMT levels are highest at around 3:00 a.m., when most of us are sound asleep, it has been hypothesized by some neuroscientists that DMT may play a biochemical role in dreaming. Notably, many people consider 3:00 a.m. to be the best time to communicate with spirits, reporting an increased frequency of paranormal activity (as well as alien abductions), which is why this time has sometimes been referred to as "the witching hour" or "the Devil's hour." Could this be related to our naturally elevated DMT levels? Filmmaker and writer Mike DiCerto has had some interesting experiences around this time of night. He wrote me to say that "every so often—around 3:00 to 4:00 a.m.—I get what I call the 'video feed.' I am awake— basically—but when I close my eyes I am peering into hyperreal worlds/ images, as if a video feed has been attached to my eyes. Sometimes it is mundane, like looking at a warehouse from the POV of a security camera, and other times super-rich and colorful psychedelic images."

However, it is just speculation that DMT plays a role in dreaming, and even if this is true, it may do more than that. Rick Strassman and others have suggested that naturally elevated DMT levels in the brain may be responsible for such unexplained mental phenomena as near-death experiences, spontaneous mystical union, nonhuman entity contact, alien abductions, and schizophrenia. There is also evidence to suggest that DMT levels rise in the urine of psychotic patients as their condition worsens.[8] Strassman suspects that DMT is likely produced in the pineal gland, and studies have confirmed that it can be found there.[9] He and others have speculated about the possibility that elevated

DMT levels in the brain may be responsible for ushering the soul into the body before birth and out of the body upon death.

I think that Strassman's landmark five-year study may be some of the most incredible scientific research ever conducted by our species. Over half of the subjects in his study reported experiences wherein they described entering an astonishing new world, one in which they were "sensing and/or interacting with external intelligences or beings." These were not reported as hallucinations, but rather as allowing a person to have a greater sense of reality than our experience of normal waking consciousness.[10]

So our species has discovered a reliable means for consistently creating experiences that sane and healthy people can only describe as contact with alien beings, and this hasn't made headlines on every news outlet around the world? Somehow this "secret" for making contact with an alien intelligence is accessible to anyone who looks into the matter, yet it remains invisible to the masses—the sleepwalkers, so to speak—who stumble through life as though in a (nonlucid) dream. But it seems that this secret was actually discovered long ago, and it was never lost to those carriers of the surviving Amazonian shamanic traditions who use the DMT-containing brew ayahuasca, which we'll be discussing later in this chapter.

Many people describe the beings that they encounter on DMT or ayahuasca as insectoid. For example, they might look like huge praying mantises. I suspect that the reason why DMT experiences often involve insectoid beings is because they are representatives of our future selves. Our future selves will undoubtedly evolve into much more complex organisms, with far more sophisticated sensory organs, with, perhaps, telepathic antennas, multiple eyes, psychic abilities, additional brain lobes, nanotechnological self-transforming abilities, and genetic blends of animal and plant characteristics. Perhaps this type of highly evolved being appears insectoid or incomprehensible to our present larval forms. But regardless of who these mysterious beings are or what DMT does in the body, since Strassman's study was approved in 1990 dozens of other scientific studies of psychedelic drugs have been approved, and a number of them have already been completed.

THE NEW WAVE OF PSYCHEDELIC DRUG RESEARCH

The new scientific studies have much more immediately practical, down-to-earth medical applications than Strassman's out-of-this-world DMT research. This flourishing body of research suggests that there is highly promising medical potential for a wide variety of these drugs: for the psychoactive drug MDMA to help treat post-traumatic stress disorder;[11] for psilocybin to relieve the symptoms of obsessive-compulsive disorder; for LSD to ease the anxieties around dying; for ketamine to treat severe depression; and for ibogaine to effectively treat drug addiction.[12] Additionally, new studies with psilocybin, the active component in magic mushrooms, have replicated earlier findings that it can promote mystical, religious, or spiritual experiences.[13] In other words, not only can psychedelics help to heal people when they're sick, they can also help healthy people optimize their potential. Other studies show that psilocybin can promote neurogenesis, or the birth of new brain cells and growth in the nervous system.[14] Perhaps most fascinating of all are the new studies that allow us to observe the inner workings of the brain in action.

DREAMING WHILE AWAKE: YOUR BRAIN ON PSILOCYBIN

Functional MRI (magnetic resonance imaging) studies with psilocybin are allowing researchers to map out the patterns of activity that occur in the brain while people are under the influence of psilocybin. In one 2012 study, researchers were surprised to discover that psilocybin's effects were associated with decreases in activity in a number of key brain areas, rather than the expected increase.[15] The areas that showed a decrease in activity are the medial prefrontal cortex and the posterior cingulated cortex, which play important roles in the regulation of self-awareness, as they tend to become activated when people are asked to think about themselves. This may help to explain the sense of ego-transcendence that many people report using this drug. Notably, the more that brain activity in these areas decreases, the more vivid the psychedelic experience. Certain regions of the brain, particularly in the left hemisphere, may have a dominating effect on brain function as a whole, suppressing creative, psychic, or unknown abilities of the more intuitive, whole system–thinking right hemisphere of the brain. This could help explain why most people tend to be right-handed: because the left hemisphere controls the right side of the body, and it appears to be the dominant hemisphere.

In other words, perhaps psychedelics temporarily shut down dominant parts of the brain that usually suppress the hidden talents of our dormant brain centers. This new understanding is consistent with the notion that Aldous Huxley put forth in his book *Doors of Perception*— that the brain normally acts as a "reducing valve" for consciousness, that it actually constrains what we normally experience so that we're not overwhelmed by the chaos of stimuli around us.

These insights may also help to explain acquired savant syndrome— when people suddenly develop powerful new mental abilities such as extraordinary mathematical or artistic talents—after traumatic brain injuries. For example, Jason Padgett, author of *Struck by Genius,* began seeing fractal geometry patterns as an intrinsic part of the world and developed extraordinary mathematical abilities after his traumatic brain injury inflicted by muggers at a karaoke bar. Perhaps the injuries are allowing previously suppressed parts of the brain to express themselves and develop?

Additional brain scanning research in 2014, at Goethe University of Frankfurt, Germany, revealed that psilocybin activates a primitive network in the brain that is linked with emotion and dreaming. Several parts of this primitive neural network, including the hippocampus and the anterior cingulate cortex, become simultaneously activated with psilocybin; this is strikingly similar to the brain-activation pattern observed when people are dreaming.[16]

According to Celia Green, a philosopher and psychologist best known for her pioneering research on perceptual phenomena such as lucid dreams and for philosophical and social commentaries, there is evidence that "during a lucid dream there may be a relative depression of function in the left hemisphere of the brain and relative activation of the right."[17]

Could this be why reading words in lucid dreams is notoriously so difficult? According to Green, "The left hemisphere of the brain is thought to be preferentially involved in the processing of information in a sequential, as opposed to a global, holistic fashion . . . and reading letters and words would seem to be an example of such serial processing."[18] We'll be discussing these reading difficulties more in chapter 4. In any case, if this is true, then what happens when the left and right hemispheres of the brain are isolated from each other?

SLICING BRAINS AND SPLITTING MINDS

Neuroscientists Roger Sperry and Michael Gazzaniga demonstrated that the right and left hemispheres of the brain are relatively independent in their functioning. Although not quite as black and white as many pop psychology texts might suggest, there are measurably distinct processing differences between the left and right hemispheres, with the left having more aptitude at verbal-analytical ways of thinking and the right hemisphere being more equipped for visual-spatial processing.[19]

What's most curious is that although we can measurably demonstrate that brain hemispheres operate relatively independently and that they influence our actions in ways that our conscious mind remains unaware of, we tend to rationalize why we make the choices we do. In other words, we often create reasons to explain why we're doing what we're doing that have nothing to do with the real cause. We know this because of studies of people who have had what are called "split-brain" operations, or commissurotomies. In some cases, people who suffer from severe temporal-lobe epilepsy require this extreme form of surgery, where the bundle of nerve fibers that connects the right and left brain hemispheres, known as the corpus callosum, is surgically severed so that an epileptic seizure won't spread from one hemisphere of the brain to the other. These surgeries have been relatively successful with regard to treating epilepsy, but there have been some very strange consequences from them too. Initially the patients didn't seem any different; however, with time the difference became strikingly apparent. I've seen absolutely bizarre videos of people who have had the split-brain operation, where it seems like two people are now residing in their brain. Sometimes one part of the body is trying to pull up a pair of pants to get dressed, while the other side is trying to pull them down!

A window into how split-brain patients see the world was discovered in a landmark experiment by Roger Sperry, which took advantage of the fact that the right side of the body is controlled by the left hemisphere and the left side of the body by the right hemisphere. Within the human eye, our visual field is equally split as well, with the left half of the image going to the right hemisphere and the right half of the image going to the left.

Sperry cleverly designed an apparatus that allowed him to project an image to one half of the eye at a time, so that the visual information signals just went to one side of the brain (and couldn't be shared between the two brain hemispheres, due to a severed corpus callosum). When a subject saw the image with his right visual field, the image went to the left hemisphere of his brain, where the language center is located. Then, when asked what he saw, the subject could easily and correctly say what it was. However, when the image was projected onto his left visual field and the visual information traveled to the right hemisphere of the brain, the subject would indicate that he had no memory of seeing anything.

Surprisingly, when the subject was asked to pick the object that he saw out of a pile of different objects before him with his left hand (which was controlled by the right side of his brain), he could do so easily. The strangest finding of all came when the subject was asked why he had chosen that object from the pile when he said he didn't see a flashing image. All of the subjects came up with reasons that had nothing to do with the reality of having perceived it with their right hemisphere. "It reminded me of a toy from my childhood" or "it just seemed interesting" were typical responses.

The implications of this remarkable research on our notions of the soul and our personal sense of self are, of course, profound, and they deepen the vast mystery of who we are, as it seems that once we cut off communication between the two major brain hemispheres each becomes what appears to be a separate person!

One might wonder, at this point, how does splitting the brain affect the way we dream? Since we know that the right hemisphere of the brain is associated with visual-spatial processing, one has to wonder if split-brain patients can even recall any visual dreams at all. According to neuroscientist Michael Gazzaniga and colleagues, who studied dreaming in split-brain patients, the answer is yes, they do have visual dreams. Gazzaniga e-mailed me saying that the 1977 study that he participated in was the only study of dreaming in split-brain patients that he was aware of, but it directly answered this question:

> This paper addresses the question of right hemisphere involvement in the visual components of dreaming. The rationale derives from an observed relation between reports of visual agnosia accompanied by dream cessation and the literature on right hemisphere specialization for visuo-spatial processes. All night sleep EEGs were recorded from subjects with partial or complete section of the corpus callosum and anterior commissure. Upon entering a EEG-, EOG- and EMG-defined REM episode, the subjects were awakened and questioned about dream content. All subjects examined in this fashion were able to recount some visual dream content. This result fails to support any notion of selective right hemisphere visual dream mediation.[20]

However, we need to remind ourselves that when we receive dream reports from people who have had split-brain surgery we are only hearing the reports from their verbal left hemisphere. I know from working with people who suffer from multiple-personality disorder that the different personalities may have different dreams at night, so it's conceivable that after a split-brain surgery each hemisphere could be having different dreams. Consider the following:

Split-brain patients also have taught us about dreaming. Scientists had hypothesized that dreaming is a right hemisphere activity, but they found the split-brain patients do report dreaming. They found, therefore, that the left hemisphere must have some access to dream material. What was most interesting was the actual content of the dreams of the split-brain patients. Klaus Hoppe, a psychoanalyst, analyzed the dreams of twelve patients. He found that the dreams were not like the dreams of most normal people. The content of the dreams reflected reality, affect, and drives; even in the more elaborate dream, there was a remarkable lack of distortion of latent dream thoughts. The findings show that the left hemisphere alone is able to produce dreams. . . . Patients after commissurotomy reveal a paucity of dreams, fantasies, and symbols. Their dreams lack the characteristics of dream work; their fantasies are unimaginative, utilitarian, and tied to reality; their symbolizing is concretistic, discursive, and rigid.[21]

Celia Green and Oxford psychologist Charles McCreery have suggested that lucid dreaming may be a state of activity in which the right hemisphere tends to dominate the left hemisphere,[22] which would seem to be the opposite of what we tend to experience in our waking state. They give four good reasons for suspecting this:

First, there is the nature of lucid dreaming considered as a cognitive "task." . . . A lucid dream seems to us to be much more naturally viewed as a task involving the manipulation of visuo-spatial imagery than as one involving the serial processing of verbal or similar symbols, and the former is an activity which tends to be correlated with greater RH [right hemisphere] activity. Secondly, there is the remarkable realism achieved by the visual imagery of some lucid dreams. Thirdly, there are the intellectual deficits displayed by some, such as the reading difficulty. Finally, and perhaps more speculatively, there are the extreme positive emotions sometimes displayed, amounting on occasion to "ecstasy."[23]

Research by Stephen LaBerge demonstrates that within lucid dreams the brain specializes in right and left hemisphere functions—just as it does when awake.[24] Because people tend to count with their left hemispheres and sing with their right hemispheres, LaBerge was able to show, using EEG recordings, that when people are singing or counting in lucid dreams, then alpha brain-wave activity is inversely correlated to cerebral activity in the relatively underutilized hemisphere. In other words, singing and counting in a lucid-dream state have the same EEG accompaniments as when performing those activities while awake. However, this finding doesn't invalidate Green and McCreery's theory, as there could still be hemispheric specialization within a system where the relative dominance of each hemisphere can shift.

Curiously, studies with patients who have undergone right hemispherectomies—i.e., in which the entire right side of the brain is removed—have shown that they dream in the same way as people with intact brains.[25] However, other studies have shown that there are some differences in dream content among right- and left-handed dreamers.[26] And our dreams may be influenced by more than hemispheric specialization of the brain, as different bodily organs may actually contain personal memories that enter into our dreams. The dreams reported by people who have had organ transplants often provide them with knowledge of the donor's name, appearance, and some behaviors.[27]

Some psychologists describe lucid dreaming and shamanic states of consciousness as hybrid states of awareness, an unholy blending of mental states that were meant to operate discretely. It seems that psilocybin experiences are like waking dreams, almost the opposite of a lucid dream. In other words, if lucid dreams bring waking consciousness into the dream realm, then psychedelic experiences appear to bring dreaming consciousness into the waking world.

PSYCHEDELICS AND DREAMING

I was eager to speak with psychophysiologist Stephen LaBerge about the relationship between psychedelics and dreaming because he had told me that his own use of LSD had partially inspired his interest in studying the mind.[28] When I asked LaBerge about the seeming correlation between psychedelic consciousness and lucid dreaming, he said, "There's a lot in common between the two states. In fact people can, in the dream state, take a dream 'psychedelic' and have it produce an effect." I replied by telling him that when my partner and I interviewed the late ethnobotanist Terence McKenna, he had told us that when he smokes DMT in his dreams he then has a full-blown psychedelic experience (which I'll be describing in detail later in the chapter). LaBerge then said to me:

> And what that shows is that what prevents us from having these experiences is not the chemical, it's the mental framework. So in a way psychedelics can be a kind of guide in revealing some of the potential in the mind. I think they have limitations in terms of taking us to the visions they show us. One can take the mistaken path of saying, well, since I had a taste of it with the substance, if I keep taking it I'll eventually get the whole thing because more of the same should help. It doesn't seem to work that way.

I also mentioned to LaBerge, as well as to numerous people online, that I found it interesting that so many people report having lucid dreams in the nights that follow a psychedelic experience. Almost every time I've ever done a psychedelic, within a couple of days I'd usually have a lucid dream. I wondered if he and others had noticed this too. Many people replied that that they had experienced this too, and LaBerge said,

> Yes, that is probably due to biochemical changes. Taking psychedelics will produce changes of neurochemical levels, which will intensify REM sleep. Basically, what you've done is you've altered the regulation of the system, and so you've pushed it away from the equilibrium, and it's going to come back and perhaps oscillate for a while until it gets back into its new equilibrium. So it's not surpris-

ing that in the next couple of nights you're going to have variations in REM sleep.

But I suspect that it's more than just variations in REM sleep. For example, drinking alcohol initially suppresses REM sleep and later causes a rebound effect with increased REM, but it seems that fewer people report that this REM-rebound effect with alcohol consumption also increases the frequency of dream lucidity. There's something different about psychedelics. I think they awaken the mind in a similar way as lucid dreaming does, by making normally unconscious regions of the mind conscious, and in so doing open up a portal or a pathway in the mind to greater possibilities. Intriguingly—and central to our discussion—both lucid dreaming and psychedelic awareness are recognized across cultures as aspects of shamanic healing.

PSYCHEDELIC PLANTS AND SHAMANIC HEALING

While scientific research into psychedelic drugs may have officially begun in 1897 with German pharmacologist Arthur Heffter's discovery of mescaline, the use of shamanic healing techniques and rituals to reach psychedelic states of mind by indigenous societies around the world stretches all the way back to prehistory. For example, ayahuasca has been used by indigenous Amazonian shamans in healing ceremonies for at least four thousand years.

During the 1960s, when people in the West first began experimenting with psychedelics on a mass scale and modern psychology failed to offer adequate models to explain the experience, many people looked to the East to find philosophies that better resonated with their experience. Hinduism, Buddhism, and Taoism offered models of reality that appear to provide some insight into the psychedelic experience. The West had yet to discover its ancient shamanic roots, which lie in the jungles of South America and Africa, where ayahuasca, San Pedro, peyote, sacred mushroom, and iboga shamanism ceremonies are practiced to this day.

Just fifteen years ago, hardly anyone outside of the Amazon jungle or Central Africa, or a small group of anthropologists and psychedelic enthusiasts, was even aware of the existence of ayahuasca or iboga. Now the influence of these profound healing plants pervades popular culture. This is especially the case with ayahuasca, as drinking the visionary tea at retreat centers in Peru has now become as fashionable for hip travelers as spiritual pilgrimages to India and Nepal were during the 1960s.

Ayahuasca has been mentioned or discussed quite a bit in the mainstream media in recent years. It has appeared in a number of Hollywood movies and on the popular television show *Weeds* (where the protagonist, Nancy Botwin, takes part in an ayahuasca ceremony). Famous musicians like Sting and Tori Amos have praised ayahuasca's benefits. In the 2012 movie *Wanderlust,* a character played by Jennifer Aniston drinks the brew made from what the Peruvians refer to as the "vine of souls." Although the Aniston character's ayahuasca experience in *Wanderlust* was grossly misportrayed in the movie, I think the fact that the sacred visionary tea was in the film at all is significant. Another example, which isn't terribly accurate either, comes from actor Ben Stiller, who does ayahuasca in the 2014 comedy *While We're Young.* A more accurate portrayal of the ayahuasca experience is found in Jan Kounen's less-known 2004 film *Renegade,* which has some wonderful scenes with uncannily accurate visual effects that are reminiscent of ayahuasca visions. However, what's important here is that ayahuasca and psychedelic shamanism are seeping into Western culture. Many people suspect that in James Cameron's popular 2009 film *Avatar,* the Na'vis' "tree of souls" was symbolic of ayahuasca.[29]

As well, relatively positive articles about ayahuasca have appeared in *Marie Claire,* the *New York Times Magazine, Elle,* and many other mainstream publications over the past few years. Yet regardless of the recent media hype and tourist attention, ayahuasca is the real deal. Many people report profound healings from using it, and it has a long track record of safe use.

The U.S. Supreme Court ruled in 2006 that the sacred Amazonian brew can be used in the United States as a legal sacrament by the União do Vegetal (UDV) church in New Mexico, and in 2009 by the Santo Daime Church in Oregon. For everyone else it's a schedule 1 drug, in the same category as heroin and LSD. This is because ayahuasca contains DMT. In the Amazon, DMT is naturally found in a number of plants and in the shrub *Psychotria viridis,* or chacruna, which is often used in ayahuasca brews. Notably, the chemical structures of psilocybin and DMT are almost identical. The only difference is that the psilocybin molecule has an oxygen atom and a phosphate group attached to it, which makes it orally active and less susceptible than DMT to breakdown by enzymes in the body.

DMT, on the other hand, is not active orally because it's destroyed in the digestive system by the enzyme monoamine oxidase (MAO). But shamans have discovered a clever way around this obstacle. Although every shaman has his own personal recipe for making the ayahuasca brew, which includes different adjunct plants, the mixture always contains plants with two key chemical elements: DMT and the psychoactive indole alkaloid harmaline. Harmaline, found in the *Banisteriopsis caapi* (ayahuasca) vine, is a substance that deactivates the body's release of MAO and is thus known as an MAO inhibitor (MAOI). This allows the DMT in ayahuasca brews to become orally active. It also slows down the experience and renders it much more comprehensible or psychologically digestible.

Of special note here is that the icaros of the ayahuasca shamans, i.e., the songs and melodies hummed during ayahuasca ceremonies to invoke the presence of particular spirits, often come to them in their dreams. According to anthropologist Charles Laughlin, dreaming has been an integral part of the "calling, selection and empowerment of shamans . . . since perhaps the beginning of the Upper Paleolithic some 40,000 years ago."[30]

The process of becoming a shaman is often not the most pleasant of experiences, and it appears that traditionally one isn't offered much of a choice in the profession. Many shamans believe that they are called to their healing roles through initiatory dreams during childhood or adolescence. According to Stanley Krippner, "Most shamanic traditions take the position that refusal to follow the 'call' will result in a terrible accident, a life-threatening sickness, or insanity. Common themes in initiatory dreams are dismemberment, death, and rebirth."[31]

There are also striking connections between ayahuasca-based shamanism and lucid dreaming on a neurological level. California Institute of Integral Studies clinical psychology professor Frank Echenhofer collaborated with anthropologist Luis Eduardo Luna to perform EEG measurements of the brain while under the influence of ayahuasca.[32] They discovered a strong synchrony in the frontal lobe over multiple frequency bands, specifically in the high beta and gamma range, which is similar to what has been found during EEG studies with lucid dreaming[33] and meditation.[34] Additionally, using fMRI scanners, research by Fernanda Palhano-Fontes and colleagues at the Federal University of Rio Grande do Norte, in Brazil, found that ayahuasca modulates the activity of a brain region known as the *default mode network* (DMN).[35] This region of the brain is known to be more active during rest than during the execution of goal-directed behavior. The results of this study support the notion that the states of consciousness induced by ayahuasca—like those induced by psilocybin, meditation, and sleep— are linked to the modulation of the activity and the connectivity of the DMN. In particular, ayahuasca intake leads to a decrease in the activity of core DMN structures, which is also decreased during meditation and sleep.

I've personally experienced what appears to be "spirit encounters" during the nights following an ayahuasca ceremony, and I often have lucid dreams during this period as well—an experience confirmed by others. These spirit encounters (for lack of a better term) often happen as I'm falling asleep, while looking around my dark room. I'll see moving, morphing energies and feel presences that seem to enter my dreams. Many people report these same types of spirit encounters, as well as other shamanic states of consciousness and lucid dreams, after drinking ayahuasca. For example, my Facebook friend and freelance writer Guy Crittenden wrote me, saying:

My drinking ayahuasca for the first time in Peru led to my having incredible visions while I was on the medicine. . . . What I didn't expect was that about two months after my return to Canada I would begin having shamanic-type lucid dreams and full-on aya-huasca visions while NOT on the medicine. These usually occurred at about 4:00 a.m. . . . I would wake up yet remain in the dark with eyes closed, experiencing the most incredible journeys. This is an ability or phenomenon I have since cultivated and actively seek out. The experiences include clouds of intense psychedelic color, white light that fills my entire visual field for a prolonged period . . . complex geometric patterns and three-dimensional tableaux and dream scenarios rich in symbolism. I believe the entheogen opened up my "third eye" . . . and removed some filters that normally keep us trapped in consensus reality. I no longer view dreams as mere hallucinations of the unconscious mind, but now think of them as visions into another dimension of reality that actually exists and is connected to the afterlife from which we emerged and to which we all will return. They never told me any of this was possible on the travel brochure to Peru!

My own experiences with ayahuasca have led to many lucid dreams and powerful visions as well. However, that wasn't the reason why I first drank ayahuasca. I went to the ayahuasca spirit initially for healing. I can personally attest to the medicinal powers of this sacred shamanic brew, as drinking it in the Peruvian Amazon healed me from childhood PTSD and cured me of the symptoms of an early trauma that haunted me for decades.

HOW AYAHUASCA CURED ME OF CHILDHOOD PTSD

At the age of three I was sexually traumatized over a period of several months by a teenage babysitter. Although I never forgot that this had happened to me, it took me over forty-five years to figure out that this was the primary reason for many of the psychological problems that had plagued me throughout my life. The earliest dream I can remember occurred when I was around the age that the trauma occurred. The dream was very vivid and extremely frightening:

I was in a room in our New Jersey apartment (that didn't really exist in waking reality) with my dad and my cousin. In the dream my dad had somehow transformed my cousin into a giant spinning toy top. She looked like a huge Hanukkah dreidel, with flat sides; it was her size, the size of a small child. The toy top was pinkish, composed of her flesh, and I could see her distorted face in the structure of the toy as it was spinning around. My dad was laughing, and I was terrified that he was going to turn me into a meat-made toy top next . . .

It's basic psychology to know that parts of us can be aware of things that remain hidden from other parts, and so despite years of studying psychology and neuroscience, years spent in introspection and meditation, years spent writing reflectively in journals, and years spent experimenting with psychedelics, I never saw the connection between my own trauma and many of the problems I was experiencing in life. It was a genuine psychological blind spot. Even in a year of psychotherapy with one of the best psychiatrists in the world, Oscar Janiger,* during a time when I was suffering from acute depression, my sexual trauma as a child never even came up in our discussions, not even once.

---

*Oscar "Oz" Janiger (1918–2001) was also a good friend and one of my most valuable mentors. As I mentioned earlier, Oz was the person who introduced me to Stephen LaBerge; this was at Oz's home in Santa Monica. Oz served on the board of directors for a foundation that funded some of LaBerge's early research, and this was how I learned about the scientific study of lucid dreaming. Oz did the LSD and creativity studies that I mentioned earlier in the chapter, and he was the psychiatrist responsible for turning many Hollywood celebrities on to LSD when it was still legal (Cary Grant, Jack Nicholson, Peter Fonda, Anaïs Nin, et al.). The interview that I did with Oz is in my book *Mavericks of the Mind,* which also includes my interview with LaBerge.

The realization finally hit me at the age of forty-nine, after a close friend made some revealing observations about me and I read up on the characteristic symptoms. This sent me into deep reflection; so many of the personal challenges I had faced throughout my life suddenly became instantly understandable. It was the missing puzzle piece that illuminated the dynamics behind maddeningly confusing aspects of my life, despite the fact that this realization seemed like such a psychological cliché. Soon after reaching these insights I had a nonlucid dream that struck a deep chord within me:

> I was at a large family gathering in a huge building. I kept getting lost and separated from everyone else in my family, and kept trying to find them. It was scary and frustrating. Later in the dream I found myself sandwiched between two teenage boys in a pickup truck. We were driving down a dark road, and I was scared and confused about what was happening. I asked the guy sitting to my right who he was. He said, "Don't you recognize me? I'm Roger."

Roger was the name of the teenage babysitter who had sexually molested me as a child. However, after realizing this insight, I was still at a loss about how to treat the primary symptoms of my trauma: having the fear circuit in my brain hypersensitized such that I overreacted with acute anxiety or near-total dissociation to stressful stimuli; being prone to clinical depression; and repeatedly reacting inappropriately in romantic relationships by being too emotionally needy or too aloof. I also had great difficulty expressing anger, suppressing it for many years, as well as problems with eating and sleeping. This emotional hypersensitivity resulted in wide mood swings, which my psychiatrist and I mistook for bipolar 2 disorder. I read around a dozen books about treating childhood sexual trauma after I figured this out, but I didn't feel like more psychotherapy would have helped me much at this point. I also tried searching for greater insight into what had happened to me during a lucid dream, without much success:

Soon after becoming lucid in a dream I tried questioning the mysterious agent orchestrating those aspects of the dream that I'm not in control of.* I was in a large department store or warehouse with no other people. I raised my head to the ceiling and asked my unconscious mind to show me the details of what had happened to me when I was traumatized at the age of three. There was no verbal response from the dream, except that I saw a large, luxurious, empty bed in front of me, with all these fluffy white covers that were messed up a bit, and the blankets were bunched up, like people had been using it for sex. The dream never spoke back in words as I was expecting or hoping. I woke up soon after that, disappointed that I didn't get a clearer message.

Around this time the memory and insights into the consequences of my trauma became a wide-open wound, and I spoke with many people who had had similar childhood experiences. For several months it was hard for me to speak about anything else. I was searching for answers, and in time my intuition urged me to treat my trauma with ayahuasca. From the stories I had heard about it helping people heal from virtually every malady from inoperable cancer to treatment-resistant PTSD, I was most intrigued. I had great trust in the sincere, sacred powers of psychedelic healing as a result of using LSD, cannabis, and magic mushrooms. Most impressively, I once had a serious foot injury miraculously heal completely overnight during a psilocybin mushroom trip. So while I was in Peru to speak at the annual Amazonian Shamanism Conference in Iquitos, I decided to try ayahuasca made from the traditional jungle plants in an attempt to heal myself from childhood PTSD.

My subsequent personal journeys with ayahuasca in the Peruvian Amazon convinced me that this magical medicinal brew can provide the most valuable and healing of all psychedelic experiences. While undergoing a series of shamanic ayahuasca journeys, I realized that the intelligence and the intention of the plants themselves play a vital role in the healing that occurs, and that they can serve as a both a doctor and a

---

*This is a technique that we'll be discussing in chapter 10.

teacher—or so it appears, and it sure seems pretty convincing. One can actually feel the spirit of the plants scanning one's body, finding wounded areas that need to be healed. One simply observes in spellbound fascination as this spirit then performs the necessary adjustments with a kind of ultraprecise and painless astral surgery that provides almost instant relief and understanding. It appears that the ayahuasca brew, as well as shamanic cacti, iboga, and enchanted fungi, contain a living spirit, an intelligent being that will communicate with you directly as she heals you. Understanding whether or not these wise and powerful beings are genuinely external to our own minds will surely remain one of the great philosophical questions for a long time to come, but wherever these wise and helpful beings come from, and whatever they are, they certainly seem to know us much better than we know ourselves.

During an ayahuasca journey this ancient intelligence often speaks to us through vivid and fluid imagery, in scenes that combine into a kind of metalanguage, the voice of dreams and even spoken words and spelled-out letters. It seems that she will use every sensory channel and symbolic medium possible, sometimes urgently so, to make absolutely sure that you get her message. Her superintelligence and profound healing abilities simply cannot be denied once they've been experienced.

The healing process for me began with that first journey using traditional ayahuasca at the home of a friend in Iquitos, Peru, where the shamanic brew is not only legal but long-respected by the culture there as a sacred medicine. Although I was geographically situated in the Amazon Basin, I did my first dose of the traditional plant brew in a completely nontraditional setting. And my first experience on ayahuasca was almost entirely sexual.

My Peruvian girlfriend and I did it alone together, in a bedroom upstairs in my friend's home, and we spent the night mostly in bed. The air was thick and muggy, and we were naked the whole time. My girlfriend purged a few times at the beginning of the journey, but I never got nauseous once, and she was fine after the first hour or so. Then we made love for hours under the influence of the ancient shamanic brew, as lights sparkled in the air and our bodies shimmered with pulsing vibrations that trailed with each movement. Spirits flew around the room, and thousands of iridescent, bejeweled snakes slithered between us, inside of us, intertwining with our blending bodies. It was an extraordinarily magical night.*

Doing this was expressly forbidden! Almost every shamanic tradition in the Amazon stresses that one should abstain from sex for several days before and after an ayahuasca experience, and most certainly not have sex while on it! But the spirits didn't seem to disapprove of what we were doing, and as I say, it was the beginning of my healing process. This experience was beyond amazing, and the next day we both felt great. My personal feeling is that this restriction on sex before or during an ayahuasca ceremony is an unnecessary, lingering Christian influence. I know that others may disagree, but I can't argue with what worked for me.

In any case, after this first journey whirling around in heaven, I proceeded further into more difficult stages of the ayahuasca healing process, facing the amplified difficulties of my early trauma. I ended up doing the traditional plant brew around thirty-five times over a period of several months, mostly alone, and with progressively stronger and stronger doses. I welcomed the spirit into my body and asked her to heal me.

During the most significant of these experiences with ayahuasca, I approached the spirit of the Amazon with a request: to be liberated from all the unreasonable fear I had experienced in my life as a result of my early trauma. The ancient psychedelic spirit's response? "Hey, dude, no problem—teaching humans how to overcome fear is one of my specialties! C'mon, I'm taking you to warrior school!" Then for the next four hours I was subjected to every one of my deepest fears, over and over, at horrific intensities, as the frightening dimensions of them

---

*I've never heard of anyone else doing this, and my having done so may shock some people. I'm including my experience here because it was an essential part of my healing process, and I hope that this information can be helpful to others. However, for most people, during an ayahuasca experience the desire to engage in sexual activity is probably the last thing on their mind.

diminished more and more, and I could feel the ayahuasca spirit making adjustments deep in my brain as this was happening. Or so it seemed.

I was simply ecstatic at the end of that particular session, feeling genuinely fearless, but also skeptical that I had really been cured of my anxieties and fears. I expressed my skepticism to the ayahuasca spirit, and she responded, "Dude, we cured your foot last year. You don't think we can heal your head too?" In any case, I waited six weeks, testing this new mental state out as my personal secret before I told another person about my experience. I truly wanted to make sure that it was real before I said anything to anyone about it. At the time of this writing it's now been over two years, and I haven't felt any unreasonable fear or anxiety since that experience. It feels like a miraculous healing. However, there were sometimes unexpected consequences to this healing that required additional psychological work, as many layers of my personality over the years had been structured around the trauma, and, once corrected, I had to work through unanticipated and sometimes difficult dynamics with people, such as those that resulted from my newly liberated ability to express anger more easily. Although difficult at times, the process was profoundly healing on many levels—physically, emotionally, mentally, socially, and spiritually.

Then, during the process of writing this book I had the following lucid dream, where it seemed that I finally got an answer to the question I had posed in the lucid dream that I described previously in this chapter:

An attractive young man from a previous lucid dream was sitting next to me in a classroom where we were both students, when I became lucid. Ever impulsive with my sexual experimentations in lucid dreams, I reached over and started fondling his penis through his pants, which he didn't seem to mind. I somehow knew that this was wrong or forbidden in the dream, but I was lucid and continued to do it anyway—because it was fun, and I figured, well, it was just a dream, right? Then I could see this very stern and angry-looking, androgynous-seeming teacher walking toward me—just as *my friend had an orgasm and ejaculated all over his pants. The menacing, androgynous teacher came right up to me, looked me in the face, and was really angry. Being lucid, I wasn't afraid, but I also realized that I couldn't fully control what was happening either, and I could see how a lucid nightmare happens. The androgynous teacher (who, most disturbingly, had the face of a gay woman that I actually know in waking life, and who was also sexually traumatized as a child) whips out this humongous penis, the size of an anaconda,* and immediately forces it down my throat! Despite being lucid, I couldn't stop this from happening, and "she" forcibly raped my mouth with this giant penis—to punish me for what I was doing to the other boy. It wasn't really painful or scary, as I was lucid and mostly just fascinated, although it was disturbing, and I could certainly see how an experience like this could be absolutely terrifying for some people. I didn't try to wake myself up during the dream, but instead reached my hand out and simply wiped it over the androgynous teacher's face. I started to do this repeatedly, and as I did so it transformed "her" face to become like moldable clay or putty. Each time I moved my hand over her face it became more pliable, less roughly defined, and less threatening-looking. Soon her whole face and body turned into an ornately designed carving or statue of a bird in a cage, with elaborate and Gothic designs around it, as her giant penis dissolved, and then I awoke.*

This dream felt profoundly healing for me, and it was clearly related to my childhood trauma. Most significantly, I was able to reexperience my childhood trauma without fear, and I transformed the androgynous rapist of my unconscious mind into a caged bird. But I don't think I could have achieved this level of psychological and emotional resolution without having done ayahuasca.

---

*One of the most common visions people have while on ayahuasca is that of an anaconda slithering down their throat. In fact, when my girlfriend and I did ayahuasca for the first time and had sex all night, at one point near the beginning of the journey she had a vision of a giant serpent slithering down her throat. This then became the foundation for a running joke between us for the rest of the night, based on the double meaning of the phrase *Un anaconda grande en mi boca!* (A huge anaconda is in my mouth!)

As anyone who has read my previous book *The New Science of Psychedelics* knows, I'm no newcomer to psychedelic drugs and plants. There was something truly special, utterly sacred, and unusually healing about doing ayahuasca made from traditional plants in the Amazon basin that made these experiences far more healing than any other psychedelic experiences I'd ever had. But maybe that's because of my expectations.

THE POWER OF BELIEF

Like dreaming, ayahuasca experiences are largely influenced by what we believe and expect, and both experiences appear to share the common factor of elevated DMT levels in the brain. Ayahuasca and other psychedelic agents appear to amplify what medical science calls "the placebo effect," or the power of the mind to affect the health of the body. This is why it's important to approach both dreams and psychedelic experiences with particular questions and intentions, to help guide the healing process. You can ask questions or direct your intentions to the awareness behind the dream or the spirit inside the shamanic experience. This may be the key to understanding their broad and mysterious healing effects, as they appear to act directly on our sense of belief, how we determine what is real and what isn't. In other words, the enormous healing power of psychedelics may lie in their extraordinary ability to affect what we actually believe to be true about reality and ourselves.

Like psychedelic agents, lucid dreaming has the ability to amplify and manifest the contents of the mind. For example, a study by psychologist, visionary artist, and professor Fariba Bogzaran found a statistical correlation between the different concepts of what an encounter with the divine might be like and those lucid dreams later recorded by subjects after they experienced them.[36] Along with psychedelic experiences, lucid dreaming has also been an important part of a number of shamanic healing traditions around the world.

SHAMANISM, SPIRITS, AND
LUCID DREAMING

In numerous shamanic-healing systems lucid dreaming has been used traditionally for locating hidden information, building physical or psychological strength, contacting spirits, communicating with the dead, and providing healing treatments for those who are sick or wounded.[37] The domains of lucid dreams are the same as those for shamanism in general—it is used for healing, guidance, and power.

One of the core beliefs that connect shamanic traditions the world over and provides a model for understanding lucid dreaming is the notion that there are other realities veiled from our five senses, higher and lower worlds that coexist with our own, parallel with our waking reality and overlapping with it to some degree. Shamans can access these "spirit realms" through "journeys of the soul," made available through dreams and altered states of consciousness.

Anthropologist Erika Bourguignon has shown how cultures that use dreams in an attempt to "control supernatural forces" correspond to the institutionalized practice of entering "hallucinogenic trance" states, and that the two states are so closely allied with the motivation to control supernatural forces that it is hard to tell where trance leaves off and dreaming begins.[38]

The ancient Egyptians appear to have practiced a form of conscious dreaming. Their written records reveal that they believed that the soul, or *Ba,* could travel outside one's body during sleep, and amazingly their word for *dream* is *resut,* which translates as "awakening"[39] and was depicted in hieroglyphs as a wide-open eye! Ancient Egyptians were the first to construct temples specifically designed for the practice of dream incubation, used for healing or receiving divine messages.

Another fascinating cultural form of disciplined dream practice can be found in Russian psychiatrist Olga Kharitidi's book *The Master of Lucid Dreams.* Kharitidi describes her extraordinary experiences with a teacher from a mysterious shamanic tradition in Siberia that has no other written record. The story takes place in Samarkand, the ancient capital of Uzbekistan, in Central Asia, where Kharitidi meets an enigmatic, perceptive, and persuasive man with unusual mental abilities who takes her on a healing journey. What's most interesting about her story is that the primary tool used by these shamanic practitioners is lucid dreaming, which they equate with death and use as a technique for removing the influence of past traumas from the mind. In chapter 10 we'll explore the idea that dreaming offers insight into what happens to one's consciousness after death as well as possibly allowing for communication with those who have passed on.

In ancient Mexico, members of the Mesoamerican Toltec culture in Tula are reported to have used lucid-dreaming practices and "power plants" such as peyote to promote healing,[40] and like the shamanic tradition that Kharitidi describes in Samarkand, it appears that the Toltec culture also equates lucid dreaming with death. In Mexican healer Sergio Magaña's book about the dreaming practices of the ancient Mexicans, *The Toltec Secret,* the author states that "you will know when you have overcome your fear of death when you start lucid dreaming regularly, because that is like dying."[41]

According to Carlos Castaneda and others, within the Toltec culture there exists a clan of "sorcerers" who have mastered the art of conscious dreaming and secretly exist to this day. Although Castaneda's wonderfully described accounts are largely dismissed by many anthropologists as fiction, there may be some truth to his reports, and he clearly had sophisticated knowledge of psychedelic and shamanic states of consciousness. Shamans among the Chontal people in Mexico are known to have used the psychoactive herb *Calea zacatechichi** for dream enhancement and for divinatory and healing purposes, a subject we'll be discussing again in chapter 5.

Among the Mekeo people of Papua New Guinea, shamans supposedly heal other people by "traveling in their dreams to power places in search of their patient's lost souls."[42] The Mekeo shamans

---

*Its English-language common names include Thepelakano (leaves of god), bitter grass, Mexican calea, and dream herb.

appear to be lucid-dream masters, capable of focusing their dreams on specific intentions for healing the ill or injured. Anthropologist Charles D. Laughlin describes how shamanistic traditions in eastern Peru, among the traditional people known as the Yanesha, use lucid-dreaming techniques to treat frightening dreams. In particular, Laughlin provides a striking example of a Yanesha boy who was experiencing nightmares about his dead father chasing him and trying to kill him. The boy was relieved of these frightening nightmares by advice from his mother, who told him to recognize in his dreams that his father was dead, that he should fly away from him and eventually confront and "kill him"—after which he was never haunted by nightmares of his father again.[43]

According to Laughlin the whole notion of "lucid dreaming" is an ethnocentric concept. He writes, "There is a lot wrong with this definition of lucidity from an anthropological point of view, not the least being its inherent ethnocentricity. It assumes a culture in which waking states and dreaming states are distinct, one being associated with active awareness and the other not. We would hardly expect that kind of distinction to be made by folks brought up in a fully polyphasic culture."[44]

Laughlin makes an important point here when he says that not all cultures make the distinction between waking reality and dreaming that we take for granted in the West. "Oh honey, that was *just* a dream—go back to sleep now," Western parents routinely say to their children in an attempt to get them to disregard their dreams as having any significance. This is an example of what Laughlin calls a "monophasic culture." In contrast, "polyphasic cultures" like those found in many preindustrial societies as well as in other industrial societies such as Japan, China, and Brazil are cultures wherein dreams and their interpretations are highly valued. According to Laughlin, Western European societies aside, there are over four thousand cultures on the planet today, and around 90 percent of them seek out and value experiences had in altered states of consciousness, and especially in dreams.[45]

As I mentioned in the introduction and will discuss at length in chapter 10, lucid-dreaming practice is an important part of several

Eastern philosophical systems, including Vajrayāna Buddhism as well as the ancient Bön religion, the latter of which appears to have shamanic roots and utilizes sacred healing plant medicines. Like psychedelic mind states, lucid dreaming has great potential for physical and psychological healing. But that's not all that these two states of mind have in common.

LUCID IN THE SKY WHILE DREAMING: PSYCHEDELICS, NIGHT FLIGHTS, AND DREAM LUCIDITY

In a discussion about the relationship between dreaming and shamanism, Charles Laughlin states that "when lucidity of dreaming and visions exceed a certain point, it is hard to tell the difference between a dream report and a vision report."[46] Additionally, Laughlin says that many anthropologists "just assume that what is being depicted [in shamanic rock art] are shamans in trance states, whereas there is ample evidence from ethnographic sources that San [Bushmen] shamans are adept lucid dreamers as well."[47]

Laughlin makes the important point that lucid dreaming and visionary states of consciousness have a lot in common. Consider the following lucid dream by English writer and occultist Oliver Fox (1885–1949),* which sounds a lot like an ayahuasca or mushroom vision:

Eventually we left the carnival and fire behind us and came to a yellow path, leading across a desolate moor. As we stood at the foot of this path it suddenly rose up before us and became a roadway of golden light stretching from earth to zenith. Now in this amber-tinted haze there appeared countless coloured forms of men and beasts, representing man's upward evolution through different stages of civilization. These forms faded away; the pathway lost its golden tint and became a mass of vibrating circles or globules (like frog's eggs), a purplish-blue colour. These in their turn changed to

*Throughout this book I refer to the writings of Oliver Fox, which was the pen name of British writer Hugh George Callaway.

'peacock's eyes', and then suddenly there came a culminating vision of a gigantic peacock, whose outspread tail filled the heavens. I exclaimed to my wife, 'The Vision of the Universal Peacock!' Moved by the splendour of the sight, I recited in a loud voice a mantra. Then the dream ended.[48]

Or consider the following lucid dream that was had by "Keelin" and reported by psychologist Fariba Bogzaran, which also sounds a lot like an ayahuasca or mushroom vision:

I become aware of being in a vast, limitless darkness that is at the same time brilliant with countless stars and very much alive. Something emerges from the darkness. It looks like some kind of living, molecular model/mathematical equation—extremely complex, three-dimensional. Fluorescent, neon-orange in color—very thin lines, very clear and sharp visually. It seems to unfold itself, multiplying, constantly changing, forming more complex structures and interrelationships. It is filling up the Universe. This growing movement is not erratic, but consistent and purposeful—rapid but at the same time determined. . . . This is the best way I can describe the space. It is rapid, yet there is a feeling that the knowledge or reality of it already exists, or that it is being born, exists in its entirety and visually manifest all in the same one moment.[49]

Similarly, journalist Damon Orion personally told me about the psychedelic lucid dreams he has: "The deeper I go into the lucid-dream state, the more beautiful the colors get. For example, in one lucid dream I looked out the window of a train I was in and saw the trippiest, most gorgeous sunset I'd ever seen (in dreams or in waking life). The swirls and blotches of color in these kinds of lucid dreams are really close to the ones you see while tripping."

Like a psychedelic experience, it can be challenging to describe what lucid dreaming is like to someone who has never experienced it. Because I've been having lucid dreams for much of my life, and because so many people I know have had them too, and because I knew that it has been scientifically verified in the sleep laboratory, it didn't even occur to me until after I started writing this book that there are quite a few people who don't believe that lucid dreaming is genuinely real, or think that it's been greatly exaggerated. I was truly surprised to speak with people who thought that lucid-dreaming reports are fabrications or exaggerations.

For example, American philosopher Norman Malcolm (1911–1990) pointed out that the only criterion we have for determining the truth of a statement about someone having a particular dream is the dreamer's own words. Malcolm says that lucid dreaming is absurd and impossible, providing this mocking example: "I dreamt that I realized I was dreaming, dreamt that I was affecting the course of my dream, and then dreamt that I woke myself up by telling myself to wake up."[50]

Charles Laughlin helps to explains why some people have trouble understanding the reality of lucid dreaming: "Without, I hope, sounding patronizing, if one has not experienced a lucid dream, then one will have little idea of just how 'real' a dream experience can be. This is no different than saying that if one has not been on a magic mushroom trip, one cannot say what it is like—or a high altitude gas balloon flight, or scuba diving, and so forth. In lucid dreaming one often has the sense of being more awake and aware in the dream than in waking life."[51]

Yes, people often report feeling more awake while lucid dreaming than they generally do during the daylight hours, and this is likely why psychologist Charles Tart has suggested that lucid dreaming can recreate the experience of many psychedelic drugs.[52] Tart found that some subjects who participated in LSD research subsequently had similar psychedelic experiences in their dreams, and some of the subjects experienced the altered state continuing for a few minutes after they woke up. This implies that a drug is not necessary to create the experience.

As I mentioned earlier in this chapter, when I asked Terence McKenna about his experience with lucid dreaming, he told me about the times when he smoked DMT in the dream state and had full-blown shamanic journeys, which agreed with Tart's hypothesis. McKenna said:

> I have dreams in which I smoke DMT, and it works. To me that is extremely interesting because it seems to imply that one does not have to smoke DMT to have the experience. You only have to convince your brain that you have done this and it then delivers this staggering altered state. How many people who have had DMT dream occasionally of smoking it and have it happen? Do people who have never had DMT ever have that kind of an experience in a dream? I bet not. I bet you have to have done it in life to have established the knowledge of its existence, and the image of how it's possible; then this thing can happen to you without any chemical intervention.

However, Ann Faraday, author of *Dream Power,* thinks differently about this. She describes having had an LSD experience in a dream before ever having taken the drug. Although she experimented with the drug later, she had her first psychedelic experience within a lucid dream. She writes, "The most extraordinary feeling came over me. Surges of energy pulsated throughout my body and I entered a 'high' in which I was completely transported on the kind of internal journey only those who have experienced psychedelic drugs would understand."[53] Additionally, several online articles tell of people having psychedelic drug experiences in lucid dreams although never having had such experiences in waking life.[54] Later, when some of these people did try the actual psychedelic drugs, they reported having similar effects to what they experienced while using their dream psychedelics. For example, my friend Heather shared the following with me:

> *Last night I had a dream about taking DMT. I have not taken DMT before. It started off with me being in this empty shop, and there was a guy in there. I didn't know who he was, but he knew who I was. He asked me questions about psychedelics. I said I have always wanted to try DMT. He told me to be very careful because of my traumatic past and to take it in small doses. Anyway . . . He told me to look in my hands, there was a black box saying*

"eat me." He told me to tap it. So I did, and out popped gold nuggets. They were very solid. He then told me to eat them, which I did. Then he told me it was DMT. I paused, and all of a sudden I started to go dizzy and fell to the floor. There were people walking around me, blurry, as I was about to pass out. It felt so real. And then it went black. Then all I could see were twins dancing in sync. More like robots. It was beautiful, and as I moved toward them they started to duplicate over and over again until I crashed. I had broken through a hole into another world. Everywhere was surrounded by grass. Even the sky. There was no free space. But there were animals, happiness, freedom. I could jump as high as I wanted to and fly through the fields. Then I noticed I was losing vision and I started to go back into the other dream, where the guy was waiting for me. He had asked me how I felt. It was as if I were not in a dream at all. I find it strange how I dreamed of going into another dream and then leaving it, going back into the original.

If Heather ever does try DMT I'd be most curious to hear how her dream journey compared. When I was first inspired to write this book I contacted Stanley Krippner and asked him what sort of connections and parallels he had noticed between the state of lucid dreaming and psychedelic awareness. Being an expert on dreams, shamanism, and altered states of consciousness, Krippner, I was sure, must have had a whole list to send me, but I was surprised by his response: "Frankly, I have never given the topic much thought. I think there are more differences than similarities between lucid dreaming and psychedelic experiences. But the problem is that there is no ONE psychedelic experience and no ONE lucid dreaming experience. So making a comparison would really be stretching it."

Since I didn't think that such a comparison was stretching any logic, I made my own list of the general connections and parallels that I've noticed between the state of lucid dreaming and psychedelic awareness. I'll be discussing these connections in greater detail throughout the book, but briefly, they are:

- Many people report having lucid dreams within days of having a psychedelic experience.

- Similar patterns of activity in the same brain regions are seen in dreaming, lucid dreaming, and in ayahusasca- and psilocybin-induced states.
- Both lucid dreaming and psychedelic experiences are used in shamanism, and both can be used for healing, creativity, improving performance, and developing personal insight.
- "Dream psychedelics" can be used within lucid dreams that have genuine psychological effects.
- Both states of consciousness perceive the world, or our mental simulation of what we believe to be the world, as having less physical stability and greater responsiveness to our mental expectations and beliefs.
- It's been speculated that endogenous DMT (a powerful psychedelic when ingested as a drug) may naturally be involved in dreaming.
- Both states are correlated with an increased frequency of psychic phenomena reports.
- Both states are commonly referred to by people as "waking up."
- Both states increase the magnitude of what appear to be sensory signals from what we believe to be the world; in both states people often describe seeing the world around them in magnificent detail.
- Both states are often categorized by skeptics as hallucinations or merely mental projections, and yet groups who have had personal experience with both states of consciousness often offer differing viewpoints on the reality of dreams and psychedelic perceptions of the world.
- Both states can help us access material in the unconscious and are powerful tools for exploring hidden dimensions of the mind.
- Both states can lead to what has been described as a "spiritual awakening," a "mystical experience," and "boundless unity."
- Both states allow for intriguing contact with what seems to be other people, the dead, and other intelligent beings.

- Both states are categorized by experiences of synchronicity.
- Both states seem to sometimes transcend logic and rationality.
- Both lucid dreaming and psychedelic experiences can be enhanced with meditative practices.
- Synesthesia is reported in both lucid dreams and psychedelic experiences.
- It's been suggested that the unconscious mind communicates with the ego using a similar personal metalanguage in both dreams and psychedelic visions.
- Powerful psychedelic experiences can lead to full immersion in alternative realities, just like lucid dreams.
- Both states can lead to the understanding that we all live inside our own personally constructed realities or mental simulations.

Much has been written about lucid dreams and psychedelic awareness, but little has been written about the striking connection between the two states, and it was largely this insight that inspired me to write the book that you're now holding in your hands. However, before we further explore the mind-bending possibilities of the interface between psychedelic and dreaming brain states, let's first review some basic physiology and psychology. In the next chapter we'll be discussing what happens in our brains during sleep and dreaming, and what function dreaming might serve in our daily lives.

2

THE PSYCHOLOGY AND PHYSIOLOGY OF DREAMING

All human beings are also dream beings. Dreaming ties all mankind together.

JACK KEROUAC

The *American Heritage Dictionary* defines *dream* as a "succession of images, ideas, emotions, and sensations that occur involuntarily in the mind during certain stages of sleep." The length of a dream, or a dreaming period, generally varies from a few seconds to around twenty to thirty minutes.[1] Whether we remember them or not, everyone has around four or five dreaming periods a night. Dreaming is one of the basic activities that every human brain does. Just as the heart pumps blood and the stomach digests food, the brain dreams. In this chapter we'll be reviewing what is known about the physical activity that takes place in the brain during sleep, what biological purpose dreams might serve, what psychological function they might have, and what language dreams speak to us in.

No one knows why we dream, or even why we need to sleep every night. According to psychologist William Moorcroft, author of *Understanding Sleep and Dreaming,* the function of sleep "persists as one of the most enduring and puzzling mysteries in science."[2] Nevertheless, we know that sleep is essential for our survival, and quite a bit is known about what happens in the brain while we sleep and dream. In 1879, German physiological psychologist Wilhelm Wundt speculated that while dreaming, the brains of sleeping people underwent marked changes in physiology. It turned out that he was correct.

THE NEUROSCIENCE OF SLEEP AND DREAMING

During the first half of the twentieth century electroencephalography (EEG), the recording of electrical activity (voltage fluctuations) in the brain using electrodes pasted along the scalp, was developed. This gave researchers a window inside the sleeping brain. Investigators discovered that sleep is not a continuous state; rather, it is a process composed of several distinct states of brain activity.

When we go to sleep each night, the states of activity that the brain passes through can be divided into two basic phases, REM and non-REM (NREM) sleep. REM stands for "rapid eye movements," and this is a neurologically active phase of sleep in which our closed eyes move around quickly. This is a time when we're most likely to be actively and vividly dreaming. NREM sleep is the more passive type of sleep, and it can be further divided into three distinct phases, known as N1, N2, and N3, which each have their own defining characteristics.

Everyone moves through a predictable pattern with these four basic types of sleep that repeat in cycles throughout each night. During the N1 stage of sleep, the brain is in a relaxed state of drowsiness, pulsing with alpha waves (8 to 13 Hz), and it begins to slow down to the rhythm of theta waves (4 to 7 Hz). During this stage of sleep our eyeballs move around slowly and we can be easily awakened. During the N2 stage of sleep the theta brain waves become punctuated by a specific type of brain wave known as a *K-complex spindle,* in which there are no eye movements during this stage. These spindles are fast, lasting only around half a second, and the waves register on an EEG monitor with a large, slow peak, followed by a small valley, which vibrates at a moderately fast frequency (12 to 14 Hz). Stage N3 sleep is characterized by the brain oscillating in slow delta waves (less than 4 Hz). There are no eye movements during this stage of deep sleep, and it is more difficult to awaken someone from this heavy state of slumber than any other stage of sleep. This is followed by REM sleep, which is, of course, characterized by rapid eye movements; the brain waves become fast, almost like in a waking state, and these are called "sawtooth waves." This is the stage of sleep when we are almost always actively dreaming, although research and scientific evidence now suggests that we may be dreaming, or experiencing some type of mental activity, throughout our sleep.

There is currently no clear physiological indication that signals that a person is dreaming within the usual sleep laboratory measurements. In other words, there is no definitive way to physically measure or determine if someone is actually dreaming; self-reports are the only way to know for certain and these don't always match up with the REM stage of sleep. That is, with one obvious exception: when a lucid dreamer can signal to researchers during sleep. Our ability to remember dream experiences after being awakened in a sleep laboratory is around 80 percent during REM sleep and 45 percent during NREM stages of sleep.[3]

Russian mathematician and esotericist P. D. Ouspensky (1878–1947) stated that careful observations of his mental states led him to believe that people are always dreaming.[4] According to Ouspensky, our waking consciousness overshadows the ever-present dreams going on in our brains, just as the sun outshines the stars in the sky during the day, but the dreams are always there despite the fact that we are usually not aware of them and only remember them under certain conditions.

There may be something to Ouspensky's idea. Sleep studies suggest that we may be dreaming all night long, and psychedelic experiences provide evidence that substantial unconscious psychological activity is always occurring below the threshold of awareness. In any case, lucid dreaming is characterized by gamma waves (20 to 50 Hz) during REM sleep, along with the active involvement of the prefrontal cortex, which performs executive functions in the brain. These brain wave cycles, characterized by N1, N2, N3, and REM, repeat throughout the night, with each of the four stages occurring about every ninety to 110 minutes. Throughout the night the periods of REM sleep grow longer and longer. This is why many lucid dreams happen to people during the latter stages of sleep, and why herbs, drugs, or supplements that promote dreaming or lucidity are most effective when taken at this time.

That's the basic pattern of sleep that we all cycle through every night. However, making the leap from patterns of electrochemical brain activity to the wild world of dreams is no easy task. It is even more complicated when we ask ourselves how has modern living affected our dream life?

ELECTRIC LIGHTING AND HUMAN SLEEP PATTERNS

Few people are aware that before the Industrial Age and prior to the invention of artificial lighting, people (or at least Western Europeans) naturally had two periods of sleep each night, with two or three hours of calm wakefulness in between. Research by Virginia Tech history professor Roger Ekirch reveals that people didn't always sleep in a single eight-hour period.[5] Ekirch demonstrates how we used to sleep over a period of around twelve hours, during which time we would generally sleep for around three or four hours, then wake up for around two or three hours, then sleep again for another three or four hours.

References to these first and second sleep periods can be found in many works of literature and medicine that were written prior to the widespread use of artificial lighting. In *The Canterbury Tales,* Chaucer writes about a character who goes to bed after her "firste sleep." Prior to electric lighting, a British physician wrote that the time between the "first sleep" and the "second sleep" was the best time for study and reflection.[6] Additionally, research by psychiatrist Thomas A. Wehr at the National Institute of Mental Health in Bethesda, Maryland, adds further support for this notion.[7] Wehr conducted an experiment in which the subjects were deprived of electric light. At first, without the glowing distraction of light bulbs or electronic devices, the participants in the study slept through the night. However, after a while Wehr noticed that subjects began to wake up a little after midnight, lie awake for a couple of hours, and then drift back to sleep again. According to Wehr this period of "non-anxious wakefulness" possessed "an endocrinology all its own."[8] Wehr observed that during this period people had elevated levels of the pituitary hormone prolactin, which causes nursing mothers to lactate as well as being involved in a large number of other functions. He described this intervening period of wakefulness as an altered state of consciousness similar to meditation, which is correlated with lucid dreaming.

What Wehr observed in his sleep laboratory appears to be the same pattern of segmented sleep that Ekirch saw referenced in historical records and early works of literature. This period of several hours of wakefulness during the night is often described as peaceful, calm, and meditative. During this time, called the "watching period," people are reported to have usually stayed in bed to contemplate their lives, converse with their partners, pray to their deity, make love, smoke tobacco, or simply enjoy their wandering states of altered consciousness. Also, according to Ekirch, it was of historical importance that during this period of calm wakefulness people "reflected on their dreams, a significant source of solace and self-awareness."[9]

So how has this change in our sleeping patterns changed our dream life? No one really knows, but this change may have interfered with our awareness of our dreams and with our dream recall. Lucid dreams tend to occur in the later stages of sleep, especially after periods of waking oneself up before returning to sleep, so this more recent sleep pattern in humans may be making it more difficult for us to lucid dream.

When I interviewed Rick Strassman he suggested that artificial electric lighting could reduce the brain's natural DMT production, which might be associated with dreaming. He told me, "With respect to the pineal [gland], pineal activity increases in darkness and during winter and decreases in increased light and in summer. Even relatively dim artificial light, indoors, has a suppressive effect on pineal function, and it may be that if generic pineal activity were related to DMT pro-duction, decreased activity through the aegis of increased ambient light during hours that were previously dark may have something to do with decreased normative DMT levels."

Personally, I think that part of the reason I have so many lucid dreams—generally, several a month—is because as a writer I don't have to follow a regimented sleep schedule. I wake up and go to sleep when-ever I want to, and I often naturally sleep three to four hours twice during a twenty-four-hour period.

So nobody really knows how much artificial lighting has influenced our dream life. But then again, we hardly even have a clue as to why we need to dream every night to begin with.

WHAT IS THE BIOLOGICAL FUNCTION OF DREAMS?

In a meme that's been floating around the Internet, one stick figure says to another, "Sometimes it seems bizarre to me that we take dreaming in stride." "Are you coming to dinner?" the other stick figure asks. "Yeah, but first I'm gonna go comatose for a few hours, hallucinate vividly, and maybe suffer amnesia about the whole experience." "Okay, cool," the other stick figure replies. This simple cartoon highlights just how weird dreaming is, and how it is even stranger that we often don't give it much thought.

Many psychologists and psychiatrists are taught that dreams are basically meaningless, mere byproducts of a sleeping brain, but some research suggests that dreaming may have a purpose, or, possibly, mul-tiple purposes. According to influential neuroscientists J. Allan Hobson and Robert W. McCarley, dreams are the result of attempts by higher brain centers to "make sense" out the cortical stimulation created by lower brain "dream generators."[10] In other words, internal stimulation is randomly produced in the lower brain centers, while the higher brain centers use this as story material to shape our dreams. For this reason Hobson proposes that dream formation is an inherently creative process.

Some research suggests that higher brain centers play a more deter-mining role in dream formation,[11] while other research indicates that dreaming may serve a biological function. Psychologists Tore Nielsen and Philippe Stenstrom have demonstrated that "dreaming about newly learned materials enhances subsequent recall of that material."[12] Some neuroscientists think that sleeping is a way for the brain to clear out its daily accumulation of unneeded memories so that it can consolidate important memories together, and there is scientific evidence to support this.[13] Additionally, REM sleep appears to facilitate brain development, as animals that are relatively immature at birth need to spend more time in this state.

One clue as to the function of dreams comes from that fact that most dreams are negatively biased and are about frightening, disturb-ing, shocking, or frustrating events. Most dreams are not sweet and pleasant, and in fact they tend to be reported as generally being more negative than waking life.[14] For over forty years the late psychologist Calvin Hall collected more than fifty thousand dream accounts from college students. These revealed that the most common emotion expe-rienced in dreams was anxiety, and that, in general, negative emotions were much more common than positive ones.[15]

People dream differently during different stages of their develop-ment, and there are also differences between how men and women dream. For example, men tend to report more acts of aggression in their dreams, and women's dreams tend to have more characters in them.[16] Also, male characters tend to predominate in men's dreams by 67 per-cent, whereas the ratio between male and female figures in women's dreams is more balanced.[17]

Another fact is that approximately 80 percent of all dreams are reported as being in color, although there is a considerable percentage of people who report they only dream in black and white. In studies where dreamers have been awakened and then asked to select colors from a chart that match those in their dreams, they most frequently chose soft pastel colors.[18] Apparently, there is a certain area of the brain where our sense of color is processed, and if this area is damaged, then color disappears from perception in waking life, from dreams during sleep, and even from one's memories.[19]

Other studies that may shed some light on the function of dreaming include those that incorporate a method whereby subjects wear glasses with vertically reversing lenses that have the effect of turning one's visual field upside-down. After a few days, the subjects adjust to this topsy-turvy condition, and the world becomes right side up again with the prismatic glasses on. During the period of adaptation, the percentage of time spent in REM sleep escalates dramatically.[20] This implies that dreaming may play a role in adjusting to altered modes of perception or sustained changes in one's environment.

In any case, if the functions of sleep still remain largely mysterious, then dreams are even more puzzling. When researchers deprive people of just REM sleep, there are no obvious physical or psychological changes. However, it's difficult to conduct REM-deprivation studies for longer than a week because the brain keeps trying to go into REM more and more each night, until the subject would need to be awakened too often to continue the research.

Also, as I mentioned earlier, additional research has shown that people not only dream during NREM sleep, they dream differently in REM and NREM sleep.[21] It appears that our conscious minds are processing memories or are involved in some sort of mental production all night long, and people have reported dreams, and lucid dreams,[22] in all stages of sleep. However, the types of dreams that people have during REM sleep tend to be more active, vivid, and anxiety- or fear-driven. Nightmares tend to happen during this stage of sleep. Meanwhile, NREM dreams are more often reported as pleasant, lacking anxiety, mundane, or boring. The primary differences between REM and NREM dreams is how one is represented in the dream. In NREM dreams we tend to be passive observers in past events, while in REM dreams we tend to play more active roles, and it is thought that these dreams are our brain's models of the future.

Some evidence suggests that people can remain healthy without dreaming. An article that appeared in 2004 in the science journal

Nature told about a seventy-three-year-old stroke patient who stopped dreaming after blood flow to her occipital lobe was disrupted.[23] Prior to the stroke, the patient remembered three to four dreams a week, and then afterward she recalled none, although all of her other mental functions appeared normal. When she was tested in a sleep laboratory and awakened during periods of REM, she reported no dreams.

Some researchers think that trying to find the function of dreams is an unrealistic goal. Canadian psychologist Harry Hunt says, "I do not know if we will find true functions of dreaming, any more than we have been able to for human existence. A self-referential, self-transforming system like the human mind will evolve its uses as creatively and unpredictively as it evolves its structures."[24] Nonetheless, dreaming may serve numerous biological functions, and in this regard I think that anthropologist Charles Laughlin best sums it up when he states:

> There really is no single function of dreaming—the functions of dreaming are manifold and depend upon the state of the brain and the time of dreaming. . . . Dreaming is the expression within the sensorium of neural models that may be developing, readjusting, and establishing connections among themselves or with other models, may be simulating or rehearsing waking experiences . . . may be working to solve problems and seek information, may be consolidating memories . . . may be expressing links between emotions and images . . . may be working through "day residue" issues, may be expressing repressed desires and emotions, may be dominated by traumatized imagery-emotion structures that remain thwarted in their development, and so forth. Dreams are, in other words, the symbolic expression in consciousness of whatever the cognitive/emotional/imaginal parts of the brain are on-about at the moment. Dream imagery may be a synesthetic experience of activities going on subconsciously elsewhere in the nervous system and the body. . . . The dream therefore is a stage upon which the brain portrays its ongoing activities (developmental, problem-solving, expression of repressed material, consolidation of memories, etc.) in often surrealistic plays.[25]

When I asked psychologist and dream expert Stanley Krippner what he thought the purpose of dreaming was, he summed up the general consensus among psychologists by saying, "It appears that . . . (REM) sleep, during which the most vivid dreams occur, served several adaptive purposes in the process of evolution: information storage, rehearsal of future activities, problem-solving, downloading of emotions, and completion of incomplete thoughts and feelings." Therefore, as Krippner and Laughlin suggest, in trying to unravel the mystery of dreaming it might be helpful to look beyond its possible biological functions and speculate about what the psychological function of dreams might be.

Certainly one's culture affects the contents of one's dreams. Consider the following quote by psychology professor Roc Morin:

> I've noticed population-specific trends as well. Violent nightmares are common in the gang-ridden border towns of Mexico and the war zone of eastern Ukraine. Scenes of nuclear war still haunt the "duck-and-cover" generation in both the East and the West. Blessings by gods and goddesses are frequently reported in heavily religious India, whereas in more secular Western populations those same functions are often performed by celebrities. I'm not the first to document the link between culture and dream content. In one study, the dreams of Palestinian children in violent areas were found to feature more aggression and persecution than those of Palestinian children living in peaceful areas; in another, African American women were shown to have more dreams in which they are victims of circumstance or fate than Mexican American or Anglo American women.[26]

When I asked Stephen LaBerge about this he told me that he thought that dreaming helped us to survive evolutionarily because it allows our minds to safely experiment with new models of the world and ourselves. However, these "models" seem oddly encoded with symbolic messages that appear to have personal meaning, which can often be gleaned by careful reflection, and this commonly feels strangely like solving a puzzle. Before we discuss dream interpretation, let's examine the following dream.

THE DEADLY GAZE OF THE FELINE DEITY

In 1997, I had the following (nonlucid) dream while visiting a friend in Herzliya, Israel:

> I was standing in a large, spacious room, filled with a crowd of other people, where there was some kind of strange animal-worshiping ritual going on. There were these bizarre and deadly creatures there that everyone seemed to be watching with adoration and worshipful servitude. Everyone there had their attention focused on the front of the room, where there was a raised, ornately decorated platform. I was with a small child whom I loved and felt protective of, and held close to me. There was another child there, up in front of the room, who had this box with him. When the child opened the box, a long coiled snake began unraveling itself out from within. The huge snake slithered atop a large white stone throne. As the snake positioned itself onto the throne, it transformed into a powerful-looking, human-animal hybrid—a deity, with a woman's body, a feline head, glowing eyes, and numerous arms or tentacles. The room was filled with intense fear, as everyone knew that this creature with the glowing eyes was going to take one of our lives at any moment. Suddenly, a bright light beam shot outward from the creature's eyes, directly at someone in the room, and that person fell right to the ground. Immediately, everyone in the room rushed up to adore the creature. The creature's eyes had stopped glowing, and they now looked like the hollow, empty sockets of a stone statue. I understood that the creature was harmless now, until its eyes filled up again. The room was aglow with a great sense of relief as everyone rejoiced, knowing that the danger was temporarily over.

This dream was quite vivid and disturbing. I awoke from it abruptly in a cold sweat. A few days afterward I flew to London, where I met with British biologist Rupert Sheldrake, with whom I was working on a number of research projects at the time. While leisurely walking around the lovely Hampstead Heath in London with Rupert, discussing our projects, I told him about my dream. Rupert seemed quite interested. He then told me that he had just (synchronistically) received a manuscript that week to review, *Blood Rites: Origins and History of the Passions of War,* by Barbara Ehrenreich. In her book Ehrenreich presents a theory for how the concept of animal and human sacrifice began in religious rituals during our prehistoric, evolutionary past, when humans were basically defenseless primates and were easy prey for wild cats. She suggests that we developed an oddly symbiotic relationship with these wild cats whereby we understood that they could eat one of us, but then afterward they would be satisfied and leave us alone. We also learned that they could provide for us and nourish us by allowing us to scavenge from their hunts of other animals.

So according to Ehrenreich, we learned to live with this reality by associating the loss of a member of our tribe with the survival of the tribe as a whole, and we thus created "blood rites," or wars, to dramatize and validate our struggle in the food chain. This ancient association, buried deep in our collective mind, may be the foundation, Ehrenreich suggests, for our association with sacrifice in organized religion, our sense of territorial nationalism, and for the seemingly suicidal passion that many people have for war. According to Ehrenreich, wars are a form of ritual sacrifice that developed as a way to reenact our primal emotions as prey animals facing the terror of a ferocious and hungry beast.

Hearing this theory after having my dream in Israel, the war-torn so-called Holy Land where the three major Western religions began with animal sacrifice, seemed to be a message from the collective unconscious about the origins of religion and war. Even more significantly, years later, while looking through a book on mythology, I found numerous depictions of Egyptian deities that were human-animal hybrids seated on thrones. Of particular interest were the goddesses Wadjet and Bastet. Wadjet is often depicted with a woman's body and the head of a snake, usually an Egyptian cobra, and Bastet is shown with a woman's body and a feline head that could be that of a cat, lion, lynx, or chee-tah. Sometimes these deities are depicted in an opposite fashion, with animal bodies and human heads, and sometimes Wadjet and Bastet are depicted as a single deity, part woman, part lioness, and part cobra. Yes, this was the deadly deity in my dream. How did this Bastet/Wadjet hybrid deity find its way into my head?

This meaningful Middle Eastern dream didn't feel personal; it felt as though I were witnessing an archetypal drama in what Carl Jung referred to as the *collective unconscious*. This term refers to a realm of prototypical information that underlies the collective dynamic of

Fig. 2.1. Seated figurine of the goddess Wadjet-Bastet, with a lioness head and a cobra that represents Wadjet (courtesy Los Angeles County Museum of Art, www.lacma.org)

all human minds and is the source of common elements and figures, called *archetypes,* in myths, fairy tales, comic books, films, and dreams reported around the world. The dream that I had in Israel seemed symbolic and transpersonal, as if it were an impersonal message, like a television broadcast that I was tuning into, and it needed to be decoded. It seemed to be what some researchers would classify as a "big dream," an unusually memorable dream that seems impersonal or initiatory, differentiating it from normal everyday dreams, which are usually about more mundane events in our personal lives. These big dreams call out strikingly for explanation, but many people believe that all dreams carry important messages. The story of how humans first came to understand the symbolic messages in dreams is lost in prehistory, but there is certainly a rich history of dream interpretation.

THE SECRET LANGUAGE OF DREAMS

According to Charles Laughlin, all societies have a "dreaming culture," that is, every human society known on the planet has within it a group of people who consider dreams to be very important in their lives.[27]

Terence McKenna stressed how important language was in our mental modeling of reality. I love his example of an infant lying in a crib, looking out of the window at this magnificent and astonishing display of bright colors and furious movement, when the child's mother points her finger at the psychedelic display and says the words that collapse that pure, pulsing sensory experience into the mechanical clucks of symbolic representation: "Oh honey, that's *just* a bird."

We also, obviously, do this with dreaming. Not only does Western culture tend to dismiss the importance, and any possible reality, of dreaming, the whole notion of a dream being a noun or a "thing" is completely deceptive. We routinely say that we "had a dream" and ask what "it" was about. But what we really experienced was a dreaming *process* while we slept, which we then try to piece together upon awakening—in our bed afterward, or within the dreaming process itself when dreaming lucidly.

The earliest notions that people had about dreams were ideas about how they were messages or revelations from deities or daemons. Records from early Egyptian and Sumerian cultures contain descriptions of dreams being sent to us by the gods; the same is true of stories in the Hebrew Bible, by the Greek poet Homer, in Grecian plays, and elsewhere in numerous historical documents. The Egyptian papyrus of Deral-Madineh, written around 1300 BCE, gives instructions on how to obtain a dream message from a god, and this appears to be the oldest manual in existence that was written to help people understand their dreams.

What all these early notions have in common is the idea that dreams come to us from somewhere other than ourselves, that they are messages sent to us by a higher intelligence or by divine or daemonic agency. Early notions of dreams also described their prophetic and healing powers.

The "dream temples" of Asclepius, the Greek god of medicine, on the island of Kos, were all the rage around 350 BCE. These temples operated as healing centers or early hospitals, where people suffering from various illnesses would come to sleep and to be healed by the power of divinely inspired dreams. Aristotle (384–322 BCE) was one of the first writers to attempt to study dreams in a systematic way, and he wrote three important treatises on the subject: *De Somno et Vigilia* (*On Sleep and Dreams*), *De Insomnis* (*On Sleeping and Waking*), and *De Divinatione Per Somnum* (*On Divination Through Sleep*). Aristotle revolutionarily said that dreams were not sent by gods and were not divine or supernatural in character, but rather follow the natural laws of the human mind. Dreams then became defined as "the mental activity of the sleeper insofar as he is asleep."[28] Aristotle pointed out that observations made while one is awake could carry over into one's dreams, like the afterimages left behind from a bright object in our visual field. These memories from waking experience, Aristotle suggested, blend with our imagination while we're asleep, and this creates the experience of dreaming. Aristotle also appears to be the first scientist to refer to lucid dreaming. In his treatise *On Sleep and Dreams* he writes, "Often when one is asleep, there is something in consciousness which declares that what then presents itself is but a dream."[29]

Some of the first experimental investigations into the nature of dreams were carried out by French scholar and physician Louis Ferdinand Alfred Maury during the 1800s. Maury carried out a series of experiments wherein he was exposed to various forms of sensory stimuli while he was sleeping, and he then reported on how the stimulation was incorporated into his dreams. For example, he dreamed that he was being tortured when tickled under his nose with a feather by his assistant. How his assistant managed to do this without waking him up remains a mystery, but the understanding that environmental stimuli could become incorporated into our dreams becomes important to the discussion in chapter 6, where I review the electronic brain machines that can induce lucid dreaming.

Maury is probably most well known for having a very peculiar and inexplicably timed dream that he used to illustrate his notion that dreams are constructed in our minds much quicker than we generally think. He describes his famous "guillotine dream" as follows:

> I was slightly indisposed and was lying in my room; my mother was near my bed. I am dreaming of the Terror. I am present at scenes of massacre; I appear before the Revolutionary Tribunal; I see Robespierre, Marat, Fouquier-Tinville, all the most villainous figures of this terrible epoch; I argue with them; at last, after many events which I remember only vaguely, I am judged, condemned to death, taken in a cart, amidst an enormous crowd, to the square of the Revolution; I ascend the scaffold; the executioner binds me to the fatal board, he pushes it, the knife falls; I feel my head being severed from the body; I awake seized by the most violent terror, and I feel on my neck the rod of my bed which had become suddenly detached and had fallen on my neck as would the knife of the guillotine. This happened in one instant, as my mother confirmed to me, and yet it was this external sensation that was taken by me for the starting point of the dream with a whole series of successive

incidents. At the moment that I was struck, the memory of the terrible machine, the effect of which was so reproduced by the rod of the bed's canopy, had awakened in me all the images of that epoch of which the guillotine was the symbol.[30]

How could this possibly have happened? Did the whole dream really happen in the flash of a second, and was the narrative actually created as Maury woke up? Or was Maury psychically aware that his bed was going to collapse in precisely that way on an unconscious level, and was this dream a form of precognition or a premonition? It's a serious mystery, although as we'll see in chapter 8, a form of psychic or precognitive awareness may actually be the more likely explanation.

P. D. Ouspensky attempts to explain this mystery by proposing that we develop the narrative of our dreams backward from the point of awakening, and not as they are actually occurring. According to Ouspensky, "The backward development of dreams means that when we awake[n], we awake[n] at the beginning of the dream and remember it as starting from this moment, that is, in the normal succession of events."[31] In other words, according to Ouspensky we formulate what we recall from our dream activity in the reverse order from which we generally think it has occured. However, reports and physiological evidence from lucid dreamers appear to contradict this notion, so the mystery remains as such.

On the cusp of the twentieth century, Austrian neurologist Sigmund Freud, the "father of psychoanalysis," put forth his theory of the unconscious with respect to dream interpretation. Freud's *The Interpretation of Dreams,* published in 1899 (subsequently revised at least eight times by the author), helped to create a scientific foundation for the notion of dream interpretation. Freud basically believed that all dreams are a form of wish fulfillment, and that they aren't usually about what they appear to be on the surface. While few people would still agree with Freud's position that all dreams represent a symbolic form of wish fulfillment, it seems that many initial lucid dreams are literal attempts to do so.

Freud asserted that dreams have symbolic or hidden meanings, that they act as a medium for the unconscious part of the mind (the part of the mind that cannot be known by the conscious mind, which includes socially unacceptable ideas, wishes, and desires, traumatic memories, and painful emotions that have been repressed) to communicate with the conscious aspect of our mind, i.e., the ego, which is nothing more than the organized part of our personality structure that functions like a miniature self. According to Freud, dreaming is the *via regia,* or "royal road" to the unconscious. In Freud's model, deities and daemons were replaced by the unconscious as the organizer of dreams—a cloaked part of ourselves that contains the vast reservoir of our memories, wishes, fantasies, and unfulfilled desires, hidden from our conscious minds.

Santiago Ramón y Cajal, a Spanish anatomist and neuroscientist who won the 1906 Nobel Prize for discovering neurons, thus founding modern neuroscience, was also a determined psychologist who believed that Freud's ideas about dreaming were "collective lies." After Freud's book *The Interpretation of Dreams* was published, dreams soon became closely associated with the notion of "repressed desires" in psychiatric circles. Cajal set out to disprove Freud's theory that every dream is the result of a repressed desire. Between 1918 and 1934, Cajal kept a journal of his dreams and collected the dreams of others, analyzing them and providing an alternative perspective to Freud's notions. Thought lost for many years, this fascinating collection was published in 2014 under the Spanish title *Los sueños de Santiago Ramón y Cajal* (The Dreams of Santiago Ramón y Cajal). However, there was no mention of lucid dreaming in the English-translated excerpts that I read.[32]

Nevertheless, it appears that Freud was aware of lucid dreaming, although he didn't have much to say about it and didn't seem to understand its psychotherapeutic potential. In the 1909 second edition of *The Interpretation of Dreams* he added the following footnote: "There are some people who are quite clearly aware during the night that they are asleep and dreaming and who thus seem to possess the faculty of consciously directing their dreams. If for instance, the dreamer of this kind is dissatisfied with the turn taken by a dream, he can break it off without waking up and start it again in another direction, just as a popular dramatist may under pressure give his play a happier ending."[33]

Freud was aware of the theories of French sinologist Marquis d'Hervey de Saint-Denys, who in 1867 published *Les rêves et les moyens de les diriger* (Dreams and How to Guide Them), about the author's detailed experiments with lucid dreaming. But for whatever reason Freud was unable to obtain a copy (an English translation is now available). Freud also corresponded with Dutch psychiatrist Frederik van Eeden (1860–1932), who first used the English term lucid dreaming while delivering a scientific paper in 1913.

According to Jung, in his collected work on dreams from the Princeton Extract Series, what we learned from Freud was "that all the products of any dreaming state have something in common. First, they are variations on the complex, and second, they are only a kind of symbolic expression of the complex."[34] What's important to note here is that although Freud and Jung, who were contemporaries, disagreed about many aspects of dreaming (and about psychology in general), Jung's work built on the foundation that Freud had established by introducing important transpersonal concepts of interconnectivity between people and terms like *synchronicity, archetype,* and *the collective unconscious.* Jung suggested that dreams might originate from both personal and transpersonal sources, and his theory of the collective unconscious may help to explain why I had that dream in Israel about the deadly feline deity. Jung's ideas, which express notions of meaningful coincidence, transcultural mental prototypes, and genetically shared aspects of our interconnected minds, developed out of his correspondence with quantum physicist and Nobel Prize–winner Wolfgang Pauli (1900–1958), and they provide valuable models for helping us understand the weird and wonderful world of dreams.

In describing the relationship between the collective unconscious, archetypes, and "big dreams," Jung said:

> Thus we speak on the one hand of a personal and on the other of
> a collective unconscious, which lies at a deeper level and is further
> removed from consciousness than the personal unconscious. The
> "big" or "meaningful" dreams come from this deeper level. They

reveal their significance quite apart from the subjective impression they make by their plastic form, which often has a poetic force and beauty. Such dreams occur mostly during the critical phases of life, in early youth, puberty, at the onset of middle age (thirty-six to forty), and within sight of death.[35]

Although it appears that Jung never specifically addressed lucid dreaming, he did report personally experiencing conscious visions that sound a lot like lucid dreams, as do some of his descriptions of using a psychological technique that he developed to help people gain greater access to their unconscious, called "active imagination." According to Jung, the active imagination is a meditation technique that can be used within psychotherapy to translate material from one's unconscious mind into visual images or a story narrative, or personify them as separate entities. Jung's approach became the foundation of many different dream interpretation systems as well as many popular beliefs about dreams, such as the notions that the unconscious mind is more knowledgeable than the conscious mind, and that by collecting sequential dreams in a series, they can be decoded as symbolic communications from the unconscious.

DO DREAMING MINDS AND SHAMANIC PLANT SPIRITS SPEAK THE SAME LANGUAGE?

Anyone who has ever experienced a shamanic journey on psilocybin mushrooms, peyote, San Pedro, iboga, or ayahuasca knows that when you close your eyes during the experience you will see a dazzling array of ever-shifting, continuously morphing images, patterns, and animated scenes. If you pay close attention to this closed-eye imagery it becomes clear that it isn't random, but rather follows a meaningful pattern, as if the botanical intelligence is trying to communicate with us.

I suspect that the closed-eye visions that one sees on a shamanic journey with sacred plants are messages spoken to us in a symbolic language much like the language of dreams. These visions may constitute a kind of metalanguage in which the basic components of the language are animated scenes with complicated and emotionally charged imagery (akin to words), which symbolically communicate a massive amount of meaningful information at once when strung together before our eyes (like sentences). In any case, it can certainly seem this way. In Simon Powell's wonderful book *The Psilocybin Solution,* this idea that magic mushrooms speak to us in the metalanguage of dreams and the unconscious is explored in great detail. This language seems ancient, protohuman—like it's the voice of the biosphere, and it may be a universal system of communication used by other life forms. Speaking of other life forms, what about their dream lives—can they become lucid too?

DO OTHER ANIMALS HAVE LUCID DREAMS?

All animals sleep, in some form or another, and dreaming evolved long before our species arrived on the scene. A recent study reveals that bees learn and store information in their long-term memory while they sleep, like humans do when they dream—suggesting that even insects may dream.[36] All terrestrial mammals enter the REM stage of sleep, accompanied by (at least partial) bodily paralysis, and many biologists believe that animals are dreaming when this occurs. Bodily paralysis presumably occurs during REM sleep so that we don't act out the behaviors in our dreams. All voluntary muscles in the body are immobilized during REM sleep by the release of certain chemicals in the brain.

Studies conducted with animals in which the natural effects of sleep paralysis are neurochemically blocked show that animals exhibit exploratory or other behaviors while in REM sleep. It appears that they are acting out their dreams, which gives us a unique window into the minds of dreaming animals. With humans there's a brain disorder called *REM behavior disorder,* in which people do the same thing. Oftentimes people who suffer from this disorder need to sleep alone in a padded room with no sharp edges.

To be conscious of one's immobilized body during a state of sleep paralysis is often quite frightening for most people, although it's really harmless. In fact, states of conscious sleep paralysis can actually be valuable springboards for lucid dreams or out-of-body experiences provided one can overcome the inherent sense of fear that naturally comes with this state (a subject we'll explore further in chapter 9). Curiously, it appears that the body is in an even deeper state of sleep paralysis when lucid dreaming than when nonlucid dreaming. A 1986 study done at the University of Texas reports that the "Hofmann reflex" is more depressed during lucid dreams than nonlucid ones.[37] The Hofmann reflex is produced by stimulating a nerve located behind the knee, the posterior tribial nerve. A response to this stimulation is a contraction of the soleus muscle in the calf, which extends and rotates the foot. The study found that this reflex was more suppressed during lucid REM sleep than during any other stage of sleep or wakefulness, including nonlucid REM sleep. It's almost as though our brain recognizes when we're lucid dreaming and physiologically compensates.

The largest amount of REM sleep known in any animal is found in the Australian platypus, which sometimes sleeps for as long as fourteen hours a day. But marine mammals and birds are different, and more mysterious. Birds only spend a tiny amount of time in REM sleep, and with marine mammals a complete absence of REM sleep is usually observed. Only in the case of one species of oceanic dolphin, i.e., the pilot whale, has there been measured a negligible amount of REM sleep.[38] However, what's most interesting is that dolphins, porpoises, whales, and birds sleep one brain hemisphere at a time, i.e., half of their brain sleeps while the other half stays awake, and then they switch. This ability to sleep with one half of the brain while the other half remains alert is called *unihemispheric slow-wave sleep* (USWS).

So one has to wonder, if dolphins and whales don't experience much or any REM sleep, do they dream? As I discussed, humans will persistently increase their periods of REM sleep if deprived of it, so it appears to serve an important biological function, whatever it is. We also know from sleep studies that people report dreaming during non-REM stages of sleep as well; it just appears to be most consistently active and vivid during REM sleep. So dolphins may experience dreamlike consciousness during these stages of sleep too. In fact, some dream researchers speculate that lucid dreaming is a hybrid state of consciousness in which one part of the brain is awake while the rest of it is asleep. This hybrid asleep/awake state would be the norm for dolphins and whales. Even though there's only the tiniest trace recordings of dolphins ever entering REM sleep, it seems that the hybrid states of consciousness resulting from their uni-hemispheric sleep patterns would be biologically ideal for lucid dreaming.

In any case, though it might be difficult to tell if dolphins dream or not, I'm confident that with time, cutting-edge dolphin researchers like Diana Reiss, author of *The Dolphin in the Mirror,* will figure out how to communicate with them well enough so they can tell us themselves. I suspect that they do dream, in some way that's different than we do, and I wonder if they can form a hybrid state of awareness where they know when they're dreaming and can influence what happens. It might be tricky to determine whether dolphins lucid dream by measuring their brain waves while they're asleep. For the most part, this can be done in humans when gamma brain waves are observed in the prefrontal cortex during REM sleep.

As mentioned earlier, the biological function of dreaming may be to assist with the brain's information processing and long-term memory storage, and it may have an additional psychological function, as a way for different portions of our mind to communicate with one another. But might dreaming have an even higher function?

DREAMING AND CREATIVITY

Dreams are creative by their very nature in that they produce a novel organization of experiences. Dreaming, or REM sleep, has been positively correlated with creativity, according to a study conducted by psychologist Sara Mednick and others.[39] In Mednick's study, people who took naps with REM sleep performed better on creativity-oriented word problems. According to Mednick, dreaming helped people combine ideas in new ways. Other studies suggest that people with high scores on creativity tests tend to recall more dreams.[40] Additional evidence suggests that creative solutions to problems encountered while awake may be worked out or facilitated during sleep, whether or not a dream is involved. In one study in which subjects were given tasks with hidden rules, those who were allowed to sleep beforehand reached solutions faster than those who were not given the opportunity to sleep.[41]

Many people have had the experience of struggling to find the solution to a problem, only to go to sleep and then wake up the next morning (or in the middle of the night) with the answer fresh in their minds, as though their brains had been ceaselessly working all night on the problem. It's not uncommon for the solution to a problem to simply require a creative association or a new perspective on one's current knowledge, which is why dreaming can be so helpful. It's also widely acknowledged that many creative artistic ideas, mathematical and scientific discoveries, and inventions have come to accomplished people through their dreams, both lucid and nonlucid. History overflows with stories of creative inspiration sprouting from dreams: Mary Shelley's novel *Frankenstein,* the tune for Paul McCartney's song "Yesterday,"* Keith Richards' riff for the Rolling Stone's song "I Can't Get No Satisfaction," Otto Loewi's understanding of the chemical transmission of nerve impulses, Friedrich August Kekule's discovery of the structure of the benzene molecule, Dmitri Mendeleev's organization of the basic chemical elements into the periodic table, and Elias Howe's invention of the sewing machine.

In Howe's famous dream (or nightmare) that led to the invention of the sewing machine in 1845, he was fleeing cannibals in the jungles of Africa. He was captured by the cannibals, and as they tried to boil him alive they kept poking him with *spears that had holes in their points.* Upon awakening, Howe realized that the secret to making his sewing-machine idea workable was to move the thread transport hole up to the point of the needle—unlike a handheld needle, where the hole is on the

---

*According to Barry Mile's account in *Paul McCartney: Many Years From Now,* "Yesterday" was not only the Beatles' most successful song, it is the most often played song of all time. A good portion of the Beatles' music also appears to be influenced by marijuana and LSD, with such songs as "Lucy in the Sky with Diamonds" and "Magical Mystery Tour."

base. This dream literally helped usher in the industrial revolution by making the mechanical production of clothing possible.

This dream also illustrates Jung's notion of how one's "shadow" can have a beneficial, creativity-enhancing aspect. According to Jung, the shadow is the dark and negative unconscious part of our personality that we lack identification with. The creative solution to Howe's technical problem about how to thread the needle of a sewing machine literally arrived in the hands of fierce and frightening cannibals!

We can all be grateful for a dream that made navigating the Internet possible. Larry Page, the cofounder of Google, attributes his inspiration for developing the Internet search engine to a dream. After waking up from a dream, Page reported wondering, *What if we could download the whole Web and just keep the links . . . ?*"[42] This was the inspiration for creating an invaluable tool that could quickly and effectively search through all human knowledge, thus radically changing the dynamics of human civilization.

Perhaps the most well-known example of how a dream can profoundly change the world comes from Mahatma Gandhi. Anthropologist Charles Laughlin writes:

> There is perhaps no more famous example of how problem solving in a dream can impact cultural change than that of the dream-inception of Mahatma Gandhi's non-violent resistance to the British *raj* in India. When the imperialist legislature passed the restrictive Rowlatt Acts after the First World War, Gandhi cast about for an adequate response. He records in his autobiography . . . that: "The idea came to me last night in a dream that we should call upon the country to call a general [hunger strike]." His idea was implemented leading to the non-violent independence movement that came to fruition in 1947.[43]

In a study designed to explore the relationship between dreams and creative problem solving, mathematician M. E. Maillet sent out questionnaires to other mathematicians asking them if any dreams ever helped them to solve a mathematical problem.[44] Out of the eighty replies he received, eight of the respondents reported that the beginning of solutions had occurred in dreams, and fifteen reported that they had awakened with partial or complete answers to mathematical problems, even though they did not recall dreaming about them.

For a comprehensive survey of how dreams have affected the creativity and problem-solving abilities of many scientists, artists, actors, writers, poets, and musicians throughout history, see Deirdre Barrett's wonderful book *The Committee of Sleep,* where a treasure chest of these anecdotes are described, as well as the results from experimental research into sleep and creativity. Perhaps less well known is the specific influence that lucid dreams have had on creativity. For example, Scottish novelist Robert Louis Stevenson, author of *Dr. Jekyll and Mr. Hyde,* said that he was "consciously making stories . . . whether awake or asleep."[45] According to Stevenson, he would sometimes wake himself up from lucid dreams when he had a good idea, to write it down before it was forgotten.

Bruce Damer, a scientist and mission visualization team leader for NASA, related to me one incident in which he used lucid dreaming to help him develop a specific mission for a NASA-funded study. Damer had a ten-year history of mission simulation and design, including the design of human missions to asteroids, rovers on Mars and the moon, and space shuttle and space station missions. He was tasked by Raytheon, the aerospace company, to support innovative ideas for the construction of a manned base on the moon. This was a difficult intellectual challenge, as it's unlikely that astronauts could spend enough time on the moon to accomplish such a task, and build the base by hand, due to radiation and a number of other factors. Damer told me that in this case he spent months "preloading" into his mind the necessary information to solve this tricky technological problem, and then he "deliberately induced a visionary, lucid-dreaming experience from his own endogenous brain chemistry." Damer also told me that he has used these natural mind-altering techniques to develop his ideas about models for how life might have begun[46] and for developing mathematical representations of how the universe may operate. He described his lucid dream about the moon-base construction technique to me:

So I was in the process of waking up, and there it was, right in front of me—this whole vibrant world including the robotic spacecraft. I still had my eyes closed, but I knew I was in a lucid-dreaming state. My consciousness had awakened into the dream, and there it was, the rack with the robotics in it—all populated and functioning. I could see how it was constructed, how it was moved to lunar orbit, and how the robots went down and started building the base under remote control from Earth. I strove to stay with it because it was showing me the whole function. I reached for a pen and paper on my bedside table and started to draw what I saw. Then, immediately, I knew that I was being disconnected from the lucid dream. But I tried to hold on to the vision and continued drawing so I could capture it all. This concept went on to being rendered as a full CAD model in computer graphics and was included in the study for Raytheon, went off to NASA headquarters, and was shown at a

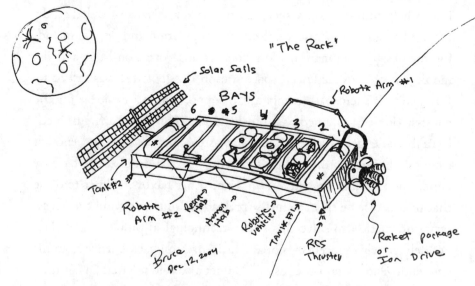

Fig. 2.2. Drawing by Bruce Damer, from his lucid dream
(courtesy of Bruce Damer, NASA, and Raytheon)

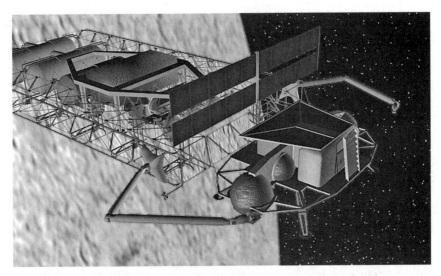

Fig 2.3. Representation of the model for the NASA project
that Damer designed via lucid dreaming
(courtesy of Bruce Damer, NASA, and Raytheon)

major conference. So that's one of my projects that emerged out of
lucid dreaming, one form of my endogenous practice.

It's strangely ironic that lucid dreaming is often characterized in the
popular media as dream control, because it can actually be such a valuable aid to the creative process by providing one with novel and original
content. British lucid-dream researcher and novelist Clare Johnson was
the first person to carry out doctoral research into lucid dreaming as an
aid to the creative writing process, and she's used it artistically herself
in writing two novels, *Breathing in Colour* and *Dreamrunner* (as "Clare
Jay"). Johnson identifies the primary qualities of lucid dreaming that
can be used in the creative process as "rational thought, ability to recall
preset tasks, heightened perception, conscious attention, detailed dream
recall, dream control, lucid suspension or the 'void,' meditative states,
and non-dual states."[47]

Johnson studied twenty-five lucid dreamers for her doctoral dissertation, twenty of whom used creativity professionally in their careers—

fifteen were writers and five were visual artists. She reported that the writers found lucid dreaming could provide assistance in overcoming obstacles, coming up with story ideas, and contributing to plot development; the visual artists also reported enhanced creativity by utilizing lucid dreaming.[48]

According to Johnson, "The dreaming mind itself could be considered to be a type of creative genius, with its spontaneous manifestation of imagery and its tendencies to original analogies."[49] When I interviewed her for this book, I asked her about the relationship between lucid dreaming and the creative process. Her response:

> Dreaming is itself a creative process: the dream is thought-responsive and translates emotions instantaneously into imagery and personalized archetypes. In lucid dreams we can observe and influence this spontaneous creativity while it is happening. Just watching our "dream film" and seeing how it responds to our thoughts and emotions is a stimulating artistic resource. When lucid we can ask the dream for inspiration with a specific project, ask to be shown "something never created before," or work on improving a physical skill like kickboxing or juggling.

Fig. 2.4. Lucid-dream researcher Dr. Clare Johnson (photo by Markus Feldmann)

Johnson suggests asking the lucid dream for creative inspiration. On her Facebook page she says, "Ask to see 'something amazing' when you next get lucid in a dream—great inspiration for art!" So I tried this in a lucid dream of my own, with the following results:

I was walking through a large warehouse or department store when I became lucid. There were no people around—just boxes piled high and what looked like store items or interesting sculptures or furniture. I was thrilled to be lucid again and quickly tried to think of what to do. I raised my head and began speaking to the spirit of the dream itself. As I was walking through the dream department-store warehouse, I said, "Astonish me!" The response came in my environment: the imagery got more vivid, more detailed, Gothic, and stranger. In particular, a huge chandelier above my head grew all these detailed octopuslike tentacles and ornately designed structures that were growing and morphing.

Artist and writer Daniel Love has a novel approach to tapping in to the creativity of lucid dreams, which I found inspiring:

The . . . technique I used to inspire my own artistic creativity was something I called "fractal dreaming." . . . Once lucid, I would seek out the dream version of my already-painted artwork (or sometimes that of my favorite artists). Once found, I would use these paintings as "windows" into other "dimensions" of the dream world, jumping through the painting itself with the intention of entering the world within the painting. More often than not, this would be successful, with incredibly mixed results. Sometimes, the dream scene would shift to something seemingly unrelated to the painting, while other times I would find myself in a far more surreal dream landscape based on the artwork itself. . . . Whatever the result, I would then seek out a scene within this new landscape, something that I believed would make an interesting painting. Once again, when I had found what I needed, I would examine and commit this image to memory, ready to record it once I awoke.[50]

Visionary artist Dustyn Lucas does extraordinary psychedelic paintings that he says are almost all inspired by his lucid dreams. He writes:

My work nowadays comes almost entirely from a lucid-dream state. I memorize the images I see; balancing on the edge of dream and reality to sketch them as I wake. From that sketch I work with oils to bring the painting forth, keeping it as close to the original dream image as possible. In this way I feel that my paintings can resonate with the viewer in a deeper place, awakening and pulling up long forgotten emotions and ideas from the waters of the subconscious.[51]

Musician Pete Casale describes composing a piano piece called "Lucid" during a lucid dream:

While making my short video on lucid dreaming for . . . [the] website World-of-Lucid-Dreaming.com I needed a nice piece of music I could use without getting sued. I started by writing a kind of clunky piano piece in a hurried kind of way, but then I got tired so I went to bed. The next morning, before waking up, I had a small lucid dream during which I decided to compose a song on a piano made out of pure energy and light. That's right, this song was written while I was asleep. It was actually about ten times as long but I couldn't remember all of it. After I woke up, I hopped on the piano and started working out how to play the song, and I established as much of it as I could remember.[52]

I corresponded with someone online who also described playing a musical instrument in his dreams. It seems that you may have more success with one type of musical instrument than with another, as Steven Nelson writes:

Last night I had a [lucid] dream where I was trying to play a piano for some people but I couldn't get a single good note out of it. They seemed disappointed so I pulled out my harmonica and started playing some gypsy-blues type music and it was effortless. All I had to do was think of a note and I could play it. I could even change to any key I wanted even though it was a diatonic harmonica. I wish the dream would have lasted longer because I could write songs like that for hours.

Clare Johnson appears to have had something akin to a shamanic experience in her lucid dreams; she describes seeing flowers that have watching eyes and entering into a bodiless void. In one lucid dream, Johnson looked at a reflection of her dream self in a dream mirror and saw miniature planets in her dream eyes. In this context, I thought that it was especially interesting that Johnson had her first experience of synesthesia in a lucid dream.

BLURRING BOUNDARIES BETWEEN THE SENSES

Synesthesia is a neurological condition in which the boundaries between the senses blur together so that when one sensory modality is stimulated, this evokes sensations in another. This naturally occurs in around 4 percent of the population—known as *synesthetes*—in some form or another, and it is commonly described in accounts where people "see" music or "taste" colors. Computer programs that display shifting patterns that morph, dance, and flash to the sound of music mimic the synesthetic effect of "seeing" music. Musical notes may also evoke particular taste sensations for someone experiencing synesthesia. A C sharp might taste minty, an F minor sweet. So for those of us unable to experience synesthesia, we can only imagine what kind of a tasty experience a good concert must be! Touch may evoke the perception of both colors and shapes, and some people with synesthesia say that acupressure, acupuncture, and massage can provide a corresponding visual experience.

Several studies show that synesthetes are more likely to engage in creative activities. Although this condition occurs naturally in some people, many people also commonly experience synesthesia during shamanic journeys or while under the influence of psychedelic drugs or plants. (Interestingly, most of the scientific articles about psychedelics list synesthesia as one of its possible effects, yet articles about the actual medical condition rarely reference the fact that psychedelics can often mimic it.)

Novelist Clare Johnson describes tactile sensations as "tasting like porridge" in a lucid dream in which she deliberately attempted to experience synesthesia when touching a wall.[53] When I asked her about her experience with synesthesia, she told me, "Over time, I taught myself to experience synesthetic perceptions at will in my lucid dreams. This helped me to understand the way synesthetes experience the world and resulted in some of the freest creative writing I've done, multisensory and strange."

Synesthesia may not only help foster artistic creation, it may also allow for new or previously unrecognized forms of artistic expression to emerge. Ayahuasca, the shamanic jungle juice from the Amazon, often produces synesthetic experiences. When I interviewed Terence McKenna, he had this to say about the experience:

> When ingested . . . [ayahuasca] allows one to see sound, so that one can use the voice to produce, not musical compositions, but pictorial and visual compositions. . . . This is actually being done by shamans in the Amazon. The songs they sing sound as they do in order to look a certain way. They are not musical compositions as we're used to thinking of them. They're pictorial art that is caused by audio signals.

Magic mushrooms often produce similar sensory-blurring experiences. Research with psilocybin showed that this active component of the magic mushroom can cause the brain to become hyperconnected, allowing for increased communication between different regions of the brain.[54]

In the last chapter we discussed how some research with psilocybin shows that it decreases brain activity, and this remains true, although additional research has demonstrated that upon receiving psilocybin the brain also reorganizes connections and links together previously unconnected regions of the brain. These connections do not appear to be random, but rather are quite organized and stable, lasting for the duration of the drug's influence, and then returning to normal. Interestingly, the researchers involved in this study stated, "We can speculate on the implications of such an organization. One possible by-product of this greater communication across the whole brain is the phenomenon of synesthesia, which is often reported in conjunction with the psychedelic state."[55]

Something similar may be going on when we're lucid dreaming, in that the experience may be linking together previously unconnected regions of the mind. In his book *Are You Dreaming?* author Daniel Love suggests that the heightened sensory experiences reported by many people in lucid dreams, along with the potential for synesthesia, are due to the more direct fashion that we experience sensory information in lucid dreams. Love writes, "Rather than being the end result of a process, starting with the processing of input from our genuine physical senses, our experience of these things in dreams all occur in the immediacy of our own brains. There is no processing to be done."[56]

Synesthesia is just one of a multitude of experiences that one can experiment with in lucid dreams; we'll be discussing many more possibilities in chapter 4. I suspect that every experience that's possible with a psychedelic plant or drug is also possible within a lucid dream. But before we start discussing all of the incredible things that one can do in a lucid dream, let's first take a look at the fascinating scientific research into the phenomenon.

3

THE SCIENCE OF
LUCID DREAMING

*A lot of what our brain does is synthesize a hallucination,
a model of the world that we proceed to live in. This is a
model reality; the real reality is completely unknowable.*

DENNIS MCKENNA

The earliest known descriptions of lucid dreaming come to us from
Hindu scriptures dating back over 3,000 years ago, in the Upanishads
and the Vigyan Bhairav Tantra, where there are instructions for how
to direct one's consciousness within a dream and during sleep. Other
ancient descriptions of lucid-dreaming meditations, from the Tibetan
Bön and Vajrayāna Buddhist traditions, are over 1,200 years old.

In the West, the earliest mention of lucid dreaming comes from
Aristotle, some 2,000 years ago. In his treatise *On Sleep and Dreams,*
Aristotle says that when we are asleep there is often something in
our minds telling us that what we are experiencing is only a dream.
However, as we learned in the introduction, the first attempt at a systematic scientific study of lucid dreaming began with the French sinologist Marquis d'Hervey de Saint-Denys, in the mid-1800s.

THE WEST AWAKENS: A BRIEF HISTORY OF LUCID-DREAM RESEARCH

In 1867, Saint-Denys' book *Les rêves et les moyens de les diriger* (*Dreams and How to Guide Them*) was published, and this landmark book is the first known record of a systematic exploration of lucid dreaming.

Originally published anonymously, Saint-Denys' detailed personal reports span a period of thirty-two years. In this remarkable book, the author describes how he became interested in dreams as a young teenager, and how he learned to become lucid in his dreams and partially direct what happened. Saint-Denys coined the term *rêve lucide,* "lucid dream," and he performed many experiments in his lucid dreams.

The first scientist in the West to explore lucid dreaming was Dutch physician Frederik van Eeden, a contemporary of Freud's who corresponded with the psychoanalyst about dreams. Van Eeden's famous first scientific paper on lucid dreaming, "A Study of Dreams," was published in 1913. This landmark paper contains the first mention of the term "lucid dream" in the English language.

Fig. 3.1. The 1867 cover of *Les rêves et les moyens de les diriger; observations pratiques,* written by the Marquis d'Hervey Saint-Denys

P. D. Ouspensky's essay "On the Study of Dreams and Hypnotism" was published in 1931. Much of it is based on detailed observations of the author's own accounts of lucid dreaming, which he calls "half-dream states." Ouspensky, a mathematician, made a number of fascinating observations as well as perhaps generalized assertions based on his own experiences, which may not be as fixed as he believed, but they were an important part of the growing body of knowledge on lucid dreaming that eventually would lead to legitimate scientific study.

In 1965, psychologist Charles Tart wrote a paper for the *Psychological Bulletin* titled "Towards the Experimental Control of Dreaming," where the idea of signaling from a dream state was first proposed. He writes, "To what extent could a 'two-way communication system' be developed, whereby the experimenter could instruct the subject to do such and such while dreaming, and the subject could report on the events of the dream while they are occurring?"[1]

Then in 1968, Celia Green, a British writer on philosophical skepticism, twentieth-century thought, and psychology, paved the way for a scientific study of lucid dreams with her seminal book *Lucid Dreams*. In this book she says, "In view of the fact that subjects very frequently report that the lucid dream arose out of a previous non-lucid dream, we may tentatively expect to find lucid dreams occurring, as do other dreams, during the 'paradoxical' phase of sleep character-

Fig. 3.2. Psychologist Charles Tart (photo by Judith Tart)

ized by fast low-voltage EEG waves, rapid eye movements and muscular relaxation."[2] It was Green's book that inspired sleep-laboratory researchers Keith Hearne and Stephen LaBerge to carry out the studies that led to the scientific demonstration that people can make conscious decisions, and carry out instructions, while their bodies are fast asleep.

SIGNALS FROM ANOTHER WORLD

While SETI (the search for extraterrestrial intelligence) researchers scan the skies and monitor electromagnetic radiation for signs of transmissions from civilizations on other worlds in vain, the first person in human history to send signals from the outer limits of the dream state to the earthbound waking world was Alan Worsley, a British shopkeeper. Worsley was recruited by Keith Hearne, who in the mid-1970s was a doctoral student in psychology at the University of Hull, in Yorkshire, England, when he conducted this experiment. Hearne had read Celia Green's book and was keen to demonstrate the reality of lucid dreaming. So after recruiting Worsley, a proficient lucid dreamer, he designed the ingenious experiment that I described in the introduction of this book.

In his book *The Dream Machine,* Hearne tells us what it was like on that magic morning when the first signals from Worsley arrived in the sleep laboratory:

> Suddenly, out of the jumbled senseless tos and fros of the two eye movement recording channels, a regular set of large zigzags appeared on the chart. Instantly, I was alert and felt the greatest exhilaration on realizing that I was observing the first ever deliberate signals sent from within a dream to the outside. The signals were coming from another world—the world of dreams—and they were as exciting as if they were emanating from some other solar system in space. A channel of communication had been established from the inner universe of the mind in dreaming sleep.[3]

Yet despite the extraordinary nature of this scientific breakthrough, Hearne's study was not immediately published. He shared the results with several other researchers, and he delivered his paper at the 1977 Postdoctoral Conference in Behavioral Sciences held at Hull University, but the research still didn't become widely known for years. Hearne submitted his paper to the British science journal *Nature,* and it was rejected because the committee thought that it wouldn't be interesting to a wide-enough audience in the scientific community; other mainstream science journals rejected Hearne's paper on similar grounds. It wasn't until 1980 that Hearne's findings about lucid dreaming were made available in a small publication called *Nursing Mirror,* which didn't receive widespread distribution.[4]

MAINSTREAM SCIENCE AND LUCID DREAMING

Meanwhile, independently of Hearne, Stanford University psychophysiologist Stephen LaBerge came up with his own study on ocular signaling from within a lucid dream. Being a proficient lucid dreamer himself, LaBerge functioned as his own test subject, and he recorded the first ocular signals from within his own lucid dream in 1978.

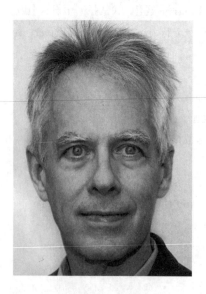

Fig. 3.3. Psychophysiologist Stephen LaBerge (photo by Patricia Keelin)

Although LaBerge also had some difficulty finding a science journal that would publish his work, he managed to get it into the peer-reviewed journal *Perceptual and Motor Skills* in 1981.[5]

More precise physiological evidence for lucid dreaming came from studies conducted at Frankfurt University and the Max Planck Institute of Psychiatry in Germany in 2009 (and later), where researchers discovered specific alterations in brain physiology that occur when people become lucid while dreaming.[6] The researchers discovered that when lucidity was attained within the dream, activity in areas of the brain associated with self-assessment and self-perception markedly increased within seconds, creating a hybrid state of awareness from the simultaneous activation of two distinct brain regions.

At a neurophysiological level, EEG[7] and functional magnetic resonance imaging (fMRi) studies[8] have shown that lucid dreaming is accompanied by increased phase synchrony* and elevated frequency-specific activity in the lower gamma frequency band centered around 40 Hz, especially in the frontal and temporal regions of the brain. The temporal and frontal lobes play an important role in decision-making, behavioral control, language, and emotions. Activity between the frontal and temporal lobes in this frequency band is related to "executive ego functions" and "secondary consciousness," which is characteristic of the human waking state and is atypical for REM sleep.[9] Yet this is what we find is going on in the brain when people lucid dream.

As a result of these extraordinary scientific studies, the contagious idea of lucid dreaming—as an understandable concept and an achievable reality—began to seep out of the sleep laboratories, through our bedrooms, and into the zeitgeist.

INFLUENCE ON POPULAR CULTURE

Although Keith Hearne was actually the first researcher to conduct a successful ocular-signaling lucid-dream study, Stephen LaBerge was the

---

*Phase synchrony occurs when neuronal groups that oscillate in the gamma range enter into precise phase locking over a limited period of time.

first to have such a study published in a peer-reviewed science journal. Additionally, LaBerge acted as an unusually charismatic promoter of lucid dreaming, helping to create a burgeoning, mainstream interest in the subject.

As I have mentioned, it was LaBerge's seminal 1985 book *Lucid Dreaming* that initially sparked my interest in the subject. This important book is currently out of print and is difficult to locate because a much briefer book by LaBerge, with the same title, was published in 2009 by Sounds True with the subtitle *A Concise Guide to Awakening in Your Dreams and in Your Life*. This shorter book is currently in print, so it's easy to confuse the two books. Much of the material in the original edition of *Lucid Dreaming* was included in LaBerge's 1990 book, which was coauthored with Harold Rheingold and titled *Exploring the World of Lucid Dreaming*, now a classic reference on the subject.

In any case, LaBerge began popularizing ideas about lucid dreaming in the late 1980s, and soon a thriving subculture arose that has influenced mainstream culture, through such Hollywood films as *Inception, Waking Life, Vanilla Sky, The Science of Sleep, Avatar, The Matrix, Dreamscape, Eternal Sunshine of the Spotless Mind, Lucia,* and *The Nightmare on Elm Street* series. What was once an esoteric subject years ago when I first interviewed LaBerge is now regularly featured in the media. It appears that the editors at *Nature* were pretty far afield when they rejected the initial papers by Hearne and LaBerge about lucid dreaming on the grounds that the topic would not be interesting to a wide enough audience in the scientific community. It's certainly of interest to the population in general.

As part of my research for this book I watched every movie about lucid dreaming that I could find. Some of the less known and more interesting titles that I watched include an amusing romantic comedy called *The Good Night,* a pretty scary horror thriller titled *Lucid,* a wonderful Japanese anime called *Paprika,* and a science fiction film about someone's rebellion against a globally oppressive system called *The Dream Parlor.* Director Rodney Ascher's documentary *The Nightmare* explores the frightening phenomenon of sleep paralysis. On television there was a *Simpsons* episode, "Treehouse of Horror VI," where Bart and Lisa had to become lucid in their dreams to stop Groundskeeper Willie from trying to murder them in their sleep—a parody of *The Nightmare on Elm Street* series. On the science-fiction series *Fringe,* Olivia has a chip implanted in her brain so that she can lucid dream on command. Lucid dreaming has appeared as a plot device in episodes of *Star Trek, Futurama, SpongeBob SquarePants,* and many other popular television shows.

Incidentally, the classic 1936 Max Fleischer animation film *Somewhere in Dreamland* is about the shared (seemingly lucid) dream of an impoverished brother and sister who enter an enchanted, toy-filled wonder world together in their dreams; there clothes sprout from trees, rivers run with syrup, ice-cream cones grow in fields, and you can ride atop animal crackers on carousels. After the children wake up to a surprise feast, the little boy even performs a "reality test" (a lucid-dream practice technique that I'll be describing in the next chapter) to see if he was dreaming or not, by poking himself in the butt with a fork.*

The fantastic dreams portrayed by cartoonist Winsor McCay (1869–1934) in his much-loved comic strip *Little Nemo in Slumberland* (which originally ran in the *New York Herald* from 1905 to 1911) contained extremely beautiful and unusually imaginative imagery reminiscent of psychedelic journeys and lucid dreams. And there's a wonderful short animated film, made in 2008 by Erica Kobren, specifically about lucid dreaming called *Oneironaut: Explorer of the Dream World* that can be found online.[10]

In addition to these popular representations, an active and growing culture of lucid dreamers exchanges useful tips and experiences on numerous Internet forums, such as Dream Views and the World of Lucid Dreaming; these people also meet at conferences such as those put on by the International Association for the Study of Dreams (IASD),

---

*As we'll see in the next chapter, as a "reality test" this would likely produce poor results, because one would probably feel the poker in the dream, just as in waking life.

a nonprofit international organization dedicated to the investigation of dreams and dreaming. Typing *lucid dreaming* into Amazon.com's search engine brings up hundreds of offers for books, electronic devices, audios, DVDs, supplements, herbs, aromatherapy oils, dream pillows, and more.

Psychologist Jayne Gackenbach did a number of studies that offer insight into some of the activities and characteristics that appear to increase the frequency of lucid dreaming. Gackenbach found that there are correlations between lucid dreaming and various other states and activities, including meditation, having androgynous gender role identities, and having better performance on an oscillating balance board as well as with playing video games.[11] Gackenbach's research draws important parallels between the effects of meditation and video-game playing, which include improved attention and spatial skills, deep absorption and flow experiences, as well as an increased frequency of lucid dreaming.[12] Gackenbach theorizes that building virtual worlds in one's mind while awake may carry over into one's dreams. As a result of Gackenbach's work, video games have been developed with the specific intention of inducing lucid dreams, such as computer scientist Sune Pedersen's *Lucid Dreamscapes*. And I would think that with the growing interest in virtual reality technology, one can probably expect to see a corresponding rise in interest in lucid dreaming.

The excitement around lucid dreaming apparently strikes a strong cultural nerve, as most people are intrigued by the idea of being awake in their dreams simply because it can be so much fun. But can it also improve our health and make us happier?

LUCID DREAMING AND HEALING RESEARCH

One of the most obvious applications of lucid dreaming is as an adjunct to psychotherapy in the treatment of chronic nightmares. Many people who suffer from chronic nightmares have discovered this on their own, since nightmares are a common trigger of lucidity while dreaming. As far back as 1921, British psychologist Mary Arnold-Foster suggested that lucid-dreaming techniques could be used to relieve the suffering of children who were plagued by chronic nightmares.[13]*

In 1967, Russian psychiatrist Vasily Kasatkin reported on a twenty-eight-year study of over ten thousand dreams, concluding that dreams could predict the onset of a serious illness several months in advance of any symptoms.[14] Medical researcher Robert C. Smith conducted a number of studies in the late 1980s that demonstrated that dreams can sometimes help predict medical problems in their early stages, thus helping to save poeple's lives.[15] These studies provide evidence that disturbing dreams could be the warning sign of an underlying medical disorder, although many frightening nightmares are psychologically based, resulting from traumas in our lives. Notably, there are differences in the types of dreams that men and women have with regard to predicting illness. Smith found that in men dreams about death and in women dreams about separation correlated with the severity of heart disease in both sexes.

More recently, lucid-dreaming therapy (LDT) has been successfully used in clinical situations to help reduce the frequency of nightmares.[16] LDT aims to train people to become lucid during sleep and to control their dreams, or at least experience them without fear, knowing that they will wake up.

One medical study found that lucid dreaming might be able to help people with chronic pain.[17] Los Angeles psychiatrist Mauro Zappaterra and colleagues presented a case study that demonstrates the complete resolution of chronic pain in a subject ("Mr. S.") after twenty-two years of suffering as a result of a healing lucid dream that occurred after two years of multidisciplinary "biopsychosocial" treatment. The authors of the study view these results as evidence for the therapeutic value of "neural plasticity," the brain and nervous system's ability to reorganize and rewire itself.

---

*More recently, Mom's Choice Award–winning author Renee Frances has written a series of books to help children who are "reluctant sleepers" stay in their beds at night, and the second book in her series, titled *The Good Night Fairy Helps Via Change Her Dream,* teaches children how to lucid dream as a way to overcome frightening nightmares. See www.goodnightfairy.ca.

Part of the rationale for investigating lucid dreams as a possible means of physical healing comes from studies that show how mental states can influence bodily functions. For example, studies by neuroscientist and pharmacologist Candace Pert (1946–2013), who discovered the opiate receptor in the brain and became a leading advocate of mind-body healing, demonstrate that purely psychological factors could influence the body's immune system.[18] In other words, the placebo effect—the ability for sham medications and fake treatments to have genuine therapeutic value—is one of the most extraordinary discoveries in medicine; it means that the mind has the power to help heal or harm the body.

Despite the reality of sleep paralysis, research suggests that you can get actual physical exercise in your lucid dreams. A fascinating study conducted by Daniel Erlacher and Michael Schredl at the University of Bern in Switzerland showed that people who repeatedly squat in their lucid dreams had significantly increased heart rates relative to strictly counting.[19] Although this kind of dreamtime exercise takes 44 percent more time as the same activity in waking life, it's possible to get a bit of a cardiovascular workout in your lucid dreams! Other lucid-dream activities also correlate with the body's nervous system. Using eye-movement trackers and EEG and muscle-tone monitors, as well as fMRI and neuroimaging techniques, in experiments that involved having people perform different activities (such as calculating mental arithmetic problems or singing aloud) within the lucid-dream state, it was found that these actions elicited the same neurological responses as identical actions performed while in a waking state.[20]

Other research, which I describe below, found that these same correlations existed for a wide range of lucid-dream behaviors, including such activities as estimating the amount of passing time, holding one's breath, or clenching one's hands. This means that the human nervous system doesn't actually differentiate between experiences that are had while a person is awake or while dreaming with lucidity. This has huge implications because it means that dreaming lucidly isn't like simply imagining that one is doing an activity; from the brain's point of view, performing a lucid-dream activity is like really doing it.

WET DREAMS AND EROTIC
LUCID DREAMS

Lucid-dream technology might offer hope for the treatment of sexual dysfunction. In a pilot study conducted by Stephen LaBerge and colleagues, subjects showed significantly heightened physiological responses to sexual activity and orgasm inside of lucid dreams, such as changes in skin conduction, respiration rate, vaginal electromyography, and vaginal pulse amplitude.[21] These results suggest that erotic activity in our dreams can have physiological consequences.

One of the natural physiological components of REM sleep is sexual arousal, as blood flow to the genitals is increased in both men and women during this stage of sleep.[22] This occurs whether there is sexual content in the dream or not, although there is evidence that increased activity occurs in the genitals when the dream is explicitly sexual. A study showed that a penile erection is firmer and stronger during a sexual dream than during a nonsexual dream, even if it is accompanied by an erection.[23]

From LaBerge's research, it appears that dream orgasms can be experienced in two basic ways—in just the brain (as in a lucid dream, when sex is consciously sought out) or in both the brain and the genitals (as in a nonlucid wet dream). Ejaculations during erotic, nonlucid wet dreams, which commonly occur in teenage boys, are thought to occur independently of the dream content, and then sometimes erotic feelings become incorporated into the dream after the genitals are physically aroused.

Nevertheless, when sexual activity occurs during a lucid dream, the physical effects are more subdued compared to the real thing in waking life. When a man achieves orgasm in a lucid dream his physical penis doesn't actually ejaculate (like in a wet dream), and his heartbeat isn't significantly elevated. Interestingly, men whose spinal cords have been injured, where the connection between the brain and the lower body has been severed, report having dreams where they experience all of the feelings and sensations of orgasm.[24] This means that even if you can't achieve orgasm in waking reality you can still orgasm in your lucid dream.

HEALING INJURIES AND ILLNESS
THROUGH LUCID DREAMING

Numerous anecdotal reports suggest that attempting to physically heal injured or diseased body parts during lucid dreams, in oneself or others, may have genuine healing effects. In fact, physical healings promoted by experiences within lucid dreams are so common that according to Robert Waggoner the quarterly publication that he edits, *Lucid Dreaming Experience,* receives one or two submissions about this per issue.[25]

Biochemist and dream researcher Ed Kellogg wrote a compelling article titled "A Personal Experience in Lucid Dream Healing," in which he describes a lucid-dream experience of healing himself of a severe infection in his right tonsil, which he had punctured with a wooden skewer while eating Japanese food: "I wake to the Lucid Dream State, decide to try healing my throat," he writes. "I look in a mirror and my throat looks healthy, but the tonsils look more like the middle section [uvula] than like tonsils. So in my dream body my throat looks healthy, but different. I program for healing to occur [using affirmations], and my throat does feel much better on awakening."[26] When Kellogg woke up from this lucid dream, he reported feeling no pain in his right tonsil, saying that it looked almost normal, and that 95 percent of the infection was gone within twelve hours of the dream.

Dream researcher Robert Moss, in his book *Conscious Dreaming,* cites many examples of how from a shamanic perspective dreams can play a role in facilitating healing. He describes how dreaming is central to the shamanic healing traditions of the Iroquois, for whom dreams are said to "provide insight into the cause of illness," which they believe "is often related to soul-loss or the intrusion of negative energies, including psychic attack and the influence of the unquiet dead." For the Iroquois, "Dreams reveal the psychospiritual causes of diseases before physical symptoms develop."[27]

Another important book about the healing ability of dreams is psychologist Patricia Garfield's *The Healing Power of Dreams,* which presents a step-by-step program for working with dreams to explore their diagnostic or medically therapeutic properties. The book is based on her extensive research and review of many case studies.[28]

Marc Ian Barasch, a former editor of *Psychology Today* and *Natural Health,* chronicles his own healing journey through dreams in his book *Healing Dreams.* Barasch presents a method for using dreams to transform one's life, and his personal experience is most compelling. He writes, "Had it really been pure coincidence I'd dreamed that a Chinese surgeon took a 'bullet' from my neck, and months later, a real Chinese surgeon— a Dr. Wang, the county's premier thyroid specialist and the spitting image of my dream doctor—had operated to remove my tumor?"[29]

According to Ed Kellogg, there are basically three types of healing assistance that lucid dreams can provide: "curative, diagnostic, and prescriptive."[30] The case that I described above, in which Kellogg seemingly healed his infected tonsil in a lucid dream, would be an example of a curative lucid dream, where a medical condition is directly healed within the dream. Using diagnostic lucid dreams, people may be able to probe their bodies and learn more about a particular medical condition or the state of their health (especially when medical science fails to provide adequate answers). In prescriptive lucid dreams one can consult with knowledgeable dream characters, or the intelligence behind the dreaming mind, for instructions on how to cure or treat a specific ailment.

An intriguing aside about lucid dreaming and illness is that for some people, being in a coma can provide an opportunity for extended periods of lucid dreaming. Stephanie Savage, the survivor of a rare muscle disease, dermatomyositis, provides a fascinating example of this. Savage fell into a coma for six weeks after being prescribed the wrong medication, and during her coma she experienced long periods of lucid dreaming:

My "dream reality" meant that suddenly I'm commenting and editing my lucid dream like a writer. At one point it's reality, and I'm editing and changing it because it's a dream, and then it's back to my dream reality. . . . Instead of seeing angels or demons or dead relatives, being a long time skeptic, I saw things that influenced my mental landscape—like science fiction movies. I think that inspired [some] episodes in my coma dream. Other things I saw in many of my dreams were serialized, like Saturday morning segments of cartoons that would rotate. Many times I would see the same scenario but with different dialogue. One of the serialized ones was where I was riding a combination of a Big Wheel bike and one of those little ice cream pushcarts. It was sort of like that, but it churned ice cream. Sometimes I was a human when I did this, and sometimes I was a polar bear cub. And sometimes, while lucid dreaming, I would think, I'm not supposed to be a polar bear cub! and I would change back into a human.[31]

Perhaps even more intriguing than the notion that we can heal ourselves in our lucid dreams is the idea that we can help heal others who are ill or injured, or learn valuable information about another person's health. Consider the following personal anecdote from author Robert Waggoner:

I became lucid in a dream and I seemed to be seeing a family member of a friend. I knew this family member had an odd illness. As I stood there observing in the lucid dream, I thought that there must be a "reason" why the family member has this odd illness. So I moved in very close and asked . . . "Why do you have this disease?" Immediately, the person responded, "I have this for . . . (this reason)." That response really surprised me! . . . I decided to wake up and write it down. Oddly, a couple of months later, I had a dream in which the dream suggested that I tell this same friend about this. . . . One evening, I did just that. Things were going quite well as I expressed the dreams, and the person responded about how the dreams had picked up on activities in his life. . . . Then I came to the above dream, and told it. Stony silence. I quickly realized that I was in very sensitive territory, so I made a hasty advance to the next dream. Years later, the friend saw me at a function and brought up the dream. He told me that the dream information was indeed correct and had picked up on a very sensitive situation that only people in the immediate family would know.[32]

Many anecdotes have been reported by lucid dreamers attempting to heal others while dreaming, with apparent success. Consider the following report, personally communicated to me by dream explorer Kelly Matthews:

> I had been studying energy healing and also reading up on lucid-dream healing. I was talking with a friend of mine, Chyrise, and she mentioned her foot had been in pain for quite some time. I asked her if I could try to get lucid in a dream and do energy healing on her foot. She agreed. That night I fell asleep with the intention of getting lucid. Now I'm in a dream, I'm with an old neighbor of mine when suddenly I realize I'm dreaming. I excuse myself from the scene and sit down on the floor. I close my dream eyes and focus all my energy on Chyrise's foot. I didn't actually see her foot but I was definitely focused on sending it healing energy. The dream was relatively short, I woke up soon after. I called her later that day and just asked her how her foot felt today without saying anything about what I had done. She told me it was the first day in a long time where she woke up and was able to walk without any pain in the morning. At that point I told her what I had done.

Although more research in this area is most definitely needed, it appears that using lucid-dreaming techniques could help to improve our health, and the health of others. And this prompts this question: Could lucid dreaming actually improve our waking performance and make us happier?

ARE LUCID DREAMERS HAPPIER, BETTER ADJUSTED PEOPLE?

Stephen LaBerge, Patricia Garfield, and other dream experts have suggested that lucid dreaming can be a method for improving performance. Certainly the previously mentioned studies support this possibility, as does the following research.

In 2011, scientists at the Max Planck Institutes in Germany became the first researchers to measure dream content.[33] Using a group of trained lucid dreamers as subjects, the researchers initially had MRI brain scans performed on them to verify that they could attain consciousness while dreaming. Before the participants went to sleep, the researchers had participants perform the task of alternating fist-clenching from left to right. They then asked the subjects to alert them with prearranged ocular movements as soon as they successfully achieved lucidity in a dream, at which point they were to perform the same exercise of fist-clenching while dreaming. Sure enough, the subjects activated the same regions of the brain in the dream state when doing this activity as they did when doing it while awake. The study found that "the coincidence of the brain activity measured during dreaming and the conscious action shows that dream content can be measured. 'With this combination of sleep EEGs, imaging methods and lucid dreamers, we can measure not only simple movements during sleep but also the activity patterns in the brain during visual dream perceptions,' says Martin Dresler, a researcher at the Max Planck Institute for Psychiatry."[34]

In England, psychologists Patrick Bourke and Hannah Shaw, lucid dreamers themselves, set out to discover whether frequent lucid dreamers performed better at cognitive tasks when awake compared with infrequent or nonlucid dreamers. Bourke and Shaw suspected that the state of consciousness that people are in while dreaming could be related to what are often referred to as "aha" moments of insight during problem solving. The study group consisted of twenty people who said that they had never had a lucid dream, twenty-eight occasional lucid dreamers, and twenty frequent lucid dreamers. All the subjects completed a problem-solving task. The frequent lucid dreamers were significantly better at solving these puzzles than the nonlucid dreamers. The occasional lucid dreamers fell in the middle, but weren't statistically different from either of the other two groups. Bourke and Shaw concluded that "results show that frequent lucid dreamers solve significantly more insight problems overall than nonlucid dreamers. This suggests that the insight experienced during the dream state may relate to the same underlying cognition needed for insight in the waking state."[35]

In Switzerland, at the University of Bern, Daniel Erlacher and Michael Schredl conducted a study to see what type of an effect mental practice during dreaming had on physical skills. The authors of the study asked people who reported frequent lucid dreams to toss coins into coffee cups twenty times before going to bed, and to then dream about practicing the coin tossing that night. In the morning, upon arising, the study participants were asked to toss coins into the cups again. Not surprisingly, subjects who reported successfully practicing the task while dreaming were more accurate with their coin tossing in the waking state compared to both the lucid dreamers who failed to practice as well as to a control group of nonlucid dreamers.[36]

So researchers have shown that people who practice a skill in their dreams can significantly improve that skill in waking life. Additional evidence suggests that lucid dreaming may help to improve symptoms of depression, and mental health in general, perhaps by giving people a greater sense of personal mastery and self-control.

FREQUENT LUCID DREAMERS SHOW BETTER SELF-REFLECTING CAPABILITIES WHEN AWAKE

Researchers at the Max Planck Institutes found that a particular brain region known to be involved in self-reflection, the anterior prefrontal cortex, is significantly larger in people who lucid dream frequently. Structural and functional MRI scans were taken of frequent and infrequent lucid dreamers, which were then compared by the researchers. The results of this study showed that

> participants in the high-lucidity group showed greater gray matter volume in the frontopolar cortex . . . compared with those in the low-lucidity group. Further, differences in brain structure were mirrored by differences in brain function. The . . . regions identified

through structural analyses showed increases in blood oxygen level–dependent signal during thought monitoring in both groups, and more strongly in the high-lucidity group. Our results reveal shared neural systems between lucid dreaming and metacognitive function, in particular in the domain of thought monitoring.[37]

This means that people who lucid dream frequently have larger regions in brain areas that contribute to greater levels of awareness, as that area of the brain is involved in controlling conscious cognitive processes. The researchers also found that those subjects in the frequently lucid group displayed more activity in this brain region during thought-monitoring tests while they were awake. This could mean that frequent lucid dreamers are better at self-reflection, or metacognition (awareness of one's thought process, or thinking about thinking), during waking life than infrequent lucid dreamers, and that lucid dreaming and thought monitoring share neural networks in the brain.

Can metacognitive skills be improved with training? Researchers at the Max Planck Institutes are trying to determine this. Meanwhile, other exciting research is taking lucid dreaming into a whole new cultural arena, by promising to make this extraordinary gift available to everyone who desires it, with the simple flick of switch.

TRANSCRANIAL ELECTRICAL BRAIN-STIMULATION RESEARCH

Probably the most important scientific research into lucid dreaming since Keith Hearne and Stephen LaBerge's groundbreaking 1970s and 1980s work came out of J. W. Goethe University in Frankfurt, Germany, in 2014. Researchers Ursula Voss and her colleagues showed that using low-current, transcranial electrical stimulation to generate gamma waves in the brain can reliably induce lucid dreaming in their sleeping subjects. This study was conducted because previous studies by Voss and others indicated that people tend to report lucid dreams during REM sleep, when their electrical brain-wave activity is in the low gamma range, which is about 40 Hz. The researchers applied transcranial alternating current stimulation—weak electrical currents along the scalp to influence the brain—to promote gamma activity in the frontal and temporal regions of their subjects' brains to see if this would provoke lucid dreaming. According to the researchers, it did—in 77 percent their subjects. The scientists concluded, "Our experiment is, to the best of our knowledge, the first to demonstrate altered conscious awareness as a direct consequence of induced gamma-band oscillations during sleep."[38]

The practical implications for this new research are profound, as it seems that once this technology is refined, miniaturized, and mass-produced, we may all be able to lucid dream on command. Meanwhile, if you're impatient for this technology to become readily available, you may wish to consider sleeping atop a lava column in the Hawaiian Islands.

GEOMAGNETIC INFLUENCE

Research by psychologist Jorge Conesa Sevilla shows that sleep paralysis (which can lead to lucid dreaming, as will be discussed in chapter 9) has been correlated with volcanic activity on the Hawaiian Islands.[39] Sevilla speculates that the cause of this phenomenon is related to geomagnetic changes that occur as a result of the volcanic activity. I found this research especially relevant to some of the studies that I participated in when I was working with British biologist Rupert Sheldrake. I did the California-based research for Sheldrake's book *Dogs That Know When Their Owners Are Coming Home* and gathered material for the book about unusual animal behavior prior to earthquakes (which constitute another example of how geologic events can influence an animal's nervous system).

Sevilla suggests a novel and risky-sounding lucid-dream method that I'd like to try sometime—going to sleep on top of a lava column in Hawaii. According to Jorge, doing so gives one a fifty-fifty chance of having an experience with sleep paralysis, which can act as a gateway into out-of-body experiences and lucid dreams. But without traveling to Hawaii and risking an unpleasant "wake 'n bake", there's still a good chance that you can achieve lucidity in a dream by just experimenting in your own bed tonight.

INFORMAL EXPERIMENTS OF THE ONLINE LUCID-DREAM COMMUNITY

It doesn't take an expensive sleep laboratory to conduct lucid-dream research. Anyone can perform his or her own experiments, and, in fact, many people do. Communities of amateur dream researchers can be found all over the Internet. These online groups offer forums where people can share reports, techniques, and the results of their dream experiences, as well as find others with whom to collaborate in shared-dream experiments.*

As with the psychedelic drug community, amateur dream enthusiasts have gone far beyond conventional scientific research, although these experiments are less rigorously controlled. For example, consider the study conducted by dream researcher Jean Campbell, who was the director of the Poseidia Institute, a parapsychology research organization in Virginia Beach. Campbell wrote a fascinating book called *Group Dreaming: Dreams to the Tenth Power,* which described a series of experiments with shared dreaming and shared lucid dreaming among a group of advanced dream explorers.

Campbell, along with nine other people, formed a research group in 1979 that planned a series of meetings in the dream state over a period of six months, to see if they could carry out predetermined tasks together. Everyone in the group agreed to record all of their dreams during this period. They would write down their dreams upon awakening, photocopy them, and mail them to a central location (this study took place in the pre-Internet days). Although there were many difficulties in verifying this research, some of the results, published in Campbell's book, are quite compelling.

---

*Following the bibliography you will find Web links to some of the forums that I'm describing.

Other informal researchers who have progressed far along in shared-lucid-dreaming studies include Ed Kellogg and Robert Waggoner. Kellogg holds a Ph.D. in biochemistry from Duke University for his work investigating the role of free radicals and singlet oxygen in the aging process, but he has been studying lucid dreaming and psychic phenomena for over thirty years. Waggoner authored *Lucid Dreaming: Gateway to the Inner Self*, the most advanced book that I've read on this subject.

In his book, Waggoner compellingly describes the results of shared-lucid-dreaming experiments that he and others have participated in. These include "dual-person-lucid mutual dreams"—shared dreams where both people are lucid—and "one-person-lucid mutual dreams"— shared dreams where one person is lucid.[40] If this subject interests you, then Waggoner's accounts will simply blow your mind. In chapter 8 we'll be exploring reports of psychic dreams, mutual nonlucid dreaming, and shared lucid dreams.

The International Association for the Study of Dreams (IASD), which I mentioned earlier, is dedicated to the investigation of dreams and dreaming. They hold regular conferences, organized to promote scientific research into the study of dreams, and to provide an educational forum for the interdisciplinary exchange of such information among the scientific community and the general public. This is an excellent

Fig. 3.4. Lucid dreaming expert Robert Waggoner (photo by Wendy Waggoner)

place to learn about the latest dreaming research, and to meet others who share your passion about dreams and lucid dreams.

But before you can cultivate your passion for lucid-dream experiences you need to be successful in achieving them. I realize that some people reading this book may never have experienced a lucid dream or have only had them on rare occasions. So in the next chapter we'll be reviewing some practical techniques that people have used to promote lucid dreaming and to develop their dream-realm skills.

4

IMPROVING LUCID DREAMING AND DEVELOPING SUPERPOWERS IN THE DREAM REALM

Dream on, dream on, dream on. Dream until your dream comes true.

AEROSMITH

Evidence supports the notion that anyone can learn how to dream with lucidity, given enough time and effort. Some people appear to be born with a natural gift for conscious dreaming and report having had spontaneous lucid dreams since early childhood, such as Will Culpepper, who sent me the following account:

I had my first lucid dream when I was about eight years old. In the dream I was in the factory that made the children's magazine Disney Adventures, *observing the huge stacks of paper and giant printing machines. All of a sudden, a man made of fire appeared behind me and started chasing me. As I ran through the factory, he shot flames out and ignited the stacks of paper all around. Suddenly, something struck my attention. Despite the fact that I was running for my life, I had the presence of mind to notice something funny about a clock on the wall. I stopped to look at it and realized that it went up to 13 instead of 12. My first thought was, That's not right. I must be in a dream. Taking a leap of faith and trust, I then told myself, Well, if I'm dreaming, then when I open this closet right here there will be a fire extinguisher. Sure enough, when I opened the closet door I found it completely empty except for a single fire extinguisher. I grabbed it, turned around, and extinguished the guy made of fire, and that's the last I remember.*

I interviewed a twelve-year-old boy from Bali named Jazz Mordant, who has been having vivid lucid dreams since the age of three or four. He told me that he often consciously intervenes in frightening dream scenarios so as to achieve better outcomes in the dream. He described dreams in which he was surrounded by scary monsters, where he learned how to control their minds in order to protect himself:

During my experiences with mind control during my lucid dreams I have been able to completely manipulate and alter the way different beings react and decide things in the dream world. The way that I do this is very simple, although it took me ages to figure out. All you have to do is give it all of your intention and think about the way you want them to act, and see it happening—and your imagination will become reality. However, I cannot control some people and beings in my dreams, as when I try to they realize this and look at me as if I'm crazy.

I'm not one of these dream prodigies like Jazz. I didn't start having lucid dreams until I was a teenager.* However, I've always had vivid dreams, and I had a lot of frightening nightmares as a young child. Then I began having lucid dreams when I was sixteen, not long after I started experimenting with meditation, cannabis, and LSD. Thanks to

---

*However, I do recall some semilucid dreams from around the age of seven or eight, where I would jump off the roof of my house and float slowly to the ground. I remember recalling these dreams while awake and thinking that I could secretly make anything happen, just by believing that I could.

the use of these mind-expanding substances and my own mental discipline, over the course of my life I've had hundreds of prolonged lucid dreams, some of which appear to have lasted for hours, and I've had a few magical periods where I seemingly never lost lucid consciousness during a whole night of sleep.

My interest in lucid dreams, and my skill at inducing and sustaining them, was largely cultivated in my early twenties through my interactions with Stephen LaBerge, whom I interviewed in 1993 for my book *Mavericks of the Mind.** In LaBerge's 1985 book *Lucid Dreaming,* I learned that one's proficiency at lucid dreaming can be improved, and that lucid dreaming is a learnable skill that improves with practicing specific techniques and setting strong intentions.

Around 50 percent of the population has experienced a lucid dream at least once in their lives, and around 20 percent of the population has around one lucid dream a month. However, only around 1 or 2 percent of the population experiences lucid dreams more than once a week.[1]

When dream researchers Robert van De Castle and Joe Dane surveyed people to distinguish potentially successful lucid dreamers from nonlucid dreamers, they found that "subjects with a spirit of adventure, who wished to explore the unknown and had a rich curiosity about the ranges of human experiences, were excellent candidates for lucidity."[2] Most lucid-dream researchers believe that the ability to have lucid dreams is present in everyone, and evidence supports the notion that anyone can get better at having lucid dreams with practice. However, frequent lucid dreaming requires continued practice and strong intent, or the frequency of one's lucid dreams will start to diminish. In other words, increasing lucid-dream frequency is more like training for an athletic sport than it is like learning how to ride a bicycle.

But wait, before we get started . . .

---

*Stephen LaBerge participated in a philosophical panel discussion about consciousness that I cohosted at the University of California, Santa Cruz, in 1994. A DVD of this event, titled *Mavericks of the Mind Live!,* was transcribed and is available as an e-book on Amazon Kindle. It's full title is *Mavericks of the Mind Live! Roundtable Discussions with Timothy Leary, John Lilly, Laura Huxley, Robert Anton Wilson, Nick Herbert, Carolyn Mary Kleefeld, Ralph Abraham, and Others.*

CAN LUCID DREAMING BE DANGEROUS?

I initially thought that this was a silly question, as one can't possibly get physically harmed in a lucid dream, and there are so many potential benefits and delights. However, after reading an essay about using lucid dreaming in psychotherapy, by Gestalt therapist Brigitte Holzinger, I began to understand why it might not be a good idea for some people to experiment with lucid-dream induction techniques. Holzinger provides a case study of one psychotic person who ended up committing suicide as a result, it seems, of his repeated experiences dialoguing with "the devil" in his lucid dreams.[3]

Negative reactions to lucid dreaming appear to be quite rare, but, as with using psychedelics, it may not be a wise idea for someone who has difficulty distinguishing reality from fantasy to start experimenting with a technique that will make one's experience of life bigger, weirder, and more mysterious than it already is. As Ryan Hurd writes, "If we grant that lucid dreaming may be powerful enough to heal, then we must also admit that it may also be powerful enough to do us harm. Otherwise, lucid dreaming is not really the medicine so many claim it could be."[4]

Hurd's warning sounds like it might apply equally well to both lucid dreaming and psychedelic journeys. However, psychophysical researchers Celia Green and Charles McCreery theorize that lucid-dreaming practices might actually be helpful for some people suffering from schizophrenia: "In the case of a schizophrenic person feeling out of control of various aspects of his or her mental life, it is possible that the experience of gaining control over at least one of them, namely distressing dreams, might have a generalized therapeutic effect, quite apart from the localized relief that might be obtained for the particular symptom."[5]

Nevertheless, a disturbing example of a negative outcome involving lucid dreaming can be found in the case of a twenty-two-year-old schizophrenic, Jared Lee Loughner, who shot a U.S. congresswoman and eighteen other people in Tucson, Arizona, in 2011. Initially judged incompetent to stand trial due to paranoid schizophrenia, in August 2012 Loughner was judged competent to stand trial, and at the hearing he pleaded guilty to nineteen counts. In November 2012 he was sentenced to life plus 140 years in federal prison. Loughner was very interested in lucid dreaming, and also had a history of using psychedelic drugs, which may have worsened his condition. Just days before the shooting he posted a series of videos on YouTube that included his observations about dreaming, one of which included the frightening statement, "I am a sleepwalker—who turns off the alarm clock." Some commentators wondered whether Loughner thought that he might have been dreaming at the time of the shooting.[6]

When my colleague Ryan Hurd was reviewing the account of Loughner in this book, he told me, "The salient point is that lucid dreaming is probably a more common symptom of schizophrenia than typically recognized, and that comes with sleep degradation and arousal disorders in the early stages of the condition. Sleep paralysis is another symptom of early-stage schizophrenia." Eerily, Loughner sent an innocent-seeming e-mail message to Hurd eighteen months prior to the shootings, asking his advice about lucid dreaming. An article on the *Gawker* website that includes Hurd's correspondence with Loughner also includes a series of fascinating excerpts from Loughner's dream diaries.[7]

Other people have raised concerns about lucid dreaming interfering with the quality of one's sleep, causing a loss of interest in one's waking life, or creating the risk of "bad trips." Although not conclusive, all of the initial studies with lucid dreamers have found these fears to be unfounded,[8] although people have had some frightening experiences during lucid dreams on occasion. In fact, Ryan Hurd confirmed that "new research shows clearly that 'bad trips' are not uncommon but probably underreported."[9]

Others have raised concerns that by lucid dreaming we interfere with the natural symbolic communication process between the unconscious and conscious parts of our mind. Yet this doesn't seem to be a concern to frequent lucid dreamers for two reasons: First, no one can ever gain complete control over what happens in a lucid dream; there's always an element of surprise, and even the best lucid dreamers, it seems, can only achieve lucidity on occasion. And second, one could argue just the opposite—that we can more effectively understand the unconscious meaning of dreams by examining them consciously while they are actually occurring. It's hard to see how being less aware and insightful about what's happening to us can be helpful.

In his book *Astral Projection,* Oliver Fox includes a list of the supposed occult dangers of lucid dreaming, such as "heart failure," "insanity," "premature burial," "temporary derangement caused by the noncoincidence of the *etheric* body with the physical body," "cerebral hemorrhage," "obsession," and "death." However, after listing these supposed dangers he states, "I would not dissuade any earnest investigator with a passion for truth. He will be protected, I believe by the unseen intelligences that guide our blundering efforts in the divine quest, and the merely frivolous inquirer will soon be frightened away by the strange initial experiences."[10]

I suspect that there's truth behind Fox's encouraging words, and that for most people lucid dreaming is a safe and healthy way to explore new possibilities. So what's the best way to get started? Studies have repeatedly demonstrated that there is a strong correlation between overall dream recall and lucid-dreaming frequency.[11]

ENHANCING DREAM RECALL

Scientific evidence suggests that we never actually lose consciousness when we go to sleep. This may sound surprising, but in studies where people were woken up during every different stage of sleep and asked what was going on in their minds, they usually had an answer of some sort. We're thinking, feeling, or dreaming the entire night, it seems, but the brain mechanism responsible for encoding our experiences into long-term memory is switched off when we go to sleep.

The explanation for this may lie in the original biological function of dreaming, which is so that we can strengthen useful memories and discard useless ones. If this is true, then it would make sense that during this process our memory systems would be unable to store new data. As we learned, REM sleep patterns are not a reliable indicator that people are dreaming, because people not only report dreams during NREM sleep, studies have confirmed that people can have lucid dreams during the NREM stages of sleep.[12] However, as many know, oftentimes remembering your dreams can be maddeningly difficult. On many mornings all I can remember from my dreams is that I was somewhere, with someone, doing something that I was very involved with. As Australian dream scholar Robert Moss writes, "The typical dreamer, after waking, has no more idea where he spent the night than an amnesiac drunk."[13]

So how can we learn how to remember our dreams? Primarily, by having the intention to do so prior to going to sleep, and by habitually recording one's nighttime experiences. It's important to make a commitment to turn on the light (or use a flashlight or an audio recorder) and write down (or record) every dream you remember when you first awaken and it is fresh in your mind. Even though our long-term memory storage system is largely turned off while we sleep, our short-term memory system still works. I've found that one partial sentence is enough to start the flow from the land of lost dreams. Just start writing. Before you know it, more and more details come back to you as you're writing the dream down or recording it.

If you don't consolidate the memory of the dream by remembering and reflecting on it in your waking state immediately upon awakening, then most likely it will be lost in the astral void—although oddly, sometimes some random stimulus during the day will trigger a dream memory from the previous night. If this happens to you, record it in your dream journal. I also find that lingering elements from dreams that vanish upon awakening may return a few moments later if I'm drifting back to sleep, and so it's important to get up and record these fragile memories at the time, before falling back asleep, if you don't want to lose them. There may also be a unique, state-dependent memory system operating within the dream itself that we can't access in our waking state, as I and others have reported experiencing memories of previous dreams while lucid dreaming.

Many successful lucid dreamers will confirm that the best way to begin one's personal experimentation with lucid dreaming is by simply learning to pay more attention to one's dreams. The best way to do this is by keeping a written record of one's experiences and experiments in the dream realm.

Keeping a Dream Journal

- The first step in enhancing dream recall is to obtain a suitable journal or notebook. Scientific research has demonstrated that being motivated and keeping a dream diary can substantially improve dream recall.[14] The more beautifully designed the journal or notebook, the more ornately decorated and magical looking, the better, I think, as this whole project is about the alchemical blending of one's imagination with reality.

- Next, one needs to get into the habit of writing down what one has experienced while sleeping immediately upon awakening. It is important to keep your journal and a flashlight right next to your bed, or, as I mentioned earlier, you can use an audio recorder if you prefer. I used a written journal for years. Now I use the speech-to-text app on my iPhone, then transfer the report to my computer and edit the text in the morning.

- Get into the regular habit of recording what happened while you were asleep. If you don't remember any dreams, then write "no dream recall," but include how you feel. When you recall a dream, write down any fragment, scene, emotion, memory, or feeling that you can remember. Write down every detail. Draw pictures or illustrate the report, if this feels appropriate. I think that it also helps to give each dream a title, like a poem or a short story, based on a central theme, as they *are* stories, first and foremost.

- One often finds that the process of writing down a few dream fragments or feelings brings back other memories from the dream, sometimes surprisingly a flood of them. The more you do this, the more you naturally enhance your dream recall, and this is the first step toward having a lucid dream.

- It's important to keep a written record, so that you can more easily examine and compare the dreams. This means that if you use an audio recorder to capture your dreams in the middle of the night, it's important to transfer these experiences into your journal for easier reference later on.

The late occult writer Oliver Fox remarks on the importance of keeping a journal of one's lucid dreams and nighttime experiences:

> What is it that our spiritual experiences, like the roseate hues of early dawn, are so fleeting, so difficult to retain in our mind? Swiftly the exaltation passes; the memory becomes blurred; we question its reality. Did that really happen? I have gone further than many people along a certain path. I have talked with Masters in another world. I have seen—though from afar—Celestial Beings, great shapes of dazzling flame, whose beauty filled the soul with anguished longing. And yet were it not for my records, the blessed written words— which ensure permanence, even though they veil and distort and make untrue—were it not for these, there are times when I should doubt everything; yes, even the reality of my Master. So hard is it to kill the skeptic in me, nor do I want to altogether; for skepticism is very useful as an aid to preserving mental equilibrium.[15]

Does consciously observing, recording, and reflecting on our dreams change them? Russian occultist P. D. Ouspensky thought so:

> Dreams proved to be too light, too thin, too plastic. They did not stand observation, observation changed them. What happened was this: very soon after I had begun to write down my dreams in the morning and during the night, had tried to reconstruct them, thought about them, analyzed and compared them with one another, I noticed that my dreams began to change. They did not remain as

they were before, and I very soon realized that I was observing not the dreams I used to have in a natural state, but new dreams were created by the very fact of observation.[16]

That observation effects measurement is a well-known conundrum from quantum physics. It appears that the very act of observation changes what we're looking at, causing a wave of possibilities to collapse into a single event. In chapter 10 we'll be discussing the philosophical implications of this perplexing insight, but in the meantime let's get to know what it's like to wake up in our dreams.

HOW TO HAVE A LUCID DREAM

As I mentioned in the introduction, there are levels of lucidity within the dream state, from what has been described as "prelucidity" to "superlucidity." In the early stages of lucidity development, one simply suspects that one might be dreaming during the dream, while in the more developed stages one can become just as aware during the dreaming state as one is during the waking state. Then, sometimes, people can even become more aware in their lucid dreams than they are during ordinary waking consciousness, and have life-transforming mystical experiences as a result.

During a low-awareness lucid dream, one may only be in partial control of one's cognitive skills, and sometimes in this state one can make erroneous judgments that seem to be obvious errors upon awakening, and one may also initially have poor impulse control. In many of the early lucid dreams that I had, I immediately rushed off to fulfill impulsive desires, and it took a fair amount of lucid-dream experience before I was able to progress beyond mere attempts to satisfy my most basic, unfulfilled desires, as I often found myself simply doing these things without really thinking. With practice, though, I was able to tame these wild impulses, which became part of the deeper, personal psychological healing that I described in chapter 1. I subsequently advanced into deeper levels of possibility with lucid dreaming.

I asked Stephen LaBerge what kind of techniques he thought were the most effective for producing lucid dreams. Before responding to this question he said, "If you were to say, 'I want to become a lucid dreamer, how should I go about it?' I would say that means you've got some extra time and energy in your life, some unallocated attention that you could apply to working on this. If you're somebody who is so busy that you have hardly the time to take a walk, you're not going to have the time and energy to do this."

This is an important point. Learning how to lucid dream takes time and effort. One needs to have the time for practicing the techniques, as well as a commitment to developing and improving one's skill over time. With persistence and dedication it appears that anyone can master these techniques. However, just taking an interest in them may be enough to start having lucid dreams. Researchers Celia Green and Charles McCreery say, "For those who wish to start developing lucid dreams, a simple prescription, which may be sufficient, is to think about the idea of lucid dreaming before falling asleep each night. Some people keep a book about lucid dreaming by their bedside and read part of it each night to focus their mind on the idea."[17]

With forty-three books about sleep, dreaming, and lucid dreaming piled next to my bedside as I write these words, I can't help but laugh when I read the above quote. In any case, be sure to keep *this* book by your bedside, and every time you see its beautiful cover art by Cameron Gray remember to question whether or not you're dreaming.

Aside from reading books about lucid dreaming before going to sleep, there are basically two ways to achieve lucidity in a dream state. The first is by maintaining a certain degree of self-awareness as one is falling asleep, staying conscious or mentally alert to a degree through the entire process of falling sleep and entering the dream state. This can be quite an amazing experience, and I find that I can only do it when I'm in a certain state of consciousness to begin with as I'm falling asleep. (Some of the herbal, nutritional, and pharmacological methods that I and others have used to help reach this state of awareness are discussed in the next chapter.)

Maintaining an alert and watchful state of consciousness as one is falling asleep can also sometimes be a bit frightening, as it involves passing through stages of sleep paralysis. I've heard people describe the experience differently, but for me it goes something like this: The process of allowing my body to fully and completely relax can produce euphoric feelings and hypnagogic imagery behind my closed eyes. As the experience deepens, and I start to fall asleep, I pass through a stage where I am still aware of my body and my surrounding bedroom, but anxiety-raising auditory hallucinations become superimposed on it. Then, as my body is humming from the euphoria of deep relaxation, I'll start to hear people talking outside my house, or I'll hear someone coming up the stairs to my bedroom. These auditory hallucinations seem completely real, and I always have to convince myself not to be afraid, that they are just dream imagery (or spirits), and there is nothing to be concerned about. This takes a lot of willpower; I've woken myself up out of the process many times, just to make sure that there really was no one in my bedroom. However, if I stay with it and surrender to the experience while maintaining lucidity, I start to see more intense hypnagogic imagery, sometimes fractal and psychedelic patterns, combined with an opiatelike bliss. Soon the shifting imagery solidifies into the environment of a lucid dream.

Dream lucidity achieved in this manner has been termed WILD by Stephen LaBerge—wake-initiated lucid dreams. One of the methods that LaBerge suggests for achieving this is by counting while falling asleep, repeating the phrase "I'm dreaming." So as one is drifting off into dreamland, one occupies one's mind with the ordinal phrases, "One, I'm dreaming. Two, I'm dreaming. Three, I'm dreaming . . . " Practicing this technique may help you to paradoxically stay awake while falling asleep, but even if you can't maintain mental alertness through the process of falling asleep, often this technique will cause you to awaken in your dream later, or so I have found and others have reported.

Maintaining a vigilant state of observing your awareness through hypnagogia (the transitional state from wakefulness to sleep) all the way into sleeping and dreaming states of consciousness can be an extraordinarily magical and blissful experience. Every night, it seems, we pass into these mentally playful, image-associating states that are truly psychedelic and absolutely delightful to experience. When I'm in them they seem instantly familiar, and it appears that I pass through these states whenever I go to sleep, but I almost always forget them. It takes a sustained effort of focused awareness to do this, and a commitment to waking up to record what happens, but the results are well worth the effort, I assure you.

This method is in contrast to the other way to achieve lucidity in a dream, which LaBerge calls DILD, or dream-initiated lucid dreams. DILD involve "waking up," so to speak, within a dream, and realizing that you are dreaming while it is already happening. This awakening to a greater sense of awareness is usually due to having an enhanced critical perspective, so that one notices something bizarre or strangely out of synch between what is happening in the dream and what one knows to be possible in waking reality. LaBerge calls these strange inconsistencies with physical reality "dreamsigns," and he says that if we remember them, they can help us recognize when we are dreaming.

One way to increase our chances of experiencing a DILD is by actively looking for common dreamsigns in the records of our dream journals. Again, this is why it's so important to have a written record, as it's generally easier to recognize common dreamsigns when one is examining them visually, in writing.

Another DILD technique, also developed by LaBerge, called the mnemonic induction of lucid dreams, or MILD, is based on memory training that is meant to be applied just after one has awakened from a dream and can easily fall back asleep. Upon awakening from the dream, this technique involves rehearsing the dream in your mind, imagining yourself becoming lucid in it as you are falling asleep, while repeating this statement: "The next time I'm dreaming, I will remember to notice that I'm dreaming."

Studies have shown the MILD technique to be the most effective DILD method for the induction of lucid dreams.[18] To learn more about MILD, WILD, and DILD, see LaBerge's book *Exploring the World of Lucid Dreaming*. Meanwhile, let's make sure that we're not dreaming right now . . .

TESTING YOUR REALITY

One of the techniques that has worked well for me is something that I also first heard about from Stephen LaBerge. It's a technique that one learns to practice throughout the day, originally developed by the late psychologist Paul Tholey, called the *critical reflection technique*. To practice this method, one gets into the habit of continuously asking oneself the question, *Am I dreaming right now?*

The idea behind doing this regularly when we're awake is that we'll carry the habit into our dreams, where we will discover that we are dreaming. Lucid-dream expert Daniel Love calculated that we spend around 11 percent of every twenty-four hours in bed dreaming, which means that if people get into the habit of asking themselves regularly if they're dreaming right now or not, then they will have a better than one in ten chance of being correct![19] However, to answer this question it's important that you actually test your environment to determine conclusively whether or not you are dreaming. If you don't get into the habit of actually testing your environment to see if you really are dreaming or not, then when you ask yourself in a dream if you're dreaming you'll be likely to just do the same thing—not carefully examine your reality, and then just conclude that you're not dreaming.

You must ask the question sincerely each time for this to work properly. Try it right now. Put down the book, look around, and genuinely ask yourself, *Am I dreaming right now?* Now, when you answer this question, be prepared to explain how you know for sure that you're correct. Remember, it's not always so obvious. The dream world can look as convincingly real as waking reality. Testing the world around you to see whether or not you're dreaming involves doing at least one of several things.

Pinch your nose: One of the easiest ways to test what reality you're in is to try breathing through your nose while pinching your nostrils closed. There's a glitch in the dream matrix here, as one can easily breathe through one's nostrils when doing this in a dream. By the way, the expression of disbelief, "I pinched myself to see if I was dreaming," would actually be a rather poor reality test in a lucid dream because one's dream state is quite capable of producing a dream sensation of a pinch that is convincing enough to fool the dreamer.

Read written words, look away, look back and read them again: Another easy test is to simply look at something written on paper, look away, and then look back and see if the same words are still there. *Expect to discover that you're dreaming while you do this.* In a dream environment, the words will almost always change when you look away and then look back again. This is the method that I use the most, as it always works for me, and for most people—but not everyone, as there are some cases where writing stays consistent in dreams. My girlfriend told me about a dream that she had where she repeatedly looked at the writing in a book, looked away, and looked back, only to discover each time that the writing was always the same, and she never achieved lucidity in that dream. It was almost as though the dream was mocking her attempts to become lucid. However, in general, although a dream environment can appear every bit as realistic as waking reality, the stability of the world is usually substantially decreased, and its fluidity, mutability, and vulnerability to our personal psychic influence is substantially increased. When I stare at written words in a lucid dream they never remain stable for more than a few seconds and always start to morph.

Pull on your fingers to see if they elongate: Robert Waggoner suggests this as an additional way to test which reality one is in. In a dream, your fingers will stretch out like Silly Putty.

Turn the light switch on or off: When you're in a dream, the light switch usually doesn't do anything when you move it, as is famously portrayed in the film *Waking Life*.

Try passing your hand through a solid physical object: First, imagine that you can do so, and then try it. In a dream it's possible to move your body through physical objects, but sometimes this takes a bit of practice. An easy way that people can do this is by simply trying to poke one's finger through the palm of the opposite hand.

Try to recall the events that led up to the situation you currently find yourself in: When I try to recall the events that led up to the situation that I find myself in, I always discover that these memories are simply not in my mind when I'm dreaming. Some people suggest using this reality test as a lucidity-trigger technique by asking oneself the question *How did I get here?* Regularly asking yourself how you got into the situation that you currently find yourself in can carry over into your dreams, where you may realize that you can't remember how you got to where you are in the dream, and consequently you become lucid.

Try using your imagination: Some other lucid dreamers and I—as well as some characters in my dreams that I've questioned—also can't seem to use our imaginations within a dream, i.e., we can't visualize things in our minds while we're in the dream state, perhaps because the world that we're in during a dream is in our imagination. However, some people report being able to do this, and these people find that whatever they visualize in their dream significantly affects the dream environment.

Reality-test reminders: Some people write messages on their hands to remind them to test their reality when they look at their hands during the day, or they use an app on their phone that sends random text messages to remind them to ask that important question *Am I dreaming right now?* One of my favorite reality-test reminders is a beautifully crafted talisman, designed by dream researchers Ryan Hurd and Lee Adams, that has ancient alchemical imagery etched into it. It's a magical, coinlike object that I carry around with me, and every time I find it in my pocket I look at it. On one side is a snake-adorned, eight-pointed sun with a celestial face, and on the other is a crescent moon within an eye, held between branching, intertwining tree limbs. "Are you awake?" it asks on the sunny side, and "Are you dreaming?" it asks when you flip

Fig. 4.1. The Lucid Talisman, designed by Ryan Hurd and Lee Adams, is available at https://dreamstudies.com/shop/exclusives/lucid-dreaming-talisman (photo by the author).

it over. This talisman turns up in my pocket during both my waking life and in dreaming situations.

Try to fly: Here's a fun reality test, although it's not something that one can easily do in just any situation. Still, it helps me—try to fly! I do this in my living room in waking reality and it carries over into my dreams. See if you can elevate yourself longer than gravity usually allows by simply jumping into the air and thinking, *I'm going to fly!* If you appear to linger in the air for even a tiny fraction longer than usual, then the situation deserves further investigation, so it's important to try it again.

Some people have been known to go through fairly complex procedures and considerable lengths to determine whether or not they are dreaming. Consider the following 1938 report from German psychologist Harold von Moers-Messmer, one of a handful of researchers who investigated lucid dreaming in the first half of the twentieth century:

From the top of a rather low and unfamiliar hill, I look out across a wide plain towards the horizon. It crosses my mind that I have no idea what time of year it is. I check the sun's position. It appears almost straight above me with its usual brightness. This is surprising, as it occurs to me that it is now autumn, and the sun was much lower only a short time ago. I think it over: The sun is now perpendicular to the equator, so here it has to appear at an angle of approximately 45 degrees. So if my shadow does not correspond to my own height, I must be dreaming. I examine it: It is about 30 centimeters long. It takes considerable effort for me to believe this almost blindingly bright landscape and all of its features to be only an illusion.[20]

However, many advanced lucid dreamers report that they simply know when they are dreaming, without having to test their reality, as one's state of consciousness is most definitely different in a dream state than in a waking state. With practice we can learn to recognize the state of consciousness that we're in while dreaming as a dream sign, to alert us to the fact that we're dreaming, thereby allowing us to achieve lucidity. The state of consciousness that one is in while in a lucid dream is a lot like the state of consciousness that one is in while tripping on psychedelic drugs or visionary plants. Have you ever witnessed people tripping on acid for their first time? They often find the wispy vapor trails that follow their hand movements to be tremendously fascinating.

LOOKING AT YOUR HANDS IN A DREAM

In Carlos Castaneda's book *Journey to Ixtlan,* the Mexican shaman-trickster Don Juan says to Carlos,

Tonight in your dreams, you must look at your hands. . . . Every time you look at anything in your dreams it changes shape. The trick in learning to set up dreaming is obviously not just to look at things, but to sustain the sight of them. Dreaming is real when one has succeeded in bringing everything into focus. Then there is no difference between what you do when you sleep and what you do when you are not sleeping.[21]

Fig. 4.2. *Reach for Your Dreams,* by Frank Alan Bella
(www.bellastudios.com)

When Castaneda saw his hands that night in a dream he became lucid and realized that he was dreaming. I read this account when I was sixteen, not long after I had taken LSD and had my first lucid dream, and it had a profound effect on me because I knew what he was talking about. Many people have had lucid dreams after reading Castaneda's account, and others have had success using a variation on this technique that is described by Robert Waggoner as "finding your hands" in a dream to become lucid. It goes like this: stare at your hands before going to sleep while telling yourself that when you see your hands in the next dream, you'll realize that you're dreaming.[22]

In the 2007 film *The Good Night,* the character played by Martin Freeman repeatedly becomes lucid in his dreams each night when he looks at his hands. In addition to being a lucidity trigger, there's something powerful about simply looking at your hands while in a lucid dream. For example, in a Lucidity Institute experiment, the participants were instructed to study their hands while in a lucid-dream state, and the reports from these experiments included bizarre variations of the hands, like having extra fingers.[23]

A contributor to a website forum, "James1982," writes about the technique of looking at your hands in a lucid dream: "The idea is that, in your dreams, your hands will never look normal. This has been my experience. Sometimes my hands will look almost like I am viewing them through a kaleidoscope, other times I will have extra fingers, or my fingers will all be of a vastly different length and thickness. A few days back I had a lucid dream where my hand became fractal, and each finger had a hand on the tip, which in turn had a hand on each finger, so on and so forth."[24]

Actually, in lucid dreams, my hands generally appear pretty normal-looking, but I have noticed that newborn infants look at their hands a lot. I've also noticed that people who first try virtual reality or LSD often spend time initially just watching their hands and fingers move. It seems that one of the first things we all do upon entering a new state of consciousness or a new level of reality is examine our hand-eye connection. There are more neural connections between the hands and the eyes than between any other two parts of the body. It was a revelation for me when I realized that there's nothing that I see more of in life than the backside of my own hands.

More than a few people have mentioned to me that they became lucid after seeing the backside of their hand in a dream, so try to let your hands be a constant reminder of dream lucidity. Also, looking at one's dream hands can sometimes help to sustain unstable lucid dreams. As I mentioned earlier, you may want to try writing the words *Am I*

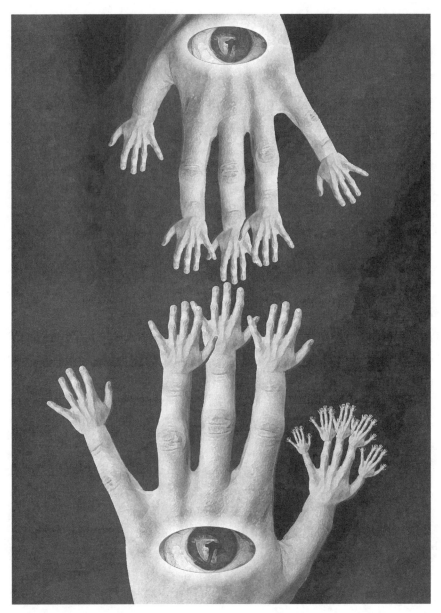

Fig. 4.3. *Infinite Lucidity,* by Bump Goose (www.itszen30.com)

dreaming? (or a symbol that carries this meaning) on the palm of your hand, and then remember to test your reality every time you see it, as this will likely carry over into the dream state.

SETTING STRONG INTENTIONS AND USING AUTO-SUGGESTION

Reminding yourself of your intention to lucid dream before you go to sleep at night can be helpful, according to some reports, and I found this to be true in my own personal experience. Doing this in a relaxed, meditative, hypnotic, or trancelike state may be especially helpful. Say to yourself, *Tonight I will be awake in my dreams.* Repeatedly visualizing or imagining oneself being awake in a dream scenario appears to help increase the likelihood of it happening. This method is an extension of a process known as *dream incubation,* which means going to sleep with the explicit intention of having a particular kind of dream. As I mentioned in the introduction, dream incubation began in ancient Greece and Egypt, where temples devoted to different deities were used by people who would go there to sleep at night in order to receive divine knowledge in their dreams, often about how to treat a particular illness.

Dream incubation works well when synergistically combined with other methods, especially those that disrupt normal sleep patterns.

Imagine that your throat is glowing: An ancient lucid-dreaming induction technique from Tibetan Buddhism is to imagine that a red lotus flower with four leaves is glowing at the base of one's throat as one is falling asleep. The Tibetan symbol *Ah* (ཨ) is supposed to be visualized, glowing in white, in the center of the lotus flower during this process. Alternatively, one can imagine a candle flame, a red pearl, or a simple white light, radiating upward from the bottom of your throat as you enter into the hypnogogic phase of sleep. This helps to sustain an aspect of your awareness into sleep, and it can also influence dream imagery, which may trigger lucidity. For example, people may see their necks glowing or radiating light after they fall asleep, which could help them recognize that they're dreaming.

The wake-up-back-to-bed method: Another technique that a lot of people have had success with in inducing lucid dreaming involves setting an alarm clock to go off in the early morning hours, during the latter part of the sleep cycle, when there's more time spent in the REM stage of sleep. This "wake-up-back-to-bed" (WBTB) method was developed by Stephen LaBerge and his colleagues. By waking up a few hours earlier than you normally would and then doing something to arouse your brain, like walking around, reading, or going to the bathroom, and then going back to sleep around a half hour to two hours later, you can sometimes induce lucid dreaming.[25] This technique becomes even more effective when combined with some of the other methods described in this book, such as the MILD technique, along with one of the dream-enhancing herbal or nutritional supplements, or drugs, described in the next chapter.

Mild sexual stimulation: Here is a lucid-dream activation technique that has worked well for me, which I haven't heard about anywhere else (but I doubt that I am the first to figure this one out). It involves very gently massaging my own genitals, keeping myself in a very mild state of sexual arousal as I fall asleep. This technique has helped me for years in achieving WILDs, when combined with the MILD technique. Another, similar technique that hasn't worked as well for me, but others say has been effective, involves holding one's arm in a raised position as one is falling asleep. This will usually wake one up repeatedly as he or she is dozing off, and the idea is that it helps to train your mind to maintain a steady state of awareness and a memory of physical reality as one is falling asleep.

Meditation: Having some form of regular meditation practice may also be helpful in inducing lucid dreaming. Various studies have demonstrated that people who meditate lucid dream more frequently than people who don't, and the longer the amount of time that people have practiced meditation, the more frequently they lucid dream.[26] Like lucid dreaming, some forms of meditation appear to be another example of a hybrid or paradoxical biological state of arousal. Some people seem to enter a state in which cortical arousal (or higher-level brain activity) is accompanied by extreme physical relaxation.[27] Additionally, it has been found that people are more likely to experience lucid dreams in the days following meditation practice compared to days when they don't practice.[28] This paradoxical state of arousal appears to occur when people have out-of-body experiences (OBEs) as well. Preliminary studies suggest that as a group, people with a tendency to have OBEs are more easily able to enter into a state in which cortical arousal is associated with muscular relaxation.[29]

Meditation is essential for developing awareness in dreams in the practice of Tibetan dream yoga (which I will be discussing in chapter 10). Personally, I started practicing Transcendental Meditation (TM) when I was fourteen. TM involves the silent repetition of a mantra in one's mind; not insignificantly, I had my first lucid dream when I was sixteen, shortly after I first tried LSD. Silently repeating a mantra as one is falling asleep can also be helpful in maintaining an aspect of waking consciousness through the process of falling asleep and into dreaming. I sometimes just repeat a simple phrase like *I'm awake* as I'm falling asleep, to keep the waking centers in my brain engaged; sometimes the continuous repetition of the words can be helpful in escorting me into a DILD. When done correctly, the body falls asleep while the mind remains awake.

In addition, as part of my lucid-dream practice, I've been developing my skill at insight meditation, or Vipassana, another Buddhist practice that cultivates mindfulness. This simply involves carefully observing the contents of one's mind without attachment—just observing, paying close attention to what one is thinking and how one is thinking. Vipassana allows you to attain a state of consciousness that transcends the mantra-repeating TM meditation practice that I had been doing since I was a young teenager. I started doing this mindfulness practice in a traditional meditative pose, sitting with my eyes closed, but now I find that I'm able to hold that state of mindfulness for a few seconds at a time as I do whatever I'm doing during the day. During the meditation, I basically just let my breath rise and fall on its own, allowing my thoughts to rise and fall on their own—like watching trees blowing in the wind—while simply bearing witness. The level of metacognition achieved by doing this allows one to escape memories of the past, anticipations of the future, and the ceaseless chattering of the "monkey mind." As a result, one's illusory sense of having a personal self dissolves into the present moment, allowing you to realize your true nature as the ever-present field of consciousness silently observing it all.

Sleep deprivation: Curiously, I have found that not getting enough sleep can sometimes trigger lucid dreaming, and going a whole night without sleep will sometimes trigger lucid dreams if I nap during the morning hours. Many people also report increased lucid dreaming when they sleep extra hours or experience disrupted sleep, and it's known that people who suffer from narcolepsy—a disorder that causes people to suddenly fall asleep—have 28.3 percent more lucid dreams.[30]

Staring at a digital clock: Spending time every day looking fixedly at a digital clock can sometimes carry over into one's dreams, where looking at it for longer than a few seconds can serve as a lucidity trigger, because the numbers won't stay fixed in a dream.

Sleep sitting up: Another method incorporated into Tibetan dream yoga practice to increase the frequency of lucid dreams is to go to sleep sitting up. I've found that going to sleep or napping with my back relatively straight, using pillows and armrests to keep my head elevated, does increase my lucid dreams. Anthropologist Charles Laughlin went to great lengths to carry out experiments that followed a Tibetan dream yoga technique, by building himself a foam-lined box made out of plywood approximately four feet higher than his shoulders when he was sitting in a half-lotus position, so that he could sleep sitting up without falling over. Laughlin reports, "Thus began a rather crazy time in my life due to the most intense dreamwork I have ever undertaken. I slept sitting up for months, and though I was never able to remain conscious throughout the night, I spent much of my sleep in lucid dreaming, wafting in and out of the waking and dream states and recording experiences on paper as I could."[31]

If sleeping sitting up sounds too uncomfortable, then perhaps try sleeping on your right side (which is also part of Tibetan dream yoga) or on your back. According to a study conducted by physician Lynne

Levitan, people are three times more likely to have a lucid dream while sleeping on the right side of their body or on their back, compared to sleeping on their left side.[32] During the course of writing this book I noticed that all of my lucid dreams occurred when I was either sleeping sitting up, on my back, or on my right side. This could be due to the possibility of certain body positions activating different sites in the brain.

Sleep somewhere new: Sleeping in unfamiliar surroundings also appears to increase the frequency of lucid dreams. A recent study, which helps to explain this, demonstrates that whenever we sleep in a new location, one of our brain hemispheres tends to stay more alert than usual while we're sleeping, similiar to the way marine mammals sleep. This may help to explain why lucid dreaming occurs more often in these situations.[33]

Sleep alone: Sleeping alone can significantly increase my ability to lucid dream because I'm generally so easily aroused when I sleep with my partner. I've found the lucid-dream state to be quite fragile, and movements by my partner can easily wake me up from a lucid dream. Going to sleep in a separate location, such as on the couch or in a sleeping bag on the floor, during the early morning hours can be a good way to avoid these unnecessary awakenings when one is experimenting with lucid-dreaming techniques. Additionally, as we learned above, sleeping in a new location can also serve as a lucidity trigger.

Sleep with the lights on: I have discovered that another effective technique for inducing lucid dreams involves leaving an overhead light on in the room where you are sleeping. This technique can be even more effective when combined with sleep deprivation. Obviously, overhead illumination makes it difficult for most people to fall asleep, but if you can fall asleep with the lights on then it may help to keep a part of your brain awake while you're sleeping. Of course, getting a good night's sleep every night is important for maintaining healthy body and brain function, so sleep deprivation and overhead illumination aren't really methods that you should use regularly.

Timing: An important factor in learning how to lucid dream more frequently is timing. There are many shifting variables and factors that need to come into just the right alignment in order to lucid dream. Some of these include your own psychological preparation and expectations, where you are in the sleep cycle, your neurochemistry, and, unquestionably, various mystery factors, as it seems that nothing guarantees a lucid dream every time. Still, timing is critical. Since we spend more time in REM sleep during the end of the sleep cycle, this is when it's best to try to increase the probability of having a lucid dream.

As you can see, there are quite a few different methods that people have developed for waking up in one's dreams over the past few thousand years, and especially so in recent years. This chapter just scratches the surface. There are some excellent books that cover methods in greater depth than I do in this chapter. Two of the best summaries can be found in LaBerge and Rheingold's book *Exploring the World of Lucid Dreaming* and Daniel Love's book *Are You Dreaming?*

MIXING, BLENDING, AND SYNERGIZING TECHNIQUES

Part of the trick to having regular lucid dreams is to combine different techniques and practice them regularly. Studies by Stephen LaBerge and others have demonstrated that combining WBTB and MILD techniques can be synergistic, and this is one of the most effective ways to train people how to lucid dream.[34] European dream researchers Tadas Stumbrys and Daniel Erlacher have found that the most effective lucid-dream induction procedures include the following steps:

1. Set your alarm clock to go off six hours after you go to sleep.
2. Go to sleep.
3. Wake up and remember a dream.
4. Stay awake for one hour practicing MILD.
5. Go back to sleep.

According to Stumbrys and Erlacher's research, if you follow these instructions, there is a 50 percent chance that you will achieve lucidity in your next dream.[35]

HOW TO SUSTAIN A LUCID DREAM

Once you start learning how to become lucid in your dreams, the most common problem you will likely encounter is that you'll get so excited in the dream that you are physically aroused into full wakefulness. Getting too emotionally excited in a lucid dream can cause one to fully wake up, so it's best to learn some form of self-control, which meditation can help with. This is one of the first lessons to learn in lucid dreaming: control of one's emotions is essential if one wishes to sustain the dream state. Self-control is not only necessary to sustaining a lucid dream, it is also necessary to controlling (or guiding) aspects of the dream. As husband-wife dream researchers Jay Vogelsong and Janice Brooks point out,

> Dream control is, at bottom, self-control, since dreams come from our minds. If controlling "them" or "it" does not always work, as LaBerge maintains, it is precisely because we often falsely conceptualize dream imagery as external to ourselves. Not only can we not control our dream selves without affecting dream imagery too, we cannot control the imagery without affecting ourselves, since such control requires monitoring our own thoughts and perceptions. It makes little difference, then, whether the dreamer wrestles [with] the fear to master the monster or wrestles [with] the monster to master the fear, since both come down to essentially the same thing: the one is a projection of the other.[36]

Another way to help sustain a lucid dream if you feel it starting to fade is to move your visual field around, looking at the tapestry of the world around you without focusing too much on the details. As I mentioned earlier, looking at your dream hands can help you stabilize an unstable lucid dream, as can trying to calm your breath, mind, and dream body. Doing "dream yoga"—posturing your dream body in a lotus position or some other yogic posture, closing your dream eyes, and meditating, all within a lucid dream—can not only help you stabilize the dream, but can promote seeing "closed-eye," trippy tryptaminelike visual patterns that other oneironauts and I have seen.

A method that I learned from Stephen LaBerge to help sustain lucid dreams works quite well. This involves having your arms in the dream fully outstretched to either side at right angles to your body, closing your dream eyes, and then spinning around in circles, like a whirling dervish. The efficacy of this technique is likely due to the involvement of the vestibular system* in the production of the rapid-eye-movement bursts in REM sleep.[37] According to Stephen LaBerge, "An intriguing possibility is that the spinning technique, by stimulating the system of the brain that integrates vestibular activity detected in the middle ear, facilitates the activity of the nearby components of the REM-sleep system."[38] In any case, not only does this technique help to sustain and stabilize a lucid dream, it gives one the option for greater control. While you're spinning around, try visualizing the environment that you'd like to be in, or who you'd like to be with; oftentimes when you open your eyes you'll find that your vision has been realized.

I can generally sense when a lucid-dream state is getting close to ending. In one experience that I didn't want to end, I did my utmost to stay there:

I could sense that the lucid dream was coming to an end soon, so I raced around asking everyone in the dream if they knew how I could stay there. No one knew. Then I came upon a wise-looking African woman wearing a long, colorful dress. Her stomach was bulging and she was clearly pregnant. When I asked her how I could stay, she just looked at me, smiled, and pointed to her stomach, implying that the only way to stay there is to be born there. Then I awoke.

---

*This is a sensory system located in the middle ear and brain that provides the leading contribution to the body's sense of balance and spatial orientation.

I had another lucid dream with this same African woman several months later:

The wise African woman (from my previous lucid dream) and I were in the back seat of a car together. As the lucid dream was dissolving, I once again turned to her and asked her how I could stay there. Then she just smiled and replied cryptically, "I'll see you when you get home."

I've pondered the philosophical significance of the wise African dream character's responses quite a bit, and I'll be discussing my thoughts on this more in chapter 9, but the point that I'm making here is that I love being aware in my dreams so much that I usually don't ever want them to end.

I've only twice experienced lucid dreams that I wanted to end. The first time was because I knew that my physical body was in trouble. I fell asleep after taking a dose of the nutritional supplement GBL (which I'll be discussing in chapter 5) with my head accidently under the covers, which obstructed my breathing. I had this powerful and disturbing lucid dream:

I had this black cloth mask over my face and a jacket on that was making me hot and uncomfortable. It was very difficult for me to breath. I kept taking the cloth mask off my face, over and over, but every time I took it off it would instantly reappear on my face within seconds. I would drop it on the floor, and then it would instantly disappear and reappear on my face. I would pull it off my face, and then instantly it would reappear, no matter how many times I took it off. And I took it off dozens and dozens of times. I would show this to the people I was with—friendly guys and a girl—and they were equally mystified by my inability to remove the black cloth from my mouth. Then I became lucid in the dream and I realized what was happening. I knew that I had fallen asleep with my head under the blanket, that I couldn't breathe, and that this was the cause of the weird experience in the dream. So I tried to wake myself up from the dream, again and again, but I couldn't. I told the other people in the dream what was going on—that I had fallen asleep with my head under the covers, and they understood, but they couldn't help me. It was very weird and disturbing. I finally did wake up, and oh, what a relief it was to take my head out from under the covers!

During that frightening experience my body was so strongly sedated from the GBL that it had to sleep, but my mind was awake and aware of the breathing problem that could have suffocated me if I didn't wake up in time. This, however, was the result of a freak accident.

The only other time that I wanted to wake myself up from a lucid dream, I did so very quickly, simply by willing myself to wake up. I did so, and I was sorry afterward that I had. This was the only time that I ever became frightened in a lucid dream due to what I was experiencing in the dream realm:

After achieving lucidity, I asked the dream to show me what it thought I needed to see. Then, rather abruptly and dramatically, the dream environment immediately began to change, shift, and get liquid or fluid, similar to melting wax. Suddenly, I found myself by a swimming pool. Then, within seconds, this unattractive, masculine-looking woman came right up to me and looked into my face. She was really scary-looking for some reason, didn't say a word, and although I didn't recognize her, she looked strangely familiar. She had short black hair, was very "butch," and was similar in appearance to the androgynous "woman" who raped my mouth in a previous lucid dream, only more frightening-looking. I wasn't sure what she was going to do—and it was definitely the most frightening figure I've ever encountered in a lucid dream. She seemed very disapproving, critical, and judgmental of me, and I got instantly scared—for reasons that I can't seem to fully understand. So I deliberately woke myself out of this dream.

I've pondered this experience a lot, and I wondered if I was being shown that a part of my mind was critical of the frivolous way that my ego had been pursuing primal pleasures in my lucid dreams. I was disappointed in myself for becoming too scared to face that woman in my dreams, and for waking myself up before I heard what she had to say. I told myself that if the opportunity ever arose again, then next time I'd see what that intimidating dream figure had to say.

Several weeks after this dream occurred, I had a partially lucid dream in which this disturbing woman appeared again—and this time I heard what she had to say. It was upsetting, I didn't want to hear it, and I lost my lucidity when I did. After becoming lucid again I impulsively began searching for sexual pleasure, and as I became more aroused . . .

> I suddenly found myself talking with a dark-haired woman who told me that she had been raped when she was younger. I became very disturbed by what she was saying and I again lost my lucid awareness. She told me that not only did she enjoy being raped but that it had been "a gift from God." This shocked me. I told her that being raped isn't a gift from God, and I tried to move away from her, but she followed me and was persistent in telling me this. I went outside the house that we were in to get away from her, and I was now in my childhood neighborhood. I went inside a car parked on the street, closed the door, and I began to scream at the top of my lungs. I was concerned that someone might hear me, and then I awoke.

Upon awakening, I realized that the dark-haired woman in the dream was the same woman who appeared in my previous lucid dream, when I asked my dreaming mind what it thought I needed to see. I've interpreted this as a message from my unconscious about the conflicting mix of disturbing feelings that resulted from my early sexual trauma, and about the fact that I can't easily tease apart these early traumas from my fruitful interest in shamanic healing and psychedelic medicine.

In any case, this previously described episode was the only lucid-dream experience, out of hundreds that I've had, where I ever became genuinely frightened by the content and sought to end the experience— *no doubt precisely because it lay at the crux of my healing.* Since it was easy for me to exit the disturbing dream, and since I generally never want my lucid dreams to end, and because most people are trying to sustain lucid dreams for as long as possible, it came as a surprise when someone who is well versed in shamanic states of consciousness seriously asked me how you can physically awaken from a lucid dream if you want to and was having trouble doing so. She told me that she had found herself in horrific lucid dreams that she couldn't control and wanted to learn how to wake up from them if she needed to.

The Ojibway people of the Lake Superior region in North America are famous for creating dreamcatchers, ornately designed circular nets that have feathers and strings of beads hanging down from them, which are hung above the bed.[39] The idea behind these seemingly magical objects is to prevent nightmares, so that the dreams that come to a person while sleeping must first pass through the filtering net of the dreamcatcher, where bad dreams get trapped in the spiderweblike, crisscrossing netting of the dreamcatcher, while good dreams drip down onto our heads through the hanging beads and feathers. Many New Age bookstores carry dreamcatchers, and I have a beautiful one hanging over the head of my bed. I tend to have a lot of good dreams, so you may want to try this too. However, if having a magically crafted dreamcatcher fails to prevent nighttime episodes of terror from jarring your mind, then research done in this area leads me to believe that it's probably healthier psychologically to confront the disturbing or dark dream forces head-on and deal with them in the lucid dream, rather then trying to escape from the situation by waking up.

Although not all researchers agree, some psychotherapists think that transforming one's negative dream images into something more positive will symbolically transform negative personality traits into positive ones, or that doing this can solve genuine psychological problems. According to Stephen LaBerge, one doesn't even need to interpret the symbolic meaning of a dream to achieve psychological integration through reconciliation or by using methods to alter the dream. LaBerge says that while the dream conflicts that he resolved may have depicted actual personality conflicts, he "was able to resolve them without even having to know what they represented," through his "acceptance or transformation of whatever unidentified emotion, behavior, or role they stood for."[40] My own personal experience leads me to believe this too. This was why the lucid dream I mentioned in chapter 1, in which I transformed my rapist, was so powerfully healing. In fact, some psychotherapists teach their clients methods for lucid-dream induction as an effective treatment for chronic nightmares.[41]

HOW TO END LUCID NIGHTMARES

If you find yourself becoming lucid in a nightmare, LaBerge and others recommend confronting the evil person, monster, demon, or dark force directly. Sometimes simply asking what the uninvited predator or beast wants, or offering a gesture of love or warmth to it, can make the creature simply dissolve or can transform it into something friendly. In that healing dream that I presented in chapter 1, I described how I transformed the person raping me in the dream into a caged bird, by swiping my hand repeatedly over the person's face.

Dream characters often seem to be fragmented parts of ourselves, and by making friends with the scary characters—what Jung would collectively call "the shadow"—in our dreams, many psychologists and lucid-dream enthusiasts believe that we integrate disconnected parts of ourselves back into the whole of our personality.

When I interviewed Jazz Mordant, the twelve-year-old boy from Bali whom I mentioned at the beginning of this chapter, he told me about how he ended his lucid nightmares:

When I was smaller I used to have nightmares, and there was one creature with a green face and strange powers that always came back. I was very scared of it, so much so that I wouldn't want to go to sleep at night. After a while my mom told me something that helped. She said to look at it straight in the eye and say, "Go away and never come back"—and I had to put all of my will, intention, and energy into making it disappear. So I did. I looked at it and said, "Go away and never come back," until the point where I was yelling. Then I saw it slowly move further away until it vanished entirely.

Asking other characters in the dream for assistance is another idea that has been reported to sometimes work, but I think that the best approach of all is just reminding yourself that your body is perfectly safe in bed, and that nothing in a dream can ever really harm you—that is, except for the emotion of fear. The terror that people experience in nightmares can have physical ramifications, such as increased heart rate and other physiological symptoms, sometimes severe enough to actually cause injury or even death, according to some researchers.[42*]

Though physical harm resulting from a nightmare is rare, realizing that one is safe within a dream can be tricky. For some people, relief in this manner may be elusive, as dream scholar Ryan Hurd points out:

I believe there is . . . potential for the slow digestion of lucid nightmares over a lifetime, in particular when we are forced to sit with existential truths and forces that cannot be resolved simply by the brave act of facing them, talking to them calmly, or absorbing their otherness into our egoic dreambodies. Sometimes more is required than courage and the ability to transform dream imagery; sometimes the willingness to be transformed is essential. Conversely the assumption that moving toward reconciliation in lucid nightmares— as opposed to killing and fighting—is always for the best also has a humanistic and ethnocentric bias that has been in favor ever since the Senoi theory* was discredited. Sometimes we still need to fight.[43]

---

*When my colleague Ryan Hurd read this he remarked, "Hard to prove death by nightmare, though! The best cases we have are the sleep paralysis nightmares of Hmong refugees in the United States in the 1980s. The deaths can be interpreted as culturally reinforced death anxiety that triggered a rare, preexisting heart condition in the young men who died. It is called SUNDS, sudden unexplained death syndrome." (See Madrigal, "Dark Side"; and McNamara, *Nightmares,* 5.)

Psychologist Patricia Garfield recommends fighting and killing aggressive dream characters as well, but only so that you can convert their negative energies into positive energies and make allies of their essences or spirits.[44] (Garfield also encourages lucid dreamers to indulge in sexual activities within their dreams as often as possible, as a way to help integrate the fragmented parts of one's psyche.) Some people, of course, express the opposite opinion, such as psychologist Robert Van de Castle, who writes, "To murder a dream character would be to commit a form of intrapsychic suicide,"[45†] Van de Castle feels this way about murdering dream characters because, if we adopt the viewpoint that the various figures that we encounter in a lucid dream can be conceptualized as components of the dreamer's personality, then it would be unwise to kill or harm some threatening figure in a lucid dream because this figure would be a part of one's self.

I found Hurd's and Garfield's perspectives noteworthy. Although they're addressing a situation that I've never had to deal with personally, I'm reminded of a friend's experience. After a friend and I journeyed together on ayahuasca several years ago, she wrote me excitedly several days later to say that she had experienced her first lucid dream. I was eager to hear what had happened. Flying and sex are two of the experi-

---

*The Senoi are the indigenous people of Peninsular Malaysia. A book written in 1954 (*Pygmies and Dream Giants* by Kilton Stewart) describes their use of dreams, and in 1972 Patricia Garfield popularized the notion that the Senoi regard dream sharing and interpretation to be of high importance for health and social reasons in her book *Creative Dreaming*. This notion evolved into what has been called the Senoi dream theory, which is a set of claims about how people can learn to control their dreams to reduce fear and increase pleasure. The belief that the Senoi generally regard sharing and interpreting their dreams as something of high importance was discredited in 1985 (Domhoff, "Senoi Dream Theory") when later researchers were unable to substantiate Stewart and Garfield's findings, which had grown into a movement. This erroneous or exaggerated belief about the Senoi was a key element in developing a new orientation toward dreams that first became popular as part of the human potential movement of the 1960s and has grown into what is now called the "dreamwork movement."

†In reviewing this manuscript, when my colleague Ryan Hurd read this he commented, "I don't advocate murder in the dream either . . . [only] the right to stand up for oneself and make better boundaries, if compromised. Fighting does not have to result in killing."

ences that most people gravitate toward initially, and I was expecting to hear something along these lines. However, I was nonplussed to learn that my friend used her first experience with lucidity to physically attack the other characters in her dream, an act she described as doing with great zeal and pleasure. I was a bit shocked to hear this, but it appears that this may have been a healthy response to the violent nightmares that have plagued her since childhood, when she was traumatized. She maintains that the experience was therapeutic, cartoony, and even fun, and she encouraged me to try it, but I never felt inclined to. In one lucid dream I threw a rock at a dream character when he wouldn't respond to me, and then felt sorry for doing so when he looked at me.

When I asked Ryan Hurd what he would recommend to someone having a lucid nightmare, he said:

> In general, I suggest that people ground themselves, remind themselves that they're safe, face their fear as much as possible, and ask for help—whether that might be a dream ally, an ancestral connection, God, the divine, or whatever is appropriate for them. Just take it as it is, and if it doesn't resolve or you wake up, don't feel too bad about it—because if it's a nice repetitive nightmare you don't have to worry, it'll be back.

In any case, it can't hurt to have a method for ending a lucid dream in one's bag of tricks. Let's say that *Nightmare on Elm Street*'s Freddy Krueger, or some other vengeful spirit that supposedly attacks people in their dreams, isn't responding to your dream hugs, and you would really rather wake up.* Or maybe you just want to wake yourself up so that you can record details from your lucid dream that you don't want to forget.

Oftentimes, emotional arousal and willpower are all that's needed

---

*My girlfriend had dreams of being chased for years, until finally she had a nonlucid dream in which she confronted the person chasing her, Freddy Krueger, and pushed him off of a balcony. Then she saw him later in the dream and said, "I don't want you in my dreams," and he vanished. She hasn't had any dreams of being chased ever since.

to physically activate the body into wakefulness. Many lucid dreamers report that they can wake themselves up from a dream by simply willing it, any time that they want to. It's hard to verbalize exactly how this is accomplished—like trying to explain how you move your body—but I can usually do it. Some people just have the natural ability to wake themselves up from a lucid dream, and many lucid dreamers deliberately wake themselves up so that they can write down ideas or experiences before they're forgotten. If you don't naturally have this ability, then here's what you might try: Just as moving your eyes or spinning around can help to sustain and stabilize a lucid dream, sitting still and focusing your attention on a fixed point in the environment can help you to physically awaken. Another technique is to try holding your breath, which you can maintain voluntary control over while you dream, and sometimes this sudden loss of respiration can shock the body into waking up.

A friend told me that as a child whenever she had lucid dreams and wanted to wake up she would jump into a body of water, and this always seemed to do the trick. (On the other hand, I've had some absolutely delightful lucid dreams where I swim around in pools of water. The kinesthetic sensation of swimming and floating is realistic, although the sensation of feeling "wet" doesn't feel quite as it does for me in the waking world. In a lucid dream the water feels real when I'm submerged in it, but my skin feels instantly dry when it emerges. Other people have also reported the same difficulty reproducing the physical sensation of wetness in a lucid dream.)

So if you do manage to wake yourself up out of a lucid dream, then you have to ask the following question . . .

AM I REALLY AWAKE?

The tricky thing to remember about waking up from a lucid dream is that you need to confirm that you really are awake and aren't experiencing a "false awakening." This occurs when you think you have woken up but are in fact still dreaming—that is, dreaming that you are in bed, having woken up. There can sometimes be layer after layer of these kinds of false awakenings, called "nesting dreams," until you finally arrive back in the true reality of your waking physical body.

I've experienced a similar phenomenon while coming out of a ketamine-induced shamanic journey, where I would repeatedly think that the experience was over and that I was back in my body and bedroom, only to discover that I was actually in some weird parallel-universe version of my bedroom. Sometimes these "false endings" of the shamanic journey would happen multiple times until I was finally back in my bedroom where I had begun the journey. I've heard others describe similar experiences with *Salvia divinorum* (such as ethnobotanist Daniel Siebert, who describes this experience in chapter 9).

TESTING OUT YOUR DREAM-REALM SUPERPOWERS

Rather than trying to awaken from nightmares, the vast majority of people who achieve lucidity in their dreams couldn't be more ecstatic. It's hard to describe just how amazing it feels the first time you achieve lucidity in a dream to someone who has never experienced it. Like a psychedelic experience, lucidity in a dream can dramatically increase the sensory magnitude of whatever it is that one is experiencing, and people often describe seeing the world around them in magnificent detail. For example, in 1902, at the age of sixteen, occultist Oliver Fox reported the following experience:

> I was dreaming! With the realization of this fact, the quality of the dream changed in a manner very difficult to convey to someone who has not had this experience. Instantly, the vividness of life increased a hundred-fold. Never had the sea and sky and trees shone with such glamorous beauty; even the commonplace houses seemed alive and mystically beautiful. Never had I felt so absolutely well, so clear-brained, so inexpressibly free! The sensation was exquisite beyond words; but it only lasted a few minutes and then I awoke.[46]

In a dream, you have the power to do almost anything imaginable, as every physical law can be bent, twisted, and broken, and you have far more control over the experience of reality than we do in the physical world. It takes a while to actually realize this, because initially we tend to assume that the dream world operates with the same forces and constraints as the waking world.

In his book *Are You Dreaming?* author Daniel Love accurately describes what it feels like to arrive in the realm of lucid dreaming: "Here, we find ourselves in a world where, like some kind of deity, we have an 'all you can eat' buffet laid out before us, containing all possible human (and beyond human) experiences ready for our personal enjoyment."[47]

What were previously ways to test to see if you're dreaming or not now become abilities with which to enjoy and explore the dream state. Pretty much whatever you believe is possible in a lucid dream becomes possible, although there appear to be neurological or psychological limits as to how much of a dream you can control. I've learned how to do many of the things that I love doing in lucid dreams by reading the accounts of other lucid dreamers. Every time I read about something that I never thought of, I add it to my list of things to try out in future lucid dreams. However, there are some people, such as Robert Moss, author of *Conscious Dreaming,* who suggest that after becoming lucid it's a good idea to let the dream unfold as it naturally would have, only with your conscious awareness carefully observing and paying close attention.

As Robert Waggoner points out in his book *Lucid Dreaming: Gateway to the Inner Self,* people can only influence their lucid dreams, not control everything that happens in them. There's still a mysterious agency (the unconscious?) that appears to be crafting everything behinds the scenes. In other words, there's no way to avoid surprises. This notion will be explored in depth when we get to chapter 10. Meanwhile, here are some of the things that your dream self is capable of doing, which you may want to try out the next time you find yourself lucid in a dream:

Fly: The first thing that many people want to do in lucid dreams is achieve lift off and fly. I suspect that this desire to feel the joy of flight comes from our current evolutionary condition as larval forms of what we will one day become—like caterpillars dreaming of becoming butterflies. Flying is easier for some than it is for others in lucid dreams. Some take to it without much effort, and others find that it takes considerable practice to do well.

I'm always thrilled when I take a test leap and feel myself linger in the air longer than gravity would allow, but I find that it takes a certain form of concentrated effort to elevate myself, to stay in the air, and to fly. However, once I get going—wow!—the soaring sensation is amazing, and the extraordinary views can be absolutely spectacular. Next time you're in a lucid dream, try jumping into the air and holding out your arms. Movement of some type may be necessary at first to convince your mind that it's possible. Try flapping your arms or swimming through the air, for example. My girlfriend says that she likes jumping from rooftop to rooftop in her lucid dreams. In the dream realm, gravity only exists if you believe it does. Also, having real-life experience in hang-gliding or skydiving can help to create the memories that build worlds from within a lucid dream.

Wild sex: This is usually the second thing that most people want to try out once they've achieved lucidity within a dream. In a lucid dream you can have sex with anyone you desire, without any of the social or biological consequences. Many people report vivid sexual experiences and orgasms that rival those in waking life, although I must say that my many personal attempts at this have had mixed and often disappointing results. Usually the dream will start to end just as I'm entering my dream girl, and I'll start waking up; sometimes the experience continues but seems to be lacking important dimensions that are present during waking-life sex. Still, it can be great fun to experiment with erotic possibilities in lucid dreams, and during the process of writing this book I did have a pretty amazing sexual experience while in a lucid dream, which I describe in chapter 10.

Passing through physical objects: In a dream state you can move your hand through what appear to be solid objects, walk through walls, or fly through any obstacle, just by thinking it is possible and then simply doing it. It takes a bit of faith to do this—to just leap into a wall or window while flying in a lucid dream—but I've just passed right through the obstacle every time, like I was simply moving through liquid.

Stretching your limbs: You can pull on the tip of your finger in a lucid dream and elongate it, as though it is composed of moldable putty (which is one of the reality tests mentioned earlier). In fact, like Plastic Man or Mister Fantastic from the superhero comic books, you can stretch and reshape your body however you please in a lucid dream. It's easy: simply pull on a part of your body and expect it to stretch.

Transforming people's faces: I learned that I could transform the faces of people around me by rubbing my hand over their faces and imagining them to look different. This can be especially fun to do during sexual encounters in lucid dreams.

Become a different sex or another species: With some practice, by closing your eyes and willing it, you can completely morph into the opposite sex or any type of animal or mythic creature in a lucid dream. This kind of shape-shifting represents another important interface between lucid dreaming and shamanism. Ayahuasca-using shamans in the Amazon are said to be able to shape-shift into jaguars, birds, snakes, pink dolphins, and other animals.

Going anywhere instantly: In a dream, you have the ability to instantly travel to any place you wish because everything is occurring within your own mind: outer space, underwater realms, other planets, fairy-tale worlds, other time periods, and fantasy paradises—all are all real possibilities. This can be accomplished by closing your eyes and spinning around in circles, by walking through a magic doorway, by crawling through a interdimensional portal (or mirror), by diving into a painting, or by utilizing whatever prop your imagination can conjure up. Eventually, with practice, you can learn how to teleport to anywhere imaginable in the blink of an eye, simply by willing it. This is an illusion, of course, as all you are really doing is shifting the contents of your mind.

Psychokinesis: In a lucid dream you can move any physical object around by staring at it and willing it to move. It works with people too. I learned about this technique when I experienced it being done to me in a lucid dream. The person in my dream looked forcefully at me, and I could feel him knock me over using just the power of his mind. He seemed to be about twenty-five feet away and was laughing. So I stood up and wondered if I could do the same thing to him. I looked at him and imagined him falling over. I could feel a release of energy, and he fell to the ground, seeming quite surprised that I too had psychokinetic powers. I realized this power in that lucid dream, and ever since then I've been able to easily move objects around with just my focused attention, with my mind willing it to do so.

Materialization: You can learn how to make anything appear in a lucid dream. The trick to learning how to do this is to use dream props to help you believe more easily. Belief is the key to making anything happen in a lucid dream. A prop is any object that can act as a bridge between what you know is possible and what you think might be possible in a lucid dream—like the aforementioned magic doorway, portal, or walk-through painting described for traveling to other locations in a dream. It may be difficult at first to simply materialize objects out of thin air, so many people find that they can make objects appear by saying out loud what they want to find when they open up a box, a dresser drawer, or a closed door. If someone has difficulty flying in a dream, a potential prop that could help might be a flying machine or a magic carpet. Novelist Amy Tan described a dream where she was able to fly with wings that she purchased for twenty-five cents. While airborne in the dream, Amy suddenly realized the impossible nature of what she was doing and began to descend. However, when she remembered that she had been flying previously, then she began to ascend again. After a series of ascending and descending bouts in the air, she realized that it was her confidence that allowed her to fly.[48]

Leaving your dream body: I've found that it's relatively easy for me to have out-of-dream-body experiences simply by willing it. I can float out of my dream body as a spirit; my floating spirit is then able to enter into and temporarily fuse with other people or objects in the dream, and then I see the world from his, her, or its perspective. Most interestingly, when I do this I find that, although my visible vantage point shifts, my basic sense of self remains pretty much the same, no matter who or what I fuse my traveling dream spirit with.

THE LIMITS OF LUCID DREAMING

While the boundless nature and countless options of lucid dreaming may appear infinite, there are limits to what can be done. The most obvious limit is time. Every moment spent lucid in a dream is precious, as the clock is always ticking. We are limited to the amount of time that our brains spend in REM sleep. Also, surely, there are neurological limits to what our brains our capable of at this stage in our evolution, which may only become apparent to us after we transcend them. Brain implants could allow us to experience undreamed-of new abilities in the future. Another obvious limit—one that can be repeatedly transcended—is the psychological boundaries of the imagination, and those limits imposed on ourselves by our own beliefs.

THE POWER OF BELIEF IN DREAMING

I have found that as you experiment more and more with your new abilities and superpowers in the lucid-dream state, it will probably begin to dawn on you that you're making assumptions that influence your dream. With this realization, the need for props to help you achieve what you want in a lucid dream slowly slips away. When we first discover lucid dreaming we carry all of our assumptions about operating in the three-dimensional waking world with us—all of our preconceptions about the nature of physical laws, and what is and isn't possible. People seem to be able to find whatever they expect to find in a lucid dream, and so learning how to control one's thoughts and emotions is key to influencing the dream state as we wish. One's thoughts in a lucid dream can instantly become realities. For example, when Saint-Denys said that he had a dream in which he'd been in a restaurant and served a dish that seemed as hard as shoe leather, the moment he said this the meal on his plate was instantly replaced by shoe leather.[49]

In a dream, everything is mutable, anything is possible, and our reality is ultimately a simulation or model constructed by our unconscious mind. As in the 2009 Hollywood science-fiction film *Avatar,* we create simulated puppet versions of ourselves in order to interact with our dream environment, which is composed of our own minds as well. Despite the fact that anything is possible in a lucid dream, recently arrived visitors to the lucid-dream realm often behave as though they are still operating on a gravity-bound planet in a physical body. This is evident in the 2010 Hollywood science-fiction film *Inception,* which was inspired by the notion of being able to lucidly share dreams, and seemed to completely lack imagination when it comes to the full range of what is actually possible in a lucid dream. The most imaginative event in all of the lucid-dream sequences in that movie was merely a city skyline folding in on itself.

The secret to successful lucid dreaming is to understand that whatever you believe to be real is what becomes real. If this isn't completely true in the waking world, our experience in the dream realm allows us to at least see its partial truth—that what we believe to be true has a massive influence on how we perceive and experience reality. Reality conforms to our beliefs. This is obvious in a lucid dream, but this truth stays generally hidden from us during waking consciousness, except when we are having a psychedelic experience. In this context, the late neuroscientist John C. Lilly's famous line about belief and reality takes on new meaning, as it certainly applies to the realm of lucid dreaming: "In the province of the mind, what one believes to be true is true or becomes true, within certain limits to be found experientially and experimentally. These limits are further beliefs to be transcended. In the mind, there are no limits."[50]

It appears that there's a continuum of consciousness between waking and dreaming, and psychedelic awareness lies somewhere in the middle. In a dream, what we believe to be true instantly becomes true. During a psychedelic experience this can happen to some extent as well, although sluggish physical laws still apply. In states of normal waking consciousness we can still learn to observe this happening, albeit much less obviously and much more slowly.

I've often wondered if what the spirit of ayahuasca said to me once on a shamanic journey is true or not. The voice said that anything that is possible in a lucid dream is also possible in waking reality once you fully awaken within it, because both realities exist within our minds. Is this what religious prophets, enlightened yogis, mystics, and superpsychics have realized? Are these people who have begun to wake up from the dream of physical reality? In other words, could Jesus walk on water because he realized that reality is just a dream? And if so, then wouldn't we all be like dream characters within the universal mind, the mind of God, realizing that we're all ultimately a single dreaming being? In chapter 10 we'll delve into some of these ideas, but first let's explore some ancient and novel methods for enhancing the dream state with herbs, nutrients, and drugs.

5

ENHANCING DREAMING WITH ONEIROGENS, NUTRITIONAL SUPPLEMENTS, HERBS, AND DRUGS

Our dreams are a second life. I have never been able to penetrate without a shudder those ivory or horned gates which separate us from the invisible world.

GÉRARD DE NERVAL

In addition to psychological preparation, there appears to be a certain neurochemical factor involved in lucid dreaming. It seems necessary to have just the right amount of mental arousal during sleep, which is not always easy to attain, and often one just has to wait for those magically balanced nights to capriciously arrive. However, besides the mental techniques for inducing lucid dreams that we discussed in the previous chapter, there are as well some neurochemical tools that one can utilize to help with lucid dreaming.

Many different drugs, herbs, cognitive enhancers, and nutritional supplements can influence dreaming, and some even have the potential to help us cultivate that special state of consciousness that promotes lucid dreaming. In this chapter, I'll be reviewing the different drugs and dietary supplements that are reputed to help with lucid dreaming, and I'll be sharing what I learned from trying most of them. As you'll see, I tried more than a few different supplements in my quest to find a formula for reliably producing lucid dreams. In fact, I tried just about every potentially dream-enhancing substance that I learned about in the course of my research.

In 2006, Thomas Yuschak, an experienced oneironaut who holds master's degrees in mechanical engineering and physics, wrote what was at the time the definitive book on using supplements to induce high-level lucid dreams and out-of-body experiences, *Advanced Lucid Dreaming: The Power of Supplements*. I'll summarize the most important information that I learned from reading Yuschak's book, and I'll build on the foundation that he laid out. Meanwhile, I highly recommend you read this valuable book from cover to cover if you're interested in the subject.

There are dozens of specially designed formulas available over the Internet that reputedly help with lucid dreaming, most of which are composed of ingredients found in this chapter. I'll provide a summary of the scientific facts about the effects, safety, and dosages of using a number of drugs, herbs, cognitive enhancers, and nutritional supplements that can enhance or influence the dreaming process. The herbs or fungi that I'll be discussing in this chapter include: *Calea zacatechichi*, *Silene undulata* (syn. *Silene capensis*), cannabis, *Banisteriopsis caapi* (a component of ayahuasca), *Peganum harmala* (Syrian rue), *Mucuna pruriens* (velvet bean), *Tabernanthe iboga*, *Piper methysticum* (kava), *Pausinystalia johimbe* (yohimbe), *Papaver somniferum* (opium poppy), *Psilocybe cubensis* (psilocybin mushrooms), *Turnera diffusa* (damiana), *Salvia divinorum*, *Scutellaria* spp. (skullcap), *Mitragyna speciosa* (kratom), *Valeriana officinalis* (valerian root), *Prunus cerasus* (tart cherry), *Artemisia vulgaris* (mugwort), and *Nymphaea caerulea* (blue lotus). All of these plants have been safely used by different traditional cultures around the world, for hundreds or even thousands of years.*

---

*Since writing this book a few other herbs have come to my attention as potential dream enhancers, which I didn't have an opportunity to research or try for this book. These include *Celastrus paniculatus* (intellect tree), wild asparagus root, *Entada rheedii* (African dream herb), and *Tagetes lucida* (Mexican tarragon).

The nutritional supplements that I'll be discussing in this chapter include: L-tryptophan, 5-hydroxytryptophan (5-HTP), choline, dimethyltryptamine (DMT), gamma-butyrolactone (GBL), melatonin, vitamin B₆, and L-theanine. These substances have been a part of the human diet or mammalian metabolism and neurochemistry since our evolutionary beginnings, but they've only become available to us in their pure forms over the last century.

The drugs that I'll be discussing in this chapter include: galantamine, phenibut, LSD, ibogaine, DXM, nicotine, huperzine A, MDMA, and oxycodone. These drugs are the riskiest substances to use, and some may have dangerous side effects, but they also hold some of the strongest potential as aids to help catalyze lucid dreaming.

Let's start with the herbs.

HERBS THAT ENHANCE DREAMING

Calea zacatechichi
Mexican dream herb

Calea zacatechichi is a medium-sized shrub that has been used by the Chontal people in Mexico for many generations to enhance the vividness and mystical aspects of dreams. The Chontal say that they use it to obtain divinatory messages during dreaming.[1]

Mexican dream herb is traditionally used as both a tea and a smokable herb, often together, just as one is drifting off to sleep. It is said to promote powerful, mythic, and larger-than-life dreams. Scientific studies with calea show that it improves sleep, dream recall, and that it increases hypnogogic imagery when one is falling asleep.[2]

I tried drinking a tea that I prepared from the leaves of the calea plant, and I smoked some of the herb in my pipe, but I had the best success using an alcohol extract tincture made from the plant by an online botanical outlet called Iamshaman (www.iamshaman.com). The tea was pretty bitter tasting, and the smoke was much harsher on my lungs than cannabis, but the herbal tincture was easy for me to ingest in sufficient quantities to obtain its psychoactive effects. I found that I needed a pretty strong dose of this stuff to get the effects I was seeking, but around four droppers full of the herbal tincture put me into a sleepy, dreamy, mild psychedelic state. Later in my experimentations I had my herbalist prepare a more potent tincture for me, but even with this enhanced tincture I required three full droppers to reach the desired effect.

My experiences with calea were reminiscent of a low dose of ayahuasca or magic mushrooms, with shifting, closed-eye visuals and enhanced hypnogogic imagery. Going to sleep under the influence of calea is absolutely delightful, especially when combined with cannabis and/or an herbal tincture made from *B. caapi* or Syrian rue, which I'll be discussing later in this chapter. Using the calea tincture before retiring definitely enhanced the vividness and detailed memories of my dreams and shifted the emotional quality of the dreams in a hard-to-define way, but it didn't seem to increase my ability to have lucid dreams.

As with a number of the herbs, drugs, and nutritional supplements that I'll be discussing in this chapter, many people report that using calea as a way to enhance dreaming appears to work best when used in the middle of the night, by waking up to an alarm clock, rather than by taking it when you first go to sleep. This is likely because we tend to dream more during the second half of our nightly sleep cycles as compared to the first half.

Calea is legal and available from many online vendors.

Silene undulata (syn. *Silene capensis*)
African dream herb

Silene undulata is native to South Africa and is regarded by the Xhosa people as sacred. The root is traditionally used by the Xhosa in shamanic initiatory rites to induce vivid, prophetic, and lucid dreaming.

Most people say that the African dream herb is best taken in the morning because it has stimulating properties, but I found it better to take at night. A lot of people report that its effects are similar to those of *Calea zacatechichi,* the Mexican dream herb.

Although silene is perfectly legal, I could only find online vendors that carried the unprocessed silene root, so I had my herbalist prepare a special tincture from this root for me to experiment with for this book. I found the tincture quite remarkable and think that someone should definitely market this. The first night I tried the thick and cloudy, cream-colored silene tincture—2 milliliters around an hour before bedtime—I had a massive flood of strange and powerful dreams. My nighttime adventures began with enhanced hypnogogic imagery, and then I had a lot of long, bizarre, complicated dreams about interactions with animal-human hybrid beings, although I don't recall ever achieving lucidity or much of the details of what I experienced.

I found silene to be somewhat similar to calea, as others have reported, although initially I thought that it was more potent. However, I now suspect that it's just different. Further experimentation with the silene tincture produced more vivid dreams, enhanced hypnogogic imagery, and insightful and fascinating near-sleep thinking. Silene is definitely a powerful shamanic plant, although I have yet to achieve lucidity with either calea- or silene-enhanced dreams.

I mentioned above that calea can sometimes feel like a mild, sleepy form of ayahuasca, with similar unfolding and morphing visions. One night after consuming some of the silene tincture the thought occurred to me that perhaps the African dream herb is like a mild, sleepy form of iboga. It's not inconceivable that the plants incorporate regional patterns that manifest as particular experiences of spirits. It feels like calea and ayahuasca could be feminine spirits, and that silene and iboga could be masculine spirits—or this could just be my nighttime fantasy.

One night when I had some of the silene tincture there were times when I was falling asleep that I started viewing this morphing stream of African and Egyptian-flavored hypnogogic visions; it felt as though the spirit of the silene plant was scanning me, just as the ayahuasca spirit is often reported to do, and showing me to myself from its alien point of view. On another occasion I tried combining the calea tincture with the silene tincture. I had been pleasantly falling asleep, in the midst of a blossoming shower of hypnogogic imagery after having earlier taken calea, when I got the idea that this would be an extra amazing night of dreams if I combined the calea with the silene. So I turned on the light and had some of the silene tincture. This turned out to be a bad idea. Within minutes the pleasant, floating hypnogogia was gone, replaced by a racing heart, mild anxiety, some insomnia, and I don't remember any dreams from the night.

Thinking back about my dream enhancement with the two plants, I remember thinking that calea was a female spirit and silene a male spirit. In a calea-enhanced dream I encountered a telepathically speaking cat, whereas I conversed with a talking dog in a silene-enhanced dream. I should have known that cats and dogs don't usually get along that well!

Cannabis sativa and Cannabis indica

Marijuana, Mary Jane, pot, weed, ganja

Cannabis affects consciousness in a number of ways that can be useful for enhancing the dream state or for increasing the probability of having a lucid dream.

Scientific studies with cannabis show that it appears to suppress REM sleep (when dreaming generally occurs),[3] and many people report that cannabis suppresses dreaming, but I suspect that this isn't entirely accurate. It's true that regular cannabis users, those who use the plant daily, often report a dramatic increase in the vividness and quantity of their dreams for several days after they stop. However, I suspect that cannabis doesn't actually suppress dreaming, but rather achieves much of the same purpose as dreaming, which serves a necessary (though mysterious) biological function. As discussed in chapter 2, scientific studies have shown that REM sleep doesn't seem to be absolutely necessary for survival, yet no one really knows why that phase of sleep can't be effectively suppressed, as the more it is suppressed the more it occurs.[4] Most mammals experience a REM-rebound effect when deprived of it, and people deprived of REM sleep quickly start to deteriorate psychologically. If the REM period of sleep is repeatedly disturbed and prevented from occurring by waking the subject up, the REM periods quickly become more and more frequent. In fact, the human research on REM-sleep deprivation that was being done had to be abandoned because it became impossible to stop REM sleep without the use of physical force, and the subjects were becoming seriously affected in an adverse manner.[5]

As discussed in chapter 2, some psychologists think that dreaming has no real purpose, that it is a meaningless, random process, or an epiphenomenon of a necessary biological function that occurs with sleep. However, many other scientists think differently. Tufts University School of Medicine psychiatry professor Ernest Hartmann writes in *Scientific American,* "We consider a possible . . . function of a dream to be weaving new material into the memory system in a way that both reduces emotional arousal and is adaptive in helping us cope with further trauma or stressful events."[6] This suggests that dreaming may be a way for the unconscious parts of our minds to communicate necessary information with our waking ego. If this is so, then it may be that the insights and creative ideas that people often report after using cannabis (especially with the *sativa* strain*) are communications from the right hemisphere of the brain to the left, as it is known that cannabis increases right-hemisphere brain activity.

Terence McKenna suggested a similar idea when he said, "In the absence of cannabis the dream life seems to become much richer. This causes me to . . . form a theory . . . that cannabis must in some sense thin the boundary between the conscious and unconscious mind . . . if you smoke cannabis, the energy which would normally be channeled into dreams is instead manifest in the reveries of the cannabis intoxication."[7]

Instead of looking at cannabis-influenced sleep as resulting in less time spent in REM, perhaps we should notice that it leads to more time spent in non-REM, therefore resulting in more deeply restorative sleep.

---

*There are many genetic varieties of the cannabis plant, which can be roughly divided into two primary strains—*Cannabis indica* and *Cannabis sativa.* The two strains have unique characteristics that differentiate them from each other, both in appearance and chemistry. In general, the psychoactive effects of *sativa* strains tend to be more uplifting and cognitively energizing, while the *indica* strains tend to be more calming and sedating. However, growers have created a widely varied multitude of genetic hybrids that complicates this simple distinction considerably.

It seems that the brain only engages in REM sleep when it needs it. Perhaps cannabis users don't need it as much? According to numerous studies, cannabis users don't display any measurable mental-health defects from regular use.[8] Also, in a scientific study in which subjects were subjected to partial REM-sleep deprivation, this increased reports of their thinking taking on a "dreamlike" quality,[9] as cannabis intoxication is reported to do.

Cannabis can act like a mild to moderate-level psychedelic, and like other psychedelic plants many people describe their reality-shifting experience with it as being similar to a waking dream. Also, cannabis can be used to increase the duration and vividness of dreams by ingesting it regularly for several days and then abstaining from using it.

Personally, using cannabis regularly doesn't seem to affect my ability to lucid dream that much. I've had hundreds of lucid dreams after going to sleep high on cannabis. As part of the research for writing this chapter I abstained from regularly using cannabis for three and a half weeks. After about five days of abstaining, my dream recall, or dream frequency, shot way up for around three nights, after which it pretty much returned to what it normally was when I was using cannabis regularly. I've always had pretty good dream recall, and using cannabis regularly doesn't seem to affect it very much, but some people claim otherwise and say that it has had a negative impact on their ability to recall dreams or to have lucid dreams. Someone wrote me while I was writing this book to say that "since quitting smoking weed entirely, I've been having a full lucid dream about once a week instead of every couple of months." However, another person wrote to me to say that he specifically uses cannabis as a way to promote lucid dreaming. This person said that he deliberately wakes himself up in the early morning hours, takes one toke of cannabis, and then goes back to sleep (as I suggested doing in the previous section on calea). He said that this promotes lucid dreaming for him.

It seems that the effect that cannabis can have on dreams varies considerably from person to person. As I noted earlier, it is also important to remember that the many varied strains and genetic hybrids of cannabis can have a wide range of different psychoactive effects. At the time of this writing, in many places cannabis is still illegal, although this appears to be rapidly changing, and a wide variety of cannabis preparations are becoming more legally available.

Banisteriopsis caapi
A primary component of ayahuasca

Banisteriopsis caapi is a vine that grows in the Amazon jungle and is one of the two primary components used to brew the entheogenic preparation known as ayahuasca. The vine contains harmaline and other harmala alkaloids, which are known in neurochemistry as reversible MAO-A inhibitors. MAO stands for "monoamine oxidase," an enzyme used by the body to break down neurotransmitters, or chemical messengers in the brain, nervous system, and digestive system. The second *A* in MAO-A means that this is an MAO inhibitor that specifically targets serotonin receptors in the body. Being reversible means that the body can still produce some MAO if it's really needed, so it's not as dangerous as some of the longer-acting and more forceful pharmaceutical MAO inhibitors like Nardil or Marplan can be when they are combined with the amino acid tyramine, which is found in a variety of different foods. Ingesting foods that contain tyramine—such as aged cheeses, red wine, and soybeans—could lead to a hypertensive crisis with harmaline because the body can't properly metabolize it. Combining harmaline with certain drugs such as other MAO inhibitors or selective serotonin uptake inhibitors (SSRIs) like Prozac is far more dangerous and could even be deadly. A number of people have died from ingesting ayahuasca with an SSRI medication.

Traditionally, the ayahuasca brew in the Amazon is primarily made from two plants, *B. caapi,* which contains the MAO inhibitor, and *Psychotria viridis* (chacruna), which contains the powerful psychedelic substance DMT that we discussed earlier and will be exploring later in this chapter. The harmaline in *B. caapi* allows the DMT to become orally active, and it also slows down the speed of the powerful psychedelic experience, thus making it more mentally digestible.

Harmaline also has psychoactive properties of its own, which somewhat resemble cannabis or a mild ayahuasca experience. It is often reported to enhance psychic abilities; in fact, one of the original chemical names for harmaline when it was first discovered was *telepathine*, because of its reputed ability to enhance telepathy during ayahuasca ceremonies. It may be that using harmaline on its own increases the amount of DMT naturally occurring in the brain by preventing its breakdown for a longer period of time.

My personal experiments with harmaline, from using both *B. caapi* and Syrian rue (which I'll be discussing next), were most interesting. I found *B. caapi* had a calming effect on my mind and that it relaxed my body, helped me sleep, and produced a mild psychedelic experience similar to cannabis, calea, and ayahuasca. *B. caapi* enhanced my experience of dreaming in a manner that was similar to my experience with calea. Furthermore, I found that calea and *B. caapi* tinctures combined are synergistic, and together they produced a moderately powerful psychedelic experience as I was falling asleep, and then dramatically enhanced the vividness and frequency of my dreams.

I obtained a *B. caapi* tincture from the same botanical outlet that I got my calea tincture from, www.Iamshaman.com, although I should point out that they advertise these tinctures for "non-human consumption." For dream-enhancement purposes I found that around two droppers full was a sufficient dose, and that with such a small amount of harmaline I needn't worry too much about dietary restrictions. The concentrated Iamshaman *B. caapi* tincture contains approximately 0.5 grams of harmaline per fluid ounce.

Peganum harmala
Syrian rue or wild rue

Syrian rue is native to the Middle East, and like *B. caapi* it also contains harmaline and other harmala alkaloids. The seeds from the plant are used in manufacturing to produce a red dye, and they also have a history of use as an incense, charm, and medicine for pain, inflammation, and other ailments. However, many people outside of South America use Syrian rue as a substitute for *B. caapi* in ayahuasca-like preparations because it's generally easier and less expensive to obtain.

I initially purchased my Syrian rue tincture from www.Iamshaman .com, although they have since discontinued this product. However, it's easy to obtain Syrian rue. I found a bottle of crushed Syrian rue seeds in the spice section of a local Middle Eastern market, and it can easily be found online.

My experience with Syrian rue for dream enhancement was similar to *B. caapi*, although I would say that the *B. caapi* experiences seemed a bit gentler than those with Syrian rue. I found that the crushed, ground Syrian rue seeds in a gelatin capsule (around a gram), a (filtered) tea made from around a teaspoon of the seeds, and an alcohol tincture made from the seeds were all quite effective.

Syrian rue is more potent than *B. caapi*, and I found that a single dropper full of the herbal alcohol tincture, which contained 75 ml of harmaline, was sufficient for dream enhancement.

Mucuna pruriens
Velvet bean, Bengal velvet bean, Florida velvet bean, cowage, cowitch, lacuna bean

Velvet bean is a tropical legume with many varied properties. It has been used in ayurvedic medicine for thousands of years, mostly as a (toxin antagonist) remedy for various poisonous snakebites. The plant contains the calming neurotransmitter serotonin (5-HT), as well as 5-HTP (a chemical precursor to serotonin), nicotine, bufotenine, 5-MeO-DMT, and DMT, the latter making it potentially psychedelic. However, the quantities of the psychedelic neurotransmitters DMT and 5-MeO-DMT in velvet bean are low and are not orally active without an MAO inhibitor, which could be dangerous to take with the herb due to its significant levels of L-DOPA, so this doesn't appear to be a safe admixture for ayahuasca. But it does offer some intriguing possibilities for dream enhancement. The amino acid L-DOPA is the direct precursor to the stimulating neurotransmitter dopamine, and this is what makes it useful as a tool for dream enrichment.

Many people report that elevated dopamine levels enhance the vividness of dreams, but for some people this can be unpleasant, increasing the frequency of nightmares.[10] However, I've had great success in pleasantly enhancing the vividness of my dreams using velvet bean and have used it effectively as a trigger for lucidity. The velvet bean extract that I used was standardized to 15 percent L-DOPA, and for dream enhancement I used two capsules that together contained 120 milligrams of L-DOPA. These high dopamine levels might keep some people up due to its stimulating effects, but I was able to sleep fairly easily with them, especially when using it with the amino acid L-tryptophan (which I'll be discussing shortly) and my Glo to Sleep mask (which I'll be describing in chapter 6). I found that when I took velvet bean in the evening I could sleep fine, and my dreams were always much more vivid, colorful, action-packed, and plentiful. It also helped me to become lucid and maintain states of easily entering lucidity for several hours. With the velvet bean I entered into states of borderland consciousness, where for several hours I would have fluid, vivid hypnogogic visions, which would gradually intensify. Then I would be able to maintain lucidity as my body fell asleep, the visions became more animated, and I entered into them. The velvet bean also helped me to "awaken" easily and repeatedly in those dreams where I wasn't previously lucid.

L-DOPA can be dangerous if taken with certain MAO inhibitors, amphetamines, or anything else that increases dopamine levels. Velvet bean extracts are available online or in most vitamin or health-food stores. In addition to their ability to enhance the vividness of dreams, they also have substantial mood- and libido-lifting properties.

Tabernanthe iboga
Iboga

Tabernanthe iboga is a perennial rainforest shrub native to West-Central Africa. It contains the powerful psychedelic alkaloid ibogaine, which is discussed in the section on drugs later in this chapter.

Some people report using microdoses of iboga for lucid-dreaming purposes. My friend Massimiliano Geraci in Italy wrote me a detailed account of his using small doses of crushed iboga root, between 300 and 500 milligrams, over a period of several weeks:

> The dream activity not only becomes more intense, the effects on acetylcholine receptors are such that a state of lucidity is induced within dreams, and this is a fundamental effect! That is, one is not simply witnessing an exceptionally realistic and immersive dream, but as the dream unfolds one can and must intervene in order to change, sometimes drastically, the course of the action. This assumption of responsibility is at the basis of the effectiveness of the therapeutic process. . . . Another key feature of iboga-induced dreams is that one is always in a state of serenity, even when the dream contents are "heavy," since you have to deal with the origin of the traumas and energy imbalances when you ingest this plant. . . . Moreover, these dreams have always been fully multisensory, with the presence of a tactile component that was unique for its intensity and that left clearly imprinted on me some specific tactile sensations for many days—and these tactile sensations acted as triggers to recall the whole dreams. Another feature of these dreams is that they are often related to one another with a narrative that unfolds and weaves over several dreams. Finally, it should be emphasized that these dreams become well etched in one's memory and continue to hover and to "speak" for several days.

Piper methysticum
Kava, kava-kava

Kava is a plant native to a number of western Pacific islands, where it is traditionally used for its sedating, calming, emotionally uninhibiting, socially lubricating, and mild anesthetic properties. The primary psychoactive ingredients of kava, kavalactones, potentiate the activity of a calming neurotransmitter called GABA (gamma-aminobutyric acid), which is the same target for powerful drugs like valium, alcohol, and GHB (gamma-hydroxybutanoic acid, often used to treat narcolepsy). However, kava is mild and safe by comparison with these potentially dangerous and addictive drugs. One often-criticized study found that kava may be dangerous for people with liver damage, but it has a long history of safe use with healthy people in the Pacific islands.[11]

While awake, I find kava to be moderately relaxing and somewhat euphoric if used occasionally, but it quickly leads to depression for me if used regularly. Different types of kava have different ratios of kavalactones, which can make the different types of kava substantially different in their effects. Some kavalactones tend to be more sedating, while others tend to have both sedating and stimulating qualities. Studies show that kava can reduce anxiety[12] and improve the quality of sleep.[13]

Personally, I've found that strong doses of kava can produce a mild, dreamy experience rich in hypnogogic imagery. I've used a number of different varieties of kava, in different forms, for years, and find that my reaction to the kavalactones has changed over time. When I first starting using kava, and for years afterward, it always put me to sleep during its initial stages. However, now I find that it can actually cause insomnia if I try to sleep right after taking it.

For dream enhancement, I found kava is better used in the later part of the afternoon or early evening. That way it doesn't interfere with my sleep and actually enhances it. Like calea and *B. caapi*, I find that kava enhances the frequency and vividness of my dreams, but not my propensity to lucid dream. The effects of kava last for around nine hours, although like the cannabinoids in cannabis or the opiates in opium, different kavalactones have different durations of action. This often causes the experience to be more stimulating and euphoric at the beginning, and more sedating and sleep-inducing toward the end.

Kava is available in most health-food and vitamin stores, and as with calea and *B. caapi*, I found the alcohol tinctures most effective and easy to use. One dropper full of the tincture was my dose for dream enhancement, although this may be strong for some people, and it's best to just start by following the instructions on the bottle. Kava is also a topical anesthetic and the herbal alcohol tincture made with it will numb your mouth, like coca leaves.*

Pausinystalia johimbe
Yohimbe

Yohimbe is derived from the inner bark of the *Pausinystalia johimbe* tree that is indigenous to West Africa. Brews distilled from yohimbe bark have been used for centuries by West Africans to enhance sexual interest and erotic performance, and to fuel their unusually impressive tribal sex ceremonies, which are reported to sometimes last as long as two weeks. Like kava, yohimbe is available in most health-food stores.

Yohimbine, the most active chemical compound in the yohimbe bark, is actually available as a prescription drug in the United States and is used for treating impotence. Some people report that high doses of yohimbe can have what are described as mild psychedelic effects that last for several hours. This includes feelings of euphoria, heightened physical and emotional feelings, and warm spinal shivers. However, higher doses of yohimbe cause some people to feel anxious, and, according to the *Physicians' Desk Reference* (PDR), people sometimes experience other mild side effects with yohimbine, including elevated heart rate, so it can be dangerous to mix with other stimulants.

I never thought of using yohimbe for dream enhancement until I read Thomas Yuschak's book *Advanced Lucid Dreaming: The Power of Supplements.* Yuschak says that using very low doses of yohimbine, less than a single milligram, can promote both dream vividness and lucid dreaming. However, yohimbine is quite potent, and it can easily cause insomnia if you take too much, which is easy to do. In my attempts to use yohimbe or yohimbine as a dream enhancer, I was never able to fall asleep while on it. I tried both herbal tinctures of yohimbe and pharmaceutical-grade yohimbine in my personal experiments. Even when taken with natural sleep aids like L-tryptophan and melatonin, which I'll be discussing soon, I still couldn't fall sleep on yohimbe

---

*To learn more about kava, see Vincent Lebot and Mark Merlin's *Kava, The Pacific Elixir: The Definitive Guide to Its Ethnobotany, History, and Chemistry.*

or yohimbine. Nevertheless, Yuschak reports substantially successful results with his yohimbe lucid-dream experiments, which is why I'm including a discussion of it here. He suggests taking a dose of 0.75 milligrams during the latter part of one's sleep cycle. However, perhaps 0.50 milligrams would be better if you're especially sensitive to stimulants.

Papaver somniferum
Opium poppy

Opium poppies are annual flowering plants that provide us with the tiny, tasty black seeds that are used to flavor bagels and buns. The poppies are also the source of opium, a famously powerful and seductive latex containing an array of pain-snuffing, euphoria-generating chemical substances such as morphine and codeine. However, most people don't know that the dried seed pods and stems, which are found in many holiday decorations, contain enough opium to make a potent tea.

I found that a strong cup of poppy tea made from around five or six medium-sized dry poppy pods could put me into a delightfully euphoric, visionary state of consciousness that promoted lucid dreaming, although most people should probably start with less than half of this dose, as overdosing on opium can be quite uncomfortable and even deadly. But when safely administered, this state of mind is rich in hypnogogic imagery that sometimes leads to sleep, and can, on occasion, develop into hours of vivid lucid dreaming.

Opium poppies are physically addictive. Overdoses can be fatal, and although the dried pods and live flowers are perfectly legal, any steps taken to convert the plant into a psychoactive drug is considered illegal. The dried pods and seeds can be purchased over the Internet from websites that sell dried flowers for decorative or crafting purposes. If one plans to ingest the tea made from dried poppy pods, it would be wise to first confirm that the pods are untreated, as some craft supply outlets will preserve the pods with toxic chemicals.

For more information about using poppy tea in a shamanic context, see Kenaz Filan's wonderful book *The Power of the Poppy: Harnessing Nature's Most Dangerous Plant Ally*.

Psilocybe cubensis, P. azurescens, P. semilanceata, P. cyanescens

Psilocybin mushrooms, magic mushrooms, shrooms

Psilocybin is the classical psychedelic, naturally found in around 175 different species of fungi around the world. Like microdosing with LSD, I have found that eating a tiny *Psilocybe cubensis* mushroom, around the size of my pinky nail, just before bedtime will often trigger vivid dreams and sometimes lucidity. Cultivating and consuming psilocybin mushrooms is illegal in the United States, but it is perfectly legal in Central and South America, as well as other parts of the world, where it is used in sacred rituals. As with other psychedelics, many people report having lucid dreams in the nights that follow a sacred mushroom experience.

Turnera diffusa

Damiana

Damiana is a small shrub that is native to parts of North and Central America, particularly Texas and Mexico. It has been used for centuries as an aphrodisiac in Central America, primarily by women who drink damiana tea prior to lovemaking, although both sexes report libido-enhancing effects with it. The damiana shrub can grow up to six-and-a-half feet tall, and the entire plant has a characteristic aroma that most people describe as pleasant—similar to chamomile—due to an essential oil present in the plant.

The dried leaves of the damiana plant, or damiana plant extracts, are available in most health-food stores. I personally prefer the alcohol tinctures, but damiana teas are also effective, and some people enjoy smoking the herb too. Although there has not been a lot of scientific research done on damiana, and no clinical studies have been conducted on its effects, chemical analysis shows that damiana contains alkaloids similar to caffeine, which can have physiologically stimulating effects, as well as other alkaloids that have calming and sedating effects.

I've personally found damiana extracts to be effective mostly as calming and sleep-inducing agents. They help to settle my mind and make it easier for me to fall asleep—and I haven't had a problem with the mildly stimulating effects of the plant interfering with my sleep, the way kava or yohimbe can. I also get some mild dream enhancement from sleeping with damiana, as it appears to increase the vividness and frequency of my erotic dreams, but it does not act as a lucidity trigger for me.

Salvia divinorum
Salvia, sage of the diviners, seer's sage, yerba de la pastora

Salvia, a native of Central Mexico, is an unusual and deeply mysterious plant that has potent psychedelic and dissociative properties. It is a perennial herb, believed to be a cultigen, which means that the plant has never been found growing naturally in the wild and has only been known to grow as a result of human cultivation.

Salvia has been used for (at least) hundreds of years by the Mazatec people in Oaxaca, Mexico, as a shamanic sacrament, to induce visionary states of consciousness, and for healing and divination purposes. It's psychoactive properties have only recently been discovered in the West.

For shamanic purposes, a handful of the leaves need be chewed for around fifteen minutes, as they are not active if eaten, and the hallucinogenic component needs to be absorbed sublingually. This is not the most pleasant of experiences, so it's hard to understand how the native people of Central Mexico discovered that the plant has these particular hallucinogenic properties. It is similarly mysterious to how the shamans in the Amazon learned to combine two relatively inactive plants to make a highly active synergistic blend, the ayahuasca brew. Salvia tastes pretty gross, so it's difficult to imagine what would compel someone to hold a handful of the leaves in their mouth for fifteen or twenty minutes. The natives say that the plant spirits told them these secrets. I can't think of a better explanation, as considering trial and error as an explanation here verges on the ridiculous when there are so many different species of plants growing around them.

In any case, as an alternative to chewing, concentrated extracts of the salvia plant can be smoked (a relatively recent discovery in the West, not practiced by the people in Oaxaca who use the plant traditionally), or it can be ingested sublingually in an alcohol tincture. It's important to note, however, that the plant is not psychoactive if the leaves or tincture are simply swallowed. When the leaves are chewed, or the sublingual tincture is held in one's mouth for fifteen or twenty minutes, the salvia produces a powerful, dissociative psychedelic experience that lasts for around ninety minutes. Smoking concentrated extracts made from the salvia plant will produce a more intense yet rapidly dissipating experience that only lasts for around ten minutes. Those ten minutes, however, can seemingly last for an eternity of subjectively experienced time, and they can easily be the very weirdest ten minutes of your life. The reality-twisting, hallucinatory voyage that salvia takes you on is due to an extremely potent psychoactive compound in the plant, salvinorin A.

Experiences with salvia are frequently reported to be among the most bizarre, unpleasant, confusing, and frightening of all psychedelic plants. I've had some extremely strange and unsettling experiences with salvia that completely rearranged my perception of reality. My personal experiences with this plant completely mystified me, and in trying to understand them I wasn't able to see how they had shamanic or therapeutic value, as they just seemed like crazy amusement-park rides designed by a sadistic alien prankster.

I once witnessed someone smoking a potent salvia extract for the first time. As expected, this person lost complete touch with external reality and became totally immersed in another world. He sat on the floor of a mutual friend's bedroom, repeating the phrase "Is that all it is? Is that all it is?" over and over, with different inflections each time. When he emerged from his salvia trance I asked him what had been going on in his mind when he was repeating that phrase over and over. "Oh, yeah," he said, "I was being shown how all of life and existence is really just this storybook on a library shelf with all of these other books that were also complete lives and worlds. Our whole world is just a storybook," he said.

After sharing an account of this experience with another friend, he related his own experience with salvia:

Next thing I knew I was scanning a bookshelf with a finger I thought to be my own, projection-wise. The finger was controlled by another force as I tried to mentally challenge its motion, to no avail. It zipped along thousands of books and pulled down a book. Before me was what I thought was the book of my life. I flipped through a few pages, and indeed it was my life printed out, complete with pictures and hyperlinks in the text, which brought me to certain arenas of my life, although vague in depiction. Then I looked at the table of contents. It was complete and looked as if my life was lived and cataloged. I had trouble getting into any chapters that were in the bottom third of the titles. There was a controversy in my head as to the naming of one chapter, probably somewhere around chapters 3–7, somewhere around there. It was strange, as it seemed like I was arguing with an unknown force or entity. I tried to focus on the ending chapters and the last pages of the book but it was like I was fighting something or someone in trying to do so. All the writing in the book was in red, and when I would highlight it, put my finger over it, the color would change to a deep red.

The similarity between these two accounts with salvia seems uncanny, and it's intriguing that as with life, dreams and shamanic journeys first and foremost are stories, meaningful narratives that we form to capture an interrelated series of events. Initially, I had a hard time understanding how salvia could be interacted with as a plant teacher or used as a shamanic healing medicine, but I also sensed that my experiences with it were important for some reason. I didn't find that my short-acting experiences with salvia influenced my dreams very much, but I did learn about a remarkable similarity between salvia journeys and a certain aspect of dreaming.

Thanks to Ross Heaven's fascinating book *Shamanic Quest for the Spirit of Salvia*, I finally understood the shamanic value of my experiences with this plant. According to Heaven, unlike the classical psychedelics, the salvia spirit speaks to us indirectly, in a symbolic language, similar to how our unconscious communicates with us in our dreams. In other words, similar to nonlucid dreams, salvia experiences are like puzzles that need to be figured out. I think that this is an important perspective, because otherwise salvia experiences can seem chaotic, confusing, and meaningless. However, like dreams, salvia experiences can be psychologically deciphered, and valuable personal meaning can be extracted from them after careful reflection on what the experience might be trying to tell us.

For example, one time after I smoked a potent salvia extract, the room that I was in suddenly had this giant mechanical conveyer belt traveling around it in a huge loop. The conveyer belt was moving forward directly ahead of me. It went up the wall in front of me, turned back toward my direction at the ceiling, and then angled itself downward when it hit the wall behind me, and then came back around again toward me, dragging and stretching me along with it as it clicked down the tracks. It wasn't until I read Heaven's book that I realized that I was experiencing a scenario that symbolically expressed a problem that was going on in my life at the time, which had to do with getting caught in repeating mental loops and running my mind around in circles.

When I interviewed ethnobotanist Daniel Siebert he told me that

> there are a lot of parallels between salvia visions and sleep dreams. Sometimes dreams are meaningful in obvious ways. They bring up material that we sometimes avoid facing head-on in our lives, and sometimes we get useful insights from our dreams. This also happens with salvia, even if you're not reading meaning into the visions; sometimes they are meaningful in obvious ways. Meaningful insights often emerge out of the experience. You might see something about yourself, or the way you've been thinking about things, something you were not aware of before. This is something that I find particularly helpful about salvia. It has been tremendously useful to me over the years, for helping me to understand myself better.[14]

Strangely—and relevant to our discussion—one of the most difficult mental abilities to maintain during a salvia experience is lucidity! With a strong enough dose of salvia, one of the first psychological effects is often complete amnesia. It seems that having a lucid salvia experience, with a dose that's strong enough to dissociate one's mind from one's body, is more challenging than maintaining lucidity during a sleeping dream.

I found medium-strength dosages of sublingual alcohol tinctures made from salvia to be the easiest way to shamanically work with the plant. These tinctures are available online where it is legal, and the legal status of salvia varies widely from place to place.

Some people have also reported vividly enhanced, crazy dreams as a result of dosing themselves before bed with homeopathic solutions made from salvia, and a small network of people who use homeopathic doses of psychedelic plants has been sharing experiences in a secret Facebook group that I followed for awhile. These are not microdoses, but rather homeopathic solutions with zero measurable trace of the psychoactive component. My girlfriend and I tried some of these solutions ourselves with intriguing results. We used a series of solutions called "The Master Sacraments" that a friend sent me from South Africa, which are said to contain the "encoded frequencies of the plant teachers."* These were solutions made from a homeopathic-like process with six shamanic plants—San Pedro, *Amanita muscaria*, iboga, salvia, *B. caapi*, and psilocybin mushrooms. My girlfriend and I both experienced some mildly mind-altering effects from these tinctures, such as a subtle feeling of presence and guidance in our creative work and in our dreams. The salvia and iboga solutions seemed to be the most effective for dream enhancement in our cases, although they all seemingly affected our dreams in subtle and different ways. I'm not sure how these homeopathic solutions work, since they have no trace of the psychoactive chemicals in them, but I found, and other people report, some rather unusual effects from using them.

Salvia is the largest genus of plants in the mint family. Notably, two other (nonpsychedelic) species of the genus *Salvia, Salvia officinalis* and *Salvia lavandulaefolia,* are known to have acetylcholinesterase-inhibiting properties. This means these two species of salvia can increase acetyl-

---

*These are legal and available online from www.mastersacraments.com.

choline levels in the brain, a factor known to promote lucid dreaming, and it is thought by some researchers that these species might be effective as lucid-dream catalysts.[15]

Scutellaria spp.
Skullcap

Skullcap is a flowering plant in the mint family. Its tiny, double-lipped, blue, purple, pink, and white flowers look similar to the skullcaps or military helmets that people wore on the crown of their heads during medieval times.

Skullcap contains a polyphenol flavonoid, baicalin, that has calming and sleep-promoting properties. It has been used historically to ease muscle tension, reduce anxiety, and help induce sleep, without being too strongly sedating. Skullcap has also been used by some people for dream enhancement and to promote lucid dreaming. In an online article about skullcap, holistic nutrition writer Kristen Ragno says, "I haven't been able to find much information out there to support my claim that skullcap promotes more vivid dreaming, with more potential for lucid dreaming and dream recall, but it sure works that way for me."[16]

In another online forum about psychoactive plant experimentation, someone named "Giz" writes:

> I have had a one-month break from cannabis, but lately I have substituted it with some herbs . . . and recently skullcap. While it is a nasty tasting smoke, leaves me zero effects when awake, I have had some intense dreams on it, lucid ones. The dreams have been really real, and I have been completely aware that I have been dreaming. I just had a dream where I smoked a bowl of weed, and I could feel the high in ways I could not imagine were possible when dreaming. This has amazed me greatly and has completely unexpected effects. I have experimented before with dream herbs such as calea but never had any effects from it. I have had lucid dreams the last 4 times I have slept with skullcap.[17]

As mentioned in chapter 1, when people ingest psychoactive drugs inside of lucid dreams, they usually work and have their desired effects.

Personally, I didn't find that skullcap influenced my dreams very much, but it did help me to relax and sleep more easily when I was over-stimulated from too much mental activity or other chemical agents. Skullcap can be ordered online or found in the herbal section of most vitamin stores, in capsules, as a dried herb for tea, and prepared in an alcohol tincture.

Mitragyna speciosa
Kratom, ketum, kratumum

The Southeast Asian herb kratom has a long history of traditional use in Malaysia, Thailand, and Indonesia. It is a fascinating psychoactive herb in the coffee family, composed of leaves that are harvested from a tree that is indigenous to Thailand. The tree is generally about thirty meters in height, with dark, shiny green leaves and yellow flowers. The leaves contain a number of relatively unstudied chemical alkaloids that may be psychoactive, including mytragynine, mitraphylline, and 7-hydroxymitragynine, which are reported to have both simulating and sedating effects on the brain.

The leaves of the kratom tree have been used as an herbal intoxicant by people in Southeast Asia since the beginning of recorded history. Dried kratom leaves are usually made into a (rather disgusting-tasting) tea, although sometimes the dried leaves are eaten by themselves as a powder for their psychoactive effects.

At lower doses kratom tends to act more like a stimulant, while at higher doses it tends to be more sedating, euphoric, dreamy, visionary, and psychedelic. A strong dose of kratom tea feels like a psychedelic opiate to many people, and it generally lasts for several hours.

Although kratom can be addictive, and the scientific studies on it are limited, from reports that I've read about moderate usage it appears to be relatively safe and not nearly as addicting as opiates can be. In fact, many people have used the herb successfully to wean themselves off of opiate addictions, and it may have valuable medical applications as a painkiller, sedative, sleep aid, and antidepressant.

My personal experience with kratom has been very positive. I've enjoyed the simultaneously stimulating and sedating properties of the herb, which can be quite euphoric. In large enough doses it puts me into a dreamy twilight state, where I have wonderful visions and blissful waves of pleasure ripple through my body. I find that large doses of kratom tea can put me into a state of consciousness where I imagine I'm doing something in the physical world, like working on my computer, and then suddenly realize that I've just been lying there with my eyes closed. It's difficult to maintain lucidity during these hallucinatory states, but it can be done, I've discovered, and maintaining lucidity while entering a strong kratom trance can open up a portal to lucid dreaming.

Kratom dosages can be standardized, but the reported strengths vary considerably from vendor to vendor, and as with cannabis there are numerous strains with mildly varying effects. The dosages that I needed for my lucid-dreaming experiences were fairly strong, usually several times the suggested dose on the package, but this might be too much for some people, so I would suggest starting with the instructions that accompany the product.

I've found kratom tea to be similar to opium poppy tea, only more stimulating and more psychedelic, and like poppy tea it also eventually leads me into hours of deep sleep. Many people use kratom as an alternative to opiates for pain relief, but not much is known about its biochemical effects, so more scientific studies on this promising plant are desperately needed.

Kratom can be ordered online, although its legality varies significantly from place to place. Some herb and head shops carry it.

Valeriana officinalis
Valerian root

Valerian is a perennial plant with pink and white flowers, native to Europe and parts of Asia, where it has been used medicinally since ancient Greece. The roots of the plant are now commonly used worldwide as a dietary supplement for their calming and sedating effects. It is thought to produce its relaxing effects because of an increase in the release of the calming neurotransmitter GABA, as well as slowing down its reuptake in the nerve terminal, so that the neurotransmitter has a longer period of activity in the brain.

"Vivid dreams" and "night terrors" are listed on a number of websites as a possible side effect of using valerian root, especially in the higher dosage range.

I've used valerian root tinctures occasionally to promote sleep and find that if used less than once a week, it works quite effectively. However, if I start using it regularly I quickly build up a tolerance, and the effects actually flip into their opposite form, that is, they start to cause anxiety and insomnia. Some people have reported this to me as well. Regardless, the valerian-root tinctures didn't seem to enhance or affect my dreams in any memorable way.

Prunus cerasus
Tart cherry, sour cherry, dwarf cherry

Tart cherries are packed with anti-inflammatory compounds like anthocyanins, which give certain fruits and berries their deep colors. Extracts of tart cherry are often used to naturally treat muscle pain and reduce inflammation. Tart cherry is also known for sometimes producing vivid dreams, so I gave it a try.

I tried 825 milligrams of tart cherry extract (standardized to contain at least 0.8 percent anthocyanosides) one night, along with some tryptophan and inositol, before bedtime. I did have vivid nonlucid dreams throughout the night, including one about being a crew member aboard a spacecraft returning to Earth from outer space. However, I woke up after only five hours, took some more of the tart cherry extract, and then couldn't get back to sleep. Even with melatonin I couldn't fall back asleep, as it seems like the tart cherry extract had some mildly stimulating properties. Later that morning, I had a cannabis cookie while working on this book, along with still more tart cherry extract. In the late afternoon I got sleepy and took a nap. During the nap I had a flood of dreams, and in one of them I became lucid:

> In the dream I noticed that while I was walking someone was pointing a handgun at me, just a few feet away, and he was tracking me with it as I moved. I started to move back and forth, trying to outmaneuver him, but his gaze and the fix of the gun were directly focused on me. Then I became lucid. No reality test or anything—I just knew that I was dreaming! And I knew that I couldn't be hurt. Curiously and confidently, I bravely faced my attacker and simply said, "You can't hurt me." I put up my hand and simply willed for it to stop any bullets. I felt a slight pressure on my hand as he tried to fire. He seemed quite surprised by my reaction. Then I started fighting back, sending psychokinetic hits or pulse punches at him, one after another, by flicking my hand and willing it to happen. Each time I hit him he flinched backward and changed form. His face became more grotesque with each hit, and then more abstract, as he eventually became overwhelmed by my psychokinetic pulses, and then I awoke.

It didn't occur to me until after I woke up that I should have tried to embrace my shadow attacker in the dream! However, I woke up from the nap feeling great, and I definitely got dream (and possibly lucidity) enhancement from using this anti-inflammatory fruit extract, which is readily available online or in health-food stores.

Artemisia vulgaris
Mugwort, common wormwood, sagebrush

Mugwort is a name used for several related species of plants in the genus *Artemisia* that have been traditionally used for their medicinal and psychoactive properties, as well as a flavoring agent in alcoholic beverages—although for dreaming purposes we are referring to the species *Artemisia vulgaris*. Mugwort is often referred to as one of the quintessential dream-enhancing, astral-projection, and psychic phenomena–enhancing herbs. It is related to wormwood, which is used to make absinthe.

The section about mugwort on the Erowid website contains a number of fascinating reports about how it enhances dreaming, without much else of a psychoactive effect. Consider the following report:

I dreamt that I was in some kind of a museum. . . . As we admired the artwork around us, the "curator" . . . came and told us that if we really wanted to see something, we should head around back to where another building was. He explained that most people couldn't see this structure because it had been cleverly hidden by mirrors to prevent curious onlookers from discovering its secrets. We all agreed that this sounded like great fun, and decided to go see it. . . . I cannot stress enough how enhanced the colors were, it was like a psilocybin mushroom trip. There were lots of people milling around, and they told me, "You've really got to see what's down there! It's amazing!" So I entered the doors of this building and found that it was really nothing more than a kind of waiting room. . . . Everyone told me to keep going, and eventually I reached what looked like an industrial elevator. Someone told me that if I wanted to see what was in this building, I had to go down the elevator. My friends were really keen on this idea, but something inside told me that I could not trust these people. I persuaded several of my friends to leave with me, but others decided to stay and descend into whatever room existed on the lower floors. My dream ended here.[18]

I found this experience most interesting, as I've also noticed how mugwort can enhance the storyline of my dreams. Consider another person's report:

First I infuse 2–3 tsp. of the dried herb in a cup of hot water for 15–20 minutes and then drink over a 10–15 minute time span just before going to bed for dream enhancement. This method for taking mugwort has worked well for me, but one thing to be aware of with this herb is to not expect dramatic results after one dose. In fact, don't expect dramatic results at all—this herb has a gentle action, it is not a hallucinogen. It does not give me a "trip" with lots of imagery. However, when I take it by the method described above, over two to four weeks I do notice a definite increase in dreaming activity.[19]

I picked up a 30 gram bag of dried herb called "Magical Mystery Tour Mugwort" for five dollars at an herb shop in downtown Santa Cruz, where I live. On the package it said "Dreaming herb: 1 tsp. per cup for relaxation or cramps. Place under pillow for astral projection." I tried a cup of strong mugwort tea before bed one evening, made of two teaspoons of herb steeped for twenty minutes. It made me a bit restless and it was difficult to sleep at first, and I didn't notice any effect on my dreams that night. However, after the following night's sleep I had around a half-dozen vivid dreams and lucid dreams in the morning, which seemed to be from the mugwort. Since then I experimented with mugwort on a number of occasions and found that it sometimes enhances my dreams, although not as much as calea and silene do, but, of course, it does so in its own hard-to-describe signature way, and sometimes for two nights. Notably, the lucid dream that I described in chapter 1, in which I transformed the face of someone raping me, occurred on mugwort.

One friend who had been sleeping with mugwort-stuffed pillows told me that it definitely enhanced her dreams, but that she had to stop because she couldn't control the dreams, and they became too forceful and dark.

As many people have discovered, I found my greatest success with mugwort as a dream enhancer when I placed a cotton pouch stuffed with dried mugwort leaves on my chest or by my pillow as I slept. I would fill up a cotton pouch with dried mugwort, pull the drawstring tightly closed, and then go to sleep with it tucked against my chest. It most definitely had a strange effect on my sleeping experience, although there were generally no lucid dreams with it (except for that one time, in which I drank mugwort tea and reexperienced my childhood trauma in a lucid dream). There weren't even very memorable dreams with this herb, but there was definitely a different type of hypnogogic experience with it, almost psychedelic in a way. It seemed as though I were becoming conscious of the plant as a spirit inspecting me—like ayahuasca—and of other spirits around me as I fell asleep. Something about the hypnogogic experience felt enhanced. I would often see visions of Hollywood-style witches with black pointed hats, cackling incessantly and stirring boiling cauldrons, as I was falling asleep. I couldn't tell if these were connections that I made by associating mugwort with theatrical witchcraft, or if I was seeing imagery from the archetypal field of the plant spirit.

Falling asleep takes longer than usual for me with mugwort, as though the mugwort aroma has a mildly stimulating effect, although others have described it as sedating. It can be smoked too, but I never tried it that way, and it's also available in capsule form. It was definitely worth experimenting with. Mugwort is anywhere from one to five dollars an ounce in bulk, and it can be found at health-food stores, herb shops, or online.

Nymphaea caerulea
Blue lotus, blue water lily

The blue lotus is a water lily thought to be indigenous to the Nile River in East Africa, where it may have been used as a sacrament or to make perfumes—although it has also grown in other locations since ancient times, such as Thailand, India, and parts of South America. Studies have shown it to have mildly sedating properties. It is sometimes used to make teas and tinctures, or as an additive to wines, as its effects are known to synergize well with alcohol. Some people report that it enhances their dreams.

I enjoyed the psychoactive effects of blue lotus tea a lot, and it helped me to sleep, but it didn't seem to affect my dreams in any significant way that I can recall. Blue lotus teas and tinctures are legal and are easily obtainable on the Internet.

NUTRITIONAL SUPPLEMENTS THAT IMPROVE SLEEP AND ENHANCE DREAMING

L-tryptophan, 5-hydroxytryptophan (5-HTP)

L-tryptophan is an essential amino acid that the brain converts to 5-hydroxytryptophan (5-HTP), another nutrient that is also sold in health-food and vitamin stores that can help with sleep. The brain converts 5-HTP into serotonin, a calming neurotransmitter, which then gets converted into melatonin, a sleepy hormone. L-tryptophan is also the precursor to DMT, but taking more L-tryptophan doesn't appear to raise one's endogenous DMT levels.

The idea behind using L-tryptophan or 5-HTP as a lucidity trigger is that it suppresses REM sleep. If you suppress REM sleep at the beginning of the night, then you'll increase it in the morning with a rebound effect, which is when you already have a greater chance to achieve lucidity.

Part of the trick to having regular lucid dreams is to combine different techniques. For example, one combination could be suppressing REM sleep at the beginning of the night with 5-HTP, so that it rebounds in the morning—after you get up at 5:00 a.m., read a book about lucid dreaming for thirty minutes, then go back to bed and practice the MILD technique until sleep sets in. Another part of the trick to having regular lucid dreams is simply sleeping well, and L-tryptophan and 5-HTP are both healthy ways to improve the quality of one's sleep. Personally, I prefer using L-tryptophan, which is metabolically one step back from serotonin, over 5-HTP, because 5-HTP makes me feel nauseated sometimes. But a lot of people use 5-HTP without any problems.

Choline

Choline is an essential nutrient, usually grouped with the B vitamins. It is naturally found in lecithin and is a precursor to the neurotransmitter acetylcholine, which is necessary for memory consolidation in the brain. Drugs that increase acetylcholine levels in the brain like galantamine are reputed to improve the frequency of dream lucidity, and taking choline supplements with these drugs is said to improve their efficacy.

I've noticed that taking a choline supplement works synergistically to heighten the memory-enhancing effects of cholinergic nootropics like piracetam (a cyclic derivative of GABA) while awake during the day, and doing this appears to assist with my dream recall when taken in the evening, as some other people have reported—although the drug is too stimulating for me to take right before sleep.

There are several forms of choline available in supplement form. Choline bitartrate and choline citrate are the most commonly used forms. These are generally inexpensive, readily available, and are not easily absorbed across the blood-brain barrier. However, what can be absorbed from them happens quickly and is metabolized fast. This could be a disadvantage if we are trying to time its action with our adventures in dreamland, or not, depending on when in the sleep cycle they're ingested. However, for lucid dreaming and dream-recall purposes GPC-choline and CDP-choline reign superior, as these forms of choline efficiently cross the blood-brain barrier, but take three and six hours respectively to reach their peak plasma levels after ingestion. These forms of the nutrient are more expensive then the forms that I mentioned previously, but they work better for dream-recall purposes and, according to many people, for the promotion of lucidity. All forms are available online and in health-food stores.

Dimethyltryptamine (DMT)

DMT is the mysterious psychedelic neurotransmitter that we discussed earlier. In its pure form the substance can be vaporized and inhaled to produce a brief and extremely powerful psychedelic experience; or it can be combined with a MAO inhibitor like harmaline to provide a more extensive experience, such as with ayahuasca.

Similar to reports from those who have used other psychedelics, a substantial number of people report lucid-dream experiences with DMT soon after the psychedelic activity of DMT dissipates. I've personally experienced this with both DMT and ayahuasca, and I've received reports from some people who have had lucid dreams the night after vaporizing DMT, or within days of having an ayahuasca experience.

The most memorable DMT-enhanced dreams that I had came after smoking an herbal blend known as *changa,* a kind of smokable ayahuasca that combines DMT and harmaline-containing plants, which I found to be truly extraordinary. Although it is also naturally found in the human brain, the brains of numerous animal species, and many plant species, DMT is considered a dangerous drug in the United States, where it is illegal. However, DMT is so common in the natural world that there are even trace amounts of it in common citrus fruits, so that every glass of orange juice contains a sprinkling of the psychedelic molecule.

Gamma-butyrolactone (GBL)

GBL is a chemical precursor to GHB (gamma-hydroxybutyric acid), a calming and sleep-promoting neurotransmitter that became known in the mainstream media as "the date-rape drug" because it is so effective at inducing sleep. GHB is a chemical precursor of the calming neurotransmitter GABA that we discussed earlier.

The primary difference between GHB and GBL, when used as a sleep aid, is that the sedating effects of GHB end abruptly after around three hours and one is suddenly wide awake, buzzing with a surge of the excitatory neurotransmitter dopamine. The sedating effects of GBL, on the other hand, linger for an additional three hours or so, and it is during this secondary period, when both GABA and dopamine receptors are simultaneously activated, that vivid and lucid dreaming becomes more frequent.

For me, GBL was the absolute Holy Grail of lucid-dream induction, although using it in the manner that I did was fraught with nasty side effects and it is now, unfortunately, illegal. Years ago, when GBL was legally sold through nutritional supplement companies, a friend purchased a case of it for me (known as Renewtrient), and I got to experiment quite a bit with it.

I discovered that when I took repeated sleep doses of the GBL, going back to sleep over and over, by the third sleep dose I would have an extensive lucid dream every time. This is where I developed the most experience lucid dreaming, and I was able to do it virtually on command. I had many dozens of lucid dreams this way and systematically explored all of the things that the hedonist and scientist in me wanted to try.

While writing this book I went back and reread my dream journals from this period, around fifteen years ago, and was spellbound by my own adventures—I had dozens and dozens of epic, jaw-dropping lucid dreams that went on and on, with intricate details from long excursions that I now just barely remember, or don't remember at all. However, also recorded are the extremely nasty withdrawal symptoms that I experienced from overusing GBL (such as days of insomnia, racing anxiety, and sweaty palms), as well as some pretty vivid and disturbing nightmares and false awakenings.

Like GHB and DMT, GBL is naturally found in the human body. GBL is still available through some European distributors on the Internet as a "wheelchair cleaner," but even as a cleaning fluid it's still illegal to ship to the United States, where, like LSD and heroin, it's considered a schedule 1 drug.

Melatonin

Melatonin is a neurotransmitter and hormone produced by the pineal gland in the brain as a response to darkness, which makes us sleepy. Metabolically, the process goes from the amino acid L-tryptophan, to 5-hydroxytryptophan (5-HTP), to melatonin. It is available as a nutritional supplement and is commonly used to help with sleep and jetlag.

I like to use melatonin during those times when I wake up in the middle of the night and can't fall back asleep. I've found that taking doses of melatonin early in the morning, after getting around five or six hours of sleep, and then going back to sleep often produces vivid, memorable, and sometimes lucid dreams.

Vitamin B₆ (Pyridoxine)

Vitamin B₆ is an essential nutrient that helps support adrenal function, helps to maintain a healthy nervous system, and is necessary for vital metabolic processes in the body. A study done in 2002 at Cornell

University investigated claims that taking vitamin B6 supplements can increase dream vividness and improve the ability to remember dreams, and it indicated that vitamin B6 can help with dream recall.[20]

There is also a disorder known as *pyrrole,* which causes the body to be deficient in zinc, magnesium, and vitamin B6, and one of the symptoms of this disorder is a lack of dream recall.

Note that one shouldn't take vitamin B6 and 5-HTP together, as this can cause the 5-HTP to be metabolized into serotonin in the digestive system instead of the brain. This may cause some uncomfortable side effects and result in less 5-HTP reaching the brain, and there is some concern that elevating the serotonin levels in one's bloodstream may cause cardiovascular damage.[21]

L-theanine

L-theanine is an amino acid analog that is found in green tea leaves and other plants. It has sedating, relaxing, mood-enhancing properties that balance the stimulating effects of the caffeine in green tea. It is found in many health-food stores and is often used to treat stress and anxiety.

Studies show that L-theanine helps to promote slower alpha waves in the brain,[22] which are associated with meditation and sleep onset. I haven't found that it has much influence on dreaming, but I do find that it helps significantly with sleep, and I often use it as part of my nighttime routine.

DRUGS AND PHARMACEUTICAL AGENTS THAT ENHANCE DREAMING AND LUCID DREAMING

Galantamine

Galantamine is a cognitive enhancer (or nootropic) used to treat Alzheimer's disease and other memory disorders. It works by increasing the concentration and action of the neurotransmitter acetylcholine in certain areas of the brain. Acetylcholine is used for memory consolidation, and galantamine is sometimes employed as a "smart drug" to help improve people's mental performance.

Galantamine is an acetylcholinesterase inhibitor (AChEI). This inhibits the acetylcholinesterase enzyme from breaking down acetylcholine, thereby increasing both the level and duration of action of the neurotransmitter. Galantamine is naturally found in numerous plants, including the red spider lily, the snowdrop plant, and the common daffodil, and it has been used for centuries in China as a memory enhancer.

Galantamine is used by many people to achieve lucidity in dreams. A lot of people rave about galantamine's unparalleled ability to help facilitate dream lucidity. For quite a few people galantamine is the Holy Grail of dream-lucidity enhancers, and it works for them every time. Other AChEI drugs such as donepezil (marketed as Aricept) and rivastigmine (sold under the trade name Exelon) have also been reported to be helpful. In fact, in 2004, Stephen LaBerge and colleagues conducted a study with galantamine and found that it increased the frequency of lucid-dreaming reports compared to a placebo.[23] (It also substantially increased reports of sleep paralysis and insomnia.) Subsequently, LaBerge filed for a U.S. patent for "substances that enhance recall and lucidity during dreaming."[24] Another study conducted in 2015 by Ryan Hurd, G. Scott Sparrow, and Ralph Carlson investigated how lucid dreams preceded by ingestion of galantamine compared with those that weren't. The results of their retrospective online survey of nineteen lucid dreamers indicated that "lucid dreams associated with galantamine were reported to have increased vividness and length, less dream bizarreness and emotionality, and much less fear or violence."[25]

Because galantamine increases levels of acetylcholine in the brain, it's helpful to make sure that your brain has plenty of the precursory material necessary to make it, which is why many people take choline supplements with galantamine.

Low doses of galantamine—between four and eight milligrams—are recommended for lucidity purposes, and it's considered best to take it in the middle of the night, after one has already completed half of the sleep cycle.

I've tried galantamine around ten times and, disappointingly, haven't had any success with it. The doses of eight milligrams that I initially used were too high and kept me awake. I was able to sleep with four milligrams a few times, but I never had any lucid dreams with this. Every time I tried using six milligrams of galantamine that dose kept me awake, despite combining it with other sleeping aids.

If galantamine does work for you, then Thomas Yuschak suggests that you shouldn't take it more than once or twice a week so as not to build up a tolerance to it. He also suggests taking the nootropic piracetam (sold under many brand names) in the morning after using galantamine, which helps to protect your acetylcholine system.

Phenibut

Phenibut* (brand name Noofen, Citrocard) is a chemical modification of the neurotransmitter GABA, which has relaxing or sedating effects. Scientific studies demonstrate that phenibut can be safely used to treat anxiety, depression, epilepsy, speech disorders, and insomnia.

Researchers have found that phenibut significantly diminishes tension, alleviates fear, and improves sleep, while enhancing memory and cognitive functioning. It feels like a cross between valium and a nootropic to me, providing both mental clarity and relaxation. It can also be quite addictive and have nasty withdrawal symptoms, similar to those of benzodiazepine withdrawal, if used more than twice a week for an extended period of time.

I've found that it significantly improves the duration of my sleep on the first night that I use it, and it increases the frequency of my dreams on the second night after using it. On the second night after doing phenibut, my ability to lucid dream is significantly enhanced. Phenibut is available online and in many vitamin shops. The best source for quality phenibut that I could find is a company called Liftmode (https://liftmode.com), which carries a number of other interesting supplements.

---

*I found phenibut so fascinating that I wrote an e-book about it, *Phenibut: A Scientific Guide to the Health Benefits and Precautions* (available on Amazon).

LSD

LSD (lysergic acid diethylamide or "acid") is the unusually potent, classical psychedelic drug that is highly active at microgram doses the size of a pinpoint. As with psilocybin and ayahuasca, many people describe the LSD experience as being dreamlike, and it is known to sometimes produce mystical experiences. As I've mentioned, I and other people have had lucid dreams several nights after tripping on LSD.* For example, at the Internet drug forum devoted to psychoactive drugs Bluelight (www .bluelight.org), on a Web page titled "Drugs that induce lucid dreaming," one finds comments like the following:

> Topmid: "LSD + MDA + weed. I slept for 24 hours after I came down and lucid dreamed the whole time."

> PredatorVision: "For me, LSD has triggered lucid dreams, especially when in combination with MDMA—I never used to get them before I started taking this drug."

In addition to triggering lucid dreams within a few nights of the initial psychedelic journey, LSD, I've discovered, can be used in microdoses or subthreshold doses specifically for lucid-dreaming purposes. I've tried doses of what I estimate to be around ten to fifteen micrograms prior to bedtime to be effective for increasing the probability of entering into a lucid dream. Taking any more than this will become mentally stimulating and tend to cause insomnia.

It is known that taking a small amount (a "microdose") of a psychedelic drug before going to sleep—an amount too small to produce a noticeable effect if taken while awake—will extend the period of REM. In 1968, biochemist Clara Torda showed that an IV infusion of five micrograms of LSD could shorten the latency of the fourth REM

---

*In the days following an experience with LSD, many people also report an increased frequency of what Carl Jung called "synchronicities," or meaningful coincidences. Both lucid dreams and synchronicities may increase in frequency due to a sustained enhancement in awareness.

period from ninety minutes in controls to one to nineteen minutes in LSD subjects.[26]

The Lucidity Institute's lucid dreaming FAQ states, "Drugs in the LSD family, including psilocybin and tryptamines, actually stimulate REM sleep (in doses small enough to allow sleep), leading to longer REM periods."[27] Also, REM sleep patterns are similar to the effects of psychedelics in evoking visual imagery and "hippocampal-septal slow waves."[28] Unfortunately, LSD is currently illegal everywhere on the planet, with the exception of its use in a handful of medical research studies.

Ibogaine

Ibogaine is a psychoactive alkaloid found in the African iboga plant (see previous section on *Tabernanthe iboga*). It has powerful psychedelic properties and is used in rites of passage and other traditional rituals among the Bwiti people of Africa. It is extremely powerful, debilitating, long-lasting, and largely unpleasant for most people, yet it has a near-miraculous ability to end chemical addictions for people overnight. Harvard researcher Carl Anderson has proposed a fascinating hypothesis about ibogaine's effectiveness in treating addictions being tied to our understanding of REM sleep.[29]

Ibogaine is currently being used in clinics around the world to treat opiate addiction, although it is illegal in the United States. I have no personal experience with this powerful plant. However, I have heard numerous reports of it increasing lucid dreaming. My friend and fellow consciousness explorer Taylor Marie Milton told me about the experiences that she had after her journey on ibogaine:

My experience with ibogaine was nothing short of enchanting and bizarre. During the depths of the 30-something-hour session, I found myself in Africa, or rather, Africa had found its way to me. I was in the most beautiful waking dream. When the session ended and I finally went to sleep, I woke up inside an actual dream—and I was lucid. There, I met guides who taught me how to navigate that realm. It was unbelievable, yet it felt more real than this third-dimensional reality. I toggled between realms for a couple hours before finally returning to normal sleep. The following night I was visited by the guides, who wished to take me on another lucid-dream adventure. Due to lack of actual rest, I politely declined and proceeded to sleep and dream as normal.

As I mentioned in the section on iboga earlier in this chapter, a number of people have reported that using low doses or microdoses of iboga root, which contains ibogaine, can dramatically promote lucid dreaming.

Dextromethorphan (DXM)

Dextromethorphan (DXM) is an over-the-counter cough suppressant, available in every drugstore, which is sometimes used by some desperate-to-get-high teenagers and a few serious psychonauts for its dissociative anesthetic properties, which can be quite psychedelic and otherworldly, and in strong enough doses can trigger extracorporeal experiences.

Although DXM's chemical structure is the mirror image of the morphine molecule, it's not considered an opiate. DXM is classified as a dissociative anesthetic, in the same pharmaceutical category as ketamine, PCP, MXE, and nitrous oxide. I tried it a few times, in various doses, and found it similar to ketamine, although it lasted much longer, wasn't as euphoric, and was more prone to producing unpleasant side effects like tachycardia.

I'm including DXM in this review because a number of people wrote to me saying that DXM helped them to lucid dream, including several people who said that taking it as directed while sick, as a cough suppressant, helped them "extremely well" with lucid dreaming. I've never had this experience using it, but I can see how it might be possible. The experience produced by a strong enough dose of DXM or ketamine is very much like a lucid dream, in the sense that one becomes completely immersed in a world that doesn't correspond to the input from one's physical senses. I've had powerful experiences with ketamine, where it seemed that I had become a disembodied deity creating virtual worlds in hyperspace, as one remains completely cognizant during the experience, and as with a lucid dream one can influence the virtual worlds with one's mind. So I can see how DXM may trigger lucid dreaming in some people. Consider the following report:

> After about a week of nightly use, I noticed something. . . . Nights in which I indulged in Nyquil, I was more conscious in my dreams. I was lucid dreaming! Something I rarely ever had but always enjoyed. The most notable experience with DXM-induced lucid dreaming was one where I was standing at the end of my driveway. I became conscious of the fact that I was dreaming and I could do whatever I wanted. As soon as I realized that, my vision went from a 2-D movielike state to a full on 3-D real-life vision. I began to move my arms in a flapping motion and I took off. I began flying. I flew down the street. I hit power lines every now and then, but since I controlled the dream, nothing happened, I just kept going. Besides this, I had a few other lucid dreams but I didn't remember them as well.[30]

I read a few other online reports of DXM helping people to enter lucidity more easily, so it appears to work for some people. However, DXM can be addictive, and there's some concern that it may cause brain damage (Olney's lesions) with repeated use.

Nicotine Patches

Nicotine is a stimulating alkaloid found in the nightshade family of plants, notably in tobacco. A nicotine patch is a transdermal patch that releases the drug into the body through the skin. It is used as an aid for people who wish to stop smoking tobacco. Many people report that wearing a nicotine patch while sleeping significantly enhances the vividness of their dreams as well as increases the frequency of becoming lucid while asleep. I haven't ever tried this, as I would be concerned about its stressful effects on my cardiovascular system. However, many others have had success with it, although I've also heard reports of it increasing the frequency of nightmares. Nicotine is, of course, extremely addictive and can have other serious health consequences. Nicotine patches are readily available over the counter in drugstores.

Another drug, varenicline (brand name Chantix), a prescription medication used to treat nicotine addiction, is also reputed to significantly enhance dreams, and someone told me that they've used it specifically for this purpose with much success.

Huperzine A

Huperzine A is an extract of the plant *Huperzia serrata* (Chinese club moss or toothed club moss). It slows down the degradation of the neurotransmitter acetylcholine, which helps with memory consolidation in the brain. It is included in many supplement formulas marketed to increase lucid dreaming.

Huperzine A is considered to be a nootropic, a "smart drug," by many people, a cognitive enhancer used to boost memory and mental performance. Like galantamine it is supposed to improve one's chances of achieving lucidity in the dream state by increasing acetylcholine levels in the brain during sleep. I've tried huperzine A a few times and found it has cognitive-enhancing properties while awake, but I've never experienced any lucid dreams with it when asleep. As with galantamine, I found that its mildly stimulating properties interfered with my sleep. But it works for some people and can be easily found online.

MDMA, Ecstasy, Molly (3,4-methylenedioxymethamphetamine)

MDMA is a most unusual and quite remarkable drug. Related to both amphetamines and mescaline, MDMA has unique psychoactive effects that many people describe as "heart-opening" or "empathogenic." It has mild psychedelic and sensory-enhancing qualities, and it reduces inhibition without affecting judgment or clarity of thought.

Although currently illegal, MDMA is being studied as a possible medical treatment for post-traumatic stress disorder (combined with psychotherapy) by the Multidisciplinary Association for Psychedelic Studies (MAPS).

I'm including MDMA here because almost every time I've tried this fascinating pharmaceutical, around two nights after having done it I've had a series of lucid dreams. This has especially been the case if I did the drug late at night and skipped a night's sleep while doing it—and then put myself to sleep afterward with valium (which suppresses REM sleep and causes a REM-rebound effect later). Other people have also reported having lucid dreams in the nights after doing MDMA.

Oxycodone

Oxycodone is a semisynthetic opiate medication used for extreme pain that is often reported to increase the frequency of vivid dreams and sleep paralysis. Like morphine and heroin, oxycodone is more powerful and euphoric than codeine or Vicodin. On those occasions when I've tried oxycodone, I found that it sometimes allowed me to stay conscious through entire nights of sleep, and I have had vivid, long-lasting lucid dreams, although at other times this didn't happen.

There is this magical combination of sleep deprivation and oxycodone use that I have experienced a few times and had extraordinary lucid dreams as a result—more powerful and lasting than with the opiate poppy tea that I described earlier. However, in the United States oxycodone is considered a schedule 2 controlled substance, with a high potential for abuse, which means that it can only be prescribed by physicians in extreme situations.

ESSENTIAL OILS AND AROMATHERAPY

I tried a product marketed as an "aromatherapy scent inhaler" for lucid dreaming. It looked like a Vick's VapoRub inhaler, and it contained a blend of four essential oils: clove, mugwort, anise, and clary sage. The directions said to inhale the scent of the essential oils before going to sleep while meditating and thinking positive thoughts. So I tried it on several nights. It smelled good and made my nose tingle, but I didn't have any lucid dreams with it.

As I mentioned in the previous section about mugwort, stuffing a cotton pouch with the dried plant and placing it by my pillow did have an interesting effect on my nighttime adventures, so I tried some essential oil made from mugwort that I bought at www.IamShaman.com. I found this magical oil to be absolutely delightful and got mildly intoxicated from just inhaling the vapors while going to sleep. It increased my hypnogogic imagery and enhanced the vividness of my dreams, although I didn't find it to be a lucidity trigger.

Atava Garcia Swiecicki, at Ancestral Apothecary, formulated an oneirogenic blend of essences from the herbs *Silene capensis* (African dream root) and clary sage, and the gemstones selenite and moonstone. All the ingredients in this magical blend, called "Dream Drops,"* are mythically related to the moon, and the formula is handcrafted on full moon nights. It is said to enhance dreaming with a few drops on one's tongue, although I haven't tried it yet.

I asked on my Facebook page whether anyone had any luck using essential oils to promote lucid dreaming. Mary Nason sent me the following response: "No luck with essential oils. However, a cologne that reminded me of someone who I pined for did work. I think it's because it was a different and emotionally powerful scent in my nose all night, so it kept me alert. Only worked that one time, like a little lucid one-night stand."

A book by Paul and Charla Devereux titled *Lucid Dreaming: Accessing Your Inner Virtual Realities* includes a chapter on essential oils and herbs for lucid dreaming.[31]

DREAM FISH

Several species of fish are said to cause vivid dreams and psychedelic experiences when eaten, due to a mysterious process called *ichthyoallyeinotoxism*. Most famously, a species of sea bream, *Sarpa salpa* (commonly known as the salema, salema porgy, cow bream, or goldline), is frequently claimed to be hallucinogenic, and the Arabic word for this fish means "the fish that makes dreams."

---

*Available at www.ancestralapothecary.com.

In 1960 a photographer from *National Geographic* magazine ate the boiled fish and reported experiencing "intense hallucinations with a science-fiction theme that included futuristic vehicles, images of space exploration, and monuments marking humanity's first trips into space."[32]

Sarpa salpa lives primarily in the Mediterranean Ocean, around Spain and part of the coast of Africa. It was known to be used as a recreational drug during the Roman Empire. I'm a vegetarian, so I didn't try eating this fish in my quest for shamanic dream enhancers, but I'd be most curious to learn more about the psychedelic or dream-inducing compound in it. The active compound in the fish—as well as several other species of fish that are also said to be hallucinogenic, psychedelic, or dream-inducing—is unknown. Some biologists think that it could be due to toxins associated with the macroalgae that accumulate in the flesh of the fish, although German anthropologist Christian Rätsch has suggested that it is due to the fact that the fish contains DMT.[33] (The Sonoran Desert toad is known to secrete a venom that contains the psychedelic compounds 5-MeO-DMT and bufotenin.)

This chapter isn't meant to be an exhaustive list of dream amplifiers by any means. There are many more dream and lucidity enhancers out there. But this is a good summary to start with, and so now let's take a look at some of the promising new electronic technologies that can help us to lucid dream.

6

EXPLORING THE POTENTIAL OF ELECTRONIC TECHNOLOGIES

If only we could crawl inside our dreams and live there.
MEG HOWREY, *THE CRANES DANCE*

The first lucid-dream machine was created in 1983 by English psychologist Keith Hearne, and there have been numerous attempts to create similar devices since then, which I will be reviewing in this chapter. Soon we'll have transcranial brain stimulators that induce lucidity during sleep whenever we like, as well as devices that allow us to record our dreams and communicate between worlds. But these technologies are not here yet, so let's start out with the simplest of devices.

THE BENEFITS OF USING A SLEEPING MASK

There are many benefits to wearing a sleep mask that covers one's eyes and blocks out light, whether sleeping or traveling on a shamanic journey. The mask minimizes any visual disturbances that might interfere with sleep, helps calm the mind, and allows one to better observe hypnogogic or psychedelic imagery. The two best eye masks that I have used with great success are called Mindfold and Glo to Sleep.

The Mindfold mask was designed by visionary artist Alex Grey. It allows one to comfortably experience complete and absolute darkness, even with open eyes. It is sold for relaxation and sensory-deprivation purposes, in addition to sleep support, and many people use it to better observe closed-eye visuals during shamanic journeys. The Glo to Sleep is a sleep therapy mask designed by Sound Oasis. Like the Mindfold, it also allows you to fully open your eyes in darkness (although the seal is not as precisely designed as the Mindfold). Inside each eye cup of the mask are four ascending vertical strips that you can charge by holding under an electric light for thirty seconds; the strips then glow in the dark. You fit the mask around your head before going to sleep. With open eyes, the four glowing strips are slightly above one's center of vision, so you have to raise your eyes to look at them. When I do this in the dark, while lying on my back, I almost immediately feel sleepy, which in turn allows me to easily enter into hypnogogic visions. With either mask it is also beneficial, upon awakening in the morning, to lie for a while with the sleep mask on so as to recall your dreams, as light appears to dissolve the details of dream memories.

A sensory-deprivation tank, which basically operates on a similar principle as a sleep mask but in this case completely blocks out all external sensory input, can also be quite helpful for inducing lucid dreaming and out-of-body experiences. I'll be discussing these isolation or floatation tanks in chapter 9. Meanwhile, let's see how the electronic technologies have evolved.

LUCID-DREAM MACHINES

Understanding that external stimuli can sometimes be incorporated into dreams, researchers Stephen LaBerge and Keith Hearne both developed electronic technologies to help induce lucid dreaming. In his book *The Dream Machine,* Hearne writes, "My idea was that if a standard signal could be incorporated into an ordinary dream, at such a level that waking would not occur, then it might be recognized by the dreamer as a 'cue' for lucidity."[1] Subsequently, Hearne developed a device that delivered mild electric shocks to the wrists of people sleeping in his laboratory, and this produced good results—half of his twelve subjects reported becoming lucid in their dreams from the point the shocks were perceived to waking, which was around a minute later.

Stephen LaBerge used infrared REM motion-detection technologies to develop the DreamLight, a sleep mask that could sense when someone was in the REM stage of sleep, and then signal to the person by flashing LEDs in the eye mask. The flashing lights are then incorporated into the dream, where they can signal the dreamer to become lucid. This has become the prototype for the two other commercial models of electronic lucid-dream machines: the NovaDreamer and the REM-Dreamer. Of course, for these devices to actually assist with lucid dreaming, people have to first train their minds to be able to recognize the flashing lights being incorporated into one's dreams as a signal that one is dreaming, as the stimuli can appear in a multitude of forms, such as police-car lights, strobing patterns, or flickering reflections.

In 1995, LaBerge tested the DreamLight with fourteen subjects, using a control group and a nonworking dummy version of the device. LaBerge concluded that "cueing with sensory stimuli by the DreamLight appears to increase a subject's probability of having lucid dreams, and that most of the resulting lucid dreams are due to the specific effect of light cues rather than general 'placebo' factors."[2]

There is also a lucid-dream induction device called a Remee, which is an inexpensive LED-blinking sleep mask that simply works with a timer, rather than the detection of REM. Since the device can't detect when one is dreaming, people have to hope that they set the timer to start the lights blinking when they're dreaming. I haven't heard any good reviews of this device, but I also haven't tried it either. Ryan Hurd says that it "may just turn out to be an alarm clock strapped to your head."[3]

There are also a number of lucid-dreaming apps available for your smartphone. *Awoken* and *Lucidity* are two apps developed for the Android operating system, and there are two others, *Lucid Dreamer* and *DreamZ,* for the iPhone. These apps offer features like binaural beats, reality checkers, alarms, and features to help you record and analyze your dreams. One of the more fascinating smartphone apps is called Shadow, which is part of a project to create the world's biggest dream database for wide-scale analysis.* According to the founder and CEO of Shadow, Hunter Lee Soik, when combined with dream reports from other app users around the world, the team can then mine the data and make new discoveries about the nature of our dreams, because over time it appears that patterns start to emerge in the collective consciousness. I'll be discussing the applications for studying clairvoyance with Shadow in chapter 8.

A British firm markets a lucid-dreaming sex toy—an alarm-clock panty vibrator called Little Rooster, which is sold as a "sex dream machine." The device works by vibrating in the underwear of the user while he or she sleeps, the idea being that the physical sensations will be incorporated into dreams, thus making them more erotic. There are both male and female versions of this device available. I haven't tried it.

However, I did experiment with a lucid-dream induction device called a REM-Dreamer as part of my research for this book, as it seemed like this was the best machine available at the time of my writing. Other devices, the DreamLight and the NovaDreamer, which were developed by LaBerge, have been discontinued, although promises of a new NovaDreamer2 model "coming soon" have been on the lucidity .com website for several years. According to a personal communication I received in 2015 from LaBerge's assistant, "LaBerge tested a newer model he called NovaDreamer2 for about five years at his 'Dreaming and Awakening' workshops in Hawaii. Rather than make that particular model available to the public, he used data gathered from those events plus advanced technologies to create a newer device. We beta-tested this one at our most recent workshop with promising results and expect to have it available for purchase by end of this year."

---

*To learn more about Shadow, see http://discovershadow.com.

Fig. 6.1. The REM-Dreamer (photo by author)

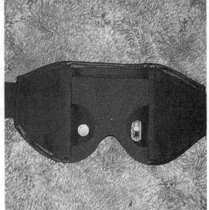

Fig. 6.2. The programmable circuitry of the REM-Dreamer (left),
which fits into a pocket (right) on the backside of the
REM-Dreamer sleep mask (photos by author)

My Experiments with the REM-Dreamer

I was especially impressed with the REM-Dreamer.* This ingenious device detects REM using infrared sensors, signaling to alert you that you're dreaming with blinking LEDs and/or beeps. You can then signal back with your eye movements from within the dream state to turn the blinking lights off once you're lucid, or adjust the intensity of the flashing signals. This machine costs $210.

---

*It's important to point out that the REM-Dreamer owes all of its ingenuity to Stephen LaBerge, as it's basically a copy of the technology that he pioneered and takes advantage of his research and development.

The REM-Dreamer arrived in a small, lightweight box that almost felt empty—significantly lighter than I expected. The device is a foam-cushioned eyeshade mask with an insertable microcircuit board that contains two LEDs, three miniature buttons, a beeper, and a tiny LCD display screen. It runs on two watch-sized lithium batteries and is programmable in numerous ways.

You can adjust the sensitivity of the infrared motion detector, which monitors your eyelids for REM activity, as well as adjust the brightness of the lights, the frequency of the flashes, and the sound volume. The REM-Dreamer has a number of features that can promote lucid dreaming, making it a fairly sophisticated piece of engineering. Like the DreamLight and NovaDreamer, it will flash the lights behind your eyes while you're in REM sleep (or make a beeping sound, if you prefer) to signal you to awaken in your dreams, and the machine records each time that it does this during the night. Most clever is the "reality testing" button positioned on the center of one's forehead when worn, which works when one is awake—with a flashing light—but fails when tried while dreaming.* The REM-Dreamer is not a toy or something for people who aren't comfortable with computer technology. It takes a good bit of exploration and experimentation to work with this device, but with time and patience it can most definitely be helpful.

The REM-Dreamer allows for two-way communication, to control the device from within the dream using one's eye movements, which

---

*The reality-test button on this device was originally developed by Stephen LaBerge for a later model of the DreamLight. LaBerge's assistant, Keelin, told me a story of how LaBerge reached the "aha" moment that inspired this innovation: "The 'Reality Testing Button' was initially conceived purely as a 'Cue Delay Button,' which would provide a means for holding off the flashing lights for the purpose of getting to, or returning to, sleep undisturbed. However, during early beta-testing of LaBerge's DreamLight (the first lucid-dream induction device ever created), a surprising discovery was made. People frequently reported either dreaming of wearing the mask or of having false awakenings in which they were wearing the mask. In either case, a button push would not work as it should in waking reality because it would only be a dream button on a dream version of the device. Either nothing would happen or something odd would happen, and if one had the proper mindset to recognize this anomaly, lucidity could be achieved. It worked brilliantly as a quick reality test, hence the adopted name."

makes it a marvel of engineering. This circuit board fits snugly into the foam-cushioned sleep mask, with each of the two little LEDs on the lower right and left corners of the board, along with a tiny motion sensor poking out through slits in the fabric.

Here's my report from the first night that I tried the REM-Dreamer:

I slept for around three hours normally, then at around two in the morning I spent around thirty minutes figuring out how to program the device. I got the settings right, strapped it to my head, and turned off the lights. Then—wow!—I had sleep paralysis, false awakenings, out-of-body experiences, and countless lucid dreams all night long! I think I must have stayed conscious though falling asleep and waking up, and falling back asleep, for around four hours. I mostly spent hours flying, talking to other dream characters, observing the incredible details in my environments, going inside mirrors as portals, talking to the dream environment itself (without any apparent responses this time), flying into outer space (always flying with at least one other person, sometimes numerous people), and having interesting sexual encounters with some of the people I met in my dreams. In my bedroom, during the states of hypnogogic sleep paralysis, it was often quite frightening—it always seemed that there were strangers walking around my home when I knew I was alone. I was mostly able to override this fear, with practice, and became convinced that all of the "people" in my home were spirits. Every time I tried to fly in the dreams I had some trouble getting airborne, and other dream characters would always either fly along with me or try to hold me down. There were just so many people in the dreams! I asked one person to stand in front of a mirror with me. Both of our reflections were clearly visible in the mirror, and I examined my own reflection carefully. I experimented with eating and smelling different foods in the dreams, and I realized that both senses were working, but in a reduced way. I tried breaking a glass, and it didn't shatter when I smashed it to the floor, almost like it was made of rubber, but then a few seconds later it broke into two or three pieces. I tried breathing through my nose while holding my nostrils closed with my fingers, and was able to easily do so. I had sex with a woman, older than myself, and noticed that it only felt like partial sexual sensations while I was inside of her. I spent a lot of the time walking around, talking to other dream characters, and carefully observing the world around me. I never lost lucidity and was able to watch aspects of the dream unfold naturally, without my influence. It was extraordinarily fun! Each lucid dream would last for a few minutes it seemed, before fading, and then I'd wake up, but easily be able to go back into more lucid dreams. I woke up in the morning with the REM-Dreamer attached to my head, having slept on my back for much of the night. I had dozens of lucid dreams, but I had no memory of any flashing lights entering my dreams. Then when I checked the REM-Dreamer to see how many times it signaled during the night to awaken me, it read zero. For some reason, the REM-Dreamer never signaled me with flashing lights the whole night, but I had more lucid dreams than almost ever before. I'm not sure why the REM-Dreamer didn't work, but the expectation of it working, and perhaps some shamanic experimentation over the weekend, combined with some sleep deprivation, probably helped. But it's a bit of a mystery why the REM-Dreamer failed to work and why I had so many lucid dreams nonetheless.

I'm including this report here to demonstrate the powerful effects that expectation can have on lucid dreaming. I have since discovered what I did wrong on my first trial: I inserted the circuit board into the sleep mask backward. Further experimentation with the REM-Dreamer revealed that this device does indeed have great potential, although I still had to make many additional adjustments. Nonetheless, this device vastly increases the number of lucid dreams I have. Here's my second report:

Wow, so many dreams and lucid dreams again this morning, my second night experimenting with the REM-Dreamer! I love this little device; it keeps entering into my dreams, cueing me that I am dreaming, and helping me to recall them and achieve lucidity. I just woke up from a nonlucid dream where I lost the REM-Dreamer in the dream and was looking everywhere for it, among all kinds of weird electronic equipment, in an apartment that was being cleared out. But I also had one lucid dream after another. The flashing lights either enter my dreams and trigger lucidity, or wake me up eventually. I had around four or five separate lucid dreams this morning; each time I became lucid within the dream rather than remaining conscious through the process of falling asleep. There were a few false awakenings, but no sleep paralysis. It's most interesting how wearing the device enters into my dreams; I find myself wearing it in my dreams and pressing the reality-test button on it, which doesn't work in the dreams. . . . In one lucid dream I was walking with a young man from previous lucid dreams, and each of us had these amazing hyperdimensional objects that we found in the street. They were around the size of our hands and were made of flat slices of metal that kept self-transforming into all of these radical, 3-D geometric structures that resembled tiny toy cities or circuit boards. My friend picked one up off of the street first and put it into my hand. At first it clamped onto my hand with these tiny metal jaws, and I got frightened. Then I became lucid from the flashing metal and realized that I was dreaming. I then began marveling at this self-transforming metal device in my hands, and said to my companion, "There is no way that this device was designed by a human being." I wanted to bring it back with me to waking reality so much, but then I awoke in this world empty handed.

Further experiments with the REM-Dreamer revealed that it was a good investment. It can really help if you're serious about lucid dreaming more frequently. Unfortunately, I found it too uncomfortable to sleep with that often and took it off a lot during the night when I was wearing it while trying to sleep.

LIGHT AND SOUND BRAIN-WAVE ENTRAINMENT MACHINES

The rhythmic sounds of rattles and drums have long been used in shamanic healing ceremonies to induce altered states of consciousness throughout the world. Repetitive percussion, flickering lights, and chanting mantras are all known to synchronize various functions of the brain and nervous system.[4] Light and sound brain-wave entrainment machines mimic this process electronically.

I've enjoyed using light and sound brain-wave entrainment devices since I've been in college, for relaxation, sleep induction, and exploring altered states of consciousness. I own several models and have had great success with them. My favorite is Mind Gear PR-2X, but they all seem fairly similar to me. These devices use LED-flashing goggles and headphones to deliver precisely timed pulses of light and sound to the senses, and the brain in turn starts to mimic the pulsing frequency patterns. In this way, the brain can be entrained in the four basic types of brain-wave patterns: beta, alpha, theta, and delta. I've used these devices primarily for meditation and relaxation purposes, although I've also had some interesting experiences combining them with psychedelic or shamanic journeys.* Although I've found these devices helpful for sleeping, I haven't had any luck with them for inducing lucid dreams. My Mind Gear PR-2X supposedly has a built-in program for lucid dreaming, but it just puts me into a relaxed state.

However, I was struck by the following idea, which might help with lucid dreaming. As discussed earlier, lucid dreaming occurs when the brain is generating gamma waves (20 to 50 Hz) during REM sleep, which are actually faster than beta waves (12.5 to 30 Hz), the type of brain waves that your alert brain is generating right now as you read these words. I wondered if a program that combines alpha (8 to 13 Hz) and theta (4 to 7 Hz) brain-wave frequencies (for inducing sleep), with just the right amount of gamma brain-wave frequencies, might do the trick of inducing lucidity during dreaming. So I wrote to Robert Austin, a developer at MindPlace, a company that designs light and sound brain-wave entrainment devices, to see what he thought of this idea, and if he had any devices that delivered gamma frequencies, as the devices that I own don't go up that high. He told me, "I've

---

*The late psychonaut Zoe7—the pen name of mind explorer Joseph Marty/Marty Joseph—wrote two fascinating books about combining psychedelic drugs and brain-wave entrainment technologies: *Into the Void* (2001) and *Back From the Void* (2005).

had a longstanding interest in gamma as well, and so the Proteus maximum frequency is 50 Hz, and the Procyon 75 Hz. Likewise the Kasina can replicate over 50 Hz, but the modulation depth starts to fall off at higher frequencies (that is, instead of switching on/off, the lights might vary between 10 percent and 90 percent brightness, due to the encoding technique used). I haven't tried using them for lucid-dream induction, but this does seem like a promising approach."

So if there's an engineering wizard out there who would like to give this a shot, please let me know. There are currently many videos available on YouTube that produce binaural beats in the gamma-wave frequency, as preparation for lucid dreaming. In any case, during the course of writing this book I experimented with a lot of electronic devices reputed to enhance my brain's abilities, and did my best to turn my loft into a miniature sleep laboratory.

BUILD YOUR OWN SLEEP LABORATORY

In his essay "Educational Frontiers of Training Lucid Dreamers," Tim Post, a doctoral student at the University of Twente, in the Netherlands, writes, "Ideally, students would own a mobile sleep laboratory at home, connected to the Internet, and upload polysomnographic recordings to sophisticated online software that is able to objectively detect and verify occurrences of lucid dreaming in support of their subjective (lucid) dream reporting."[5]

While having a professional sleep laboratory built in your home is still quite expensive, personal electronic fitness and sleep trackers that monitor your full sleep cycles, including REM, are available for a few hundred dollars. This information could be useful if you're really serious about studying your brain and your dreaming cycles. I considered purchasing one as part of my research for this book but decided that I didn't need it, as my REM-Dreamer measures how many times a night I spend in REM sleep, and that was sufficient for my purposes. Nevertheless, if you are interested in doing a more sophisticated analysis of your sleep cycles, neurologist Christopher Winter tested various personal sleep monitors to see how accurately they measure sleep cycles.[6] He says the Basis Peak Ultimate Fitness and Sleep Tracker (around $220) performs best and provides the most information about one's sleep cycles.

Currently, there are two similar, promising lucid-dream induction devices in production that go beyond what has been achieved thus far: the NeuroOn and the Aurora. These devices look like mini sleep laboratories in a mask, measuring and recording numerous biosignals with great accuracy. The NeuroOn, by Intelclinic, not only measures EEGs, but also electrocardiograms (ECG) and electroculography (EOG)—which means that it measures brain waves, eye movements, and muscle tension. This device has primarily been developed as a way to optimize one's sleep patterns by measuring and tracking one's polyphasic sleep cycles, but it also has the ability to detect REM, as well as the ability to send flashing light signals to the user to alert the person and help induce lucid dreaming. The Aurora, by iWinks, also has built-in EEG and EOG monitors for measuring brain waves and eye movements, and an accelerometer for measuring body motion and displaying sleep-staging actigraphy, or recordings of gross motor activity. It measures sleep cycles and, like the REM-Dreamer and similar devices described above, allows you to program personalized light and sound cues for lucid-dream induction. Both of these devices should be available at the time of this book's publication.

These electronic technologies for brain enhancement are certainly amazing, but I suspect that they'll seem quaint in just a few years compared to some of the extraordinary technology that is just around the corner. In fact, with computer technology and artificial intelligence advances accelerating so rapidly these days, some people are starting to wonder if digital appliances are actually becoming conscious and mindful entities. If so, can they dream too?

WHAT DO COMPUTERS DREAM ABOUT?

Artificial neural networks—computer programs that simulate how networks of neurons in the brain process information—are able to simulate dreaming in computer models, which can result in some highly

Fig. 6.3. Photo of the author
by Keana Parker,
run through Google's
Deep Dream program

imaginative artwork and bizarre imagery reminiscent of psychedelic visions.[7] One program of this type is called Deep Dream, which I've had great fun running personal photos through, as in the photo above.

At Google, an artificial-intelligence (AI) research team built a highly advanced computer vision system that is able to visually differentiate between objects. These AI networks can be trained to recognize objects and then seek them out of the surrounding environment. Unexpected results can occur when the computer is instructed to detect objects that aren't really there, for example, instructing the computer to locate animals among clouds in the sky. The computer is able to find (or "hallucinate") and display a surreal orgy of animals in the clouds, and these images look a lot like ayahuasca or mushroom visions to me. The gallery of AI-generated dream images compiled by Google researchers is a treasure trove of extraordinary surrealistic artwork.[8]

Aside from being able to peer into the digital dreams of machines, other developments in computer technology and neuroscience are allowing us to recreate images directly from patterns of electrical activity in the visual cortex of our brains, thereby opening up the possibility that we can record videos of our dreams to view later when we're awake, and then share with others.

RECORDING AND SHARING OUR DREAMS

A team of Japanese scientists in Kyoto have already created the rudimentary technology for recording dreams. Using an MRI machine, a computer model, and thousands of images from the Internet, they've been able to record the neurological patterns of their sleeping subjects and translate those patterns into visual imagery with 60 percent accuracy.[9] This technology is premised on the fact that our brains create predictable patterns of electrical activity for different kinds of visual stimuli, and over time a computer algorithm can learn how to correlate each of those patterns with different classes of visualizations. Although still in its early stages, this promising technology could one day soon allow us to record our dreams so that we can play them back later, study them scientifically, or even share them with friends on social media.

Additionally, cognitive neuroscientist Frank Tong and his colleagues at Vanderbilt University are learning how to decode and reconstruct the patterns of neural impulses that compose what we see in our visual fields, our dreams, and our imaginations, on low-resolution visual grids.[10] This technology already allows us to reconstruct what a person sees from that person's brain activity, and it is getting more sophisticated all the time. Currently, images reconstructed from brain activity clearly show what type of symbol a person is viewing. The day is not far off when we'll be able to directly project our imaginations into a collectively shared space.

Lucid-dream researcher and computer consultant Daniel Oldis wrote a fascinating article about how we'll soon be able to record and share our dreams like movies—because the technology to do this already exists. In addition to the research that I described above, which can record rudimentary visual imagery in our dreams, Oldis also describes using technologies that record dream speech and dream body movements. He describes a device that uses electronic sensors placed over the voice box (and other muscles involved in talking) that are sensitive to the subvocal muscle potential and capture what we say in our dreams. This is now possible using an electronic "smart tattoo" (patented by Motorola) that can be placed over the vocal cords and record at least part of our dream conversations.

Additionally, body-tracking technology can be used to record (and reconstruct) our dream body's movements through an electromyography sensor—as the body movements in dreams send nerve signals to those muscles involved in the dream behavior (despite the fact that physical movement is generally suppressed during REM sleep). By combining visual images with corresponding speech and movement, Oldis envisions being able to create multisensory videos from our nightly dreams. Once these technologies improve, shrink, and become more affordable, we could all be recording and sharing our dreams every morning.[11]

Besides being enormously fun and fascinating, these technologies could allow us to study the reality of shared lucid dreams—which we'll be discussing in chapter 8—by providing the records from two people to compare.

COMMUNICATING FROM OUR DREAMS

As noted in the introduction of this book, in 1975, when the first Morse Code–like, left-right-left-right eye signals from sleeping lucid dreamers were transmitted to researchers in the waking world, a whole new medium of communication was born. Those faint signals were the first transmissions from the dream realm to the material world, and as a species, we're literally building a communication and transportation system between these worlds. The REM-Dreamer that I own allows me to communicate with the device from within the dream state by moving my eyes up and down. This is the first-ever commercially available electronic device that allows one to send information directly from one's dreams to operate its functions. It isn't difficult to see where this technology is leading us. With controlled eye movements or breathing patterns—or possibly more directly with just brain-wave activity—we'll eventually be able to communicate complex information from lucid dreamland to the waking world.* It won't be long before there's a smart-

---

*Technologies that allow the brain to directly control a computer or robotic limb with neural impulses are currently being developed with greater and greater sophistication. (See Regaldo, "Thought Experiment.")

phone app that allows people to text their friends in waking reality from the dream realm, and someday it may even be possible for people in lucid dreams to speak with other lucid dreamers while they're dreaming. Brain-wave sensing technology will allow people to remotely operate computers with their minds, and perhaps most incredible of all, it will soon be possible for people to lucid dream whenever they want to.

LUCID DREAMING ON COMMAND

In 1988, I wrote a science-fiction novel called *Brainchild,* about a neuroscientist who creates an electronic technology that induces lucid dreaming at the touch of a button. It looks like science fiction is now fact. As mentioned earlier, German researchers have developed methods of inducing lucid dreaming with transcranial electrical brain stimulation. So the technology to induce a lucid dream on command is already here. While the cost of this technology is currently prohibitively expensive for the average person, it is obviously just a matter of time before it is miniaturized and mass-produced inexpensively. With the further development of nanotechnology and neuroscience, it seems that we'll all soon have precise control over dialing and tuning in to our dream states.

Looking farther into the future, it seems that lucid dreaming and space travel may someday merge in different ways. In his book *Are You Dreaming?* author Daniel Love speculates that lucid dreaming could one day be used by astronauts for maintaining psychological health during long space-travel missions—something like the holodeck on *Star Trek.* Or maybe we'll discover that lucid dreaming is itself a form of space traveling, and we'll learn to migrate to these other worlds with greater efficacy as our species continues to evolve.

One thing is for sure: whatever and wherever our dream worlds are, they're already populated. In the next chapter we'll be looking at how to best interact and get along with the natives of slumberland.

7

COMMUNICATING WITH DREAM CHARACTERS, ARCHETYPES, SPIRITS, AND DISEMBODIED ENTITIES

It is one great dream dreamed by a single Being, but in such a way that all the dream characters dream too.

ARTHUR SCHOPENHAUER

According to Jung, dreams may be considered communication exchanges between different (possibly unconscious) "parts of the self" with the "conscious self," and that these "intra-psyche communications" are necessary to keep the larger self from fragmenting.[1] From this perspective, dream symbols and characters are seen as the language that the different parts of ourselves use to speak with one another, and dreaming assists with the reorganization of the self.

However, try explaining Jung's theory of intrapsyche communication to someone in your next lucid dream, and that character is likely to give you the same perplexed response as anyone in waking life. One of the most important things that we first need to come to terms with

216

as we start exploring lucid dreams is understanding that we not alone in the dream realm. Our dreams exist in a world populated by countless other people and beings, who often seem every bit as conscious and intelligent as those we meet in waking life. Lucid-dream expert Robert Waggoner describes this well:

> Inexplicable and unexpected events will occur. The lucid dreamer will still feel surprised and bewildered by novel situations and creative comments of dream figures. While the lucid dreamer will likely continue to treat dream figures as mental projections, the idea may occur that different types of dream figures exist. Some dream figures comply with requests willingly, some ignore the lucid dreamer altogether, and some seem to act like independent agents with their own knowledge, volition, and agenda.[2]

Jung eventually was forced to question his own assertions about "intra-psyche communication" when he repeatedly encountered a perplexing figure in his dreams whose name was Philemon, whom Jung described as a winged elderly man wearing a simple robe:

> Philemon and other figures of my fantasies brought home to me the crucial insight that there are things in the psyche which I do not produce, but which produce themselves and have their own life. Philemon represented a force that was not myself. In my fantasies I held conversations with him, and he said things which I had not consciously thought. For I observed clearly that it was he who spoke, not I. He said I treated thoughts as if I generated them myself, but in his view thoughts were like animals in the forest, or people in a room, or birds in the air, and added, "If you should see people in a room, you would not think that you had made those people, or that you were responsible for them." It was he who taught me psychic objectivity, the reality of the psyche. Through him the distinction was clarified between myself and the object of my thought. He confronted me in an objective manner, and I understood that there

is something in me which can say things that I do not know and do not intend, things which may even be directed against me.[3]

During some periods of my life when I was having regular lucid dreams, I began to befriend and seemingly establish relationships with other people (or repeating dream characters) I met in my dreams. When I would try to explain to these people that we were all in a lucid dream, they were almost always very resistant to this idea at first. They most certainly didn't think that they were merely aspects of me, as Jung originally asserted. Initially, when I showed some people in a dream that I possessed superpowers such as the ability to fly, they actually got upset with me and tried to pull me back down to the ground when I was demonstrating this ability. However, in later lucid dreams this changed, and I was eventually able to teach my dream characters how to fly too.

As my lucid dreams became more and more frequent, I met people in them who made me question the reality of my experience and made me wonder whether they were fabricated by my own brain—similar to my experiences with DMT and ayahuasca. It seems as though this "place" where lucid dreaming occurs is an independently existing alternative reality or realities where some people live their day-to-day lives. However, on rare occasions, some of the other characters that I've met in the dream realm seemed to be, like me, other dreamers who temporarily came to this place through the process of lucid dreaming. I once met someone in a lucid dream who seemed to be another dreamer recognizing that we were in a lucid dream together. I wonder if someday I'll meet this person in waking life and discover that he wrote a lucid-dream report that matches mine:

> We were inside an elevator with other people, when I said something about how this was all a dream to everyone. This young man across from me immediately looked at me in recognition, and we excitedly grasped each other's shoulders, looking into each other's eyes, exclaiming, "Wow! We're in a dream! This is so cool!" We were in total disbelief that we could be there together, inside a place that we got to by dreaming. It seemed impossible, yet somehow there we were.

Not everyone experiences such a pleasant exchange with his or her lucid-dream characters. Consider what one of the first scientists to study lucid dreaming had to say about his unpleasant dream characters.

FREDERIK VAN EEDEN'S DEMON DREAMS

Psychiatrist Frederik van Eeden first described his experience with lucid dreaming to the Society for Psychical Research in London in 1913, although he had his first personal experience with the phenomenon in 1897. He was a proficient lucid dreamer, with hundreds of recorded lucid dreams. Van Eeden was curious about whether or not a deceased person he encountered in his lucid dream was the genuine consciousness of that person from waking life or not. He wondered the same thing about the "demons" or "low creatures" that he encountered in his lucid dreams, which he would banish by "invoking God." Van Eeden writes, "Whether these beings have a real existence or whether they are only creations of my fancy, to see them and to fight them takes away all of their terror, all of the uncanniness, the weirdness of their tricks and pranks."[4]

To realize that one is dreaming while it is happening usually instantly alleviates any circumstantially based fear, but, as we have seen, this is not always the case. Sometimes other dream characters appear to have their own will and agendas, or even a sense of volition that is at odds with our own. Consider the following: "The Catholic monk known as Father 'X,' whose rather Lovecraftian elaborations on his decades of conscious sleep experiences appeared now and then in *Lucidity Letter,* had similar difficulties [as Van Eeden] with morbid and malicious dream characters. He too concluded that the 'beings' must exist outside his own mind, perhaps as spirits of the dead trapped in a transitional afterworld or as residents in another space-time continuum."[5]

Here's another example. On an Internet forum, someone going by the name of "Sir Domino" describes a lucid dream that he had where he called all of the characters in his dream together for a conference in a large room. After they all took their seats, he told them that this was all his dream, and that his physical body was outside of this reality, asleep in bed. He goes on:

> I received a bunch of people being snarky, some laughing, and a few with looks of deep concern, even fear. I continued, saying that when I wake up, the dream would end. Several begged me to never wake up. Another asked what would become of them. And still another asked me if I was God. I did my best to answer their questions, but they all became quiet, and I had one raise her hand, stand up, look me in the eyes and say that she was real, that this was the only reality she knew, and that she was afraid of becoming nothing and dying when I woke up. She begged me to reassure her that she wouldn't be gone. The most I could do was tell her that I would remember all of them, especially her, when I awoke, and that they would probably continue to exist in the universe of my mind, perhaps subconsciously. She then asked me what the point of their [lives were] if they were nothing more than characters in my dreams. I didn't know how to answer this, and then another guy spoke up and said that perhaps they were all a part of me, that maybe . . . without them I couldn't be who I needed to be when I woke up. Another chimed in and said that was the feeling they were getting as well, that they were all representations of deeper personalities that make up who I am.[6]

So the first question we need to ask ourselves is . . .

ARE DREAM CHARACTERS JUST MENTAL PROJECTIONS?

One of the biggest philosophical and ethical questions facing lucid dreamers is whether the characters we encounter in our dreams have a genuine, independently existing sense of awareness, with their own thoughts, emotions, willpower, and autonomy. Some people initially assume that dream characters are illusory projections of their own minds, while others maintain that they are conscious spirits from another realm, or independently aware and autonomous fragments of our own minds. In his book *Are You Dreaming?* Daniel Love writes, "Time and time again in both my dreams and as confirmed in my discussions with (and reports from) other lucid dreamers, the consensus is that dream characters pass all of the criteria we would expect when dealing with any genuine waking entity."[7]

Robert Waggoner described using an intriguing technique to help distinguish the difference between what may be autonomous beings in our dreams and our own mental projections. While making love to an attractive character in his lucid dream, Waggoner questioned her reality and said, "All thought forms must disappear." Waggoner's dream lover immediately vanished after he said these words.[8] If one experiments with this technique it seems like it might lead to some compelling insights—or, perhaps, even more perplexing questions.*

However, whatever mechanism that causes certain dream imagery to remain and other imagery to vanish may not necessarily be capable of providing us with an accurate representation of what are and are not projected thought forms. It's a very tricky situation. Since dream characters respond to our beliefs or expectations about them—conscious or unconscious—uncovering their true nature may prove difficult, as the following example from Janice Brooks' lucid dream illustrates: "When a Frankenstein monster appeared in a dream mall one time Janice knew that her reaction would determine how it behaved. Rather than running away and being chased as in similar dream situations in the past, this time she went right up to the creature and shook its hand, and it acted like a friendly, sophisticated gentleman, walking and talking with her and proposing a business partnership."[9]

Brooks and her coauthor, Jay Vogelsong, are not only skeptical

---

*Stephen LaBerge suggested another, perhaps more definitive, way to check this, by asking a dream figure to do a certain type of math problem where using a carry-over number is required, because if dream figures don't possess their own consciousness then they shouldn't be able to perform this type of mental calculation. In a transcript titled "Conversation Between Stephen LaBerge and Paul Tholey in July of 1989," he says, "How do you do mental arithmetic? How do you compute 5 times 5? The answer simply appears. It's not conscious, it's automatic. But when you have to do arithmetic that involves carrying a number, you store that number in consciousness."

of the possibility that dream characters have any sort of independent existence, they don't even think that our dream characters represent fragmented parts of our own minds that we can form acts of psychological reconciliation with. In response to the warnings that some psychotherapists express about acting aggressively against dream characters, the authors state, "Such concern seems to be based on a combination of waking-world ethics and what amounts to superstitious deification of the unconscious. We feel that any code of behavior in lucid dreams should be a matter of personal taste and principle—and context-specific taste and principle at that—rather than wariness regarding unproven psychological aftereffects."[10] Nevertheless, Stephen LaBerge and others report incidents where the resolution of dream conflicts resulted in the resolution of actual personality conflicts,[11] so the mystery remains.

One runs into similar philosophical problems in trying to determine if the entities that appear to communicate with us on DMT, ayahuasca, or sacred mushroom journeys have a genuine independent existence or not. Many people report encounters with seemingly independent beings while on shamanic journeys. These have been described as "extraterrestrial scientists," "self-transforming machine elves," and "giant intelligent praying mantises"; they are also alleged to be ancestors or dead friends, plant spirits, or talking animals, and can take on numerous other forms. As with dreams, some people think that these beings in the shamanic realms are illusory projections of our own minds, while others maintain that they are conscious spirits from another realm. I suspect that the resolution of these intertwined mysteries will reveal a truth far more complex than any of these assumptions allow for.

MYSTICAL EXPERIENCES AND MULTIPLE SELVES

When someone has a mystical experience as a result of a psychedelic agent like psilocybin or LSD, they generally report that the mental boundary between their personal-body ego-self and a larger, universal cosmic Self dissolves. With this dissolution comes a sense of union or unity with what has been called "the Universal Mind," "the Source," "the One," "God," and other terms. In this state of consciousness it appears that one's ego is a persistent illusion, or not really what it seemed to be, and that all people or personalities are really just different variations of the one and only mind that ever exists.

Now apply this insight to the characters in our dreams. Even if our dream worlds are composed of consciousness, independent agents may exist within them, the same way that we exist as independent agents inside the universal mind. Following this train of thought, we have to then ask: if one of our dream characters had a mystical experience, would he or she claim to have achieved divine union with us, the brain's "overmind"? I wonder . . .

Each person, it seems, is a holographic representation of the entire universe. Could we all just be characters in the dreaming mind of God, and could all of the dream characters inside us be people who dream too? And what about what's inside of them? Does this insane craziness just keep going on and on, like a never-ending fractal, or a nested infinity of Russian dolls, of dreams within dreams within dreams? What if someone were to fully "wake up" within the "dream" of waking life? Would this person have the extraordinary superpowers that we possess in our lucid dreams? Is this what religious prophets and mystics are?

These are all cogent philosophical questions to ponder, although I suspect that no one really knows the answers. We'll pick up on this subject again in chapter 10. For now, let's put these perplexing philosophical mysteries aside and discuss more practical matters. So whoever or whatever the characters in our lucid dreams really are, when we meet them in their world, how should we react?

DREAM-REALM COMMUNICATION ETIQUETTE

Evidence gleaned from many reports of lucid dreams suggests that it's probably wise to treat the characters we meet in our dreams—or on our shamanic journeys—with the same respect we give to people in waking life, as well as the same discernment in evaluating their intentions. These characters may be a part of ourselves, isolated fragments of our minds, and as such they may have their own inner lives, just as we do. Treating them as we would like to be treated seems to be the best course of action, regardless of what they are. I think that it would be foolish to risk hurting another being—or another part of ourselves—by mistreating a dream character.

Not surprisingly, just as in the waking world, there appears to be different types of characters inhabiting our lucid dreams. However, with time, one begins to learn that most lucid-dream characters fit into three basic categories, which Waggoner describes well in his book *Lucid Dreaming*. These types seem to match my own experience. Briefly, some characters in lucid dreams seem like they're sleepwalking, rather mechanical and relatively stupid, with low levels of awareness, responding like moldable puppets. Others appear to have surprising intelligence and their own sense of free will. In this second category it seems that some of these independent agents are parts of our own minds, while others appear to be visitors, or the spirits of other dreamers. Then there is a third category, that of wise beings, guides, or guardians who teach us things and seem to know more about us than we know ourselves. The most fascinating encounters that I've had in dreamland have been with these wise beings.

ENCOUNTERS WITH WISE BEINGS

Sometimes the characters with greater awareness in our lucid dreams will try to teach or educate us about certain things, and some extraordinary dream characters appear to us as wise or angelic beings. In my experience, the forms these wise beings frequently assume are those of little children. I've read accounts of people who see these wise beings in lucid dreams as angels, or as old men or old women, or as people with glowing bodies, which I haven't ever seen myself.

The wisest being I ever encountered in a lucid dream was a little girl who seemed to be around the age of five. She communicated with me telepathically by touching her forehead to mine and saying, "Let's do the bunny hug." The moment our foreheads touched was one of the most powerful experiences of my life. I woke up crying and still get teary-eyed thinking about that superwise, supercompassionate, fully understanding "little girl" who blew my mind and my heart wide open. It seemed like she could see into every part of me, that she understood me completely and loved me very deeply.

Then there are those wise beings I've conversed with in my dreams and lucid dreams over the years whom I actually once knew as human beings when they were alive. Terence McKenna, Timothy Leary, and Oscar Janiger have all appeared numerous times in my dreams as wise, spiritually advanced beings who have shared revelations and insights with me about the nature of self, mind, reality, and death.

Maybe before we can understand what our dream characters are we need to first figure out who we are. Like the hookah-smoking caterpillar in Disney's animated adaptation of *Alice's Adventures in Wonderland,* we're forced to ponder that incessant rhetorical question: "Who . . . are . . . you?"

OH MY GOD, IT'S ME!

Sometimes people report seeing double or twin versions of a certain character within a lucid dream, that is, two figures of the same person. I've never experienced this, but I have had nonlucid dreams in which a person I know splits into two characters in the dream, like a dark and light version of the same individual. Sometimes we also encounter twin versions of ourselves in lucid dreams. For example, oneironaut Janice Brooks experienced "a stray double of herself [who] attempted to flee in terror when she wanted to round it up and merge with it."[12]

I have met a physical duplicate of myself in a lucid dream, but my experience was quite different from Brooks':

I was dreaming that I was walking across a city street, and I became lucid the moment that I saw a physical double of myself, slightly younger than my present self, walking out of a subway station or building entrance. I walked up to him immediately, fully lucid, and tried to think of what we could do. This was the first time I have ever seen a double of myself in a dream. As I examined his (i.e., my own) face, he grew slightly shorter and his face seemed to melt or morph a bit. Then I said, "Let's see if we can merge!" He was very cooperative but didn't speak a word. I hugged him and tried merging our two bodies into a single body, but we stayed separate. I very vividly felt the sensation of our skin touching, and then decided instead to see what it what be like to be sexual with "myself." I looked at my physical double and focused on how cute "he" looked. Then I started massaging my physical double's back, and soon we were sensuously kissing each other's necks, getting sexually aroused—when I awoke.

After having this dream I familiarized myself with the German term *doppelgänger,* which means "double walker," a physical duplicate of oneself. The word is taken from German fiction and folklore, where encountering one's doppelgänger is often seen as an omen of bad luck or a harbinger of approaching death. Having this lucid dream was like picking the Death card in the tarot and realizing that the seemingly chilling literal interpretation of physical death could in reality be referring to a positive transformation. In truth, the encounter with my doppelgänger never turned out to be an omen of bad luck at all, and my experience of meeting him was clearly positive, so I took the encounter to be a good omen in my life. After reading about all the people who died after seeing their doppelgänger, such as Percy Bysshe Shelley, I wonder if these tragedies weren't due to a lack of erotic connection between their twin psychic selves? During the course of writing this book I read about someone else who also had a positive sexual encounter with a doppelgänger in a lucid dream, so I'm not the only one to view this type of experience as more about transformation than tragedy.

According to dream scholar Ryan Hurd,

The doppelgänger encounter occurs in times of stress, at life's crossroads, and especially during times of emotional upheaval. They often carry messages and portents that the conscious mind does not want to hear. They can be insistent, angry, or stone cold in demeanor. Sometimes they know information that we simply did not have access to. This unsettling truth is unexplainable by the current paradigm of science.[13]

To add even more complication to the mystery of who we are both in our dreams and when awake, it's important to note that our sense of self in dreamscapes isn't always constant; it can shift.

ALTERNATING IDENTITIES AND ALTERED STATES

Our sense of identity in dreams isn't static; it can completely change form, it seems. I've had nonlucid dreams where I think about what someone else is thinking in the dream, and then suddenly I see the world from that person's perspective. This is a relatively common experience, I've learned. Consider the following examples of shifting identities in dreams and shamanic states of consciousness.

A friend described a nonlucid dream to me in which she kept repeatedly dying in different ways, and each time she died she would then keep waking up in the same bed, as a different person—different sex, age, and ethnicity. She would notice this as she walked by the mirror and saw her own reflection. I wondered if this might be a memory of the reincarnation process and was fascinated by her continual change of identities in the dream.

From his cross-cultural study of dreaming, Stanley Krippner describes the dream of a Brazilian woman that is a good example of how one's identity can shift within a dream:

> I dream that I see an Indian man who is running. He has a knife in his hand and is being chased by a leopard. I watch him fight with the leopard and am frightened. But then I stop being a witness and become the Indian in the exact moment that the leopard jumps on him. I think I wake up and recall the dream, but actually I am still in the dream. But this time I am the leopard, and I attack the Indian.[14]

One is reminded here of that famous story by the ancient Chinese philosopher Zhuangzi (Zhuang Zhou): "Once upon a time, I, Chuang Chou [Zhuang Zhou], dreamt I was a butterfly, fluttering hither and thither, a veritable butterfly, enjoying itself to the full of its bent, and not knowing it was Chuang Chou. Suddenly I awoke, and came to myself, the veritable Chuang Chou. Now I do not know whether it was then I dreamt I was a butterfly, or whether I am now a butterfly dreaming I am a man."[15]

The Marquis d'Hervey de Saint-Denys dreamed that he witnessed two people quarreling. Saint-Denys sided with one of them and thought of what he would say if he were in that person's place. Then, instantly, he became that other person in the dream.[16] After reading about Saint-Denys' experience I was reminded of the late Joseph Marty/Marty Joseph (described on his Amazon page as "a paranormal investigator, cartographer of altered states of consciousness and writer who explores the nature of reality and the psyche, parallel universes, and realms of existence beyond through a fusion of lucid dreaming/astral projection, mind technology and psychedelic mind-states"). As Zoe7, he writes about an experience that he had with a large dose of the dissociative hallucinogen dextromethorphan (DXM), "As I'm returning back to my home office I'm in for another surprise. 'I' am standing next to the recliner smiling at 'me' coming from the kitchen. In other words, there is a twin of 'me' looking back at me. This other 'me' looks so real, it's almost as though I am looking at my reflection in a mirror. But the instant I become startled by this particular occurrence, I become the 'me' that's standing next to the recliner, smiling at the thought of this episode, which has just popped into my mind!"[17]

Robert Waggoner describes a different kind of mind-blowing, identity-questioning lucid-dream encounter in his book *Lucid Dreaming*. In this encounter a lucid dreamer describes telling a dream character that she is a character in her dream. The dream character refuses to believe that she is a character in the dreamer's dream, and instead insists that the dreamer is a character in *her* dream. So finally the dreamer says, "Well, watch this," and she demonstrates her dream superpowers by flying around and doing other tricks. However, her dream character responds by doing the same thing, such that neither can influence the other's point of view.[18]

In the wonderful Japanese animated film *Paprika,* about lucid dreaming and dream-recording technologies, one lucid-dreaming character says to a character in her dream, "Why won't you listen? You're a part of me!" To which her dream character smugly responds, "Have you ever thought that maybe you're a part of me?"

I offer these thought-provoking reports of alternating identities to show that we're not always who we think we are in our dreams. Yet even more philosophically perplexing are the reports from people with multiple personality disorder.

MULTIPLE PERSONALITY DISORDER AND DREAMING

As noted in chapter 1, splitting the brain through surgery appears to split the mind as well. Even more bizarre are the symptoms of multiple personality disorder, or MPD (sometimes known as dissociative identity disorder). This psychiatric disorder is marked by severe dissociation, in which many separate selves reside within the same brain. MPD is caused by severe physical and/or emotional trauma at a very early age, an age so young that a unified personality never emerges from the brain as it develops. This disorder is debilitating and can even be life-threatening. Instead of a single, cohesive personality, the person develops a multitude of relatively independent personalities or "alters" that compete for control of the brain—from a few to many hundreds. Each personality functions almost like a unique person, with a consistent perspective and individual sense of self, complete with personal memories and even unique medical conditions, reactions to drugs, allergies, eye color, and perhaps most fascinating of all, independent dreams at night. When I worked as a psychiatric counselor in my twenties, the MPD patients with whom I worked confirmed this and told me that all of their alters had their own individual dreams. It really is a truly uncanny and mysterious phenomenon.

It genuinely seems like each alter in someone who suffers from MPD is a separate person. It really seems undeniable when one experiences this directly, but how can this possibly be? Is someone with MPD possessed by more spirits than the rest of us, or is this another case of splitting brains and slicing minds? Examining the mysteries of MPD really helps us get to the core questions of who we really are. The cause of this disorder is always due to severe and repeated physical, sexual, or emotional trauma prior to one's first birthday. I think that this early trauma prevents a consistent, integrated field of personality from organizing our brain's activity into a whole pattern, resulting in a myriad of competing states with only relative stability, each with cooperating functions. So personalities are created to be able to function in certain social situations and are called forth by an overseeing, organizing personality when needed, or by conditions of overwhelming stress.

Psychologist and dream researcher Deirdre Barrett says that "dream characters, at the very least, may be analogous to . . . (MPD) alters and other dissociated ego states." She sees the dreaming process as a way to help illuminate the mysteries of MPD, and she suggests that

> dreaming may . . . be a more literal precursor, whose physiological mechanisms for amnesia and projection of dissociated identities get recruited in the development of MPD. There are constellations of cognitive and personality processes that operate outside conscious awareness and normally are observable primarily in dreams. Extreme early trauma may mutate or overdevelop these dissociated parts and call upon them to "wake up" and function in the external world.[19]

So dreaming may help to explain MPD, but do people with MPD ever have lucid dreams? Yes, they do, but it's not always a pleasant experience, it seems. It appears that the alters can function as disruptive independent agents within the lucid dreams of people suffering from MPD. Consider the following report by someone with MPD:

> The first alter I ever met was in my dreams, and I did not know who or what it was. Since I was a child I would lucid dream, where you know

you are dreaming and you are aware that everything in your environment is you. However in my dreams, objects would show up, usually obstructive, that were not a part of "me." Like a teacup where one should not have been, or a windfall of trees over a road I was traveling on. I would remove or circumvent the offending obstacle or thing and go about my merry way dreaming until another bigger obstruction would appear. This would repeat with bigger and more obvious obstructions. The whole thing would culminate with an "entity" attacking me. This entity never looked the same but always had the same eyes. It was definitely not "me." It did not like to be seen and it hated "me" with a hatred I never imagined possible. I would wake up in sleep paralysis having gruesome hypnopompic hallucinations, and wondering what the hell had just happened. It was terrifying.[20]

Frightening lucid dreams like this one may not seem that surprising when one considers the history of severe trauma that results in this medical condition. However, I think there is much to be gleaned here that is relevant to anyone who dreams. I believe that MPD is an exaggerated condition that highlights neural dynamics that in reality we all share. In other words, everyone has multiple personalities—it's just that some people's personalities are more orderly than others, so for most people it's not a disorder. According to the late author Robert Anton Wilson, "One psychic told me I sometimes channel a medieval Irish bard; another told me I sometimes channel an ancient Chinese Taoist philosopher, an alchemist. I think every writer channels 'Entities' and I suspect we all have thousands of 'Entities' within each of us that can function as if they were independent spirits. I don't believe in the single ego. I think we have multiple egos and when one starts communicating we're likely to think it's the spirit of the dead or something like that, but it's just another part of ourselves."[21] Lucid dreams offer fertile ground for integrating the different "personalities" that comprise aspects of oneself that the person may not even be aware of.

Psychological treatment of MPD usually involves one of two methods: an attempt to integrate or unify the personalities, or an attempt to form a cooperative "community" among them. These also seem like good strategies for any of us to use in approaching a hostile or threatening figure in a lucid dream; it's also probably a good approach to take in encounters with noncorporeal beings during a psychedelic or out-of-body experience.

SHAMANIC ENCOUNTERS WITH SPIRIT ENTITIES, OR UNTAPPED REGIONS OF OUR OWN BRAINS?

We know that it is common for people to report experiences of spirit contact during ayahuasca journeys and other shamanic adventures. During these experiences it often seems like the presence of invisible entities can be felt, and that communications occur with these seemingly noncorporeal beings. It's also not unusual for people under the influence of ayahuasca or sacred mushrooms to believe that the spirit of the plant is scanning them, healing them, and communicating with them.

Ever since I first began exploring the far reaches of consciousness I've been intrigued by experiences with "the Other," the orchestrating intelligence behind our dreams, the voice of the ayahuasca or mushroom spirit, or the supposed communications from extraterrestrials, gods, angels, daemons, ghosts, or spirits that I've alluded to throughout this book. Pondering my own experiences of this nature brings on a flood of questions. Are these beings really independent from our minds? Are they different entities or the same one? If they're different, then are they connected to one another in some unimagined way? If they are independent from us, then where do they reside? How is it that these mysterious beings often know us better than we know ourselves? Are these spirits just aspects of our own unconscious minds? Could the brain have more than one conscious system? Are there limits to my cognitive abilities that prevent me from understanding this?

I've thought about these perplexing questions for many years and the whole matter is still as utterly mysterious as it ever was. However, when pressed, I'll admit that I suspect that this mysterious entity may actually be the right hemisphere of the brain, while the human ego, the miniaturized model of "I" in one's mind, is generally identified with the language-using, left hemisphere of the brain.

It seems (and the split-brain studies that we discussed in chapter 1 offer additional evidence) that the two hemispheres of the brain could actually be different people. We assume that the dominant left hemisphere—the part of us that talks and writes—is the totality of our being. But the nonverbal right hemisphere may have been silently observing us (the left hemisphere) since birth. Perhaps the right hemisphere may be able to observe the left hemisphere directly, but not vice versa? This might help to explain how intuitional nudges, dream messages, inspirations, and psychedelic insights occur—that is, from the left hemisphere's perspective.

The right hemisphere, our "subliminal twin,"* may communicate with the left hemisphere in the language of dreams, visions, and intuitions. I once had a psychedelic vision on a shamanic journey with magic mushrooms in which I saw my own brain from an elevated perspective. All of the folds and crevices of the two brain hemispheres subtly rearranged themselves into male and female forms, so that the two hemispheres were passionately making love to each other.

Reconnecting the fragmented or disconnected components of our personalities and uniting the polarizing forces within us is an important aspect of development in many spiritual and shamanic traditions. Unifying the male and female aspects of ourselves is a goal in many mystical traditions, from tantra to alchemy, and scientific studies suggest that people who tend to be more neuronally androgynous tend to have more lucid dreams.[22] As we become more whole and inclusive in our development, and we examine the ego-self from a more transcendent vantage point, it simply vanishes into the void, like Rumpelstiltskin, when we speak his name aloud.

---

*Subliminal Twin is video-performance artist Hana Theobald's clever stage name, which I think captures the mysterious relationship between the two brain hemispheres quite well.

SPEAKING ONE'S NAME OUT LOUD

P. D. Ouspensky wrote that it was impossible to say one's name aloud in a lucid dream:

> A man can never pronounce his own name in sleep. If I pronounced my name in sleep, I immediately woke up. And I understood that we do not realize that the knowledge of one's name for oneself is already a different degree of consciousness as compared with sleep. In sleep we are not aware of our own existence, we do not separate ourselves from the general picture which moves around us, but we, so to speak, move with it. Our "I" feeling is much more obscured in sleep than in a waking state. This is the chief psychological feature which determines the state of sleep and expresses the whole difference between sleep and waking state.[23]

Ouspensky offers an interesting train of thought here; nevertheless, I've certainly experienced a clear sense of "I" in my lucid dreams, and Stephen LaBerge claims to have spoken his name aloud in a lucid dream without physically awakening.[24] In fact, LaBerge says he had no trouble doing this and thought that others who do only did so because their beliefs set up unnecessary psychological constraints.

Psychologist Patricia Garfield experimented with carving her name in a lucid dream:

> In . . . "Carving My Name," I proceeded to do just that on the door where I was already carving. I read it and realized why Ouspensky . . . believed it is impossible to say one's name in a lucid dream: The whole atmosphere vibrated and thundered, and I woke. It's not impossible to say one's name in a lucid dream, but it may be disruptive if you expect it to be so.[25]

Although both LaBerge and Garfield say that they think others experienced this inability to articulate their name in lucid dreams due to their expectations, my experience with trying this has been fraught with unexpected challenges—and I had no knowledge of Ouspensky's idea about this when I first experienced an inability to voice my name out loud in a lucid dream. I've tried in many different lucid dreams to form some type of postdream connection with what seems to be fellow dreamers that I've met there, by trying to exchange our earthly names and contact information. So far, I've found this to be completely impossible, almost as though a law of physics in this other reality prevents me from doing so—although I've wondered if this could be related to my tendency to stutter as a child.

For some reason, I find it impossible to tell other characters I meet in a lucid dream that my name is David Jay Brown, or that I live in California, even though I can clearly think this while in the dream. Every time I've tried to, the words simply do not come out, and everyone else in the dream appears to have the same difficulty. In one lucid dream, when I was trying to exchange contact information with a fellow dream character, he suddenly got the bright idea to write it down on a piece of paper:

Brilliant, I thought! Why hadn't I thought of that? However, when he handed me the piece of paper and I looked at it, the letters were, of course, continuously changing, and they almost seemed to be mocking my frustrating attempt to understand them. I looked at the paper and saw a long string of strange and obscure, ever-shifting symbols—some in English, and some in what appeared to be alien hieroglyphics. However, at the end of the letters there was a comma followed by an "M.D." It was like some higher order of intelligence was preventing this type of exchange in the dream and even making fun of my attempt to do so.

Lucid dreams like this make me wonder—is information ever exchanged during a dream, or is it just processed and rearranged? Does dreaming involve intrapersonal or interpersonal communication, or both? In the next chapter we'll be exploring the possibility that a dream can be an interpersonal experience and that new information can be obtained.

8

DREAM TELEPATHY, PSYCHIC PHENOMENA, MUTUAL DREAMING, AND SHARED LUCID DREAMS

A dream you dream alone is only a dream. A dream you dream together is reality.

JOHN LENNON

Despite a commonly held belief in the reality of psychic phenomena among a majority of the general population, surprisingly few people are aware that there have been numerous, carefully controlled scientific experiments involving telepathy, psychokinesis, remote viewing, and other types of psychic phenomena, which have consistently produced compelling, statistically significant results that conventional science is at a loss to explain. Most scientists today are unaware of the substantial scientific evidence for psychic phenomena resulting from over a century of parapsychological research.

The reason why so few people are aware of these results, it seems, is due to a number of factors: the experimental effects are relatively small or modest; developments in the field have been rather slow and gradual; the mechanism behind the effects isn't well understood; a good portion of the research was initially conducted in secret; and uninformed critics of this kind of research have been outspoken about the supposed impossibility of the results. Perhaps also some people are frightened of the results because they imply that the boundaries between our minds are much fuzzier and less defined than we often think.

Nonetheless, hundreds of carefully controlled (and many times replicated) studies, in which psi researchers continuously redesigned experiments to address comments from their peers and critics, have produced results that demonstrate small but statistically significant effects for such psi phenomena as telepathy, precognition, and psychokinesis. This research demonstrates that the human mind can acquire information, seemingly without the mediation of the recognized human senses or the processes of logical inference.

According to psychologist Dean Radin, a meta-analysis of this research demonstrates that the positive results from these studies are significant, with odds in the order of many billions to one.[1] Princeton University, the Stanford Research Institute, Duke University, the Institute of Noetic Sciences, the U.S. and Russian governments, and many other respectable institutions have all spent years researching these mysterious phenomena, and conventional science is at a loss to explain the results. This research, which was originally published in numerous peer-reviewed scientific journals over the past century, is summarized in Radin's remarkable book *The Conscious Universe: The Scientific Truth of Psychic Phenomena*. Just as fascinating as the research into psychic phenomena is the controversy that surrounds it.

In my own experience working with British biologist Rupert Sheldrake in researching the possibility of telepathy in animals and other unexplained phenomena, I discovered that many people are eager to share personal anecdotes about their experiences with psychic phenomena like remarkable coincidences, uncanny premonitions, precognitive dreams, and seemingly telepathic communications. In these cases, the scientific studies simply confirm people's life experiences. However, many scientists with whom I've spoken with haven't reviewed the evidence and remain dubious that there is any reality to psychic phenomenon, mainly because the mechanism isn't understood. Nonetheless, surveys conducted by Sheldrake and myself reveal that around 78 percent of the population has had unexplainable psychic experiences, and scientific evidence supports the validity of these experiences.

Sheldrake views the reports of psychic phenomena as evidence for his morphic field theory. He defines a morphic field as "a field within and around a 'morphic unit' which organizes its characteristic structure and pattern of activity."[2] In physics, a field is defined as "a nonmaterial region of influence," and a morphic unit could be anything that changes form over time—a quartz crystal, a cannabis plant, a human being, a collective of human beings, a biosphere, a galaxy, a universe, or even the multiverse. A morphic field underlies the form and behavior of morphic units at all levels of complexity, Sheldrake says, and this term includes biological, behavioral, social, cultural, and mental fields.

Sheldrake thinks that these fields are shaped and stabilized by means of "morphic resonance" with similar, previous morphic units, which are themselves under the influence of fields of the same kind. In other words, every flower is resonating like a tuning fork with all of its previous botanical relatives. As a result, these fields contain a kind of cumulative memory and tend to become increasingly habitual, so that the more frequently something happened in the past, the more likely it is to happen in the future.

When I asked Sheldrake if he thought that there is a morphic field for dreams, mystical experiences, and other states of consciousness, he replied,

> I think that any organized structure of activity—which includes dreams and some mystical experiences, and altered states of consciousness—any pattern of activity has a structure, and insofar as these mental activities or states have structures, then these structures could indeed move from person to person by morphic resonance. And indeed, in many mystical traditions it's thought that

through initiation people are brought into that particular tradition and resonate, or in some sense enter into communion with, or connection with, other people who followed in the tradition before. So in Hindu and Buddhist lineages you often get the idea that through initiation and the transmission of the right mantras and so on, the initiate comes into contact with the guru, the teacher, and the whole line of those who've gone before. There is a similar idea in Christianity, the idea of the communion of saints. Those who participate in the Christian sacraments, particularly the Eucharist, are in contact, not just with other people doing it now, or other people who happen to be around, but somehow in some kind of resonant connection with all those who've done the same thing before.

As we're learning in this book, there is an important link between dreams, mystical experiences, and psychic phenomena. Many case reports of paranormal events occur while the person is in some kind of altered state of consciousness, like a psychedelic experience or a dream.

PSYCHEDELIC EXPERIENCES AND PSYCHIC PHENOMENA

Many people report experiencing meaningful psychic experiences with psychedelic drugs, not to mention a wide range of paranormal events and synchronicities that seem extremely difficult to explain by means of conventional reasoning. A questionnaire study of 150 experienced marijuana users conducted by psychologist Charles Tart found that 76 percent believed in extrasensory perception (ESP), with frequent reports of experiences while high that were interpreted as psychic.

Psychiatrist Stanislav Grof and psychologist Stanley Krippner have collected numerous anecdotes about psychic phenomena that were reported by people under the influence of psychedelic drugs, and several small scientific studies have looked at how LSD, psilocybin, and mescaline might affect telepathy and remote viewing. For example, psychologist Jean Millay told me that in 1997, students at the University of Amsterdam in the Netherlands did research to establish whether or not the use of psilocybin could influence remote viewing. This was a small experiment, with only twelve test subjects, but the results of the study indicated that those who were under the influence of psilocybin achieved a success rate of 58.3 percent, which was statistically significant.[3]

A good source of information about the relationship between psychedelics and psychic phenomena is the new edition of the 1964 book *ESP Experiments With LSD-25 and Psilocybin: A Methodological Approach,* by Roberto Cavanna and Emilio Servadio, which was republished in 2010, with a preface by Charles Tart. In the preface Tart states that, "this study remains as important today as when it was first published."

In a classic episode of an early black-and-white television show about extrasensory perception called *One Step Beyond,* which aired from 1959 to 1961, host John Newland eats two psychedelic mushrooms and performs extraordinarily well in a series of experiments designed to test his telepathic and clairvoyant abilities. The episode is called "The Sacred Mushroom," and it can be found on YouTube.

A great review article by Stanley Krippner and psychologist David Luke, which summarizes all of the psychedelic research into psychic phenomena, can be found in the Spring 2011 *MAPS Bulletin* that I edited, about psychedelics and the mind-body connection.[4]

When I conducted the California-based research for Rupert Sheldrake's book about unexplained phenomena in science, *The Sense of Being Stared At,* one of the experiments that I ran involved testing blindfolded subjects to see if they could sense being stared at from behind. A particular person with whom I worked reported an unusually high number of correct trials while under the influence of MDMA. I'd love to run a whole study to see if MDMA-sensitized subjects are more aware of when they're being stared at.

It is especially common for people to report experiences with telepathy, clairvoyance, precognition, remote viewing, and psychokinesis while using ayahuasca. In fact (as I mentioned in chapter 5), when the chemical structure of an important psychoactive component of ayahuasca was first discovered, now called "harmaline," one of the original suggestions for its name was "telepathine," due to the psychedelic brew's common association with telepathy.

There have only been several studies with ayahuasca that also demonstrate certain health benefits, but this is an area that is just crying out to be explored carefully and in depth. Future studies with ayahuasca could examine its potential and accuracy as a catalyst for psychic phenomena. All of the traditional studies that have been done with psychic phenomena that have generated positive results could be redone with subjects dosed with different psychedelic drugs or hallucinogenic plants to see if test scores can be measurably improved. In any case, increasing our psychic abilities may open the human mind up to new, unimagined possibilities—and it appears that we can all do this when we dream.

DREAM TELEPATHY RESEARCH

In 1886, early psychic researchers Edmund F. Gurney, Frederic W. H. Myers,* and Frank Podmore, of the British Society for Psychical Research, collected 1,300 pages (two volumes) of case histories from people who had experiences with psychic or unexplained phenomena. This massive collection is a gold mine of rare information. Of these many case histories, 149 of them were about "dream telepathy."

However, despite these many cases, the authors remarked, "Millions of people are dreaming every night, if anywhere the range of possibilities seems infinite. Can any possible conclusion be drawn from such chaos of meaningless and fragmentary impressions?"[5] Indeed, it's like the proverbial search for matching needles in a monster haystack. "For this reason," psychologist Stanley Krippner says of these early investigations, "it was necessary to develop research strategies that would address the questions of coincidence and chance."[6] And that's exactly what he and his colleagues did.

Compelling evidence for the notion that people can transfer

---

*Frederic W. H. Myers died in 1901, and two years after his death his book *Human Personality and Its Survival of Bodily Death* was published.

thoughts or mental imagery to someone who is dreaming comes from research done in the 1960s and 1970s by Krippner and psychiatrist Montague Ullman at the Maimonides Medical Center's dream laboratory in Brooklyn, New York. There they performed thirteen formal experiments and three groups of pilot studies over a decade. A wide range of experimental procedures were tried during these studies. In one of their repeated experimental designs the researchers had subjects sleep in a sound-proof room while wired to EEG monitors. Lab assistants carefully observed the brain waves of the sleeping subjects, and when they saw that a subject had entered into REM sleep they immediately alerted a participant in the study who would act as a telepathic sender. That person would then mentally focus on the target photo, which was randomly selected from hundreds of classic art reproductions. Ten minutes later, the lab assistant would wake up the subject via an intercom and ask the person to describe any dreams that he or she had just had. Additionally, in the morning, the subject would then be asked to guess which one of eight possible photos was the target image based on the content of their dreams from the previous night.

Remarkably, the results from this study were reviewed by independent judges, who declared them to be statistically significant about two thirds of the time, with the statistical odds of twenty-two billion to one that this occurred by chance. This means that the subjects could correctly identify target materials much more often than would be expected by chance by using dream content. According to Krippner, the target photo material appeared to be incorporated into dreams in a manner that was "similar to the ways that day residue, psychodynamic process, and subliminally perceived stimuli find their way into dream content. Sometimes the material corresponding to targets is intrusive . . . and sometimes it blends easily with the narrative. . . . At times, it is the central focus of the dream . . . at others, it is peripheral. . . . It can be either direct . . . or symbolic."[7]

Weather conditions, oddly enough, seemed to have an effect on these results. As part of this investigation, neuroscience researcher Michael Persinger ran a correlation between the accuracy of the subjects reporting dream imagery that matched the chosen art print images and the weather conditions during each telepathy experiment. Persinger found that the accuracy increased on relatively calm nights with little sunspot activity, compared to nights marked by electrical storms and high sunspot activity.[8]

If the subject of dream telepathy in general interests you, then the book that Krippner and Ullman coauthored on the subject, *Dream Telepathy: Experiments in Nocturnal Extrasensory Perception*, is essential reading.

Krippner also conducted a pilot study in dream telepathy using entire audiences at rock concerts as telepathic senders to investigate the possibility that a large number of people might be effective in facilitating dream telepathy. As a preliminary study in 1970, the entire audience at a Holy Modal Rounders rock concert served as telepathic senders, and five volunteers who were each located within a hundred-mile radius of the concert location in New York City served as telepathic receivers.

Fig. 8.1. Psychologist Stanley Krippner (photo courtesy of Dr. Stuart Fischer)

The audience was instructed to visualize different birds from around the world, as well as the mythological phoenix, and there were some intriguing responses from the receivers that suggested results were above chance. This preliminary research inspired a six-night pilot study involving the Grateful Dead and their audiences in 1970. Two receivers at the Maimonides Dream Laboratory in Brooklyn were hooked up to EEG monitors, and they were awakened right after REM periods, whereupon images that consisted of randomly selected paintings projected onto a large screen in front of the audience were telepathically sent by the audience at the concert to the receivers. When independent observers examined the dream reports and paired painting selections, there was a significant success rate in one of the two subjects.[9]

There have been a number of attempts to replicate Krippner and Ullman's research at the Maimonides Dream Laboratory, although the procedures and the results have been inconsistent.

Psychologists Simon Sherwood and Chris Roe at the University of Northampton in England reviewed all of the home-based studies that attempted to replicate Krippner and Ullman's research up to 2003. In these studies, subjects slept at home and were not awakened directly after REM. Although the results of these studies were much less robust than Krippner and Ullman's work, they nevertheless demonstrated some degree of effect unexplainable by conventional science.[10] The authors of these studies concluded:

> Combined effect size estimates for both sets of studies . . . suggest that judges could correctly identify target materials more often than would be expected by chance using dream mentation. Maimonides studies were significantly more successful . . . than post-Maimonides studies, which may be due to procedural differences, including that post-Maimonides receivers tended to sleep at home and were generally not deliberately awakened from REM sleep. . . . Nevertheless, home dream ESP research has been successful and continues to be a less expensive and less labor-intensive alternative to sleep-laboratory-based research.[11]

A study conducted in 2013 by psychologist Carlyle Smith at Trent University, in Canada, collected data that seemed to suggest that people can intentionally dream details about the personal problems of an unknown person simply by examining a picture of the target and then "incubating" or planning to dream about that person's problems.[12]

Evidence and anecdotes suggest that one can become receptive to information during sleep in ways that conventional science is at a loss to explain, but is it really possible to discover previously unknown knowledge in one's dreams?

CAN PSYCHIC DREAMS REVEAL NEW INFORMATION?

Stanley Krippner and colleagues report on a fascinating dream by a woman named Dolores, who dreamed that she heard a knock at the door, and when she went to answer it she saw a strange, shadowy man there whose face was concealed. The mysterious man simply said, "I want to sleep here tonight." Dolores didn't open the door, got nervous, went upstairs, and telephoned the emergency operator for help. However, to her surprise, as she heard the would-be intruder going around her house, trying to open up the locked doors, the emergency operator said, "Oh yes, we know who he is. His name is Nisrock." Several days after this dream, Dolores found herself in a library, where she randomly opened up a book and read the caption: "Nisrock, the winged Babylonian god who takes the souls of dreamers to the place of the dream."[13]

Was this just a random coincidence or a forgotten memory? Did Dolores's dreaming mind retrieve the name Nisrock out of the collective unconscious? Or did she have a precognitive dream? What about the famous historical example of President Abraham Lincoln's seemingly precognitive dream in 1865? A week before his assassination, Lincoln supposedly had a dream in which he saw people gathered around a corpse in the White House, and some people were crying. In the dream Lincoln inquired as to who the dead person was, and a soldier replied, "the president. He was killed by assassination."[14]

Could dreams like these really be predicting the future, or are they just illusory coincidences occurring from a post hoc perspective? Some people think that precognitive dreams are occurring all the time, we just forget them, and that this could help to explain the uncanny sense of déjà vu that we sometimes experience.[15] Perhaps when we recognize some place or situation as being familiar, even though we've never encountered it before in waking life, this is because we've already seen it in our dreams.

It appears that different parts of our bodies may actually contain memories and information that can influence our dreams. There are cases where the dreams of people who have had organ transplants provided the recipients of the organs with uncanny knowledge of the donor's name, appearance, as well as some of their behaviors.[16]

In more than a few cases it appears difficult to distinguish whether a psychic influence in a dream could be the result of telepathic, precognitive, or clairvoyant factors, but there is scientific evidence to suggest that the human brain is capable of precognition, so it's not inconceivable to think that premonitions about future events could influence our dreams. For example, psychologist Dean Radin did a series of fascinating experiments that comprise what he calls "presentiment research," and these investigations provide compelling scientific evidence for precognition. Radin had his subjects hooked up to a galvanic skin-response measuring device, which records changes in the electrical conductivity of the skin. This has been correlated with strong emotional reactions and is the basis for using polygraph tests as a method of measuring honesty and detecting lies. Radin's subjects were seated in front of a computer screen, which randomly displayed a series of photographic images. The majority of these images were emotionally neutral or pleasant, such as images of natural scenery or smiling people. However, some of the images were inserted specifically because of their ability to shock people—such as sexually explicit photos or images with disturbing violence—and these were randomly interspersed with the neutral and pleasant scenes. As expected, when the subjects saw a shocking image, there was a significant shift in their electrical skin conductivity.

Notably, however, the spike in skin conductivity began several seconds before the subject actually viewed the shocking image. Somehow the body already knew what to expect before the person actually saw the image on the computer screen.[17] Furthermore, these results have been independently replicated in labs around the world.

Even crazier and more mysterious than the presentiment research is the study that reveals how our brains can predict the reactions of our conscious minds before we make decisions.[18] In one study, researchers at the Max Planck Institute for Human Cognitive and Brain Sciences demonstrated that our individual choices and decisions are actually made by our brains seven seconds before we become consciously aware of the choices and decisions. Subjects could freely decide if they wanted to press a button with their right or left hand; the only condition was that they had to recall when they made the decision to use that particular hand. The researchers scanned the brains of these subjects using fMRI machines while this decision-making process was occurring, to see if they could predict which hand the participants would use before they were consciously aware of making the decision. By monitoring micropatterns of activity in the frontopolar cortex, the researchers discovered that they could predict which hand the participant would choose a full seven seconds before the subject was mindfully aware of the decision. However one interprets these mysterious results, they appear to require a revision in what we regularly refer to as "free-will."

In any case, according to anthropologist Charles Laughlin, the view that the soul may leave the body during sleep is very common cross-culturally, as is the view "that useful information may be accrued during the wanderings and adventures of the soul."[19]

I once had a lucid dream in which I was dancing with an elfish blonde-haired woman who seemed very similar in appearance and personality to a woman I met for the first time two days later. When I met her, she seemed instantly familiar from my dream. The Hebrew Bible contains fifteen prophetic dreams, and almost everyone has at least heard of people having psychic dreams of some sort. Many people report some type of seemingly precognitive dreaming, or of having dreams about events before they happen or as they are occurring. This type of dream is actually a fairly common occurrence. In two studies, groups in Virginia were asked, "Have you ever had a rather clear and specific dream that matched in detail an event during or after your dream, and that you did not know about or did not expect at the time of the dream?" In each group, 36 and 38 percent of the subjects replied affirmatively.[20] Around a third of the precognitive dreams in these studies were confirmed within twenty-four hours. Other surveys suggest that more than 50 percent of the general population reports experiencing at least one precognitive dream.[21] But were these confirmations due to the brain's ability to create good models for estimating the future, or can dreams genuinely reveal something that wasn't previously known to the dreamer?

Dreams collected from numerous people prior to large-scale disasters could provide clues. According to Ryan Hurd, "It's well known in psychotherapeutic circles that many clients dreamed of the Twin Towers falling down right before September 11, 2001, when the United States suffered its greatest terrorist attack."[22] Rupert Sheldrake collected a number of stories from people who had seemingly precognitive dreams of the 9/11 attack for his book *The Sense of Being Stared At*. In fact, my own brother, Steven Ray Brown, who was living in Manhattan at the time of the attacks, told Sheldrake that on the morning of September 11, 2001, he dreamed he was "in the stairwell of the World Trade Center with a lot of people trying to get out."[23]

While working on his Ph.D., Keith Hearne ran two experimental trials to see if he could telepathically communicate a four-digit number to his subject while he was having a lucid dream in his sleep laboratory. While neither trial produced a direct hit, the second trial produced three out of the four digits, although in the opposite sequence.[24]

Oliver Fox writes about using the opportunity in a lucid dream to review the college exam that he was scheduled to take the next day:

> On the eve of sitting for an examination in machine construction, I willed to dream of seeing the paper that would be set. I dreamed that I was taking the examination, and knowing that I was dreaming,

attempted to memorize the questions upon the paper. On awakening, I remembered two: (1) Sketch and describe some form of steam-separator. (2) Sketch a grease-box suitable for a goods-truck. The next day, when I actually took the examination, I found both these questions upon the paper. They did not appear as complete questions by themselves, but were sections of others. The first was a likely question; but a perusal of past papers (made after the dream) showed that the second question had not been asked for many years.[25]

Fox goes on to say that he would have been able to bring more questions back had reading in the dream not been so difficult. He describes how the letters blurred together, faded away, or changed when he tried to read them, and grasping one letter at a time took great mental effort and focused concentration.

Now consider the following experience, personally reported to me by my friend Ian Koslow:

It was my freshman year at the University of Florida when I had my first lucid-dream experience. When I realized this was a real thing that people all over the world practiced, I was extremely excited and became almost obsessed with it in the sense that I was talking about it all the time and telling everyone about it. This led to a conversation with a friend in my dormitory who was interested in this concept, and we would excitedly talk about the implications and experiments one could do while in a lucid dream. We were interested and curious to know if the "dream characters" one interacts with in a lucid dream had any reality to them, or if they were just mental projections of the dreamer. We wanted to come up with an experiment, so I asked my friend if there was anything about her that I didn't know but might be able to discover in a dream, which could then be verified. She told me that she had a freckle somewhere on her back, just one, so I could find her in a lucid dream and see if it was there. The next time I was in my dorm room and I achieved lucidity, I instantly remembered the experiment and set out to find her. While in the hallway, a friend (someone who had heard me telling people about lucid dreaming and doubted its validity) approached me and began shouting, which woke me up. The following time I achieved lucidity, also while in my "lucid dorm room," I remembered the experiment, except this time I decided I would intend for her to enter my room, which she did. She came over to me and I lifted her shirt to reveal her back. There, dead center, right above her buttocks was a lone freckle. I remember thinking that was very interesting but I didn't think it could possibly be in the right location, I guess, because of how central it was (also because for whatever reason when I imagined where it might be I had a feeling it was on the side). When I woke up from the dream I ran straight to her dorm room and told her I had found the freckle. We were both very excited. She approached me and I put my finger right where it had been in the dream on her back and then lifted her shirt. We both couldn't believe it; my finger was on the freckle.

Ian also sent me the freckled girl's account of what happened:

The freckle story—I remember it like this: we were talking about lucid dreaming, and if the people you meet in your dreams were real—or if our brain processes everything (we see through clothes) but we just access specific parts of the brain, so we don't realize we see everything . . . and so we said that you were going to try to find a freckle of mine. A few weeks go by, and you came to my dorm room and said you thought you had found it—and you were convinced there was no way you could be right. And then you put your finger right over it.

Were these lucky coincidences or genuine psychic perceptions? Regardless, it appears that telling psychic dreams to the wrong people can get you into big trouble. Stanley Krippner describes a situation where someone named Steve Linscott dreamed about a gruesome murder in 1980 that seemed to weirdly correspond with an actual murder that night in a nearby apartment building. When he was encouraged by friends to tell the police about his dream, they actually arrested him for knowing too many accurate details and after the initial trial he was put in prison with a forty-year sentence. Luckily, appeals by his defense attorney were successful in liberating this misunderstood psychic dreamer.[26]

Some people consider precognitive dreams to be more of a warning or a possibility that could be avoided, rather than a window into a distant location or the future. Krippner suggests that "a precognitive dream may represent a premonition; it may give one a chance to actually change the future, as if the dreamed events do not have to happen or can be modified in some way. In other words, some precognitive dreams appear to represent mutable premonitions (warnings) rather than immutable 'destiny' over which one does not seem to have much control."[27]

Although studies have demonstrated compelling evidence for precognition, conducting scientific research on precognitive dreams is pretty tricky, as they seem so unpredictable. However, a most fascinating dream clairvoyance project is currently underway.

SHADOW AND THE QUANTIFICATION OF DREAMS

The world's largest dream clairvoyance experiment is currently in progress and anyone is welcome to participate. Dream researchers Hunter Lee Soik and Jason Carvalho have created an iPhone app called Shadow that allows us to quantify our dreams. According to Soik, "Shadow is the world's first alarm clock that helps people remember and record their dreams. It transcribes your dreams, pulls out the keywords, strips away any data that could identify you, and pushes it to a giant global data cloud—where other Shadow users can see global dream patterns and find dreamers like them around the world."[28] Soik's project is an extraordinary opportunity to gain insight into the collective dreaming mind on our planet. At any given moment, half the world is sleeping and dreaming, and we spend a third of our lives in this mysterious state of consciousness, yet most of this valuable information is quickly forgotten. The Shadow app helps to capture these dreams before they fade, while they're still fresh in our minds. It works like this: After a gradual awakening, with escalating volume and vibration, the app records your dreams in a digital journal, by voice or by typing text. Then the report is entered into a global database that allows for thousands of time-stamped transcripts to be searched through by keywords. The idea behind this ingenious project is that clairvoyance could be identified through specific keyword spikes before a major event.*

But perhaps even more intriguing than the possibilities of tele- pathic, clairvoyant, and precognitive dreams is the notion that two or more people can share the same dream.

MUTUAL DREAMS

Some people report sharing dreams with other people—both lucid and nonlucid. Although the details are subject to different interpretations, it really does seem that is possible for two or more people to share the same content of their dreams around the same time.

Shared dreams have been recorded throughout history. The Assryian king Assurbanipal and his priests reported a mutual dream in the sev- enth century BCE. The king was interested in his dreams and he recorded them in a journal. One morning he and his priests claimed to have shared the same dream, which involved inspiration from the god- dess Ishtar. Apparently the goddess rose before them in this collective dream and promised to lead them into battle. This historical dream sup- posedly encouraged the king's army to fight more valiantly and win the battle.[29] Carlos Castaneda claimed that Mexican Toltec shamans taught him techniques for achieving mutual lucid dreams as part of his appren- ticeship.[30] And sometimes closely bonded people in a group setting will report experiencing the same closed-eyed visions on ayahuasca, magic mushrooms, and other psychedelics. I've personally had this kind of experience while tripping with girlfriends. We would describe the same visions as we were experiencing them, and had some uncannily similar, seemingly shared, lucid-dream-like experiences on ketamine journeys.

---

*To learn more about Shadow and to participate in the project, see www.discovershadow .com.

When I interviewed Robert Waggoner, he told me about a mutual dream that he experienced while in college:

One night I dreamed that I went to one of the suites in my dormitory, where each suite had five single rooms, with five people living there. This was in a particular women's suite. I made love to each of the women in this dorm suite, all of whom I knew in waking life. I remember the final one to whom I made love, who was actually the most attractive of the five. She told me how unworthy and unloveable she felt. And even though we were making love, in another way it was more of a heart sharing, it wasn't some physical act, it was much more of a deep kind of heart-sharing spiritual engagement. Anyway, when I woke up in the morning I thought, Wow that was a strange dream. *And as I was walking to class that day, one of my friends yelled out across campus, "Hey Romeo!" He was shouting at me. And I asked him why he would call me Romeo, and he said in that dorm suite two of the five women remembered that night I had come to them in the dream state and made love with them. So that just totally stunned me. And being a young guy from Kansas, I was embarrassed that my dreaming self had gone out there and done that, and two women had reported it. So that was my first experience with a mutual dream, which three people—the two women, and myself—recalled. We remembered the same fundamental experience. Now when it gets to lucid dreaming, you're consciously aware, and you have the capacity to either seek out other dreamers and try to help them become lucidly aware, or somehow engage their dream. So in my book I have various experiences where lucid dreamers have claimed to have done that.*

However, when I spoke with Stephen LaBerge, he was somewhat skeptical of the phenomenon of mutual dreams:

I haven't really experimented with that. I consider it to be theoretically possible, but it's not something that I felt was of developmental value first of all. There are many aspects of dream control that I haven't pursued. I've emphasized instead controlling myself and my responses to what happens instead of making it magically different, because I've wanted something that would generalize to the waking state. In this world we don't have the power to magically make other people appear and disappear. There have been a few people who've said, "I can visit you in your dream," and I've said, "Okay, do so." But I've never experienced an unequivocal success that I remember. I think the problem is that we tend to bring mental models from the waking state into the dream state. So we have expectations in the dream, especially in a lucid dream. Here it is, it's all so real, and hey, you two people look perfectly real to me so you'll remember this conversation later, right? Now why would I think you'd do that, any more than I would think this table would remember this conversation? One of the things you have to do in developing skill with lucid dreaming is to be critical of your state of mind. So you wake up from a lucid dream and you think, *Did I make some assumptions that were inappropriate or do something that didn't make sense?* So you can therefore refine and clarify your thinking and build up mental models that are appropriate to the dream world. I dreamed in a lucid dream that I was flying above the San Francisco Bay, and I had the thought, *My body is asleep over there, I'll go visit it.* And I woke up and said, "What? This is a dream! Your body's not in there or you'd be in trouble if your body's asleep in your own dream, how could you wake up?" People who don't make that extra effort don't tend to learn.

Nonetheless, dream researcher Linda Lane Magallon has collected dozens of reliable, mutually verifiable reports from people who say that they have shared dreams in some form or another.[31] Magallon distinguishes between mutual dreams, which occur when two or more people have similar dreams on the same night, and shared dreams, which she says occur when two or more people dream of one another in a common place and time, and independently recall similar details from the dream. However, in this book I (and others) don't make this distinction and use the two words interchangeably. Some people report meeting in nonlucid dreams; others report having uncannily similar "meshing" dreams, which according to Magallon involve sharing the same dream plots with another dreamer without seeing one another. And there are groups of advanced lucid dreamers all over the world that are informally attempting to meet in their dreams, and are having a compelling degree of success. According to Magallon, often all that is necessary to have a shared dream is the mutual intention to do so. But shared dreaming, especially shared lucid dreaming, is an elusive phenomenon, Waggoner told me:

> Shared dreams seem to be one of the most fascinating areas of dreaming and lucid dreaming. But of all the experiences that a person can seek out and try to have, I think they seem like some of the most elusive. These are hard to achieve even for experienced lucid dreamers. What's most likely to happen is that one lucid dreamer becomes lucidly aware and then interacts with another dreamer, and gets some information.

My friend Milo in Connecticut e-mailed me accounts of two dreams that he seemed to have shared with his girlfriend. He said they both "discussed it in depth immediately after it happened." The night before the second of the two shared dreams, Milo said, "I remember making eye contact with my girlfriend before going to sleep that night. I recall it so clearly because it was that rare kind of eye contact where it feels like you can touch each other. I still have the image of her huge black pupils, and the sensation of being engulfed, or slipping toward falling, immediately before the light went out." Milo goes on to describe the dreams that they both seem to have shared, in terms of concurrent content (Milo wasn't actually present in her dream, although she was in his). For each, the dream occurred in a large barn, where they were covertly working to thread a rope through a pulley system in order to hoist stuff up to protect a small pack of puppies. In their dream they also each encountered his girlfriend's brother, whom Milo hadn't previously met, and his physical appearance in the dream matched his physical appearance when Milo actually met him later.

I've personally had experiences with transpersonal dreaming on a number of occasions. The first time I experienced this was as a child. My brother and I both recall having a mutual nonlucid dream during childhood. My brother was around the age of four and I was around seven. We often woke up before our parents did and enjoyed imaginative role-playing games in which we would pretend to be different characters. One morning we began telling each other about the dreams that we had had the night before, and after a few sentences of going back and forth with our descriptions, we became convinced that we had shared the same dream. Many of the details are now forgotten, but I vividly recall that the dream took place aboard a spaceship; my brother was there, and my grandmother, with birthday cake in her hair.

During the writing of this book I experimented with the possibility of sharing lucid dreams with my girlfriend, Becca, and with others:

> I was in a classroom, and the instructor was handing out these forms. I looked at the first two questions on the form, and the instructions were so complex that I couldn't figure out what to write. Becca was sitting next to me, at another desk, and she had no trouble filling out the forms. It wasn't a test, just a form, but the questions were just too complex, with weird mathematical equations and obscure references in them. I tried to explain to the instructor that I couldn't understand the questions on the form, when I awoke. Then, upon awakening, Becca reported her dream to me, where she described us as being at desks in a classroom together. She said, "The dream was that you were, at first, teaching me how to write better, because I wasn't good with my punctuation, but for some reason in the dream I couldn't comprehend anything you were saying. You would be telling me one thing, and I'd do the complete opposite." I found it telling that we both had dreams of being in a classroom together, that we both had difficulty understanding what was going on, and that we both saw each other as understanding things better than ourselves.

Becca sent me the following report of visiting me in a lucid dream that she had one night when we were apart. Unfortunately, I have no memory of this, despite the fact that she did her best to rouse me in her lucid dream:

I had to find David, my love! . . . Then I saw him. . . . I was so thrilled! . . . I ran up to him and he suddenly changed once I was up close. It was David, but it was like he was motionless. I remember saying "Hey! David, its Becca! Can you see me? Are you dreaming? Why don't you look happy to see me? What's the matter? Is that really you?" I couldn't control myself; I had so many questions. After receiving nothing but a smile and a few laughs in return for so many of my questions, I felt a little unsure of what to do next. I figured since I was in a dream I would take advantage of the situation. I took his hand and I could feel the warmth of it. He held on tightly to my hand, to my surprise. I remember getting on my tiptoes and kissing him . . . he kissed me back! It felt so real. . . . But why wasn't he talking? He wasn't saying anything at all, yet he was going along with anything I did physically to his body. . . . He was mimicking me. I thought, This is just my imagination, that's why. *I looked at him and I remember seeing his eyes. . . . When I looked deep into his eyes, I saw myself. I saw how perfectly happy I was. I wanted to do so much with him. I had a crazy thought to have sex on the moon with him. I figured if I was dreaming then it was possible. I asked him "Do you want to go to the moon with me?" He replied, "Should we go to the moon?" My heart felt like it skipped a beat! He talked and he sounds just like he does in waking life. Still holding hands, we walked down this road and I was thinking,* How in the world are we going to get to the moon? *The more we walked, the darker it got outside. I couldn't wait any longer. I stopped and turned to face him. I let go of his hand and unzipped his pants. I got down on my knees and started giving him oral. I remember the feeling of excitement and I felt like I was getting wetter and wetter. As I was giving him oral sex, I took both of his hands and leaned him down toward me. He sat down on the pavement. . . . I remember getting on top of him, and as soon as his penis entered me, we ended up on the moon. It was bright and not what I was expecting. I saw no stars, nothing. I just knew we were on the moon. I was trying to focus on David, but my mind started to wonder.* How am I going to get off *of the moon? Why isn't David talking? If I can make his penis hard, then why doesn't he want to talk now? What if he really knows that I'm taking advantage of him in this dream? The more I thought about these things, the softer his penis got. Oh my goodness, can he hear my thoughts? Next thing I knew, the moon we were on turned into some type of cardboard image of the moon, and we were on this stage. I was fully clothed. I ran up to the front of the stage and saw no one in the crowd. I only saw bright lights. I then turned around to get David, and he was gone.*

The puppetlike way that my physical double responded in Becca's dream, with such low levels of awareness, is typical of how many lucid dreamers report shared dream encounters with other dreamers (appearing in their dreams), who they suspect haven't achieved lucidity.* It's also how Becca, in her dream body, responded to me in one of my lucid dreams, when we were making out together, without her saying a word and just politely cooperating with my advances.

So when a person in a lucid dream encounters a partner in a zombie-like state, seemingly sleepwalking, the idea is to help wake the person up and achieve lucidity within the dream. You'd think that having the most beautiful woman in the world wrap her dream lips around my penis would be enough to rouse me, but apparently it's not so easy to awaken a slumbering, unconscious dreamer in a lucid dream—that is, if this isn't all just happening in one's imagination.

Further experiments with Becca brought more seemingly shared dreams, where one or the other of us would become lucid. For instance, I had a lucid dream where we were dancing together erotically and acrobatically in a large, low-gravity room, while she had a nonlucid dream that night where we were splashing paint around, playfully wrestling and tickling each other in a large spacious room. In both dreams we were alone together in a large open room, doing something creative and fun with our bodies.

---

*Noteworthy also are the similarities between this dream version of me that Becca encountered and the mute and easily cooperative physical duplicate of myself that I once encountered in a lucid dream, which I described in chapter 7.

During a period several years earlier, when I had a different partner and was attempting to share lucid dreams regularly, there was one experience that stood out as a distinct possibility:

One morning I found myself walking around in my bathroom with my lucid-dreaming partner and I noticed that there were bookcases lining the walls. Since there are no bookcases in my bathroom, I realized that I must be dreaming. I got excited, immediately turned to her and said, "Wow, we did it—we're in a lucid dream together! Do you think you'll remember?" She replied that she wasn't sure, and then the dream began to fade. "Oh please remember," I pleaded. "Look at your hands!" I said, "look at your hands and try to remember!" Then the dream faded and I woke up.

I looked at the clock. It was 9:10 a.m. and I immediately e-mailed my friend. Her response arrived a few hours later. Unfortunately, she didn't have any memory of the dream. However, she had been up in the early morning and had then gone back to bed at 8:30 a.m., with the specific intention to dream lucidly, which I didn't know. Although she didn't recall the dream that I had, she was asleep at the time, and with the intention of having a lucid dream, and she didn't recall any other dream during that time period either. So maybe we did share this dream, and it wasn't encoded in her conscious memory. When I asked her in the dream to try to remember, she said she wasn't sure if she would remember it or not; later she confirmed to me that this was indeed what she would have said.

Oliver Fox famously described an attempt to meet up with two other friends in a lucid-dream experiment. Fox and one of his friends appeared to share memories of a dream meeting that night, but there was no sign of the third friend, who, they discovered, had no memory of dreaming that night.[32]

Curiously, since I began this project, a number of people have reported having shared dreams with *me*. I've received around a half-dozen reports from people I know online who say that they've personally sought me out—and found me—in their lucid dreams. I have no memory of any of these experiences, but find them most intriguing, and I encourage people to keep trying.

I asked the question "Have you ever had a shared lucid dream?" on my Facebook page and received some striking responses, such as this one, from Chris Topher Moule:

I shared a dream with another person, but it wasn't lucid. During this time (summer of 2007) I was recording my dreams in a notebook immediately upon awakening so that I could recognize themes and, hopefully, recognize dream states while I was still dreaming (and achieve lucidity). I was living in South Korea at the time, teaching English, and came upon a [Aleister] Crowley fan once at a bar, late at night. He and I talked enthusiastically about magick, [Israel] Regardie, Crowley, and his fascination with DMT and mushrooms. Despite my love of psychology and altered states, my few experiences with psychedelics had left me with PTSD-like symptoms and so I prefer to listen to the experiences of others and live vicariously through them. He loved that I was a receptive listener, but we didn't exchange contact information. Months later, in the cold of winter, I happened to meet him again on a bus. He came and sat next to me and relayed the details of a dream he had in which he was lost in a giant house, carrying a coffin-shaped gray guitar case. He heard music and followed it to a room where I was playing in a band. I was in a hurry to finish the song so I could attend to some matter, but I didn't have a guitar case, so he gave me his. As he told me this I felt my reality unhinge because I suddenly recollected the dream that he was describing. I didn't tell him that I'd had the same dream, only from my own perspective. I don't know why I didn't tell him. Probably because I didn't really believe it myself. I later went home, flipped through my notebook, and found that the dream was exactly as he described it. I immediately started paying more and more attention to my dreams, and absolutely nothing else like that happened again (though I did get better at achieving, though not maintaining, lucidity). This other person and I met again under even more unusual circumstances. It was nearly a year later when I heard a knock on my apartment door (still in Korea). It was him. He was looking for somebody else who lived nowhere near me, but he'd somehow mixed up the address and was at my door—another very curious coincidence. We chatted over tea, then he left, and that was that.

According to anthropologist Sylvie Poirier, Australian Aborigines claim they commonly experience shared dreams: "It was not uncommon for two individuals to say that they shared the same dream. Both dreamers usually have shared the same camp overnight and found themselves in the same dream setting and action."[33]

Lucid-dream researchers Ed Kellogg and Robert Waggoner appear to have had some success in achieving mutual lucid dreams in intentional experiments. Kellogg had one experience that was particularly striking, when in a lucid dream he participated in an archeological dig with a friend from waking life, Harvey Grady. Both Kellogg and Grady wrote down their dream experiences separately before sharing details of the dream and were struck by the uncanny similarities.[34] When I spoke with Waggoner, who is a friend of Kellogg's, he described it this way:

Ed Kellogg, a good friend of mine and an incredibly experienced lucid dreamer, reports lucidly dreaming of interacting with Harvey Grady. . . . And in the morning when he talked to Harvey, or later when he contacted Harvey, Harvey claimed that he also was lucid and wrote down his experience, which was very similar to Ed's experience. But even in that experience you'll see where one of them will claim they were in the Sonoran desert, and the other one will say, no, it seemed more like the hill country in Israel. So sometimes, as Ed would put it, at the structural level you'll have things match up, but then at the naming level they don't exactly match up.

A number of anthropologists have famously reported having shared dreams while doing fieldwork in different cultures. A good summary of these experiences can be found in Charles Laughlin's *Communing with the Gods,* in the chapter on transpersonal dreaming. British psychologist Ann Faraday also offers many examples of mutual dreams in her book *The Dream Game,* and British writer Hornell Hart had a number of dreams that he seemed to share with his wife; these experiences and the mutual dreams of others are reported in Hart's book *The Enigma of Survival.*

Many people believe that shared dreaming is a learnable skill that improves with practice, and it's easy to start practicing with one or more partners. So how do people do it? According to British psychologist Robin Shohet, who developed a systematic approach to dream sharing, a basic technique that many people use simply involves gathering together a group of people who agree to meet in the same dream, at the same time, and to remember the details of what happened when they awaken.[35] Agreeing on a common dream environment to meet—a place that all parties know well from waking life—appears to be helpful, and the more closely the parties are bonded emotionally the greater the likelihood of sharing dreams, it seems.

Emotional bonding appears to be a crucial factor in many psychic dreams, and few personal bonds are closer than those between a mother and child. Not surprisingly, many of the psychic and shared dreams that are reported are between moms and their kids. According to Stanley Krippner, the reason for this "is thought by some investigators to originate in the intrauterine period of mother-fetus symbiosis" that "may have developed in the early postnatal period as an emergency channel of communication."[36] Krippner's suggestion makes sense to me, as I can think of another factor to help explain this phenomenon. I think we may have already discovered an important element in what makes this type of mother-child telepathy possible. What I suspect is this: It is known that when a fetus is developing in the womb, some of the child's brain cells will actually travel through the umbilical cord, into the mother's bloodstream, whisk past her blood-brain barrier, and then become incorporated into the mother's brain for life.[37] So unless you have an identical twin, the only person in the world who has some of your identical brain cells is your mother. Furthermore, I suspect that sharing genetically identical brain cells promotes telepathy, perhaps through some type of molecular or cellular resonance. Personally, my own mom has surprised me on numerous occasions by casually mentioning things in an offhand way that seemed to reveal very personal information about my experiences that she couldn't possibly have known by conventional means. According to some telepathy studies done by psychic researchers, some of the best-performing subjects in their studies were identical twins, who have genetically identical brains.[38]

In any case, most shared dreams appear to happen spontaneously, without any planned meeting or intention. For example, Ryan Hurd told me about a shared dream that he had with his young child:

> I think that I had a shared dream with my toddler once. It was about a year ago, when he was two years old, sleeping next to me in bed. I had a lucid dream in which I was in California, with cliffs overlooking the ocean, and I flew down into the water and landed right into a boat. I was floating in the water, and that was basically the dream. Then when I woke up from that, my son stirred in his sleep and said, "Blue water, boat," and that was it. Then he went back to sleep. I was very surprised and taken aback, as he's not a sleep talker, and he only had around fifty words at that point anyway. So it was remarkable, and that made me think, Wow, that's a mutual dream. But I wonder if it happened because our heads were right next to each other, almost like being too close to the router.

All this evidence for shared dreaming doesn't necessarily mean that two people are actually sharing the same physical space in a dream, as these reports could be examples of dream telepathy, where just dream content was shared. Stephen LaBerge devised an experiment that if carried out successfully would allow us to determine if there's an objectively shared dream world or just telepathically shared dream plots occurring:

> I propose that there is an empirical test: Two oneironauts could have simultaneous lucid dreams while being monitored in a sleep laboratory. They would agree to meet in their lucid dreams and signal simultaneously. If the experience were truly a mutual dream—that is, if the lucid dreamers were actually sharing a dream-world—

simultaneous eye-movement signals would show up in their polygraph recordings. If, on the other hand, they reported carrying out this task in a mutual lucid dream but did not show simultaneous signals, we would have to conclude that they were at most sharing dream plots. Let us be sure to appreciate the significance of such an experiment. If the mutual lucid dreamers fail to show simultaneous signals, it would be neither surprising nor especially significant. However, if they did prove to produce simultaneous eye-movement signals, we have incontrovertible proof for the objective existence of the dream world. We would then know that, in certain circumstances at least, dreams can be as objectively real as the world of physics.[39]

I would be most curious to learn about the results of an experiment like the one LaBerge suggests. In the final analysis, the question of whether shared dream reports are the result of an objectively shared dream space or the telepathic communication of dream plots remains mysterious. Providing an additional puzzle to this mystery, it's known that people don't just report sharing lucid dreams with other people, they also report sharing them with their pets.

TELEPATHY WITH PETS
AND SHARING DREAMS
WITH ANIMAL COMPANIONS

Many animals appear to dream more than humans do, and some may lucid dream as well. So maybe I shouldn't be surprised that a few people wrote to me saying they shared dreams or lucid dreams with their pets, and they believe that there is a reality to this. Sometimes people also tell me that the animals speak to them in their native language during dreams.

Considering the animal research that I have conducted in the past, I found these reports of interspecies psychic dreams compelling. During the three-year period in which I worked closely with Rupert Sheldrake doing the California-based research for his book *Dogs That Know*

When Their Owners Are Coming Home, I became aware that many people have experiences with their pets that conventional science is at a loss to explain.

Ed Kellogg wrote a fascinating essay about some lucid-dream experiences that he had with Shazam, his pet dog:

> In the 40 years since the Maimonides studies . . . it has become clear, through both scientific research and first hand reports, that individuals can become telepathically linked in dreams, and can even experience one another in a consensual way in a shared intersubjective dreamspace. However, considering the fact that many animals dream physiologically just as humans do, it should not surprise us that, given the strong bonds between humans and their animal companions, that psi-dreaming might connect humans with other species as well.[40]

Kellogg describes a lucid dream in which he flew to the moon, landed on the lunar terrain, and when he looked back toward Earth he saw Shazam flying through space to join him. He also provides several compelling examples of cases that might be genuine shared dreams between humans and their animal companions in his essay.

In some Native American traditions, young hunters and shamans are taught to recognize dreams about specific animals that represent the whole species and are said to become their spirit allies, power animals, or totem animals that help with their future hunts. In South America, many shamans are said to be shapeshifters and can take the form of different animals, such as jaguars, owls, and hummingbirds.

Personally, I often have dreams about cats, and have for much of my life. People transform into cats, and cats have human qualities in my dreams. I've also had recurring dreams about caring for a small kitten that I love, that communicates telepathically with me and keeps getting lost. I was taking care of a friend's cat recently and noticed that when the cat slept on my bed he would enter into my dreams, but I have yet to experience a shared lucid dream with an animal companion.

DREAMLAND GEOGRAPHY

While falling asleep one night I remembered a place that I frequently visit in my dreams. It is a place that I have forgotten many times and remembered many times—a town, somewhat similar to where I grew up, but different, more magical. In particular there is a small store there not far from a train station, on the edge of the town, where they sell rare underground comic books, enchanted toys, trading cards, and candies, as well as witchcraft and sorcery supplies. I'm always delighted to enter this place in my dreams.

Once I started to regularly record my dreams, I soon realized that there are a few environments that I keep returning to. These places are generally hybrids of different areas where I've lived, but there are certain combinations that keep recurring and seem to have some degree of continuity from dream to dream. I often find myself in places that are mixtures of locations that I have lived in or visited, like California beach towns surrounded by mountain landscapes and forests, or combinations of New York City, my hometown in New Jersey, college dorms, neuroscience labs, and different resorts and compounds, with South American, European, or Middle Eastern cities often blended in. There's also this recurring road or pathway that runs through mountains and woods that I sometimes follow; it begins in the grass fields just beyond my childhood elementary school, and it leads to foreign and enchanted lands.

Although I often forget the places that I visit in my dreams during my waking state, I sometimes remember them upon returning to a dream, it seems. In other words, it appears that I have an independent, state-dependent memory system operating in my dreams that I have trouble accessing in my waking state. There is something haunting and magical about these places that I regularly visit in my dreams that is hard to explain, but it seems like these places are truly enchanted and have an independent existence from my own mind.

When I posted a summary of what I have just said on my Facebook page, psychic researcher Jean Campbell responded with this comment:

"I once created a map of my dream geography." I found this comment intriguing, so I decided to do the same. I was inspired to create a geographic display of my dream realms, like J. R. R. Tolkien's map of the Middle Earth. Using Venn diagrams to show how the areas overlap and blend together, I discovered that there are five or six basic domains where my dreams occur, although where one domain ends and another begins is sometimes hard to discern, and new environments pop up all the time. I would suggest that you try this too, by reviewing your dream journal and making notes of the recurring environments you find yourself dreaming about. You can then draw a map that shows the different domains of your personal dream world.

The flexibility of time and space will be explored in the next chapter, as time and space appear to operate very differently in the metaphysiological dream realm. Many of my lucid dreams begin in quite ordinary environments such as a dream version of my own bedroom. This is an especially common starting point for me when I enter into lucid dreaming from a state of sleep paralysis, which I'll also be discussing in the next chapter, along with out-of-body experiences and the possibility of entering into higher dimensions of reality through lucid dreams. Although dream environments may initially start out as seemingly ordinary places, they can quickly lead us into immensely profound mysteries.*

---

*Afternote: It eventually happened that my girlfriend and I had what we believe to be a shared lucid dream. This happened in the early morning hours, after we both had episodes with sleep paralysis. I entered a stable lucid dream and soon set out to find my girlfriend. I found myself in our bedroom, where she was sleeping in her usual spot. I shook her awake excitedly, and she sluggishly came around. "We're having a lucid dream right now," I said. "No, we're not," she responded. "Check your nose and see!" I exclaimed (i.e., try breathing through your closed nostrils). Becca did this and suddenly said, "Oh, my god, you're right—we're dreaming right now!" Then I awoke into physical reality. A short while later, Becca woke up and remembered an uncannily similar experience as a "false awakening." She said that she was having a lucid dream, and then thought that she had woken up in our bed. During this "false awakening" I was with her, telling her that she was still dreaming. She didn't believe this at first, but heard me tell her to try breathing through her closed nostrils, which she did, and then she realized that she was still dreaming.

9

OUT-OF-BODY EXPERIENCES, PARALLEL UNIVERSES, AND ALTERNATE DIMENSIONS

Our truest life is when we are in dreams awake.

HENRY DAVID THOREAU

Some people think that dreams occur outside of our bodies. In fact, some cultures don't even have a word in their native tongue for *dream* in the Indo-European sense discussed in this book.[1] In other words, what we call dreams may be considered by others to simply be experiences in other domains of reality, and their sense of identity may incorporate memories of experiences in dreams and other states of consciousness besides just waking life. According to anthropologist Charles Laughlin,

> For many peoples, dreaming is a portal into a parallel reality. . . .
> People who have dream cultures do not merely believe the dream
> to be real, they experience the dream world as real—just as we
> Westerners are conditioned to experience our waking state as reality,
> despite ample phenomenological and neuropsychological evidence
> that everyday reality too is but a construct of our brain.[2]

For example, among the Sambia tribe in Papua New Guinea, dreams are considered to be occasions when the soul leaves the body and roams freely in different places. The Ramamuri people of Northern Mexico consider dreams to be as real as the events in waking life, and the Kalapalo people of Central Brazil say that a part of the self rises out of the body and wanders around during sleep. The Mapuche natives of Chile believe that dreaming involves a journey of the soul outside of the body, where it can observe faraway places and distant events. They believe that dreaming can serve as a channel of communication—between the dreamer and other dreamers, as well as between the dreamer and the spirit world. Although Mapuche shamans utilize dreams in their healing work, all people in Mapuche society are considered to have this extraordinary potential for genuinely traveling in their dreams.[3] For the Zuni in the American Southwest, it is believed that during sleep the soul can travel not only to other places, but to the past and the future. Among the Quiche Maya in Central America, dreaming may involve visits with the dead. The Aguaruna tribe of Peru also believe that their souls can travel during sleep.

The belief that an aspect of our minds separates from our physical bodies during sleep has been thought to be the cultural origin of the belief in a soul that transcends the body's life. For example, German philosopher Friedrich Nietzsche (1844–1900) famously wrote in his book *Human, All Too Human:*

> In the ages of the rude beginning of culture, man believed that he was discovering a second real world in dream, and here is the origin of all metaphysics. Without dreams, mankind would never have had occasion to invent such a division of the world. The parting of soul and body goes also with this way of interpreting dreams; likewise, the idea of a soul's apparitional body: whence all belief in ghosts, and apparently, too, in gods.[4]

However, although dreams are clearly correlated with specific brain states, that doesn't mean that's where they are actually occurring. In other words, to use the example of a radio, the patterns of electrical activity in a radio are correlated with the sound coming from the box, but that doesn't mean that those sounds are originating from the box that houses the radio, as young children might initially think. As we know, the sounds are being broadcast by a radio station tower that is some distance away, and the radio receiver is just picking up the transmitted signals.

Our brains may operate on a similar principle and be more like transceivers of information than generators of consciousness. This model might help to resolve some of the mind-bending paradoxes that we're going to encounter in this chapter. Also, it may not be a black-and-white situation; like a computer, perhaps the human brain can be publicly "online" or privately "offline," depending on the situation. Locating the source of our internal experience can become even more perplexing when we observe that there's a lot of overlap between lucid dreaming and what people report as out-of-body experiences (OBEs).

WHAT IS AN OBE?

An OBE is when someone has the distinct feeling, and accompanying viewpoint, of being conscious outside of his or her physical body. Around 10 percent of the general population has had an OBE at some point in their life,[5] and the phenomenon can take a number of forms, although there are some general characteristics.

An OBE can sometimes spontaneously occur when one is in a very relaxed state, although it can also happen during states of trauma, shock, or near-lethal accidents, as well by means of deliberate techniques, the ingestion of certain drugs, and the practice of specific mental exercises. OBEs generally begin in a waking state; you feel something like a ghost, or a point of awareness, that can leave the physical body and occupy and perceive the immediate environment outside it. Some people find the experience frightening, while most seem to find it pleasant or at the very least interesting. I've personally had dozens of OBEs and have found using a sensory-deprivation tank (which I'll be discussing later in this chapter) to be immensely helpful in being able to launch such journeys.

Of course, without any conclusive evidence, no one really knows if there's truly an independently existing, freestanding, objective reality to the environments experienced during OBEs or not, although that doesn't prevent people from holding strong opinions about the matter one way or another. Later in this chapter I'll be reviewing some of the evidence for and against both notions, but here I'd just like to point out that a number of studies demonstrate that there is a statistical correlation between the frequency of reported experiences with lucid dreaming and the frequency of OBEs.[6]

The primary similarity between lucid dreaming and OBEs is that in both states of consciousness we create models of the world that are largely independent of any recognized sensory stimuli. In both states we retain a clearheaded memory of waking reality and experience a direct continuity with our everyday ego. Additionally, in both OBEs and lucid-dream environments, the world that we find ourselves in tends to be much less stable than what we generally experience as waking reality.

The primary difference between an OBE and a lucid dream is that in an OBE people often first have the actual experience of leaving their physical body and seeing it sink below them as they rise. Because of this aspect of the phenomenon, and the fact that people often find their extracorporeal selves in environments that closely resemble the one that their physical body is in, they often believe that the environment experienced within an OBE is a genuine representation of reality. Lucid dreamers, on the other hand, generally regard their experiences as being imaginary.

According to one study of 450 people who had OBEs and 214 people who didn't, 66 percent of the first group reported at least one experience with dream lucidity, whereas only 48 percent of the second group reported lucid dreaming.[7] Additionally, there are many experiences that aren't clearly classifiable as one or the other, and sometimes each can lead to the other.

Regarding the similarities between lucid dreaming and OBEs, there are basically two schools of thought. One view is that lucid dreaming and OBEs are both forms of imaginary world-building wherein the brain creates a model of reality entirely from stored memories and imagination. The other view is that lucid dreaming and OBEs are distinctly different states of consciousness, with OBEs occurring outside of the physical body in a literal sense.

Robert Monroe (1915–1995) was a radio broadcasting executive who became known for his research into altered consciousness and founding the Monroe Institute, a Virginia-based educational and research organization devoted to the exploration of human consciousness. He authored best sellers like *Journeys Out of the Body, Far Journey,* and *Ultimate Journey.* Monroe writes in response to this question about OBEs: How do you know that they aren't just a type of dreaming?

> In the OBE, the individual is near-totally conscious, as our civilization defines the state. Most if not all of your physical senses are replicated. You can "see," "hear," and "touch"—the weakest seems to be smell and taste. Your perspective is from a position outside your physical body, near or distant. In a near state, it is usually from a location impossible for you to "be" with your physical state, such as floating against the ceiling. In a far location, it could be in Paris when you know you are in New York physically. You can observe events taking place, but you cannot change or significantly affect them. You can verify the authenticity of such events subsequently if you so desire. You cannot participate to a major degree in this physical activity because you are not "physical." It is the extreme reality of the OBE that sets it apart from a dream. It is as "real" as any physical life experience.[8]

However, as we've learned, the world within a lucid dream can seem every bit as real as any waking-life experience. Monroe says the most common difference between a lucid dream and an OBE is that the environment in a lucid dream has the ability to change, unlike the environment in an OBE[9]—but I wonder if this isn't simply due to one's expectations.

When I interviewed psychologist Charles Tart about OBEs, he said:

The typical thing about an OBE is that a person feels like their mind is perfectly normal, and therefore the situation they find themselves in is ridiculous and impossible. This is different from being in a dream, for example, where you're (from our waking perspective) out of your body all the time. When you're dreaming, you don't know that you're not occupying your physical body in a normal way. You're in dream consciousness. And it's the clarity of consciousness in an OBE that causes people to think that this simply cannot be really happening. People generally feel perfectly awake, perfectly conscious, and yet they're floating up to the damn ceiling. So they automatically think, *This just can't be happening!*

Many OBEs that are not related to shock or trauma begin with sleep paralysis, and this state may offer some insight into the mysterious, seemingly extracorporeal phenomenon of the OBE.

SLEEP PARALYSIS AND OBES

In sleep paralysis, the muscles of the body become limp and paralyzed during REM sleep, such that we don't act out the behaviors in our dreams. Sleep paralysis occurs when we wake up and are still in this state of bodily paralysis. Some people believe that the psychedelic neurotransmitter DMT is released in our brains during these periods of paralysis.[10] Although sleep paralysis can be quite scary, it's always temporary and harmless. On the positive side, it can also be a gateway into lucid dreams and OBEs.

Sleep paralysis occurs when our brains are in a hybrid state between waking and REM sleep—when our minds wake up and our day-to-day egos come back online, while our bodies remain asleep. In this odd state of mind, dream imagery often blends with perceptions from our open eyes, and this can be quite frightening. People experiencing sleep paralysis often feel like they are in their bed, as they should be, having just woken up from sleep, but are completely unable to move a muscle except for their eyes. It can be a terrifying experience, partially because

Fig. 9.1. Artist Henry Fuseli's famous painting from 1781, *The Nightmare,* of a woman lying immobilized on her back with her arms outstretched as an incubus sits atop her chest, is a depiction of sleep paralysis that captures its scary aspect quite well.

you suddenly find yourself unexpectedly paralyzed, and also because it's common to see and/or feel a dark, menacing figure attempting to do you harm while you're in this frozen state. This dark figure generally moves toward you, stands beside your bed, or sits on your chest with its hands on your neck or forehead. This is perhaps where the notion of the incubus/succubus originated—supernatural or demonic entities that supposedly seduce us in our sleep and drain us of our vital life force.

My friend Pandora Spocks had an OBE that she describes as different from her experiences with sleep paralysis and lucid dreaming, although it sounds somewhat similar. She drew the following picture of the event, telling me that it is a depiction of her "astral body being pulled out" of her "body through her mouth, before it went into a wormhole."

Fig. 9.2. A drawing by Pandora Spocks of her OBE experience

Pandora recounted the story of this bewildering event to me:

I have only had one OBE so far in my life. Although I had asked for the experience I believe it was accelerated by fasting and a severe bout of depression I was experiencing at the time. The reason I believe my bout of depression helped me have this experience is because I had lost all fear of leaving my bodily vessel. In the months leading up to the experience I would half leave my body, but fear prevented me from fully leaving. On the night in question I felt a scratching in my throat, then my astral body was pulled out of my mouth by masked figures depicted in this drawing. I then flew into a wormhole and arrived in a place that I was told was a school for the astral. I was taught to fly and move things with my mind as well as schooled on the various rules of the astral realm. After the experience I came back into my body with a THUMP and woke instantly in a state of exhilaration and excitement. I am an adept lucid dreamer and have experienced sleep paralysis. This experience felt like neither of these, and I have yet to replicate it. The feeling of being free from the bodily vessel was truly incredible and liberating. I am convinced my astral body left my meat suit.

Occultist Oliver Fox describes his first experience with sleep paralysis. He was naturally frightened and said that it seemed "imperative" that he remain as "calm as possible." He writes, "To this end I mentally repeated the Binomial Theorem and several other mathematical formulae."[11] I'll have to try that some time, when I'm faced with sleep paralysis, or some other situation that requires a heightened sense of calmness—just start repeating the Binomial Theorem in my head!

HOW TO LAUNCH AN OBE FROM SLEEP PARALYSIS

I haven't tried repeating mathematical theorems to calm my mind yet because I have learned to joyfully embrace my episodes of sleep paralysis. This took me a while to learn. Consider the following experience I had:

> I woke up in my bedroom, in the midst of sleep paralysis that lasted a few minutes. I tried not to get scared when I couldn't move my limbs—they just felt too heavy, like I was hypnotized, or like a magnet was holding them to my bed. Then I kept hearing people talking downstairs or outside my house, and this just frightened me too much—I had to check to make sure they were hypnogogic hallucinations, so I deliberately woke myself up fully. Then, when I realized that I was completely alone, I was sorry that I didn't try to have an OBE or lucid dream from the sleep-paralysis state. It can be very hard to control one's fear in that state sometimes, as the voices that one hears can sound so real.

As described, initially when this happens there's an instinctive jolt of fear, which isn't terribly different from the initial fear that swells up in one's head after taking a deep toke of vaporized DMT. However, as with DMT, and as many other people have discovered, I learned that the fear can be controlled, and sleep paralysis can become a glorious gateway into OBEs and lucid dreams.

I've had a number of lucid dreams and OBEs that began with sleep paralysis and then developed with my recognition of having a second body, with phantom, astral, or dream limbs that I could move, despite my paralyzed physical body. This largely occurred during my many experiences floating in sensory-deprivation tanks. The secret, I learned, to staying calm during sleep paralysis is to focus on my sense of personal identification with my dream body rather than with my physical body. Doing this requires a slight mental shift. Instead of becoming frustrated and panicked because my muscles won't respond to my intentions, I focus my attention on the phantom feeling that responds to my attempts at physical movement. By focusing on the sensation of my phantom-limb movement, I begin to shift my sense of identity away from my physical body and into my dream or astral body. Initially, there's a sense of dual consciousness—an awareness of both bodies—but then my experience of the dream body overshadows any sensory perception coming from the physical body.

I've also noticed, as have other psychonauts, that it appears that I can see my surroundings with my eyes closed during sleep paralysis, while on ayahuasca, or in certain other states of consciousness. On ketamine I was once able to see the stars through my ceiling. Could this be perception of the environment via one's astral body, or merely a model constructed by the brain from memory? In any case, once I've shifted my sense of identity away from my physical body and into my dream or astral body, I'm able to easily lift myself out of my body by simply sitting up or rolling over while in the dream body, and then floating free.

FLOATING UPWARD AND THE EVOLUTION OF GETTING HIGH

Most people who have had OBEs report an experience of rising up out of the physical body, gaining an elevated viewpoint or a higher perspective, such that you're looking down at your body. Although it does happen, people rarely report sinking downward out of the body, or leaving it horizontally. If the essence of our conscious mind is indeed composed of a material substance, then like helium it seems to be lighter than our atmosphere, because people who have had OBEs consistently report rising up toward the ceiling, not sinking down into the floor.

This makes sense to me in terms of a larger evolutionary context. If one studies the history of human civilizations, it seems that those areas of the world where people have been the most culturally experimental and technologically innovative have steadily moved westward. The planet continually spins on its axis, from east to west, at 900 miles an hour. This means that migrating west is really moving against the direction of the planetary spin. From an extraterrestrial vantage point (i.e., high off the planet), moving west can be seen as a climb upward over time, as though humans have been faithfully ascending a giant mountain for thousands of years that reaches from India to Hawaii. The whole notion of "East meets West" implies that this process has come full circle, and that perhaps we are currently preparing for extraterrestrial migration, as our aerospace technology will soon be allowing us to do so.

These westward migration patterns also make sense to me within the larger context of an evolutionary perspective. It appears that there is an evolutionary momentum behind all of human progress, moving it ever and ever upward, i.e., getting "high." Our early ancestors climbed up and out of the ocean onto dry land. Then they grew taller, stood up on their hind legs, and began climbing up into trees. Some took off into the air and learned to fly; we eventually learned to do so as well with our advanced technology.

The central locus of consciousness in every animal species is always located near the top of its head—as close to the heavens as physiologically possible—which has the highest perceptual vantage point. When I've journeyed with ayahuasca, LSD, or magic mushrooms, it sometimes felt like the locus of my consciousness literally shifted from the center of my head to a point that is actually a few inches above my head.

It is no accident, I realize, that people refer to cannabis intoxication as a "high." Consciousness has been literally evolving higher and higher for eons—the brains of animals have evolved into higher and higher positions of physical elevation throughout our evolution, and consciousness has been rising upward, against the force of gravity, toward the stars. This may be because there is such thing as a soul, a portion of our conscious mind that always rises to the top of a biological system and survives physical death—by rising toward the heavens and then, perhaps, moving into another dimension of reality. This soul may have a physical form that our current science is yet unable to measure or detect.

If this is correct, then it appears that the human soul weighs very little, if anything at all, and can float upward freely when no longer attached to the human body, like a helium balloon.

This evolutionary momentum to ever-elevate our souls may also help to explain the nearly universal love of flying dreams, and why flying is often one of the first things that people try doing in lucid dreams. Perhaps we're like caterpillars dreaming of our future form as butterflies, carrying our lighter-than-air souls skyward into the heavens.* However, before we become convinced of the reality of an immortal soul and determine that OBEs and lucid dreams are occurring anywhere other than inside of our skulls, let's review what the skeptics have to say about this.

SHIFTING MODELS OF REALITY

Many people have experienced being startled awake by the sensation of falling as they enter the first phase of sleep, and in fact we commonly use the phrase "fall asleep" to describe the beginning of the sleep process. Some researchers have theorized that the brain's perception of weightlessness—due to a severance from bodily sensations—may account for the experiences of floating, flying, and falling that many people report as they approach sleep and dreaming.[12]

The sensory isolation that comes with sleep onset may help to explain the sensation of weightlessness that many people experience during OBEs, and more than a few researchers believe that searching for the validity of OBEs or psychic phenomena in lucid dreams is misguided. Consider the following, in which the authors describe entertaining notions of psychic or extracorporeal possibilities as lapses of judgment within the lucid dream:

---

*In the late psychologist Timothy Leary's "8 Circuit Model of the Brain"—which is described in many of his books, psychologist Robert Anton Wilson's books, my own books, and those of others—an OBE occurs in the eighth and highest brain circuit: "the metaphysiological circuit," which supposedly transcends the body by being centered in one's atomic nuclei, rather than in the DNA of our cellular nuclei.

Even lucid dreamers who know better can suffer from time to time from naïve confusions about this state, since the dreaming mind readily takes up all sorts of notions at which the waking mind might scoff. Many a nominally lucid dreamer will ascribe oneric oddities to jumping around in time or between parallel lives. We would sometimes wonder if people in the real world could see us in some ghostly form, or imagine that someone met in a dream must literally be that person dreaming at the same time rather than a mental image.[13]

If the authors of the quote above think that entertaining the possible reality of OBEs within the lucid dream state is misguided, then I wonder what they think of people like me who entertain these ideas in their waking state? The authors go on to say that "some dreamers further limit lucidity by carrying excess mental baggage in the form of favored occultist, metaphysical, or psychological theory into their dreams, employing it as dogma rather than investigating its validity."[14]

Similarly, it appears that some researchers also limit their speculations about what is possible within lucid dreams by employing the dogma of scientism, and the authors quoted above don't seem to recognize their own contradiction here, as they appear to be assuming that conventional scientific models don't need to be tested, and that all other models must be wrong. How do we know what is possible within a lucid dream unless we test all of our assumptions? It may be a mistake to assume that dreaming only takes place within the brain. As we discussed in the last chapter, there is ample evidence to suggest that the boundaries between our dreaming minds are not so clearly defined. British psychologist Sue Blackmore has an interesting perspective on this matter. As we've learned, lucid dreaming is correlated with specific brain states, and while statistical correlations don't always imply causation, sometimes they do, and the origin of consciousness remains the grandest of mysteries. Maybe OBEs and lucid dreams are all happening in the brain.

In her essay "A Theory of Lucid Dreams and OBEs," Blackmore explains how our brains create models of reality using a combination of sensory input and memory.[15] Although she distinguishes between OBEs and lucid dreaming on a phenomenological level, Blackmore classifies them both as a type of insufficient reality modeling. Blackmore says both OBEs and lucid dreams utilize unstable mental models of reality constructed by the brain without any sensory input or bodily restrictions, so that they are built entirely from memory and imagination. "Lucid dreams, false awakenings, and OBEs can all be seen as the natural result of our normal modeling process coming up with models of reality that are not predominantly input-driven," she writes.[16] Blackmore offers a compelling perspective, and Occam's razor beckons us to accept the simplest model that explains all of the data. But does this theory really do that? According to Blackmore, without normal input from the senses, all of our models of reality are constructed from memory or guesswork. This would mean that OBEs are merely a very convincing hallucination of sorts, and that no new information can be gained from them about the external world. Support for Blackmore's theory that OBEs are really a type of lucid dream come from an investigation she conducted with people who have experienced OBEs, in which she found that 85 percent of her respondents said they had experienced OBEs while resting, sleeping, or dreaming, rather than when they were fully awake.[17]

Oxford psychophysical research director Celia Green presents a similar theory to explain lucid dreaming, seeing ghostly apparitions, false awakenings, OBEs, and other unexplainable phenomena by suggesting that during these experiences one's entire visual field becomes a temporary hallucination (which she calls a "metachoric" experience) due to variations in the process of sleep paralysis.[18] Green believes that these phenomena are all hallucinatory and are due to the intrusion of processes that are normally associated with sleep into waking consciousness. She sees this as a satisfying solution to the mystery of how the sight of hallucinated apparitions can seamlessly integrate with one's normal perceptions of the world—because, she says, the whole visual field is actually hallucinated, as it with is with false awakenings and lucid dreams. Green conducted a survey similar to Blackmore's, in which she found that most OBEs take place when people are in bed, ill, or resting, with a smaller percentage of people reporting OBEs while under the influence of different drugs.[19]

In 1991, Stephen LaBerge examined 107 lucid dreams as part of a study and found that 9 percent of them included OBEs. Additionally, in a questionnaire study of 572 people, in which 452 respondents claimed to have had at least one lucid dream, 39 percent reported having at least one OBE, and only 15 percent of the respondents who never recalled a lucid dream claimed to have had an OBE.[20] LaBerge appears to agree with the perspective offered by Blackmore and Green, but adds an interesting twist:

> I propose that dreams result from brain activities using internal information to create a simulation of the world, much like the process of waking perception, minus sensory input. According to this assumption, human dreaming is the result of the same perceptual and mental processes that we use to comprehend the world when awake. In order to understand dreaming, we need to understand perception, and vice versa: from this perspective, to perceive is to dream. More precisely, perception is dreaming constrained by sensory information; dreaming is perception independent of sensory information.[21]

According to LaBerge to "perceive is to dream," which implies that we're always dreaming. Perception, in this sense, is a certain kind of dreaming—dreaming constrained by sensory input. In another words, dreaming is perception without any sensory input.

Evidence from a neuroscience study suggests that there are measurable physiological distinctions between OBEs and lucid dreams. In 1984, Australian psychologist Harvey Irwin conducted a comparative study of lucid dreams and sleep-initiated OBEs. He found that most OBEs were unlike lucid dreams, because during an OBE the brain-wave patterns would often show alpha activity, but hardly any REM. This means that whatever the subjects were actually doing during this period, they weren't dreaming.[22]

When I asked Stephen LaBerge what he thought about the relationship between lucid dreaming and OBEs, he said:

It's a complicated topic and I devoted an entire chapter to it in *Lucid Dreaming* because it's something you have to deal with carefully. I think they're not what people naively think they are, which is literally that you're leaving your physical body in some ghost body in the physical world. Let's take what happens in an out-of-the-body experience. Typically a person is lying in bed, awake—at least they think they are. Next thing they know, they feel themselves separating from that body, as if they have a second body that floats out of the first one, and then they may look back down and see what they take to be their physical body. So let's just examine that idea for consistency. Now, I'm floating up here, and then I look around at the bedroom and notice that there's a window where there shouldn't be, or there's no window where there should be. So I say, "Oh, I guess that wall there is not exactly a physical wall, maybe it's an astral wall, and of course then that's an astral floor, an astral bed—and what's that down on the astral bed that a moment ago I thought was my physical body?" It's an astral body or a dream body. Therefore, what happened to the assumption that I'm moving in physical space? It's suddenly evaporated. The reason people find it so compelling is that it feels like you leave your body, and since it feels like it, that's what you believe is happening. In our experiments in the laboratory, out of about 100 lucid dreams that were recorded, about 10 percent of those had out-of-body phenomenologies. So we analyzed the physiology associated with the out-of-the-body-experience type of lucid dream compared to the other lucid dreams to see if there's some characteristic that predicts that a person is likely to have a dream in which they think they're out of their body. And what we found was that there was much more likelihood of a brief awakening before the experience. Now, I think the way the OBE takes place—in the typical form, which is in association with sleep—is: you're lying in bed, you wake up, you're awake. It's from REM sleep, so you're now in the context of going back into REM sleep, and what happens is that you fall asleep without knowing it. Suddenly the sensory input is cut off and you've now got the memory of the body instead of the sensory perception of the body. A moment ago your body had weight, but now that gravitational force has been cut off there's not sensory input for it, so it suddenly disappears and, I propose, it's the same thing that happens when you pick up an empty carton of milk, expecting it to be full. Suddenly your body flies upward, and you feel as if there's a force going up that compensates for your mental model of your body weight. When you perceive that the weight is less than expected by your mental model, you explain that as an upward force.

Along with LaBerge's skepticism that we have astral bodies, many conventional neuroscientists simply regard OBEs as "disjunctive kinesthetic hallucinations" or as "neural instabilities in the brain's temporal lobes" and as "errors in the body's sense of itself."[23] However, if this is true, then one has to wonder why the U.S. and Russian intelligence agencies spent over twenty years studying a method for obtaining classified information, apparently with some success, called remote viewing.

REMOTE-VIEWING RESEARCH

Remote viewing is generally described as a type of clairvoyance, or the psychic ability to perceive information from a distance, without using any of the known sensory channels. Although the person who is doing the remote viewing doesn't lose awareness of the physical body, he or she is in a trance that's been described as "a mild form of OBE."[24]

Remote viewing has been scientifically studied by the U.S. and Russian intelligence agencies as a method for obtaining classified information from other countries, and it has had some success. Although the information gathered from remote viewing was eventually judged to be too unreliable for practical use, some of the results appeared to be uncanny. Side-by-side comparison of some of the drawings made by remote viewers with satellite photos of their targets sometimes looked eerily similar. Perhaps best known is the time that these studied remote viewers were able to help locate a downed Soviet plane in Zaire.[25]

Because it seems that some people have a genuine ability for remote viewing, the phenomenon was seriously and intensively studied by the U.S. government from 1972 to 1995. At that time, the Stargate Project,* established by the U.S. Defense Intelligence Agency and the CIA, investigated claims of psychic phenomena and researched remote viewing for military applications at the Stanford Research Institute in Menlo Park, California.[26]

While it seems that remote viewers don't make useful spies, it does appear that they have some genuine ability to gather information from a distance in a manner that is currently unrecognized by science.

Then there is Robert Monroe's fascinating research.

JOURNEYS OUT OF THE BODY AND THE MONROE INSTITUTE

The late radio broadcasting executive and paranormal research pioneer Robert Monroe began having a bewildering series of spontaneous OBEs in 1958, after he started experimenting on himself with different sound patterns to study the possibility of learning during sleep. In 1971 Monroe published a book describing these experiences, *Journeys Out of the Body*. It became an instant classic in the field and popularized the term out-of-body experience.

In 1977, Monroe founded the Monroe Institute in Faber, Virginia, to study OBEs and other unexplained phenomena related to altered states of consciousness. The Monroe Institute† has conducted research into how sound technologies affect brain-wave states, with the goal of developing methods, techniques, and programs for expanding human potential. In recent years the institute has shifted its focus from pursuing evidence for the existence of an astral body to convince materialistic skeptics, to focus instead on developing a more qualitative understanding of OBEs and other altered states. It has produced a wealth of data

---

*This project actually went by a number of names over the decades that it was secretly carried out, including "Gondala Wish" and "Sunstreak." This secret project was declassified in 1995 under executive order no. 1995-4-17.

†An overview of the Monroe Institute can be found at www.monroeinstitute.org.

suggesting that there is an independent reality to what people experience when they have OBEs.

The Monroe Institute developed a patented auditory technology for inducing OBEs and other altered states of consciousness called Hemi-Sync, which blends multilayered, binaural-beat sound frequencies into different left and right outputs that the brain combines while listening, causing the two hemispheres to synchronize. These auditory patterns have been shown to alter brain waves and enhance sleep, meditation, or certain types of mental performance, while in some people they can produce OBEs and other unusual states of awareness. This hemispheric synchronization is similar to the brain-entrainment technologies discussed in chapter 6. My own personal experience with the Hemi-Sync audio CDs has been relaxing and trance-inducing, but I haven't had any lucid dreams or OBEs with them.

Although I find Monroe's work fascinating, his experiences are so at odds with my own OBEs that I'm not sure what to make of them. His writings remind me a bit of Carlos Castaneda. His books are filled with great, compelling stories, and clearly the author had substantial experience with exploring and expanding consciousness. But some of the stories just seem a bit too fanciful to me—almost as though he had these fascinating OBEs and then used his imagination to embellish on what happened. Could he really be describing genuine journeys to other realms in his astral body, or unusually stable lucid dreams? Maybe. In many cases it seems like the lucid dreams he reports describe environments that seem as stable as the material, waking world. I wish I could have had the opportunity to interview Monroe for this book.

Unlike Monroe's *Journeys Out of the Body*, which seems to contain possible exaggerations to me, Oliver Fox's 1938 book *Astral Projection: A Record of Out-of-the-Body Experiences* seems more believable. Fox's book appears to be an honest attempt at an early scientific or systematic investigation of this mysterious phenomenon, although his reports are clearly influenced by occult beliefs about astral projection. Fox writes at length about his lucid dreams, which he calls "dreams of knowledge," and sees them as being a portal into a state of existence outside of the body.

I haven't read about anyone conducting any of the "reality tests" (that we discussed earlier, to determine if one is dreaming or not) during an OBE, and I would be most curious to learn what the results of such an investigation were.

Reading Sue Blackmore, Celia Green, Oliver Fox, and Robert Monroe (whose works are cited in the bibliography of this book), I get the impression that each of them is attempting to squeeze this huge, gaping mystery into small conceptual boxes, and oftentimes their theories seem strained when trying to account for the variety of strange phenomena reported or what is known scientifically. What happens during an OBE is deeply mysterious, and accepting it as a genuine extracorporeal experience or classifying it as merely a hallucination is, I think, premature. We just don't know enough about what this mysterious phenomenon is to make such confident assumptions, as there appear to be examples that make all of these models seem inadequate.

One of the most intriguing OBE studies was conducted in 1968 by Charles Tart.[27] The study was done with a single woman—Miss Z— who reported frequent OBEs over a period of four nights in Tart's sleep laboratory. The subject was attached to an EEG monitor, and a five-digit code was placed out of sight and out of reach, on a shelf above her bed. During the experiment, Tart monitored the equipment behind an observation window in the next room. On the first three nights Miss Z said that she couldn't see the number, but on the fourth night she reported the number correctly as 25132. However, this study has been criticized because Tart admitted to napping during the night, and skeptics say that the subject might have secretly concealed a mirror and telescoping rod in her pajamas and peeked at the shelf when she thought Tart was asleep. The critics' explanation sounds a bit farfetched to me, but the study hasn't been replicated either. I trust Tart's research, but I'm a bit dubious. I mean, you'd think that if such a thing were possible, the Monroe Institute, or someone, would have replicated this by now. However, OBEs may not be that easy to control.

Another intriguing OBE study was conducted in 1966 by Stanley Krippner and colleagues at the Maimonides Dream Lab in Brooklyn.

This study was conducted with a medical student who claimed that he was able to leave his body while he was asleep.[28] In the sleep laboratory the researchers built a little shelf, and before the subject went to sleep Krippner had somebody throw some dice to get a random number, which directed him to an envelope. Then he opened the envelope up and put the picture inside of it into a tray on the shelf. That night the subject tried to go out of his body to view the picture. According to Krippner, when the subject said he was out of his body, the EEG recordings showed a strange pattern with very slow alpha waves, which you usually don't see while someone is dreaming. The subject reported seeing a picture of a sunset that matched the target image—"Indian memories of a perfect sunset." Although this first trial was successful, the subject was not able to return for more research because he had to go back to medical school. Did the medical student in Krippner's OBE study see the photo with his astral body? Or did he read Krippner's mind? Or was it just a lucky guess?

Whatever the case, there's additional evidence to support the notion that consciousness can exist independently of the body from the field of thanatology, the study of the near-death experience (NDE).

RESEARCH INTO THE NEAR-DEATH EXPERIENCE

No mystery in life is grander than death, and it appears that some people may get something of a preview of what comes after the ultimate demise of the body. A NDE is an umbrella term for a mysterious class of experiences with similar characteristics that are reported to occur when some people come close to dying and their heart actually stops. Within seconds of when the heart stops beating, all brain function ceases. If consciousness is dependent on the brain, then people shouldn't be able to remember what happens during these periods, and they certainly shouldn't be able to remember events from vantage points outside of the bodies. Yet they do. People report these NDEs all the time. According to a number of surveys, around 10 percent of people who have come close to dying report an experience of nonordinary peacefulness combined with an OBE, along with contact with a loving light or departed loved ones.

Some research suggests that there is a connection between NDEs and lucid dreaming. According to lucid-dream researcher Jayne Gackenbach, two studies have found that people who have had NDEs are more likely to experience dream lucidity.[29] Penny Sartori, Pim van Lommel, and Sam Parnia are three of the world's leading medical researchers into the NDE. Intensive care nurse Penny Sartori conducted the first long-term clinical study of the NDE in the United Kingdom and has shown that people who have had NDEs can sometimes perceive highly accurate, verifiable facts about their resuscitation that they could not have known otherwise.[30] Likewise, Dutch researcher and cardiologist Pim van Lommel, who has been studying the NDE for more than twenty-five years, also conducted important research into this phenomenon and reported findings that are incompatible with conventional science as well—as conventional science doesn't have an explanation for perceptions that occur outside of the body.[31] Van Lommel's research and conclusions are summarized in his book *Consciousness Beyond Life: The Science of the Near-Death Experience*.

A professor of critical-care medicine and the director of resuscitation research at State University of New York at Stony Brook, Sam Parnia summarizes his thought-provoking studies of the NDE in his book *Erasing Death: The Science That Is Rewriting the Boundaries between Life and Death*. In 2008, Parnia launched the world's largest study into NDEs, involving 2,060 patients from fifteen hospitals in the United Kingdom, the United States, and Austria.[32] The study examined a broad range of mental experiences in relation to death and attempted to test the validity of conscious experiences using objective markers to determine whether the claims of awareness compatible with out-of-body experiences correspond with real or hallucinatory events. Parnia and his colleagues planted signs in hospital rooms that could only be read from near the ceiling, and it appears that some patients were able to view these. Additionally, there were some accurate reports about what was going on in the operating room when patients were supposedly unconscious, sometimes from a vantage point significantly elevated in relation to their bodies. After reviewing the results of the study, Parnia and his associates concluded that in some cases of cardiac arrest, the memories of what people see during an OBE may correspond to actual events. This is especially remarkable when one considers that these OBEs occurred during periods after the patients' hearts had stopped, when there was no measurable brain activity.

When I interviewed psychiatrist and LSD researcher Stanislav Grof, he told me that some out-of-body experiences can happen to people not only when they are in a state of cardiac death, but also when they are brain-dead. Cardiologist Michael Sabom described a patient named Pam, who had a major aneurysm on the basilar artery and had to undergo a risky operation. To operate on her, the surgeons had to basically freeze her brain to the point that she stopped producing brain waves; at the same time she had one of the most powerful out-of-body experiences ever observed, with accurate perception of her environment. Following the operation, she was able to give an accurate description of the surgical procedure, to the point where she could draw the instruments that were used.[33]

While some skeptics understand that new information can be gathered through remote viewing or OBEs, they point out that some form of telepathy could help to explain this more easily than postulating the real existence of a second body and another world. In other words, perhaps our brains are capable of gathering information from other brains, through means currently unrecognized by science, and then build models of reality incorporating this new information.

When I asked Stephen LaBerge about what he thought of NDEs, when people feel like they're leaving their body, he said this:

> Another factor that can produce an OBE is the ability to dissociate. There are some people who can much more readily than others detach themselves from their current experience. Once you detach, it's possible then to reconstruct a view of reality that involves you outside the situation somehow. For most people for that to happen they either need the context of REM sleep, or they're falling off a mountain, or they've just been declared dead, or something. That's

quite an emotional shock—it's enough to produce dissociation, which then allows you to reorganize the experience. Now you hear stories about people in near-death experiences seeing things that they shouldn't be able to see and that sort of thing. Well, I don't deny them that, there may be some paranormal information transfer occasionally in these experiences. But I think we underestimate how much knowledge we have about our surroundings through other senses. I don't buy the account that we leave in some second body. That second body—does it have a brain in there? What are the fingers for? If you pulled an eye out, would it look like an eye or is it just a mental model of an eye? It seems clear that that's what it is. It's one of those ideas that people are very attached to for some reason, and I think it's a misplaced sense of the value of individual survival. They think, *This proves that I survived death because I was there!* Yet I don't think that's what we want, to survive death. Why would we want these funky monkey forms to persist forever?

But how could this mental modeling happen when metabolic activity in the brain has ceased? Maybe some lingering traces of (currently unmeasurable) brain activity will someday account for this. Or perhaps the boundaries between what is inside and outside of our minds is not as clearly defined as we usually think. It's incredibly tricky trying to figure out what is real and what is hallucinatory when it comes to dealing with OBEs and NDEs, and one can't help but wonder if they provide evidence for the soul's survival after the death of the body.

PROOF OF HEAVEN?

Neurosurgeon Eben Alexander wrote a best-selling book about his NDE called *Proof of Heaven,* which I enjoyed. However, despite the compelling story, I think that it is naive to assume that anyone's NDE is really proof of a heavenly afterlife.

Alexander tells a fascinating story about his visionary experience during a weeklong coma due to a rare case of bacterial meningitis (i.e., a brain severely infected with *E. coli* bacteria). A number of people recommended Alexander's absorbing book to me because his NDE uncannily resembles experiences that many people have reported with powerful psychedelic substances like ayahuasca, DMT, and ketamine. The similarities are truly remarkable, and it appears as though Alexander had a shamanic journey into the underworld and paradisical realms of nonlinear time, very similar to what many people describe on shamanic journeys. His beautiful descriptions of being immersed in the deep, dark bowels of the earth, and then soaring high into the light-filled heavens on the wings of a giant, ever-morphing butterfly are mesmerizing. The wings of the colossal butterfly are "intricately-patterned, alive with indescribable and vivid colors," like a "Persian carpet." An angelic, blue-eyed companion with high cheekbones accompanies him, explaining the spiritual secrets of existence.[34]

These experiences, and the climax of merging into the core of the godhead, seem very similar to the OBEs that people have described while under the influence of ketamine and DMT. Alexander is a wonderful writer, and he tells an astonishing story, but at the end of the book, in a couple of brief paragraphs, he quickly discounts endogenous DMT or ketaminelike neurochemicals—psychedelic molecules that are naturally found in the brain—as possibly playing a role in his NDE.

Although only speculation, current evidence seems to support the notion that a flood of DMT and perhaps also ketamine-like molecules may be released in the brain when we are close to death, and that this may help to account for the commonly reported NDEs that people have of leaving their body when they come close to dying. Alexander claims that the higher brain centers in his neocortex, where the receptors for the DMT molecules bind, were "off-line," "inactivated," or "shut down."[35] However, according to neuroscientist (and outspoken atheist) Sam Harris, this isn't necessarily true, that the brain scans that Alexander had don't reveal enough information to really know this.[36] Additionally, serotonin 2A receptors—the receptors in the brain that DMT binds to—can be found in deeper brain regions, such as in the hippocampus and the thalamus.[37]

Alexander's book presents compelling evidence for higher dimensions of reality, but he tries to squash his amazing, language-transcending (his description) experience into proof of a Christian belief system instilled in his childhood. The author presents compelling evidence for the existence of other realms and mysterious dimensions of consciousness—what psychonauts describe as a good "trip report"—but interpreting this as proof of an ancient, Bible-founded religion seems like a bit of a stretch to me. It appears that Alexander just didn't have an adequate model for explaining his mind-blowing experience. His medical training was clearly inadequate for doing so, he admits, but he also ignores (or is unaware of) scientific studies done on DMT by Rick Strassman, as well as the whole history of shamanic traditions. Alexander discounts DMT and ketamine experiences as being "dreamlike" or "chaotic," but he really should look at the research to see that almost every subject describes their DMT experiences as being hyper-real—as he does his NDE—that is, as seeming even more real than physical reality.

Nevertheless, just because I suspect that DMT or ketaminelike molecules may play a role in the NDE doesn't mean that I don't think that experiences like this might provide evidence for a true reality, a higher dimension of consciousness, and result in genuine spiritual insights. Rather, I just suspect that DMT and ketamine may also provide actual portals to the same mysterious realities and strange dimensions that Alexander experienced and that shamans have accessed throughout human history.

Despite the fact that body-mind dualism reigns supreme in Western philosophy, the truth is that on a scientific level it's exceedingly difficult to separate the mind from the body—that is, to define where one ends and the other begins. Consider the following studies, which provide some additional evidence for the notion of an astral body.

PHANTOM-LIMB RESEARCH

In Rupert Sheldrake's book *Seven Experiments That Could Change the World,* the author proposes doing research with people who have experience with a phantom limb, i.e., the feeling of a ghostly appendage where someone's missing limb used to be. Specifically, he proposed two different experiments to see whether or not there's actually a physical reality to the phenomenon. The first type of research Sheldrake suggested involves running tests with two subjects, someone who is behind a closed door and another person on the other side of the door who has a phantom limb. The person with the missing limb would randomly insert his or her phantom limb through one of six regions in the door, and the person on the other side would have to guess which one of these regions the phantom limbs were placed through. A second type of experiment could also be conducted, with a blindfolded amputee who would have to guess whether another other person was touching his phantom limb or not.

Sheldrake conducted some actual preliminary research with this first type of experiment that yielded promising results.[38] In a series of trials, three subjects sat one at a time behind the door and felt for the phantom arm, silently noting their guesses on the score sheet provided. Overall, there were 273 trials, involving the same three subjects. By chance, 16.7 percent of the results should have been correct. However, the overall success rate was 23.1 percent—significantly higher than chance. It's important to also point out that people may vary in their ability to sense the phantom limb—if indeed they can—as some subjects clearly perform better than others. The most successful subject in Sheldrake's research had a success rate of 33.9 percent, and the subjects doing the guessing were people who trained in subtle energy medicine or claimed to have dowsing abilities.

Research into the phenomenon of phantom limbs has also been conducted by Robert and Suzanne Mays, who together have studied phenomena related to near-death experiences for over thirty-five years (although neither has had a near-death experience). In 2007 and 2009 they conducted several experiments with a subject who reported phantom-limb sensations in the missing fingers of her left hand, with which she would "touch" people on the back of their heads. These studies produced some fascinating results. The Mays observed that the subject with the phantom fingers could "sense the presence of her left phantom fingers through interaction with the fingers of the other hand, with another person's body or with an object's surface. She senses the presence through physical sensations such as warmth, pressure or tingling in her left finger buds, palm, wrist, arm or other areas of her body." Additionally, the authors of these studies reported that after the subject had "been using her phantom fingers for a time in such 'feeling' situations, her hand usually shows increased skin color, and her finger buds at times show observable twitching." The subject could "touch" another person, "and that person can generally sense the interaction." The researchers ran two preliminary blinded trials of randomized "touch" and "no touch" cases. They provided immediate feedback to six subjects, and two subjects got nearly perfect scores detecting a phantom-finger touch versus a control stimulus (which was a leather mitten held on a yardstick).[39]

Regardless of whether we have an astral body or not, or exist as a field of consciousness beyond our physical forms, it's possible for us to perceive realities that are independent of our (bodily) sensory input on command with a certain class of powerful psychedelic substances.

PSYCHEDELIC OBES

A few psychedelic drugs and plants can consistently produce experiences that many people report as occurring outside of their physical bodies. This is especially true for DMT, ketamine, and salvia. However, these experiences differ in many important ways from both conventional OBEs and lucid dreams.

Like lucid dreaming and conventional OBEs, during psychedelic OBEs we create clear-headed models of a world that is largely independent of any recognized sensory stimuli. However, these worlds are rarely as ordinary-seeming as physical reality, and even the surreal world of our dreams seems fairly normal compared to the hyperspatial dimensions experienced on DMT, or the fractal layering of worlds experienced on ketamine or salvia. However, I've also heard of a number of cases where people under the influence of salvia report being in different physical locations—and different time periods—than where their bodies are actually located. For example, when I interviewed ethnobotanist Daniel Siebert, he offered a personal example of this very phenomenon:

> Then, suddenly, my eyes opened, and I found myself back in my body, back in physical reality. I looked around and felt greatly relieved. But then, a moment later, as everything came into focus, I realized that I wasn't in the right place, temporarily or physically. I found myself standing in a familiar place—it was the home of my maternal grandparents, but it was as it was when I was a small child. This alarmed me because I knew it wasn't right. I had somehow stepped out of this disembodied state seemingly into the wrong place in my personal history. It didn't feel at all like a vivid memory; it felt like I had literally stepped back into time in the wrong spot. Everything seemed completely real in the environment around me, and that frightened me. I panicked. Somehow I returned to a disembodied state, unaware of any physical reality. Then it happened again. I suddenly snapped out of it and opened my eyes. I looked around, and once again I was in the wrong place. I was at a friend's house. It was familiar to me, but it wasn't where I was supposed to be. This cycle repeated several times, returning again to a disembodied state, regaining awareness of physical reality, and finding myself in the "wrong" place.[40]*

I've personally had a number of psychedelic experiences where my consciousness entered a state in which I lost all awareness of the physical waking world, where I was only aware of an alternative reality. These experiences occurred after using ketamine, salvia, DMT, and several other shamanic aids. Once, on an ayahuasca journey, I became aware of how closed-eye visions originated in two forms, through two different visual systems, and I could see how the experience of going

---

*This is also an example of someone experiencing "false endings" during a psychedelic journey, which I described in chapter 4, similar to the "false awakenings" that are commonly reported with lucid dreams.

into a psychedelic OBE was created. During this experience I would stare at the back of my closed eyelids and see visual imagery unfolding in the space before me. Additionally, I could visualize imagery in my imagination, which would be greatly enhanced by the DMT-amplified state of consciousness and take on a life of its own. These were like two different visual realities competing for my attention. I could distinctly separate what I was seeing from these two different systems, and then I watched as they started to merge. When the two different visual systems merged so that I was seeing into my imagination, this started to take on the characteristics of a lucid dream or a psychedelic OBE, in the sense that I would become completely immersed in a new reality without any loss of awareness or clarity of mind. Many of these experiences were similar to lucid dreaming in some ways, especially those with ketamine, although I had somewhat less control over my environments in the psychedelic spheres. A number of times when I had these kinds of experiences I wondered if I had truly died.

When I asked psychologist Charles Tart how a NDE is similar to, as well as different from, a psychedelic experience, he said:

> I wish that I could say we have a lot of studies that have made detailed phenomenological comparisons, but of course we haven't. The NDE is, of course, centered around the fact that you think you've died, which is a pretty powerful centering device. It usually includes the feeling of moving through a tunnel, toward a light, contact with other beings, and a quick life review. A psychedelic experience may not have all of these characteristics. Some of the characteristics may be present, but certain details of the NDE may be missing, like the quick life review or the speedy return to normal consciousness. Now, this is interesting. This is one of the very vivid differences between psychedelic experiences and NDEs. With NDEs you can feel like you're way out there somewhere, and then "they" say that you have to go back, and bang! You're back in your body and everything is normal again. With psychedelics, of course, you come down more slowly and don't usually experience a condensed life review. So that's

what the major difference is. But psychedelic experiences also reach over a far wider terrain of possibilities. Let me tell you something about the life review. It's extremely common in NDEs for persons to undergo a life review, where they feel as if they remember at least every important event in their life, and often they say every single event in their life. Sometimes it even expands out into not only remembering and reliving every single event in their life, but also into knowing psychically the reactions of other people to all their actions. For some it must be horrible, because it seems that you would really experience their pain. I very seldom hear people say anything about a life review on psychedelics. Yeah, occasionally past memories come up, but not this dramatic review of a person's whole life.

One of the psychological models that I've used to help understand OBEs and lucid dreaming is psychologist Timothy Leary's (1920–1996) "eight-circuit model of consciousness." In this model, there are eight levels of function in the human brain; lucid dreaming and OBEs correspond to the eighth level, or circuit, "the metaphysiological circuit"— that part of the mind that supposedly extends beyond the brain and body, by being centered in one's atomic nuclei, rather than in the DNA of our body's cellular nuclei. Besides NDEs and states of consciousness activated by certain drugs like ketamine, salvia, and DMT, another effective method for reaching this eighth circuit is to float naked in a sensory-deprivation tank.

SENSORY-DEPRIVATION TANKS AND OBES

When I was in college, I worked on weekends at a sensory-deprivation tank center in West Hollywood, California, called the Altered-States Mind Gym. I used to float in the tank for hours every weekend after closing. A floating body leads to a floating mind, I quickly discovered.

Sensory-deprivation tanks—also sometimes called *isolation tanks* or *flotation tanks*—were invented by the late neuroscientist John C. Lilly in 1954, while he was a researcher at the National Institute of Mental Health. At the time that Lilly invented the tank, many scientists believed that if all stimuli were cut off from the nervous system, then our brains would simply fall asleep. Lilly demonstrated that this wasn't so. When our brains are separated from channels of sensory stimuli, whole new vistas open up within our minds, and many people have experiences that are similar to lucid dreams or psychedelic journeys. The tank provides a soundproof, light-proof environment where one floats in a warm pool of water so densely saturated with Epsom salt (800 pounds in eleven inches of water) that one buoyantly rests on the surface of the water without sinking, like visitors to the Dead Sea. The water and air temperature inside the tank are precisely controlled so that they are maintained at exactly skin surface temperature (93.5 degrees Fahrenheit). As one floats in the tank, all physical boundaries begin to blur and dissolve; the body relaxes profoundly, and the mind expands into new dimensions. It feels as if one is floating in zero gravity, and after floating for a while, all sensation of the physical body vanishes. The tanks are used for relaxation, meditation, health improvement, and for the exploration of altered states of consciousness.

The first OBEs that I had initially started in the sensory-deprivation tank as frightening episodes of sleep paralysis. It would happen almost every time I floated in the tank for over an hour, and the first dozen times or so I panicked each time and frantically tried to regain control of my body. One day when I wasn't floating I reflected on this experience—how each time my body became paralyzed I would get really scared and struggle to move my body, but then everything would always be okay after a short while. I realized that there was a compelling aspect to this experience that I wanted to explore. Every time my body became paralyzed in the tank, I would attempt to raise my arms out of the water and they wouldn't move—but something did. When I went to lift my arm up, a phantom limb or astral arm would move with my intention. So, I thought, what if I didn't panic and remembered that the paralysis was temporary? Could I then experiment with my astral limbs?

The next time I floated in the tank, sure enough, the sleep paralysis happened again. This time I refused to get scared. I couldn't move my physical body but I was able to move ghostly limbs without difficulty. I was able to easily lift myself out of my body, and—wow—liberation! What extraordinary freedom! I could easily do somersaults with my astral body in midair. This was immensely joyful, absolutely delightful, and I would then go exploring my environment, which eventually developed into either a lucid dream or a nonlucid dream.

These experiences are the closest I've ever come during my waking state to having the kind of traditional OBEs that are commonly reported with near-death experiences. The only significant difference is that I never saw my own physical body lying where it should be.

I have also had traditional OBEs within lucid dreams, and in these situations I experienced leaving my dream body within the dream environment. One night I found myself repeatedly floating up toward the ceiling of a strange room, out of my body, only it wasn't happening in material reality, it was happening in a lucid dream. I was having an out-of-the-dream-body experience.

The environments that I immediately find myself in, after it appears that I'm leaving my physical body during episodes of sleep paralysis, have always been slight variations of the room that my physical body is actually lying immobilized in. It's like a parallel-universe version of my room, and the astral environment is always more mutable, like in a dream, but not quite that mutable.

Of course, skeptics will say that this is due to the fact that my brain is creating inaccurate models of reality from memory and imagination, and perhaps so. However, when I'm actually in these states of consciousness I can't help but wonder if some physical objects, beings, and environments have correlating representations in both our physical waking world and other dimensions of reality—what are often referred to as the astral realms. This would help to explain countless reports of sensing presences or feeling unusual energies at sacred sites and haunted houses. Perhaps there really are certain kinds of physical places that have correlating astral environments where spirit tribes like to hang out . . .

SACRED SITES, HAUNTED HOUSES, GHOSTS, AND SPIRITS

My home in the Santa Cruz Mountains of California is not far from the Brookdale Lodge, a large resort hotel built in the early 1900s that has a colorful and tragic history, and which is considered to be haunted by many ghosts. Every book on famous haunted houses in California contains information about this legendary lodge, with a brook running through its dining room, as over the years many apparitions have supposedly interacted with resort guests.

I spent a fascinating night at this supposedly haunted lodge with some friends a few years ago, and we did have some mysterious, unnerving experiences on that occasion.* Ever since then I've read and thought a lot about the many reported ghost sightings there. Then one night, while falling asleep, I thought that there might be a crossover realm between the physical and astral environments, and I wondered what it would be like to visit the Brookdale Lodge and other haunted locations in an OBE state. I have yet to try this, but perhaps at certain levels of awareness our minds become conscious of a level of reality where the physical and astral meet. These seemingly thinly veiled locations where astral beings or spirits supposedly congregate might allow for a kind of crossover between realms. So depending on the psychological type or personality of the spirits and the particular social climate of these unusual places, they could seem either haunted or sacred to people who are sensitive to these levels of reality.

Like me, Oliver Fox discusses having an OBE in which he describes not seeing his physical body where it should be, lying on the bed. He explains this by suggesting that although the room he was in looked as vivid, or more so, than usual, what he was seeing was the astral representation of the room. Since he was occupying an astral representation of himself, he couldn't see his physical body lying on the bed, because it was an astral representation of the bed in this parallel reality that he was seeing. He writes:

---

*For an account of my paranormal experience at the Brookdale Lodge, see the second edition of Aubrey Graves' book *The Haunted Brookdale Lodge*.

It will be noted that I could not see my body when I looked for it upon the bed, and this has been my general experience, yet other projectionists state that they can see theirs. It has been suggested to me that if I am functioning in my astral body, I should be able to see only the astral counterparts of the objects in the room; and therefore to see my physical body a sort of "downward clairvoyance" would be necessary, as its astral counterpart would be no longer coincident with it. Perhaps other people have this power and I do not possess it. But, fundamentally, different states of consciousness are the result of being able to respond to different rates of vibration; and for this reason it may be the projectionist when exteriorized lives to some extent in a world of his own, and no two experimenters will ever get precisely similar results, because they will not respond to exactly the same range of vibrations. This is true, but to a much smaller degree, even in waking life.[41]

If there is any truth to this notion it might help to explain why OBE environments can seem to contain slight variations from their physical counterparts. In my experience—and in many other reports—the environment that I immediately enter upon exiting from my body often seems identical to the room that I am physically in, except there will be an extra window or door, or a piece of furniture that shouldn't be there.*

Of course, we need to keep reminding ourselves that Sue Blackmore and other skeptics of the OBE phenomenon suggest that they occur because our brains produce imperfect mental models or inadequate simulations of reality based on memory and imagination, not perception. Once again, I'm reminded of the account told by Zoe7, recounted in chapter 7, when he experimented with the hallucinogenic dissociative anesthetic DXM. I've puzzled over that account for years. I just can't help wondering what was really occurring when he returned from

---

*I've also noticed that sometimes when I get high on cannabis indoors my perception of the physical environment can subtly shift, so that out of my peripheral vision it appears as though aspects of the room have elongated or changed in odd, dreamlike ways. These perceptual shifts remind me of how some astral environments have appeared.

that trip to the kitchen and saw another version of himself standing in his office while he was standing at the door, before suddenly switching perspectives and becoming the other version of himself in the office. Could it have been Zoe7's astral or dream body that got up to go to the kitchen while his physical body remained in bed, and he didn't even realize it because of the chemically induced dissociation? It's a common idea—as portrayed in the film *The Sixth Sense*—that many people who have died don't realize that they're dead. Can this also happen sometimes with some OBEs?

In any case, I asked Ryan Hurd what he thought of this idea. Did he think that physical objects had astral correlates in the OBE realms? "Yes, I think so," he said. "The concept of apotropaic objects is key here, as they are objects that traverse worlds. Liminality is superimportant in ritual protections and in household archaeology the world over. Apotropaic amulets have made a big difference in my own relationship to sleep paralysis."

Hurd describes a memorable lucid dream or OBE where he is in a dream or astral version of his bedroom, and he takes a piece of obsidian that is actually in his waking-world bedroom and inserts it into his astral eye area, like an old computer-game cartridge, and this, he reports, clarifies his vision and stops the pain in his eyes.[42] So it appears that astral objects and bodies may operate in ways that are quite unlike what we experience in the physical world. Could this dual-dimension representation help to explain why certain objects are regarded as sacred or cursed, because of their corresponding characteristics in another level of reality? Numerous lucid-dream explorers have written about the magic of locating emotionally charged possessions from the waking world within their lucid dreams, and the enchantment that comes from carefully observing these treasures and toys within the dream. This can be a most delightful experience. After I've studied a sacred object or artistic creation in a lucid dream, that object then takes on new dimensions in the waking world, and always connects me back to the dream.

OBEs stretch the limits of what we know to be biologically possible;

however, quantum physics may offer insights into OBEs, lucid dreaming, and the outer limits of shamanic consciousness.

CONSCIOUSNESS AND QUANTUM PHYSICS

There are some types of dreaming that are difficult to understand using models developed from biological sciences like neuroscience. These include telepathic dreams, shared dreaming, and precognitive dreams. Studies conducted in quantum physics, however, may help to shed some light on these nighttime mysteries.

The famous "double-slit" light-beam experiment from quantum physics—first conducted by English physician Thomas Young in the early nineteenth century and replicated many times, in ever sophisticated ways—informs us about the strange nature of reality. The results from these experiments appear to indicate that the type of measurement that we make of light determines whether it appears as particles (photons) or a wave (oscillations in matter that involve energy transfer).

The basic version of the experiment is quite simple and goes like this: A light source such a laser beam is directed toward a plate that contains two parallel slits in it, and the light shines through the slits to a screen behind the plate. The crazy, odd, counterintuitive, and most bizarre and difficult thing to understand about the results of these experiments is that the act of observation plays the determining role in whether the light appears on the screen as a coherent wave or as a series of random particles. In other words, when one watches or records the light shining into the slits, particles can be seen entering one slit or the other, and then this appears on the screen that way. However, if the light beam is unobserved or not recorded going through the slits, then the light actually travels through both slits simultaneously and creates a wave pattern when observed on the screen. How can the act of observation possibly determine how the light travels and appears? No one knows, but these experiments have been verified many times and provide a foundation for engineering many of the technologies that we rely on today. According to the mathematics that are used to express this phenomenon in quantum physics, the reason for this is because, prior to observation, every possible outcome for any event exists simultaneously. Then the act of observation or measurement "collapses" this wave of multiple possibilities into a single event that can no longer be changed.

One model for interpreting the results of these experiments is the theory of parallel universes, which attempts to solve this mysterious problem by suggesting that every possible outcome for every event branches off into its own parallel universe, moment by moment. Could dreams or OBEs be journeys into these other universes?

Another important study from quantum physics, also replicated many times in ever more sophisticated ways, provides evidence that whenever two particles interact with each other in a certain way, they are forever more connected in a way that appears to transcend our ordinary notions of space and time. This important understanding provides the foundation for Bell's theorem, which states that no matter wherever or whenever we observe a single particle, we instantly affect its strangely connected twin, no matter how far apart in the universe the two are. This understanding may help to explain Jung's concept of synchronicity, or meaningful coincidences.

Contemplating the results of these quantum physics experiments causes me to suspect that there's a much greater link between my mind and reality than most people commonly think. If one takes the results from these well-verified experiments seriously, then one has to accept that we're literally co-creating the universe by observing it.

This understanding of the deep nature of reality that quantum physics has been able to reveal sounds a little bit like how the mind manifests creative ideas into physical actions and material things. I can also personally relate to the notions of being a particle or a wave. When I'm alone, with just my own mind, I feel like I'm a wave—undefined, with blurry boundaries, and more fluid. When I'm with other people I feel like I'm a particle—sharply defined, distinctly bounded, and more separate. It seems that my own mind can be either a wave or a particle, depending on whether or not I'm being observed by others.

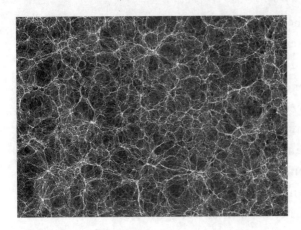

Fig. 9.3. A network
of galaxy superclusters
in deep space
(photo by NASA)

Ever since the beginning of quantum physics,* a number of its
most prominent researchers have become interested in the relationship
between physical reality and consciousness. Carl Jung and physicist
Neils Bor corresponded with, and influenced, each other. In his book
How the Hippies Saved Physics, MIT physicist David Kaiser examines
the connection between the development of quantum physics research
and the exploration of psychedelic states of consciousness. Numerous
physicists have drawn parallels between physics and mysticism, and
between physics and the wisdom of Eastern philosophy. Physicist Fred
Alan Wolf suggests that the universe itself may dream, and that we
dream because the universe dreams. Wolf theorizes that dreaming is
the basis for consciousness, and that it is through dreaming that we are
able to manifest a sense of ourselves.[43]

High-powered telescopes reveal that the universe can be seen on
a macroscopic level as an intricate network of galaxies, a cosmic web.†
Some areas are almost empty, like dark voids, while other areas are
densely packed with galaxies, in superclusters. These superclusters are

---

*Quantum physics has its origins in Max Planck's solution in 1900 to the black-body
radiation problem, and it was further developed with Albert Einstein's 1905 paper that
offered a quantum-based theory to explain the photoelectric effect. Early quantum theory was profoundly reconceived in the mid-1920s.
†Galaxies, of which there are between 170 and 200 billion, are clusters of stars. A galaxy can range between just a few thousand stars to over a hundred trillion. The Milky
Way galaxy, where our solar system resides, contains around 500 billion stars.

the largest-known structures in the universe, and photos of them look startlingly like images of neural connections in the brain. Could our whole universe exist inside of a cosmic, ever-dreaming brain?

Could the universe in fact be a giant nervous system, a cosmic brain, as the late psychologist Timothy Leary and others have suggested? And if the universe is a giant brain, is it alone, or are there others?

DO DREAMS ALLOW US TO VISIT PARALLEL UNIVERSES OR HIGHER DIMENSIONS?

Numerous people have described their lucid dreams or their visionary experiences with ayahuasca and magic mushrooms as being akin to entering a higher dimension or a parallel universe. Physicist Michio Kaku's theory about multiple universes coexisting within a larger multiverse may help to explain how this mind-bending possibility could be a reality, and why there are basically two different types of creation myths in our world.[44] Some cultures believe that the universe had a beginning, and that it will one day have an end, but others think that the universe is timeless and eternal. Kaku proposes that within an eternal, timeless multiverse, new universes with finite life spans are continually bursting into existence, living out their lives, and then dying. If this theory is true, then it helps to explain the mystery behind our conflicting Creation myths—as well as where our consciousness might actually go when we lucid dream or journey on ayahuasca.

Sometimes people report that the universe that they return to after a shamanic experience ends is not the same universe that they started out in. Consider the following experience with *Salvia divinorum* reported in the *Entheogen Review*: "There have been a few times when I smoked *Salvia divinorum* and was not sure (and still am not sure) that I really returned to the same reality I left from. Funny little details—like all of the people I know being acquainted with an advertising cartoon called *Charley the Tuna* that I seem to have no recollection of whatsoever."[45]

I had a similar experience, in which I dreamed I smoked some *Salvia divinorum* and then awoke a few moments later. Every so often I can't help but wonder if all of my life since that moment hasn't really just been a salvia voyage that actually began in another universe, a universe that I remember now as a dream . . .

Physicists tell us that the universe has ten dimensions, although our bodily senses only reveal four.[46] Besides having a shamanic journey or a lucid dream, one of the best ways to gain an understanding of what the higher dimensions of reality might be like is to read English theologian Edwin A. Abbott's 1884 classic satirical novella *Flatland,* about someone from a two-dimensional world encountering a third dimension.

There's a popular story that I find intriguing that has been passed around on the Internet, about the strange case of a mysterious traveler arriving in the Tokyo airport. The story has been rewritten in various forms, and it now appears on a number of strange-but-true and ghost-story type websites. As far as I can tell, this story first appeared in a book coauthored by British writer Colin Wilson, who passed away in 2013.[47] It goes like this:

Supposedly in 1954, a businessman arrived in the Tokyo airport with a passport, driver's license, currency, and other official papers from a country that no one in Japan had ever heard of and couldn't be found on any map. This professionally attired man was said to have claimed that his country, a place called Taured, was almost a thousand years old, but when he tried to locate it on a map of Western Europe he is said to have indicated that Andorra, Spain, was where he thought his country should be. Allegedly the mysterious traveler had never heard of Andorra, Spain, so the Japanese custom officials were confused and unsure of what to do with this enigmatic and bewildered visitor who claimed that he and his colleagues had been doing business with Japanese companies for years. That night he is said to have mysteriously vanished from a guarded hotel room high above the city streets, and no one knows what happened to him since then.

Whether or not this story is true remains a mystery, as I couldn't locate an earlier source for it, but it certainly can be a fascinating possibility in pondering the existence of parallel universes. As I mentioned earlier, this notion, a common motif of science fiction, stems from a theory that some physicists subscribe to as a way of explaining one of the mysteries of quantum physics—how every possible outcome can simultaneously exist in an unobserved event. The "multiple universe theory" is one possible solution to the mystery of how Schrödinger's cat* could be both alive and dead at the same time, because in this model there is one universe where the cat dies and another where the cat survives.

If the theory of parallel universes is correct, then it may offer some clues as to where we go in our dreams and shamanic voyages—that is, if they're not just masturbatory constructions of our minds. For a lot of people dreams are experienced as real. According to anthropologist Charles Laughlin, "Many peoples believe that their dreams are real— that they are experiences had by their dream-selves wandering around in another dimension of reality."[48] When I asked psychologist Stanley Krippner about this possibility—that dreams might allow us to visit other dimensions and parallel universes—he said:

> I have talked with shamans who believe that they can travel to other dimensions of reality during their dreams, and perhaps they can. Psychologists know very little about the "imaginal world," that terrain that goes by such names as the *collective unconscious* and the *akashic field*. Many ordinary people have dreams about future events or about what another person is doing or thinking, but to claim that they enter a parallel universe every night is a notion that lacks empirical evidence. And such a claim diminishes the wonders of the neuropsychology of dreams.

---

*Schrödinger's cat is a famous thought experiment devised by physicist Erwin Schrödinger in 1935 that helps to illustrate the paradoxical nature of a phenomenon in physics known as *quantum superposition,* which recognizes that multiple events can exist simultaneously prior to observation. Whether or not a cat in a sealed box has been poisoned is linked to a random subatomic event that may or may not occur, and before checking, both outcomes simultaneously exist.

Another possibility is that dreams and shamanic experiences are occurring in parts of the universe composed of dark matter or dark energy.* Astrophysicists tell us that the 200 billion galaxies that are detectable by our best telescopes add up to only 4 percent of the whole cosmos! Around 96 percent of the universe is composed of this dark matter or dark energy that we can't see or measure. Nobody knows what this stuff is, but we know that it's there, and there's a lot of it, because it massively outweighs all the atoms, in all the stars, in all the galaxies, across the whole detectable universe.

Psychiatric researcher Rick Strassman speculates that the worlds and beings that people experience under the influence of DMT may be composed of this dark matter or dark energy. When I interviewed Strassman about this he said, "Maybe one day we will develop a dark-matter or parallel-universe camera, take pictures of what we see there, and then compare it to what a DMT subject witnesses in his or her altered state. That way, we would establish the objective existence of the beings and their world."

Dark matter and dark energy may be what dream worlds, and possibly astral worlds, are composed of as well, and the yet-to-be-discovered physics of these exotic energies may help to explain why time doesn't seem to operate in dreams the same way that it does in the waking world.

TIME DILATION WITHIN DREAMS

Although early studies by Stephen LaBerge and colleagues demonstrate that ten seconds experienced in a lucid dream equals about ten seconds in waking-world time, other more recent studies indicate that dreams

---

*Dark matter is a hypothetical substance that is nevertheless believed by most modern astronomers to account for around five-sixths of the matter in the universe. It has not been directly observed, yet its existence and properties are inferred from its various gravitational effects: on the motions of visible matter; via gravitational lensing; its influence on the universe's large-scale structure, and its effects in the cosmic microwave background. Likewise, dark energy is an undetectable form of energy that much of the universe appears to be mysteriously composed of.

may occur in slow motion. This may help to explain why it's common for people to dream that when they're being chased, or have to run for some reason in a dream, it feels like their legs are caught in molasses and they can hardly move.

Psychologist Daniel Erlacher and colleagues at the University of Bern, Switzerland, conducted a study to analyze brain activity during sleep to see how the brain reacts to action in a dream, as well as the passage of time.[49] Erlacher used lucid dreamers as subjects in his study, and he had them carry out an activity in their dreams such as counting, walking, or doing gymnastics. Notably, it took the subjects 50 percent longer to carry out these activities in dreams than in waking life.

Among the dream reports and anecdotes I've read that I find the most compelling are those that deal with dreams in which time is stretched in ways that seem impossible. I've found a number of stories on the Internet about people who claim to have experienced days, weeks, months, or even years living the life of another person, only to then snap back into their beds and discover that this all happened in a single night. I've reviewed several accounts like this from people who were dreaming, and one from someone under the influence of the psyche-delic dissociative drug DXM. A few reliable people have personally told me that they have experienced this—including my own girlfriend—and there are plenty of stories on the Internet, such as the following:

> The dream itself wasn't really that exciting but the duration and realism were astonishing. . . . I went into bed. . . . When I got my eyes opened and my blurry vision got better I found myself in a hospital bed with nurses around. All confused, I asked all the right questions: What happened? Where am I? Who are you? I was told that I had an accident and had been in a coma for a few weeks.

He then goes on to describe his experience in the dream hospital, where he discovered that he was not only a different person, but a different sex (female), and that people there already knew "her":

Anyway, to make a very, very long story short, I got out of the hospital. Went back to school, graduated. Went to university, met my future husband, became a chemist, we bought a house, I got two kids. None of this felt like a dream. Time wasn't quirky, lights lit up perfectly, I read newspapers, was bored, excited, menstruating, sick and in love. And it would have definitely hurt had [I] tried to fly or walk through walls. I had to live all the dull moments and the most exciting ones.

He recounted this dream life as seemingly going on for what felt like twenty years. He struggled with his memories from before the dream, to understand how this could possibly be happening, when one night during a storm, she—i.e., the woman he was in the dream—lost control of the car she was driving, smashed into a tree, and then woke up from the dream as his old self again, back in his bed, as if only a single night had passed.[50]

Some people believe that it's possible to subjectively experience years in a lucid dream while their bodies merely age a single night. This concept was toyed with in the film *Inception,* and there are numerous online discussion groups that take up this subject.[51] I've never been able to do anything like this—changing the nature of time in my dreams—but it seems conceivable to me, as I suspect that time and space are ultimately mental concepts. I've certainly experienced a sense of time dilation on psychedelic voyages, especially with DMT, where it felt like hours or days were compressed into just a few minutes of clock time.

I posted the following request on my Facebook page: "I'd be curious to hear from anyone who has ever experienced an unusual sense of time dilation during a dream or a shamanic journey, where an experience that lasts for around an hour in waking reality is experienced as days, months, or years in another reality." My friend, Italian writer Massimiliano Geraci, said, "Time dilatation? Ever heard what happened to the sage Narada when he asked Lord Vishnu to explain to him the concept of maya?" Geraci provided me with a link that told the story:

Narada went to Vishnu and asked him the meaning of Maya. . . . Vishnu said, "I will explain after you quench my thirst. . . ." Narada went to a river to fetch water. But as he was collecting the water, he saw a beautiful girl. He was so drawn to her that he followed her to her village and asked her father for her hand in marriage. The father agreed and the two got married. Before long, Narada was a father and then grandfather and then great grandfather. . . . Suddenly one day, it rained. And the rains refused to stop. The river swelled and broke its banks. Water rushed into Narada's house, and to his horror, swept away his wife, his children, his grandchildren and his great grandchildren. He screamed and shouted for help as the water dragged him under. Suddenly he . . . found himself . . . before Vishnu. "Narada," said Vishnu, "where is my water? I am still thirsty." Narada did not understand. Where was his family, his wife's village, the river? "Where does this pain and suffering come from, Narada?" asked Vishnu. . . . "I thought you had full knowledge of Maya before you set out to fetch water for me." Narada bowed his head in realization. He knew Maya but had never experienced Maya. . . . Unless one experiences Maya, one will not be able to empathize with those who are trapped in it.[52]

According to Hindu philosophy, learning to see through the illusion of maya can take lifetimes, but how is time actually experienced in a lucid dream? Studies by Stephen LaBerge seem to demonstrate that the time that elapses in a lucid dream generally corresponds to our experience in waking time, while Daniel Erlacher found that dreams seem to move in slow motion. Yet we also know that dreams are notoriously affected by what we believe. Is it possible to hack into the dream realm and change the nature of time through our beliefs, or is this one of the biological limitations of lucid dreaming?

Only more research will determine this, but mystical experiences might shed some light on this subject. In the next chapter we'll be examining how lucid dreaming can be a path to spiritual awakening.

10

CONSCIOUS DREAMING AS A PATH TO SPIRITUAL AWAKENING

*O you who fear the difficulties of the road to annihilation—
do not fear. It is so easy, this road, that it can be traveled
sleeping.*

SUFI APHORISM

*You are dreaming . . . from then on I was watchful, even
in dreams, to separate the real from the unreal.*

YOGANANDA

Morpheus is the Greek god of dreams; his name means "shaper of dreams." The related word *morph* is often used to describe the shifting, transformative nature of a psychedelic vision or its digital representation, while *morphine* is the name of that powerful, dream-inducing opiate drug. Notably, Morpheus is also the name of the captain of the flying ship Nebuchadnezzar* in the classic science-fiction film *The*

---

*This flying ship was a hovercraft in the film, and it was named after the biblical king of the same name, the ruler of the Babylonian Empire from 634 to 562 BCE. In the Book of Daniel there is story about the king awakening from a powerful dream, only to have his memory of the dream frustratingly dissolve a few seconds later. Nebuchadnezzar believed that the powerful dream must have been divinely inspired, so he sent strict

Matrix, which presents the idea that everything we think of as reality is really a computer-generated simulation—much like lucid dreaming.

Neo, the hero of *The Matrix,* gains his strength through realizing that reality is created by his mind, a concept that resonates with much of Eastern philosophy. For example, the word *buddha* means "awakened one." To be awake, in the Buddhist sense, means to wake up from the dream or illusion of being a separate self, so in some sense all lucid dreamers are buddhas, at least temporarily, when they realize that the world around them is a dream is composed of their own mind.

The parallels between becoming lucid in a dream and having a mystical experience in waking reality are truly striking and thought-provoking. In both cases, you become acutely aware that the person you think you are is just a temporary illusion, and in both cases you remember that you have another existence that you have forgotten about. In both cases, having this experience of "awakening" generally brings an immediate sense of joy, a profound loss of fear, the lifting of an amnesia that you didn't even realize was present, and the delightful realization that so much more is possible than you had previously thought. Celia Green expresses this well when she explains how frequent lucid dreamers sometimes come to view all of life as a kind of dream:

> The idea that the whole of life might be in some sense a dream, which seems more characteristically to occur to habitual lucid dreamers, consists in admitting a qualitative distinction between waking life and ordinary dreams, but going on to consider that there may be an equally qualitative distinction between waking consciousness and some "higher" form of consciousness. The relationship between this supposed higher state of consciousness and normal

---

(continued) instructions to the diviners, astrologers, and wizards in his kingdom, saying that they must tell him what his dream was and what it meant or else they would all be killed. When the prophet and dream interpreter Daniel prayed to God to reveal the king's dream and its meaning to him, and the king was satisfied with the response that Daniel gave, his life—and the lives of his fellow diviners in the kingdom—were saved. In the film *The Matrix,* Morpheus references the biblical king when he says, "I have dreamed a dream . . . but now that dream is gone from me."

consciousness would be analogous to the relationship between normal waking consciousness and non-lucid dreaming.[1]

Throughout this book we've considered the possibility that dreams might be more real and meaningful than many people commonly believe. Now, paradoxically, we are asked to consider the possibility that both dreams and what we experience as the waking world may be illusions, and be equally unreal.

Stephen LaBerge expresses well how we can recognize the illusory nature of dreams, and he describes how we can learn to see what we think of as the "real" world as actually being the inside our own mind in a dream:

> Lucid dreamers realize that they themselves contain, and thus transcend, the entire dream world and all of its contents, because they know that their imaginations have created the dream. So the transition to lucidity turns dreamers' worlds upside down. Rather than seeing themselves as a mere part of the whole, they see themselves as the container rather than the contents. Thus they freely pass through dream prison walls that only seemed impenetrable, and venture forth into the larger world of the mind.[2]

Consider Celia Green's further assessment:

> It seems possible that the failure to make the necessary distinction between a lucid dream and a non-lucid dream arises in part from a psychological resistance in recognizing the uncertain philosophical status of the "external world" of waking life. In order to preserve our belief in the unquestioned status of the physical world, and our secure grasp of "reality," it is perhaps desirable that dreams should be regarded as something as distinctly unreal as possible. If it becomes clear that they can rival the waking world in perceptual precision and clarity, and that the state of a person's mental functioning in a dream can seem to be not much different from that of waking life,

we may start to ask ourselves uncomfortable questions about how good a claim to superior reality our waking life actually has.[3]

With the attainment of lucidity in a dream comes the memory that one has another life as a human being on earth. Does this experience have parallels in the mystical experiences of the waking world? Yes, it does, and when this happens people often say that they remember having a spiritual existence that transcends their biological life, sometimes along with what are referred to as past-life memories. Some people also say that these memories can influence our dreams.

MEMORIES OF PAST LIVES

There are many people who claim to have memories of living lifetimes as other people, and some significant scientific research has been conducted to verify these claims. The work of psychiatrists Ian Stevenson, Brian L. Weiss, Stanislav Grof, and others provides many compelling examples of cases where it appears that, at the very least, personal information or traumas have mysteriously traveled from the death of one person and into the birth of another.

Stevenson worked at the University of Virginia School of Medicine for over fifty years, was its department head for ten years, and is the author of three hundred scientific papers and fourteen books about reincarnation. He collected hundreds of cases that he believes provide evidence of past-life memories, and instances where birthmarks correspond with the wound on a deceased person that a child was said to recall. If you're interested in reading Stevenson's work, a good place to start is his book *Twenty Cases Suggestive of Reincarnation*.

Brian Weiss is a Yale University–trained clinical psychologist who had been treating a patient who began discussing what appeared to be past-life experiences while in hypnosis, and although Weiss was skeptical at first, he later became convinced that these memories were real, after confirming elements of his patient's story through public records. After becoming convinced of the validity of his patient's experience,

Weiss began using a technique called past-life regression in his therapy. He offers some compelling evidence for his convictions in the book *Many Lives, Many Masters*. Weiss believes that a lot of common phobias, recurring nightmares, anxiety attacks, and even physical ailments are rooted in past-life experiences, and that people can learn to overcome these ailments by understanding their cause in a previous lifetime.

A number of psychotherapists besides Weiss have incorporated the doctrine of reincarnation into their practice. These practitioners generally refer to themselves as past-life therapists and have formed an organization called the Association of Past-Life Therapy and Research.

Psychiatric researcher Stanislav Grof, who conducted more LSD studies than any other scientist on the planet, has described how there were numerous examples in the therapeutic psychedelic sessions that he ran where he encountered convincing evidence for past-life memories among his subjects, such as unexplainable knowledge of obscure historical facts or archaic languages.[4]

The late "psychic sensitive" Edgar Cayce advocated the study of dreams and promoted the idea that dreams may reflect past-life experiences. Cayce's work has had a big influence on many people. According to its website, the organization that he founded, the Association for Research and Enlightenment (A.R.E.), boasts "centers in 37 countries, and individual members in more than 70 countries,"[5] with around 25,000 members.[6]

Additionally, and most significantly, the concept of reincarnation—that one's essential awareness transcends death and progresses through numerous incarnations—is basic to the religions and philosophies of most Asian, Australian Aborigine, tribal African, and Pacific Island cultures, and is also found in many Native American tribes. Clearly, the concept of reincarnation has great appeal to many people.

However, even if confirmed as true, past-life memories may not be personal; they could be experiences that arise due to interacting with information that is stored in the collective unconscious, and their possible existence doesn't necessarily imply that the person experiencing the memories has lived before as that separate unit of consciousness. However, confirmation of these kinds of memories certainly stretches the limits of what we currently know to be true, and Weiss's accounts of people healing through past-life regression therapy are most compelling.

When I spoke with psychologist Ralph Metzner about this subject, he told me:

> I have for many years now included past-life regression methods in my psychotherapy practice, if the search for causal factors of present problems in childhood or in prenatal experience, as well as from parental influences, has been unproductive. Past-life regression therapy uses a light hypnotic trance state, in which the practitioner guides the client to ask questions of their inner/higher self— questions about past-life connections to their current-life issues. Such approaches can be very revealing and bring about profoundly healing changes in attitudes. Successful past-life regression therapy does not require commitment to any particular belief system or theory of reincarnation. An openness to the possibility is the only prerequisite and, as in any healing practice, it is the results that count. Many people, myself included, have reported flashes of insights and seeming memories of other lives during group or shared psychedelic experiences.

I have a friend who told me that she often has dreams in which she is other people, of different ages, ethnicities, and both sexes; something I've rarely experienced myself. In one particularly arresting dream of hers (mentioned in chapter 7), she said that she died repeatedly in the dream and then immediately woke up right after dying each time, in the same bed, in the same bedroom—but as a different person. My friend said that this happened many times in her dream, and that she could see her reflection as different people in her bedroom mirror when she seemingly awoke after each "death" in the dream. When she told me about this I couldn't help but wonder if this dream was based on memories she had of previous incarnations, or possibly on a memory of the reincarnation process.

Could commonly recurring nightmares or emotionally charged dream themes that seem to have no relationship to one's current life be caused by the residue from events that occurred in a previous lifetime or lifetimes? This is a question that no one can really answer, but the question becomes especially interesting when we compare it to how we think about our current life when we achieve lucidity in a dream. In a lucid dream we know for certain that we have at least one other life—as the person lying in bed who is having the dream—and that other existence in the waking world unquestionably has a huge influence on what one experiences in the dream realm.

According to past-life researchers, memories from a previous life can come to people while they are either awake or when they are dreaming. Stanley Krippner explains: "When this information comes from dreams, the dreamers visually experience themselves participating in a scene during some earlier time before their present lives. At other times, the dreamers simply observe the scene in a dream. In either case, the dreamers claim that they cannot account for these images by events in their present life situation."[7]

When I interviewed Robert Waggoner I asked him about the possibility of using lucid dreaming as a tool to explore past-life memories. He responded with some words of caution:

I did a paper . . . on seeking past-life experiences while lucidly aware, because I realized as I went deeper into lucid dreaming that seemed a possibility. Normally, I don't talk about this and share it too much with lucid dreamers because there are some difficult aspects of seeking out past-life information in lucid dreams. I'll give you an example: For a period of about nine months, that's what I did in lucid dreams—I sought out past-life information. And it began to seem that I had awakened within my larger awareness, past-life . . . I'll just call them "selves" or "awarenesses." So one day I was at my local grocery store doing the daily shopping. I was pushing my cart along, and I could feel one of these newly awakened awarenesses within my stream of consciousness. And as "we" turned the corner and came to the meat counter, I could hear it say clearly in my head, *Oh my— they keep cut up dead pieces of animals where they store their food.* So imagine a meat counter in your normal grocery store. You have sixty or eighty feet of steaks and pork chops and chickens, all basically dead animals chopped up. Of course, the Robert-me had never considered that. But this larger awareness, or different awareness, that I'd kind of woken up by virtue of seeking out past-life selves in the lucid-dream state was utterly horrified by this. And so the caution that I'm trying to bring out is that a lucid dreamer . . . has to keep clear in your head what your thoughts are and your stream of consciousness, and not get confused by other streams of consciousness that you might have awakened. So that's one of the interesting things that a person can do. But I do think that the flexible or the malleable nature of space and time that we oftentimes see in our dreams and lucid dreams means that in dreaming, and also lucid dreaming, we oftentimes have experiences that connect with past lives. And also sometimes the dream symbols that seem so odd and unusual to us, I assume . . . must have connections with either past-life memories or other incarnations that we're just not aware of in this ego-life.

Notably, both the practice of lucid dreaming and a belief system based upon the concept of reincarnation are part of the structure of Tibetan Buddhism.

TIBETAN BUDDHISM AND LUCID DREAMING

Lucid-dreaming methods have been used for thousands of years in different shamanic and religious traditions, and perhaps no tradition has a more developed and integrated system of lucid-dream training than Tibetan Buddhism.

Tibetan Buddhism is a branch of Buddhist philosophy that resulted from the cultural integration of the Mahayana branch of Buddhism developed in India, which incorporated many of the tantric techniques of Hindu traditions and the shamanic Bön tradition of Tibet, which already had a long history of developing sophisticated techniques for training people how to dream with lucidity.* Lucid dreaming is also a part of Hindu traditions, where the practice is referred to as "dream witnessing."

As mentioned earlier, the word *buddha* is Sanskrit for "awakened one." It's important to reemphasize the significance of this term in our discussion here, as the term "awakening" is given to both the experience of arising from sleep and to gaining a sense of greater spiritual awareness.

The philosophy of Buddhism began around 2,500 years ago, in the foothills of the Himalayas, with the spiritual awakening of Siddhartha Gautama, a wealthy Sakyan prince who left his palatial life of luxury to see the world and reach enlightenment—that is, to awaken to a deeper understanding of reality. As the story goes, Siddhartha's birth was heralded by a prophetic dream. Siddhartha's mother, Queen Maya, reportedly dreamed that a white elephant with six tusks ran into the palace, loudly trumpeting. It circled her bed three times and then dove into her womb, through the right side of her ribcage. Upon awakening, Maya interpreted the dream as an omen that her child would bring a special gift to the world.

As a young man, Siddhartha left his lavish palace of cushioned luxury, whereupon he then shockingly encountered all of the suffering and misery in the world that he had been carefully sheltered from in the palatial bubble of his gated kingdom. Undeniably changed by what he had witnessed, Siddhartha became a sannyasi, an ascetic who renounces the ordinary world. He practiced meditation with other ascetics and nearly killed himself attempting to reach his goal of spiritual liberation

---

*When my colleague Rebecca McClen Novick, an accomplished Buddhist scholar, read this sentence, she remarked, "To clarify, although Mahayana does contain much of what is considered by the Theravada tradition—the other main Buddhist tradition—to be the 'original' teachings of the Buddha, much of it is contested by Theravada practitioners as apocryphal. The Tibetan branch of Mahayana involves a lot more ritual and tantric influence than other Mahayana traditions, such as the practices in China that were influenced by Taoism, or the traditions of Vietnam, Japan, and Korea."

as a result of methods that involved starvation and other forms of extreme asceticism. Dissatisfied with his spiritual progress using the traditional methods, Siddhartha eventually committed himself to stubbornly sitting under a Bodhi tree until he finally "woke up," or awakened to his true nature.

Supposedly Siddhartha just sat there meditating for forty-nine days straight under the Bodhi tree, fighting against an army of ferocious demons until he finally came to realize the illusory nature of the physical universe—as well as the "self"—within the larger reality of consciousness. From this experience, Siddhartha built his philosophy and created a spiritual practice that teaches people how to reach the state of consciousness that he attained under the Bodhi tree, by recognizing desire and attachment as the cause of all suffering, and by being kind and learning how to tame one's mind.

Well before Buddhist philosophy merged with the indigenous Tibetan Bön tradition, it appears that Siddhartha himself encouraged lucid dreaming. According to Buddhist scholar and lucid-dreaming teacher Charlie Morley, "In the Pali Vinaya, the original rulebook for monks and nuns, the Buddha actually instructs his followers to fall asleep in a state of mindfulness as a way to prevent 'seeing a bad dream' or 'waking unhappily.'"[8] Later, when Buddhism traveled to Tibet and merged with the more shamanic Bön tradition, the resulting system not surprisingly placed a lot of emphasis on teaching practices that promote conscious dreaming, and for thousands of years the Tibetans have refined and mastered their techniques.

Dreaming plays an important role in Tibetan Buddhism for many reasons. Dreams are used to help predict future events, to receive spiritual teachings, and to find the location of reincarnated masters. However, it is the practice of dream yoga, which incorporates advanced techniques that include lucid dreaming as a method of helping people to recognize the illusory nature of everything, including oneself, that is unique to Tibetan Buddhism. In his book *Openness Mind*, Tarthang Tulku, a Tibetan lama, writes about how "advanced yogis are able to do just about anything in their dreams. They can become dragons or mythological birds, become larger or smaller or disappear, go back into childhood and relive experiences, or even fly through space."[9]

Despite how attractive these awesome superpowers might seem to the average person, they are discouraged for wish-fulfillment purposes by dream yogis, who regard the pursuit of these pleasures as trivial distractions that prevent one from reaching higher spiritual realizations.*

According to Tibetan Buddhist philosophy, dreams and death are closely linked. Dreams are seen as an important example of illusion and impermanence, as well as a training ground for teaching us how our minds create temporary, ever-shifting models of reality. Our nightly dreams are understood within this perspective to be dreams within a larger dream, secondary illusions within the primary illusion of waking life, where death is seen as a portal, a passageway for transporting one's soul from one lifetime to another through a region of the universal mind known as the *bardo,* the intermediate place between realms.

Using the terms *region, place,* and *realm* in the previous sentence could be misleading, as the bardo is not actually a location, but rather a transitional state of consciousness; it translates literally as "intermediate state." Dreams are considered to be similar to the postmortem bardo, and descriptions of the bardo are often reminiscent of the state of being experienced on a psychedelic journey. In fact, the very first guidebook written by Westerners for planning and navigating a healthy psychedelic journey, *The Psychedelic Experience,* by Timothy Leary and colleagues, was modeled on the Bardo Thödol, or Tibetan Book of the Dead, an ancient manual on how to meditate while dying and how to recognize opportunities for spiritual liberation and navigate the postdeath bardo to consciously reincarnate.

According to Johns Hopkins psychologist Katherine MacLean, "A high-dose psychedelic experience is death practice. You're losing every-

---

*I, however, see the lucid dreaming superpowers more as lures set up by a higher intelligence to help us evolve. As with psychedelics, many people are drawn to lucid dreams for pleasure-seeking thrills and unexpectedly wind up spiritually transformed by surprising mystical experiences.

thing you know to be real, letting go of your ego and your body, and that process can feel like dying."[10]

In Tibetan Buddhism, dreaming and the bardo state are recognized as being so similar that dreaming is used as a path to spiritual liberation, in the practice known as dream yoga. This practice is considered essential to recognizing illusory states for what they really are and to developing valuable abilities for use at the moment of death and thereafter. The basic idea behind Tibetan dream yoga is that if someone can learn how to extend meditative awareness throughout sleep and dreams, then he or she can apply this ability to dying and death when the time arrives. Just as a dream is seen as a bardo between falling asleep and waking up, so the postdeath bardo describes an intermediate state between death and rebirth, which is said to be dreamlike in nature. The primary goal of dream yoga is to extend the transcendent state of lucid awareness developed during lucid-dreaming practices while alive into the postdeath bardo while dying and immediately afterward.

Dream yoga can be used as a powerful tool for spiritual growth, although it seems that simply lucid dreaming can also benefit one spiritually. When people regularly experience lucid dreams, over time it appears that they will naturally begin to progress through predictable developmental stages.

STAGES OF PSYCHOLOGICAL AND SPIRITUAL DEVELOPMENT WITH LUCID DREAMING

In Robert Waggoner's book *Lucid Dreaming: Gateway to the Inner Self,* the author describes five developmental stages that he has observed in himself and in others as they lucid dream.[11] Waggoner's insightful descriptions of these different stages ring true for me, and for others. Briefly, these unfolding mental stages involve a process of discovery and a phase where one needs to overcome temptations, fears, and defenses. This is followed by a period in which one learns how to transcend one's personal assumptions about what is possible. If the practice continues, it eventually leads one to direct contact with the unconscious dreaming mind, as well as to an inquiry into spiritual or philosophical questions about the nature of reality.

Waggoner's five developmental stages are:

Stage 1: personal play, pleasure, and pain avoidance. Initially, most people don't understand how much power they actually have in their lucid dreams, and so they mistakenly assume that the same restrictions in waking reality apply to the dream realm. One functions at this level by simply seeking out pleasurable experiences and avoiding painful ones, while marveling at the extraordinary sensations in this new world: *Wow, I'm awake inside of a dream!*

Stage 2: manipulation, movement, and me. At this second stage you begin to understand that you can influence what happens in your dreams through your intention and willpower. This is when you come to understand that you have amazing superpowers in this new environment, and that the laws of dream physics respond to your expectations: *Wow, I can fly through walls!*

Stage 3: power, purpose, and primacy. This is the stage that unfolds when you begin to gain mastery over the general direction of your dreams and start carrying out systematic experiments to determine what is possible and what the limits of this world are: *Wow, I can change the entire dream environment and make anything appear!*

Stage 4: re-reflection, reaching out, and wonder. This stage of development emerges when a dreamer learns how to directly address and communicate with the larger dreaming mind, the unconscious: *Wow, I can speak directly with the mind behind my dreams and get answers to my questions!*

Stage 5: experiencing awareness. This ineffable, ego-transcending stage emerges when you seek out the foundation of consciousness at the core of the dream, and then experience nondual awareness beyond the dream: *Wow, "I" don't really exist!*

Walter Evans-Wentz (1878–1965), an American anthropologist and scholar of Tibetan Buddhism whose writings helped transmit Buddhism to the West, described these stages similarly, albeit a bit differently:

> The yogin is taught to realize that matter, or form in the dimensional aspects, large or small, and its numerical aspects, of plurality and unity, is entirely subject to one's will, when the mental powers have been efficiently developed by yoga. In other words, the yogin learns by actual experience, resulting from psychic experimentation, that the character of any dream can be changed or transformed by willing that it shall be. A step further and he learns that form, in the dream-state, and all the multitudinous content of dreams, are merely playthings of mind, and, therefore, as unstable as mirage. A further step leads him to the knowledge that the essential nature of form and all things perceived by the senses in the waking-state, both states alike being sangsaric [i.e., samsara, the repeating cycle of birth, life, and death]. The final step leads to the Great Realization, that nothing within the Sangsara is or can be other than unreal like dreams.[12]

For many people the initial lure of lucid dreaming comes from the desire to engage in fantasies and thrills, like flying and sex, and many people never develop past this phase into the higher stages. However, some people learn to ignore the superficial elements of the dream and interact directly with their personal (or the collective) unconscious.

SPEAKING TO THE DREAMING MIND

Perhaps the most valuable activity to carry out in a lucid dream has only been mentioned in passing thus far in this book and has yet to be discussed fully. I am speaking here of interacting with the invisible agent orchestrating the dream environment, characters, plot, and action behind the scenes: your "conscious unconscious,"* Brahman, Morpheus,

---

*This delightful term was coined by Robert Waggoner in his book *Lucid Dreaming: Gateway to the Inner Self.*

or whoever or whatever it is that shapes our dreams. By deliberately addressing the dream environment itself with questions, one can explore one's unconscious in an uncannily direct way.

As we've learned, it's a common misconception that lucid dreaming means that one can control one's dreams. Being lucid just means that you're awake in your dreams and can influence what happens. However, no matter how much creative influence you can have on the structure of your dream characters and environment, there will always be an element of surprise, there will always be things going on that you didn't intend, and there is simply no way that you can imagine all of the details so quickly when influencing a lucid dream such that you can control every aspect of it. Clearly, there is some other agency or intelligence (or mechanism) operating behind the scenes here, and whatever it is, we can learn to communicate with it directly.

I learned about this ingenious technique from Robert Waggoner, who writes:

> Some experienced lucid dreamers . . . maintain that the potential of lucid dreaming includes communicating with another layer of inner awareness. These lucid dreamers report using a counterintuitive technique of ignoring the dream figures and objects, and lucidly addressing questions or requests to a nonvisible awareness behind the dream. . . . The fascinating responses and interactions with this inner awareness appear to meet the characteristics outlined by . . . Jung as necessary to show that a "subject, a sort of ego" exists within the "unconscious." . . . Approached thoughtfully, lucid dreaming appears to allow lucid dreamers to engage this second psychic system, or inner layer of awareness. If true, this discovery could radically alter the future of psychology and science.[13]

When I interviewed Waggoner I asked him how he first discovered this technique, and if he was surprised to get a response the first time he directly addressed the dream itself. He replied:

You know, I was astounded to get a response. What happened was
. . . in the mid-1980s I became part of a lucid-dreaming group that
corresponded each month, and all of us had a monthly goal. One
month the goal was to find out what your dream figures represent
when you become lucidly aware. So that month I was off on a business trip in Chicago. I went to sleep that night remembering that I
had that goal to achieve in a lucid dream. I became lucidly aware,
followed someone into an office setting, and I looked around. There
were four people there—a receptionist woman, a woman sitting at a
table reading a magazine, another well-dressed woman in a corner,
and this kind of avuncular older gentleman to my left in a three-
piece suit. So lucidly aware, I stepped up to him and said, "Excuse
me, what do you represent?" Then it surprised me that instead of
him responding, a voice boomed out from above a partial response.
The partial response didn't make total sense, so I just asked the
awareness up there to clarify it, and then a full answer came forth.
So in the morning I thought, *Why didn't the dream figure respond?*
Why did this voice boom out, from above the dream figure, the
response? So after that I decided that I was going to experiment with
this and see if there's an awareness behind the dream, if there's a
larger consciousness that exists within the dream state—because so
often in our life we're taught to focus on other people, other figures,
other creatures, other objects. It's rare that you would focus on just
space, or an awareness that has no visible form.

One can also use a variation of this technique that was developed
by Ed Kellogg.[14] Kellogg suggests first finding a blank piece of paper or
a closed furniture drawer in the dream. Then you ask the question you
have in mind out loud, turn away for a few seconds, and then read the
paper or open the drawer to see the dreaming mind's written response.
Note, however, that written words are notoriously unstable in lucid
dreams. If you'd like to try Kellogg's technique in a lucid dream, I suggest reading the response quickly and not looking too long at the words,
as they typically will start to change when you do.

As I've mentioned throughout this book, I've experimented with Waggoner's technique numerous times and have had some good results with it. During my first attempt to do this in a lucid dream, I had the following experience:

> After achieving lucidity in the dream, I walked into a small room lined with tiny shelves, from floor to ceiling, that were filled with row after row of cute and artistically designed toys and little sculptures. When I first entered the room I was looking for other people or a wise being to speak with, but there was no one there. Then I remembered that I had wanted to try speaking to the dream itself. However, when I tried this I ran into some difficulty. I tried to say my question out loud, but I couldn't get the sound out of my mouth for some reason. I tried doing this over and over a few times, and then, finally, I was able to just barely pronounce a few words to my surrounding dream environment. I asked, "What does this dream mean?" Then a few seconds later I heard a barely audible voice, with lots of static and electronic-sounding interference, like from an old transistor radio with a weak signal, coming from somewhere behind me in the room. The voice simply said, "Look." So I looked more closely at the rows of colorful little toys around me. There were these tiny purple teddy bears dressed in enchanted wizard hats, and dozens and dozens of other little magical objects. I wasn't sure what the message that I was supposed to see was, and I soon awoke.

After awakening it occurred to me that the lucid dream seemed to be showing me that it was possible to establish a more direct communication link with my conscious unconscious but that the connection was weak and needed to be strengthened. With time and practice I was able to do this, and I received fascinating responses by asking the dream to "astonish me," "show me the details of what traumatized me at the age of three," and "show me what you think I need to see." I've also had fruitful interactions when asking for assistance with various creative projects, which is something that a lot of people seem to report success with.

Another good request is to have the dream show you what a mystical or spiritually transcendent experience is like. With some practice, this orchestrating intelligence behind your dreams can become your personal genie in the dream realm as well as your spiritual advisor. I use this technique like an oracle and take my most important questions to it. I don't always get answers to my questions right away, as sometimes the answers will come in future lucid dreams, but I often get responses that affect me in profound ways. However, I usually get a response around five or ten seconds after asking the question. One time I asked the dreaming mind what it thought I needed to hear, and I opened up a box, expecting to find a piece of paper inside with a note written on it. Instead I found that there was a huge stack of papers inside, with endless notes written on the pages. I wasn't able to remember any of the written words upon awakening, but I got the message that my conscious unconscious sure had a lot to say to me!

Speaking to the mind behind the dream seems similar to setting an intention or asking a question before embarking on a psychedelic journey. Writing down a question or specifying one's intention before an ayahuasca or mushroom voyage will often lead to very direct answers or guidance during the experience. Something inside of us listens when we ask these questions, it seems, and when we're in the right state of consciousness we can divine responses and wisdom from this oracle within.

Who is this mysterious orchestrator of our dreams that responds to our inquiries? Maybe it's not a single voice; perhaps it's a collective of sorts. I'm not convinced that the same voice is always responding to my inquiries in every lucid dream. When I interviewed Ryan Hurd about this, he said, "Is it one thing, one system in the unconscious? I doubt it is one thing. There's really no guarantee that you are in conversation with your higher self when you ask a question beyond the dream. The voice could be representing any number of self-constructs, or even your expectation of a conversation with your higher self. It can be tricky. But the practice certainly brings novelty into the dream, that's for sure."

Sometimes it seems as though our responsive unconscious mind has a sense of humor. Consider the following, from Buddhist scholar and lucid-dreaming teacher Charlie Morley:

> I remembered my dream plan and put it into action. I called out to the dream: "What is the essence of all knowledge?" Instantly, a huge game show–style computer screen manifested in front of me with the question written across it in big digital lettering. The letters were so big that I could read them easily without them blurring. Three dots appeared after the question mark, indicating that I was about to receive the answer. I tried hard to keep my excitement under control but it was really difficult! Then the answer finally manifested. The computer screen read: "The essence of all knowledge is? . . . Obtainable through lucid dreaming."[15]

Morley also discusses a technique that I've found helpful—calling out to the dream and asking it to stabilize lucidity. This can help give you more time in the lucid dream to explore its mysteries.

Perhaps the most profound mystery of all that one can seek some illumination on through lucid dreaming is what happens to us when we die.

DREAMING AND DEATH

Around five hundred years ago English playwright William Shakespeare wrote in *Hamlet,* "To die, to sleep, To sleep, perchance to Dream; Aye, there's the rub, For in that sleep of death, what dreams may come . . ." These immortal lines draw our attention to the possibility that dreaming may offer us a window into the afterlife.

The ancient traditions of so many cultures speak of dreaming and death together, proposing that the dreaming process offers insight into what happens to us after we die. There are countless examples: We know that Tibetan Buddhism offers profound techniques in dream yoga, regarded as training for death and beyond. Russian psychiatrist Olga Kharitidi, in her book *The Master of Lucid Dreams,* says the primary tool used by the shaman-healers of Central Asia is lucid dreaming, which the shamans equate with death. In Thomas Mann's wonderful 1927 novel *The Magic Mountain,* the protagonist, Hans Castorp, resolves his questions about the mysteries of life and death by means of his experiences with lucid dreaming. The Sanskrit word *Vsvap* means both "to sleep" and "to be dead," and this is the root of the English word *dream.*[16] The Dunne-za people of the Doig River region of British Columbia believe that their prophets are able to "transverse the trail to Heaven at will in their dreams," which they equate with a pathway to the afterlife.[17]

I tried exploring this timeless philosophical mystery in a lucid dream once. I reasoned that if I could commit suicide in a dream (without really harming myself), then I might be able to gain some insight into what actually happens to consciousness after death. I have this suspicion that a part of me already knows what happens to us after we die, despite my inability to consciously access this knowledge. So, after thinking about this possibility, the next time I found myself in a lucid dream I decided to give it a try. One night in 1999 I had the following experience:

> I was being pursued in a large warehouse by some threatening figure in the dream when I became lucid. I found a private section in the building that I was in, and after repeatedly confirming that I was indeed dreaming— more so than usual, as there was no room for error—I conveniently found a handgun located in my right hand. I pointed the gun at the side of my head, took a deep breath, and bravely pulled the trigger. After the bullet fired, the next thing I knew I was bodiless, in a dark, silent void, alone with just my thoughts. It wasn't unpleasant, but it was certainly much less dramatic than what I was expecting, and I soon awoke.

There was no tunnel, no bright light, no loving presence, or any sense of special peace; it was just my consciousness, alone in a dark, silent void. After reflecting on this experience, I now suspect that this wasn't necessarily my unconscious mind's vision of death so much as its vision of death by suicide. In reading about the near-death experiences of others, it seems that most people have positive encounters when they begin to depart from life, with one primary exception: when suicide is attempted. This is when hellish experiences are often reported, and one of these hellish NDEs is being alone in a dark, silent void (although my experience in the dream wasn't this unpleasant).

I wasn't the only one who tried to commit suicide in a lucid dream, however I was one of the more successful. The Marquis d'Hervey de Saint-Denys recounts how he also tried to commit suicide in lucid dreams but always ran into obstacles that prevented him from succeeding in his attempts. In one experience he tries to cut his own throat with a razor, but his "instinctive horror of the action" prevents him from carrying this out, and in subsequent lucid dreams, when he considered shooting himself, he reports that locating and operating a pistol in the dream always took too long.[18]

In Celia Green and Charles McCreery's book *Lucid Dreaming: The Paradox of Consciousness during Sleep,* the authors provide several more examples of people who tried to commit suicide in lucid dreams but were also unsuccessful, as the dream faded or they awoke when they tried crashing a van or jumping under some moving cars.[19]

However, there are also reports of people having near-death experiences in nonlucid dreams that differed from my experience within a lucid dream. I've read a number of accounts of people who died in their dreams as a result of accidents and then had OBEs and transcendent spiritual experiences, all within the dream, but they weren't lucid.

When I asked Stephen LaBerge what he thought about consciousness after death, he said this:

> Let's suppose I'm having a lucid dream. The first thing I think is, *Oh, this is a dream, here I am.* Now the "I" here is who I think Stephen is. Now, what's happening in fact is that Stephen is asleep in bed somewhere, not in this world at all, and he's having a dream that he's in this room talking to you. With a little bit of lucidity I'd say, *This is a dream, and you're all in my dream.* A little more

lucidity and I'd know you're a dream figure and this is a dream table, and this must be a dream shirt and a dream watch and what's this? It's got to be a dream hand and well, so what's this? It's a dream Stephen! So a moment ago I thought this is who I am, and now I know that it's just a mental model of who I am. So, reasoning along those lines, I now think I'd like to have a sense of what my deepest identity is, what's my highest potential, which level is the realest in a sense. With that in mind I have this lucid dream in which I am driving my sportscar down through the green, spring country-side. I see an attractive hitchhiker at the side of the road, think of picking her up but say, *No, I've already had that dream, I want this to be a representation of my highest potential.* So the moment I have that thought and decide to forego the immediate pleasure, the car starts to fly into the air and disappear, and my body too. There are symbols of traditional religions in the clouds—the Star of David and the cross and the steeple and Near Eastern symbols. As I pass through that realm, higher, beyond the clouds, I enter into a vast emptiness of space that is infinite, and it is filled with potential and love. And the feeling I have is *This is home! This is where I'm from and I'd forgotten that it was here.* I am overwhelmed with joy about the fact that this source of being is immediately present, that it is always here, and I have not been seeing it because of what was in my way. So I start singing for joy, with a voice that spans three or four octaves and resonates with the cosmos, in words like "I Praise Thee, O Lord!" There isn't any "I," there is no "thee," no "Lord," no separation somehow, just a sort of "Praise Be!"

My belief is that the experience I had of this void is what you get if you take away the brain. When I thought about the meaning of that lucid dream I recognized that the deepest identity I had there was the source of being, the all and nothing that was here right now, that is what I am too, in addition to being Stephen. So the analogy that I use for understanding this is that we have these separate snowflake identities. Every snowflake is different in the same sense that each one of us is, in fact, distinct. So here is death, and here's the snowflake, and we're falling into the infinite ocean. So what do we fear? We fear that we're going to lose our identity, we'll be melted, dissolved in that ocean and we'll be gone. But what may happen instead is that the snowflake hits the ocean and feels an infinite expansion of identity and realizes what I am in essence—water! So we're each one of these little frozen droplets and as such we feel only our individuality, but not our substance. But our essential substance is common to everything in that sense, so now God is the ocean. So we're each a little droplet of that ocean, identifying only with the form of the droplet and not with the majesty and the unity. There may be intermediate states where, to press the metaphor, the seed crystal is recycled and makes another snowflake in a similar form or something like that, but that's not my concern. My concern is with the ocean, that's what I care about. So whether or not Stephen or some deeper identity of Stephen survives, well, that'd be nice if that were so, but how can one not be satisfied with being the ocean?

Additional evidence that dreams might serve as a portal into what happens to consciousness after death comes from encounters that people have reported with deceased loved ones in their dreams.

COMMUNICATING WITH THE DEAD

Many people have reported having meaningful contact experiences with friends and family members who have died in lucid and non-lucid dreams. Sometimes practical information is passed along in these encounters, as in the case of poet and painter William Blake (1757–1827), who dreamt that his deceased brother taught him an engraving technique that he used after the dream.[20] Other people have resolved conflicts, finished uncompleted dialogues, and also exchanged personally meaningful information in dream encounters.[21] When I interviewed psychologist Stanley Krippner, who has studied dreams like this for many years in great detail, he said, "There are numerous examples of what I call 'visitation dreams,' and I doubt that all of them can be written off as coincidence, prevarication, or wish fulfillment."

Psychologist Patricia Garfield wrote a fascinating book on this topic, *The Dream Messenger: How Dreams of the Departed Bring Healing Gifts.* Garfield writes,

> Sooner or later, all of us will have to endure the trauma of the death of a significant person in our lives. . . . Regardless of your beliefs about whether there is an afterlife or not, one thing is certain: you will dream about the person who recently died. . . . Whether these dreams are actual contact with spirit or images conjured up by our own needs is not the issue: what we know is that we dream about the people we have lost, and that these dreams are extraordinarily vivid and emotionally charged and can alter the life and belief system of the dreamer. In the dream world, unfinished dialogues can be completed and conflicts resolved.[22]

I've personally had some beautiful, heartwarming encounters with friends and loved ones who have passed on in lucid dreams. The late psychiatrist Oscar "Oz" Janiger, the friend who introduced me to Stephen LaBerge and the scientific study of lucid dreaming—and was the psychiatrist who treated me for depression—has appeared in quite a few of my lucid dreams. In one particularly striking one, Oz and I walked around arm-in-arm in this beautiful utopian village. He explained to me that this was where he was now living. My memory of that encounter with Oz, which occurred a few months after he died, is as real and vivid as any memory that I have of him from waking life, and it affects me in a deeply emotional way, although, of course, that doesn't necessarily mean that it was real.

I also once had a nonlucid dream as an adult where the cat from my childhood, Fritzy, had somehow come back to life. She was really old and fragile in the dream, but I was overjoyed to see her again. The dream left me feeling really happy when I awoke.

My girlfriend told me about a lucid dream that she had one morning, in which she met up with her father who had passed away several years earlier. She described becoming lucid in the dream while looking at the stars in the sky, after which a woman pointed to the door of a bar and said, "You're going to miss your chance." Rebecca walked over to the bar and . . .

I pulled the door handle, looked around inside, and saw a few people chatting and playing pool. There was a big group of people by the bar. No one seemed to notice that I walked inside or paid any attention to me as I walked in the room. I walked to the side of the wall where the pool sticks were kept. I picked up a pool stick and couldn't get over how real it felt in my dream hand—the weight of it and all the textures were just like waking life. I walked around toward the back of the pool hall, carrying my pool stick with me, to where there were fewer people, and I was trying to decide which table I wanted to play on. I picked one, bent down to get the balls out from under the table, and realized that I didn't have any money for the quarter slot. Luckily, I'm in a dream, so I don't need any money, I thought. I used my fingers to turn the metal lock on the case that the balls were in and started putting them on the table. As I was doing this I noticed someone standing on the other side of the pool table. I looked up and . . . it was my dad! I was stunned and felt like my heart was going to explode with joy! (And to be honest, I felt a tad bit of fear, because I know that in waking reality my dad has passed away.) "Don't look at me like that—we going play or what, girl?" he said. "Girl?" Yup, that's my dad, no question about it. From there we played a game of pool. I was shooting the balls in left and right. My dad was really impressed, I could tell by his expression. I was making almost every shot, Dad really didn't even have that much of a chance to play. Toward the end of the game I shot a ball and it bounced off the table and rolled into a dark room. Inside the dark room sat a Christmas tree with a lot of gifts underneath. As my dad walked over to the room, he said, "You are getting good, girl, real good!" and he started looking for the ball. As I was sitting there waiting for him to come back, I woke up.

My favorite passage in Garfield's book comes from someone who had the following experience about encountering a deceased relative in a dream: "I am astounded to see my dead uncle alive again, singing, laughing, and making jokes; I say, 'My God, what are you doing here? You're dead!' He smiles and replies, 'Honey, when you die, you lose your body, not your sense of humor.'"[23]

Within death lies the deepest of mysteries, and biological termination gives meaning to life—but maybe there is consciousness beyond life and death . . .

MYSTICAL EXPERIENCES AND NONDUALISTIC CONSCIOUSNESS

As I previously mentioned, it seems that persistent lucid dreamers will eventually report having spiritual, religious, or mystical experiences within their lucid dreams. This propensity for fostering mystical experiences is a common feature that lucid dreams share with psychedelic or shamanic states of consciousness.

A mystical experience is often described as a state of nondualistic awareness. In this ineffable state, conceptual opposites unify and personal boundaries dissolve in an all-encompassing reunion with the bedrock of consciousness. During a mystical experience the distinctions that separate one's awareness from the rest of the world melt away, the ego vanishes, and there is a profound sense of interconnectedness with all of existence, which many people describe as orgasmic. In lucid dreams you achieve this state when you move into what is beyond or behind the dream itself. When I interviewed Ryan Hurd he attempted to describe his experience in this state of consciousness:

About eight years ago . . . I woke up in the middle of the night into a nondual experience that felt a lot like cosmic love as I hear other people describe it. I shared a flow of energy that was bigger than me. I was part of it, but it was also separate from me, and we were . . . but it was . . . I was . . . Ugh—there's just no words! You try to get

Fig. 10.1. Lucid-dream researcher Ryan Hurd (photo by Brian Furry)

into it and it all just falls apart. It was heart-centered, it was glorious, confusing, and I just did not exist as I now define myself. But I would not call that a lucid dream, it was something else entirely. I mean, from a technical standpoint, a lucid dream has to be dualistic, you have to have a witness for metacognition to take place, to know that you're dreaming.

In 2006, investigators at the Johns Hopkins School of Medicine published the results of a six-year project on the effects of psilocybin, in which more than 60 percent of the participants reported having had "complete" mystical experiences. These experiences were rated as being among the most personally meaningful and spiritually significant of their lives, and they were indistinguishable from the reports of religious experiences by mystics throughout history.[24] Recall that earlier we learned that psilocybin's action mimics some aspects of conscious dreaming in the brain.

A study done by psychologist Fariba Bogzaran, founder of the dream-studies program at John F. Kennedy University, demonstrates that merely expressing the intention of wanting to have a spiritual experience in a lucid dream can lead to actually having one.[25] According to Bogzaran, practicing intention and incubation prior to sleep are the two most important factors in cultivating spiritual experiences in a lucid dream. In another study done by Bogzaran she describes the difference between ordinary lucid dreaming and "multidimensional dreams" or what she refers to as "hyperspace lucidity," where lucid dreamers report experiencing a transformation of their dream bodies into particles of light, or when the dream body disappears while awareness continues.[26]

I've had many mystical experiences in both psychedelic states of consciousness and lucid dreams. As a teenager, the combination of LSD, nitrous oxide, and reading the work of philosopher Alan Watts activated full-blown religious experiences within me that kick-started my spiritual development and deeply influenced the course of my life. Likewise with lucid dreams. I've had deeply moving, profoundly transformative mystical experiences when, for example, within a lucid dream I sat down, closed my dream eyes, and simply started meditating. It seems that all that is necessary to have spiritually illuminating experiences within a lucid dream is the intention to have such experiences.

Consider the following lucid dream I had one morning while writing this book. It began with my persistent sexual pursuits, resulting in the first time that I ever actually achieved realistic sexual intercourse within a lucid dream, as for many years something always prevented me from doing this. Although the pleasurable sexual encounter appeared to contain a punch line of sorts, the dream ended with a powerful spiritual experience:

I finally succeeded in actually having realistic sex in a lucid dream—well, sort of. I found a willing partner but had some trouble getting all of her clothing down past her butt. She was on all fours, sticking her butt out and wiggling it, but there were so many layers of clothing to pull down— four or five layers of pants, pantyhose, underwear. I finally got them all down, got an erection, and entered her. Once I was inside of her it felt wonderful and completely real. I was really enjoying the delightful sensations, knowing that my time there was limited, and I was trying to see if I could actually orgasm in the dream. However, before I could come, the woman turned into a rubber doll. Actually, she became just a partial, life-size doll's body, just the backside and butt, made out of rubber or latex, and she was hollow, there was no front to her. I realized with a sudden shock that I was just having sex with this rubber thing. Then I realized that I wasn't alone in the room, which was a classroom of sorts. I noticed that a little boy was sitting in a chair watching me trying to have sex with this doll of a partial woman. Despite being lucid and knowing that I was dreaming, I couldn't help but feel embarrassed. This little boy then became part of another child; they seemed biologically connected somehow, and they didn't seem too concerned with what I had been doing with the rubber doll. Most interesting of all was my encounter with a different little boy whom I met later in the lucid dream in the upstairs bedroom of an unfamiliar house, who was around five years old. I was thinking that I was going to ask him about his dreams. I wanted to ask the dream characters in my dreams about their dreams! Then, at the exact same instant in time, we both asked each other, "What are your dreams like?" I was really surprised by this simultaneous expression, and I said to him, "How did you know that I was going to ask you that?" Then he looked at me with an expression of wisdom that I've never seen another dream character possess and confidently said, "It's because we're the same person." I was utterly shocked that he knew this, as I've never had a dream character say that to me in a lucid dream before. Usually it's me telling them that we're the same person. I asked him how he knew this, and his face became more animated, cartoonlike almost, and he said something that seemed very wise and funny, that seemed to contain these clever puns and have multiple meanings, but I can't remember what he said or even if I fully understood what he was saying at the time he said it. After he told me this I closed my eyes in the bedroom with the little boy, raised my head toward the ceiling, and asked the dream intelligence to show me the "highest spiritual experience." Then "I" simply dissolved into an egoless, light-filled awareness, before I awoke.

This brightly lit, nondualistic awareness that I experienced in my lucid dream is sometimes referred to as the "void."

THE VOID

The term *void* describes a type of nondualistic awareness that can be reached in lucid dreams and other shamanic states of consciousness. It transcends both the physical world and the dream world and is sometimes distinguished from other types of nondualistic states of consciousness. It seems that the term can actually have several meanings, although it generally implies a state of mind or a purity of awareness that lies beyond the perception of separation or form.

In a personal communication, New Zealand–based lucid-dream researcher Peter Maich sent me his description of this state:

> I feel there are two places that dreamers call the void. The first is in the early stages of a wake-induced lucid dream, when you drop or phase to a light sleep state and retain awareness of this state change. At this point it gets eerily quiet as the sense of hearing is the first to shut down, and you can be in a darkness that feels like an open space that will often precede hypnogogic imagery. The second place is entered from within a lucid dream, and I describe this as the space between dreams. In the early days I would enter this space and quickly transit to a new dream. Now I am able to spend time there and see it as a place of its own, with potential for adventure.

I found Maich's experiences intriguing. He describes at first feeling uneasy in the second type of void, with its dark, formless space (reminiscent of the state I experienced after committing suicide in a lucid dream, only this state appears liberating whereas mine felt confining). But then in time he becomes comfortable enough to explore: "Over a series of dreams I've had a lot of entries into the void and found that if I just accepted being there I would remain for longer periods. In time I also started to lose the uneasiness that seemed to accompany me at first.

The more time I spent in the void, the more I seemed to lose any sense of self, and it got to the point where I felt I existed as pure awareness."

It seems that the void is an egoless state of awareness, beyond the body and all form. However, it appears that descriptions of it, even using the distinctions that Maich made, don't always match up: my own experience of the void was filled with light, while Maich experienced darkness or emptiness. It appears to be inherently difficult to describe this experience using language, *which is based upon the perception of distinctions*. Nevertheless, Maich writes:

> In the void there is blackness that seems to be all around and has a presence. It is not seen with eyes, but experienced with a set of inner senses that combine to create the awareness. This awareness is very hard to define in normal terms. There is nothing to touch, and I have nothing to touch with, as there is no energy or dream body either. There is thought and full access to memory and the ability to leave to another dream if desired. I suspect what is happening is a shutdown of all sensory input and no recall of sensory data to construct a dream with.

When I interviewed Robert Waggoner, he described his own unique experience of the void: "I began to fall asleep at night, and the entire night there'd be nothing but blue light. So there were no figures, no symbols, no action, no plot, no me. It was just blue light." Descriptions of the void often seem reminiscent of the goal of Tibetan dream yoga, which is to reach what is called the "clear light," a nondualistic state of mystical consciousness. Ryan Hurd describes his experience with the indescribable like this:

> Since I was a child I have had conscious dream experiences that take place in immense, spacious realms devoid of light or objects. Sometimes these spaces are truly voids and my own dream body does not exist. Other times these spaces become filled up with abstract geometric patterns, or multicolored buzzing particles that

resemble the "snow" from a television set. I call this the "cosmic snow" because it is literally the stuff dreams are made of.[27]

I've experienced this state of consciousness, or something similar, after inhaling the vapors of 5MeO-DMT, which is chemically similar to, but phenomenologically different from, N,N DMT, which is the type of DMT that I've been referring to throughout this book. Both compounds are naturally found in the human body. People often report seeing an insane multitude of endlessly morphing, multihued forms and hyperdimensional alien worlds after ingesting N,N DMT, but after ingesting 5MeO-DMT, the most common report is that of being immersed in a bright white or clear light. It's as though these two basic forms of DMT represent the all and the void, everything and nothing.

In psychonaut Zoe7's book *Back from the Void,* the author describes the void as "a primordial point of origin as well as a point of extinction. It is the Alpha and the Omega—a way station for recycling soul and all

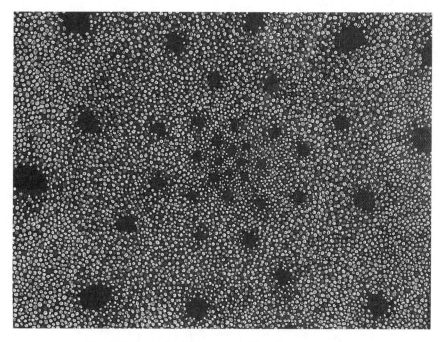

Fig. 10.2. *Entoptica,* a painting by Ryan Hurd
based on his lucid "void" experience

of Creation. The Void can be thought of as an 'instance' in which nothing exists. It's a point when All That Is was not."[28]

From this description it seems like the void might be a good place to visit if one wants to begin fresh and start anew. Dissolving into the void and reemerging involves a kind of death and rebirth of the ego or personality. So when I needed to reorganize my life from the ground up, that's just what I did, and this book encapsulates my healing journey, transforming years of misunderstood pain and confusing darkness into newfound strength and guiding light.

BIOCENTRISM AND AYAHUASCA

Biologist Robert Lanza presents a theory in his book *Biocentrism* that may provide some important insights into the nature of reality and dreaming. Lanza proposes that the universe is actually created by the perceptions of conscious, living creatures. He turns the whole notion that life evolved from an inanimate universe on its head, by interpreting the results of experiments in quantum physics in a direct and practical manner and suggesting that the physical universe evolved from life, consciousness, and observation, not vice versa.

If reality requires observation to exist, then how could a universe without observers ever have evolved? asks Lanza. He suggests that this is why everything in existence fits together so perfectly—why the whole universe seems to be so perfectly designed just for us, why all of the improbable cosmic factors seem so precisely orchestrated for our arrival: because we created the universe through life's observations, those moment-by-moment acts of choosing one possible event out of the always infinite availability of quantum-possibility waves.

I realize that this sounds paradoxical on the surface, and I can't summarize all of the details of Lanza's fascinating theory here, but I bring it up because the combination of reading *Biocentrism* and doing ayahuasca in the Amazon transformed my life in such a way that I can only say that I feel like I'm always living inside of a lucid dream when I'm awake, or inside a model within my own mind. These two factors conspired to turn my worldview inside out. While I conceptually understood for many years that I wasn't actually experiencing the "real world," and instead was experiencing a mental simulation of the world, it wasn't until I did ayahuasca and read Lanza's book that something clicked in my mind, and this knowledge suddenly became clearly experiential. I now experience the world as being inside my mind, instead of my mind being inside the world. It's difficult to explain how this conceptual shift occurred, because I realize that every time I try to explain it, it sounds like I'm saying something that I already knew before the conceptual shift occurred, and many other people already know, which seems obvious. All I can say is that something shifted inside me that made this knowledge experiential in a way that I hadn't ever realized or anticipated before.

I'll do my best to explain what happened. Up until this shift occurred, despite what I already knew, it always appeared that I was inside a body-brain system, looking out at the world through the windows of my senses. Now, I knew from studying neuroscience and taking LSD that I wasn't directly seeing the world around me, but rather viewing a simulation of reality created by my visual cortex from a sea of electrical signals. I already knew that the world exists inside my mind, not vice versa—but I wasn't experiencing it that way.

The model of myself that I naturally had in my head was completely backward. I wasn't looking out at the world through the windows of my senses; I was experiencing a simulation of the world inside my mind. This means that, like in a lucid dream, everything around "me" (including what I thought was my body) isn't the (directly unknowable) physical world (or my body), as I had thought my whole life, but rather the inside of myself. The reason why consciousness may survive death—and anything is possible—is because on the level of our subjective experience, which is all that we ever really know, the universe exists within our own minds.

All that exists in everyone's experience of this universe is consciousness and its contents. What we think of as our bodies and the world are actually concepts inside our minds. The most consistent, constant image, in both dreaming and waking states of consciousness, is the image of one's body. So ubiquitous is this image that we normally take it for granted, without regarding its true nature. But it's important to understand that the image of one's body is not equivalent to a physical body; rather, it is a concept created in one's mind. Gaining this perspective is tremendously liberating, and with it comes the ability to psychically influence the world and manifest synchronicities within reality to a greater degree. Everything is interconnected because everything is inside our minds. While obviously not as pliable as a dream, physical reality is much more responsive to our thoughts than many people realize. It may be that physical laws are themselves mental constructs within a larger, more universal mind. The best metaphor for understanding this shift that occurred in me is by saying that now it is like my whole life is happening within a lucid dream. Whatever I do and wherever I go, it's clear that I'm always inside the center of my own mind. I think that what I've been experiencing is what some people refer to as "lucid living."

According to Tibetan dream-yoga master Tarthang Tulku, once one realizes that life is like a dream, in the sense that all experience is subjective and we never directly experience an objective world, then our self-identities become less rigid and "even the hardest things become enjoyable and easy. When you realize that everything is like a dream, you attain pure awareness. And the way to attain this awareness is to realize that all experience is like a dream."[29]

THINKING OUTSIDE THE MATRIX

Okay, here's a thought experiment: Imagine that you wake up tonight inside a dream. *Ah, wonderful!* you think, so excited to be lucid while dreaming, wondering what you'll do next and how you'll sustain the dream. Then let's say you're able to indulge in all of your wildest fantasies, live like a deity, and the dream lasts and lasts. You're just marveling at how awesome all this is when you start to realize how strange it is that you still haven't woken up. So you have some more fun and then start to think that it really is time to get back to your body and waking reality, when you realize that you can't. Nothing you do to try to wake yourself up works. Maybe your body is in a coma, or perhaps you've died, but whatever the case, you now find that you're stuck inside your dream.

Now imagine that you just start living your life from within this dream world. Days and nights go by, and soon you want to start discovering the nature of this new reality, so you become a scientist in the dream. You observe everything carefully and carry out experiments. You make discoveries about the nature and limits of this world, and you start to think that you've gained some kind of an understanding of this reality—until you remind yourself that every measurement and calculation that you make in this reality is done using measurement tools that are composed of dream matter. Every act of measurement is actually made using . . . what? A mental concept, not anything material. And then everything that is actually being measured is also just a mental concept. It suddenly occurs to you that aside from your own existence, nothing else can be perceived with any certainty, because everything that you can sense is composed of your own mind. Now, how would this situation differ from the situation that we find ourselves in right now, here in waking reality, I wonder?

This thought experiment leads to a similar state of philosophical confusion, about what level of consciousness or reality we actually exist in, as an ancient Hindu myth about a hunter and a sage, from the Yogavasistha Maharamayana of the harbinger-poet Valmiti, a philosophical treatise and compendium of dream narratives that dates back to as early as the first millennium. I discovered this remarkable story around six months after writing the thought experiment above. In this story within a story, a demon goes through various incarnations as different insects and animals before incarnating as a human being who is a hunter. The hunter wanders through the woods and comes upon the home of a sage, who becomes his teacher and tells him the following story:

> I studied magic. I entered someone else's body and saw all his organs; I entered his head and then I saw a universe, with a sun and an ocean and mountains, and gods and demons and human beings. This universe was his dream, and I saw his dream. . . . I saw his city

and his wife and servants and his son. When darkness fell, he went to bed and slept, and I slept too. Then his world was overwhelmed by a flood at doomsday; I, too, was swept away in the flood. . . . When I saw that world destroyed . . . I wept. I still saw, in my own dream, a whole universe, for I had picked up his karmic memories along with his dream. I had become involved in that world and I forgot my former life. . . . Once again I saw doomsday. This time, however, even while I was being burnt up by the flames, I did not suffer, for I realized, "This is just a dream." Then I forgot my own experiences. Time passed. A sage came to my house . . . and as we were talking . . . he said, "Don't you know that all of this is a dream? I am a man in your dream, and you are a man in someone else's dream." Then I awakened, and remembered my own nature . . . that I was an ascetic. And I said to the sage, "I will go to see that body of mine (that was an ascetic)," for I wanted to see my own body as well as the body which I had set out to explore. But he smiled and said, "Where do you think those two bodies of yours are?" I could find no body, nor could I get out of the head of the person I had entered, and so I asked him, "Well, where are the two bodies?" The sage replied, "While you were in the other person's body a great fire arose that destroyed your body as well as the body of the other person. Now you are a householder, not an ascetic."[30]

After the sage tells this story to the hunter, who is now in a state of amazement, the hunter lies down in bed in silence and says, "If this is so, then you and I and all of us are people in one another's dreams."[31] Missing the sage's point, the hunter leaves and goes through more incarnations, finally becoming an ascetic, and eventually achieving liberation.

WHY IS WAKING UP FROM THE DREAM OF LIFE FORBIDDEN?

Due to a consistent (possibly deliberate?) mistranslation of a Hebrew word in the Bible by Saint Jerome in around 450 BCE, seeking guidance through one's dreams became equated with witchcraft for more than a thousand years, and many authorities in the Roman Catholic Church prohibited dream interpretation.[32] Like psychedelic states of consciousness, dreams can seem threatening to those in authority, perhaps because they expand our notion of what is possible.

Funny, isn't it, that with the advent of electronic dream machines like the DreamLight or the REM-Dreamer, one of the most commonly reported interpretations of how flashing LEDs are incorporated into the dream is as police lights? Sometimes I wonder if it's against the rules to become lucid in our dreams, or in waking life. Some people seem to think so, and perhaps the band Cheap Trick was on to something in 1979 when they sang, "The dream police, they live inside of my head."

This book contains secret information that can get you into trouble if used unwisely. In the Book of Genesis (3:5) it is forbidden to eat from the Tree of Knowledge because one's "eyes will be opened and you will be like God." As with the forbidden fruit in the Garden of Eden, I suspect that the real reason that psychedelic plants and drugs are illegal is because they wake us up from the dream of life, and many people are culturally programmed to believe that we should stay asleep.

Life is like a game in many ways, and the first rule of this game of games is to unquestionably accept what your senses tell you as reality. To get along here on Earth, we all need to accept the basic assumption that everything we see, hear, touch, taste, and smell is "real." Anyone who thinks otherwise is, of course, crazy.

The acceptance that life is actually real is universally experienced and rarely questioned—but how would you know if you were imagining the universe into existence or not? It appears that waking up from the dream of life is an inherently difficult process. It almost seems as though there is a built-in inhibition to discovering this, as though it is a deliberate part of the design of the universe. Perhaps it is. Regardless, there appears to be a huge increase in the number of people in the world today who are interested in lucid dreaming, as well as psychedelic states of awareness, and I suspect that this growing trend will continue into the future. It seems like the whole world is starting to wake up, and perhaps this is part of the overall design that is unfolding too.

STEPPING INTO THE FUTURE

In the 1949 Broadway musical *South Pacific*, Bloody Mary sings these famous lines, "You gotta have a dream, if you don't have a dream, How you gonna have a dream come true?"

I find it interesting that the word *dream* refers both to our nightly adventures in slumberland and to our ideal vision of what we'd like most in our lives. During the process of writing this book about lucid dreaming many of my longtime dreams, of the second kind, surprisingly did come true—with regard to my career, my home, and my romantic partner. Somehow the process of increasing awareness in my dreams brought me greater balance and health, as well as more love and abundance in my life.

After my shamanic healing in the Amazon, the dynamics of my life began to substantially shift, and it was during this period that my lucid dreams began to increase in frequency—which helped inspire me to write this book. It seems that the timing of my personal journey is in synch with the culture at large, which is now exploding with an interest in lucid dreaming, and we're making enormous scientific advances at an accelerated rate. I think that this interest in lucid dreaming and our understanding of it will grow into a sophisticated science, opening up magnificent new possibilities for our species. Terence McKenna echoed this sentiment when he told me:

> I've had lucid dreams, but I have no technique for repeating them on demand. The dream state is possibly anticipating this cultural frontier that we're moving toward. We're moving toward something very much like eternal dreaming, going into the imagination and staying there, and that would be like a lucid dream that knew no end, but what a tight, simple solution. One of the things that interests me about dreams is this: . . . They are more powerful than any

yoga, so taking control of the dream state would certainly be an advantageous thing and carry us a great distance toward the kind of cultural transformation that we're talking about. How exactly to do it, I'm not sure. The psychedelics, the near-death experience, the lucid dreaming, the meditational reveries . . . all of these things are pieces of a puzzle about how to create a new cultural dimension that we can all live in a little more sanely than we're living in these dimensions.

I suspect that our species' interest in lucid dreaming is an extension of our planet's 4.5-billion-year evolutionary process, and I see consciousness explorers as the leading edge of our biosphere's emergence into new frontiers. I think these frontiers—the realms of consciousness that we find in our dreams or in shamanic states of mind, and perhaps those that hover beyond death—could be genuine geographical realms, where we can, and eventually will, set up transportation and communication systems.

We're connecting and wiring the different realms together, turning our imaginations inside out. Soon we'll be able to lucid dream on command, record our dreams, and electronically share them with one another, and this may be part of what we were designed to do as a species. Ultimately, this could be just the beginning of a new evolutionary adventure that is currently beyond our comprehension.

I'll end my speculations here and let yours continue. Good night and sweet lucid dreams. May all of your dreams come true!

NOTES

Introduction.
Exploring the Secret Realm
of the Waking Dream

1. Morley, *Dreams of Awakening,* 19. Morley notes that this was the first song to ever be sung within a lucid dream by Stephen LaBerge's research team.
2. For a good discussion of the levels of lucidity that are achievable within the dream state, see Waggoner and McCready, *Lucid Dreaming, Plain and Simple,* 24–25.
3. Van Eeden, "Study of Dreams."
4. Saint-Denys, *Les rêves.*
5. Hearne, *Dream Machine,* 17–18.
6. LaBerge et al., "Lucid dreaming verified."
7. LaBerge, *Lucid Dreaming: A Concise Guide,* 61.
8. Peters and Price-Williams, "Towards an experiential analysis," 398–99.
9. Krippner, "Psychology of shamans," 10–12, 38–40.
10. Hurd, "Lucid Dreaming as Shamanic Consciousness."
11. Castaneda, *Teachings of Don Juan, Separate Reality,* etc.
12. Kharitidi, *Master of Lucid Dreams.*
13. Brooks and Vogelsong, *Conscious Exploration,* 253.
14. https://en.wikipedia.org/wiki/Eckankar.
15. Brown, "DMT Research and Nonhuman-Entity Contact" in *Frontiers of Psychedelic Consciousness,* 148.
16. Waggoner, *Lucid Dreaming,* 63.
17. Hoyle, "Science Wakes Up."

Chapter 1.
Shamanic Plants, Psychedelics, and Mind-Body Healing

1. Carey, "LSD Reconsidered."
2. Richardson, "Psychedelic Drugs."
3. Dobkin de Rios and Janiger, *LSD*; and Fadiman, *Psychedelic Explorer's Guide*.
4. Kärkkäinen et al., "Potentially hallucinogenic."
5. Shulgin and Shulgin, "DMT Is Everywhere," 249.
6. Servillo et al., "N-Methylated tryptamine derivatives"; and Servillo et al., "Citrus genus plants contain N-methylated tryptamine derivatives."
7. *DMT: The Spirit Molecule* (film). "Terence [McKenna] was very . . . he was a good promoter" (00:16:47) . . . "Basically he said it's the ultimate metaphysical reality pill" (00:16:53).
8. Murray et al., "Increased excretion of dimethyltryptamine."
9. Barker et al., "LC/MS/MS analysis."
10. Personal e-mail communication from Rick Strassman to the author on August 9, 2014.
11. Mithoefer et al., "Safety and efficacy."
12. For a comprehensive summary of the medical research into psychedelics since 1990, see my e-book *Psychedelic Drug Research*.
13. Griffiths et al., "Psilocybin can occasion mystical-type experiences."
14. Catlow et al., "Effects of psilocybin."
15. Carhart-Harris et al., "Neural correlates."
16. Tagliazucchi et al., "Enhanced repertoire"; and "Your Brain on Magic Mushrooms."
17. Green and McCreery, *Lucid Dreaming*, 26.
18. Ibid., 109.
19. Springer and Deutsch, *Left Brain, Right Brain*.
20. Greenwood and Gazzaniga, "Dream report."
21. "Behavior of Split Brain Patients."
22. Green and McCreery, *Lucid Dreaming*, 159.
23. Ibid.
24. LaBerge and Dement, "Lateralization of alpha activity."
25. Montplaisir, "REM sleep dream mentation."
26. McCormick et al., "Handedness."
27. Garfield, *Creative Dreaming*, 18 (see the story of Claire Sylvia).
28. This discussion with LaBerge appears in my book (with Rebecca Novick) *Mavericks of the Mind*.

29. E. Davis, "Ayahuasca," 12–13.

30. Laughlin, *Communing*, 275.

31. Krippner, Bogzaran, and de Carvalho, *Extraordinary Dreams*, 136.

32. Echenhofer, "Dynamics of healing."

33. Voss et al., "Lucid dreaming."

34. Lutz et al., "Long-term meditators."

35. Palhano-Fontes et al., "Psychedelic state."

36. Bogzaran, "Experiencing the divine," 28.

37. Hurd, "Unearthing the Paleolithic Mind."

38. Bourguignon, "Dreams."

39. Szpakowska, "Through the Looking Glass," 31.

40. Magaña, *Toltec Secret*, 47.

41. Ibid., 87.

42. Laughlin, *Communing*, 251.

43. Ibid., 156–57.

44. Ibid., 134.

45. Ibid., 64.

46. Ibid., 276.

47. Ibid., 277.

48. Fox, *Astral Projection*, 90–91.

49. Krippner, Bogzaran, and de Carvalho, *Extraordinary Dreams*, 39–40.

50. Malcolm, reference 51: https://en.wikipedia.org/wiki/Lucid_dream.

51. Laughlin, *Communing*, 139.

52. Tart, "High Dream," 171–76.

53. Faraday, *Dream Power*, 294–95.

54. Gillis, "Dream Trips"; and Kay, "Psychedelics."

Chapter 2.
The Psychology and Physiology of Dreaming

1. J. Hobson, "REM sleep."

2. Moorcroft, *Understanding Sleep and Dreaming*, 227.

3. Nielsen, "Mentation."

4. Ouspensky, *On the Study*, 295–96.

5. Ekirch, *At Day's Close*.

6. Ibid., 300–308.

7. Wehr, "In short photoperiods."

8. Ibid.

9. Ekirch, *At Day's Close*, xxvii.

10. Hobson and McCarley, "Brain is a dream state generator," 1347.

11. Antrobus, "Neurocognition of Sleep"; and Solms, "Dreaming and REM sleep."

12. Nielsen and Stenstrom, "What are the memory sources?"

13. Van der Helm and Walker, "Sleep and emotional memory processing."

14. Valli et al., "Dreams are more negative."

15. Hall and Van de Castle, *Content Analysis*.

16. Domhoff, "Dreams of Men."

17. Hall and Van de Castle, *Content Analysis*, 164.

18. Alleyne, "Black and White."

19. Edelman and Tononi, *Universe of Consciousness*, 53.

20. Zimmerman, Stoyva, and Metcalf, "Distorted visual field"; and De Konick, Prévost, and Lortie-Lussier, "Vertical inversion."

21. Hartman and Zimberoff, "REM and non-REM."

22. Dane, "Non-REM."

23. Pilcher, "Dreamless woman."

24. Hunt, "Some relations," 226.

25. Laughlin, *Communing*, 126–27.

26. Morin, "What People around the World Dream About."

27. Laughlin, *Communing*, 23.

28. Pace-Schott, *Sleep and Dreaming*, 197.

29. Aristotle, *Works*, 703–6.

30. Maury, *Le sommeil*, 133–34.

31. Ouspensky, *On the Study*, 289–90.

32. Ehrlich, "Read the Lost Dream."

33. Freud, *Interpretation*, 611.

34. Jung, *Dreams*, 5.

35. Ibid., 77.

36. Riley, A. "Bees learn while they sleep."

37. Brylowski, Levitan, and LaBerge. "H-reflex suppression."

38. Serafetinides, Shurley, and Brooks, "Electroencephalogram."

39. Kaufman, "Dreams Make You Smarter."

40. Schredl, "Creativity and dream recall."

41. Wagner et al., "Sleep inspires."

42. Page, transcript.

43. Laughlin, *Communing*, 251.

44. De Becker, *Understanding*, 85.

45. Stevenson, "Chapter on Dreams," 206–30.

46. Damer and Deamer, "Coupled phases."
47. Johnson, "Magic, Meditation," 46.
48. Ibid., 50.
49. Ibid., 46.
50. Love, *Are You Dreaming?* 226–27.
51. Lucas, portfolio.
52. Casale, "Lucid."
53. Johnson, "Magic, Meditation," 47.
54. Petri et al., "Homological scaffolds."
55. Ibid.
56. Love, *Are You Dreaming?* 206.

Chapter 3.
The Science of Lucid Dreaming

1. Tart, "Towards the experimental," 88.
2. Green, *Lucid Dreams,* 128.
3. Hearne, *Dream Machine,* 11.
4. Hearne, "Insight into Lucid Dreams."
5. LaBerge et al., "Lucid dreaming verified."
6. Voss et al., "Lucid dreaming."
7. Hobson and Voss, "A mind to go out of."
8. Voss et al., "Lucid dreaming."
9. J. Hobson, "REM sleep."
10. *Oneironaut.*
11. Gackenbach, "Video game play."
12. Gackenbach and Hunt, "Deeper Inquiry."
13. Arnold-Foster, *Studies in Dreams,* 30–31.
14. Kasatkin, *Theory,* 6–9.
15. R. Smith, "Traumatic dreams" and "Do dreams reflect."
16. Taitz, "Clinical Applications."
17. Zappaterra, Lysander, and Pangarkat, "Chronic pain resolution."
18. Pert, *Molecules of Emotion,* 28.
19. Erlacher and Schredl, "Cardiovascular responses."
20. Dresler et al., "Dreamed movement."
21. LaBerge, Greenleaf, and Kedzierski, "Physiological responses."
22. Karacan et al., "Uterine activity."
23. Fischer, Gross, and Zuch, "Cycle of penile erection."
24. Rycroft, *The Innocence of Dreams,* 111.

25. Waggoner and McCready, *Lucid Dreaming, Plain and Simple,* 163.

26. Kellogg, "Personal Experience," 6–7.

27. Moss, *Conscious Dreaming,* 14.

28. Garfield, *Healing Power.*

29. Barasch, *Healing Dreams,* 5.

30. Kellogg, referenced in Waggoner and McCready, *Lucid Dreaming, Plain and Simple,* 17.

31. S. Davis, "Being in a Coma."

32. Waggoner, "A Look at Lucid Dreams."

33. Dresler et al., "Dreamed movement."

34. "Scientists Measure Dream Content."

35. Bourke and Shaw, "Spontaneous lucid dreaming."

36. Erlacher and Schredl, "Applied research."

37. Filevich et al., "Metacognitive mechanisms."

38. Voss et al., "Induction of self awareness."

39. Jorge Conesa Sevilla presented this unpublished research in a Web-based seminar hosted by Ryan Hurd on the Evolver social network, www.evolvernetwork .org, on November 20, 2014.

40. Waggoner, *Lucid Dreaming,* 211.

Chapter 4.
Improving Lucid Dreaming and Developing Superpowers in the Dream Realm

1. Stumbrys and Erlacher, "Science of Lucid Dream," 81.

2. Van de Castle, *Our Dreaming Mind,* 457.

3. Holzinger, "Lucid Dreaming," 42–44.

4. Hurd, "Unearthing the Paleolithic," 296.

5. Green and McCreery, *Lucid Dreaming,* 129.

6. Laughlin, *Communing,* 465–66.

7. Daulerio, "Lucid Dreams Deferred."

8. Green and McCreery, *Lucid Dreaming,* 120–21.

9. Chapters by Riboli, Holzinger, and Dahl, in *Lucid Dreaming,* eds. Hurd and Bulkely.

10. Fox, *Astral Projection,* 120–21.

11. Schredl and Erlacher, "Frequency of lucid dreaming"; and Erlacher et al., "Incidence of lucid dreaming."

12. LaBerge, "Lucid Dreaming: Psychophysical Studies"; and Stumbrys and Erlacher, "Lucid dreaming during NREM."

13. Moss, *Conscious Dreaming*, 72.

14. Reed, "Learning to remember"; and Schredl, "Questionaire and diaries."

15. Fox, *Astral Projection*, 157.

16. Ouspensky, *On the Study*, 272.

17. Green and McCreery, *Lucid Dreaming*, 114.

18. Stumbrys and Erlacher, "Science of Lucid Dream," 87–89.

19. Love, *Are You Dreaming?* 81.

20. Translated by Beth Mugge in LaBerge, "Lucid Dreaming in Western Literature."

21. Castaneda, *Journey to Ixtlan*, 83–84.

22. Waggoner and McCready, *Lucid Dreaming*, 34–36.

23. Levitan et al., "Look and feel."

24. James1982, "What's the deal."

25. Edelstein and LaBerge, "The best time."

26. Gackenbach, Cranson, and Alexander, "Lucid dreaming"; and Hunt and Ogilvie, "Lucid Dreams in Their Natural Series." in Gackenbach and LaBerge, eds., *Conscious Mind, Sleeping Brain*.

27. R. Wallace, "Physiological effects."

28. Gackenbach and Bosveld, *Control Your Dream*.

29. Green and McCreery, *Lucid Dreaming*, 158.

30. Dodet, et al., "Lucid dreaming in narcolepsy," 487–97.

31. Laughlin, *Communing*, 415.

32. Levitan, "Sleep on the right, as a lion doth . . ."

33. Masako, Bang, Watanabe, and Sasaki, "Night Watch in One Brain Hemisphere," 1190–94.

34. LaBerge, Phillips, and Levitan, "An Hour of Wakefulness"; and Stumbrys and Erlacher, "Science of Lucid Dream," 85–89.

35. Stumbrys and Erlacher, "Science of Lucid Dream," 87–88.

36. Brooks and Vogelsong, *Conscious Exploration*, 77.

37. J. Hobson, *Dreaming Brain*, 111.

38. LaBerge and Rheingold, *Exploring the World*, 143.

39. Krippner, Bogzaran, and de Carvalho, *Extraordinary Dreams*, 67.

40. LaBerge, *Lucid Dreaming: The Power of Being Awake*, 179.

41. Holzinger, "Lucid Dreaming," 39.

42. McNamara, *Nightmares*, 5.

43. Hurd, "Unearthing the Paleolithic Mind," 300.

44. Garfield, *Creative Dreaming*, 112–15.

45. Van de Castle, *Our Dreaming Mind*, 449.

46. Fox, *Astral Projection*, 32–33.

47. Love, *Are You Dreaming?* 200.

48. Epel, *Writers Dreaming*, 282.

49. Saint-Denys, *Les rêves*, 141.

50. Lilly, *Programming and Metaprogramming*, xvi.

Chapter 5.
Enhancing Dreaming with Oneirogens, Nutritional Supplements, Herbs, and Drugs

1. Mayagoitia, Diaz, and Contreras, "Study on *Calea*."

2. Ibid.

3. Freemon and Al-Marashi, "Long-term changes."

4. Revonsuo, "Reinterpretation of dreams."

5. Sampson, "Psychological effects."

6. Hartmann, "Why Do We Dream?"

7. McKenna, "Trialogue: Cannabis."

8. Lehrer, "Does Marijuana Make You Stupid?"

9. Nielsen et al., "Partial REM-sleep deprivation."

10. "Parkinson Disease."

11. Baker, "Tradition and toxicity."

12. Boerner et al., "Kava-Kava extract."

13. Lehrl, "Clinical efficacy of kava."

14. Brown, *Frontiers,* 208.

15. Stumbrys and Erlacher, "Science of Lucid Dream," 93.

16. Ragno, "Why skullcap is one of my all-time favorite medicinal plants."

17. Shroomery.

18. Erowid Experience Vaults.

19. Ibid.

20. Ebben, Lequerica, and Spielman, "Effects of pyridoxine."

21. Yuschak, *Advanced Lucid Dreaming,* 102–3.

22. Gomez-Ramirez et al., "The deployment."

23. La Marca and LaBerge, "Pre-sleep treatment."

24. LaBerge and Levitan, *Substances That Enhance.*

25. Hurd, "Initial Findings."

26. Torda, "Contribution to serotonin."

27. www.lucidity.com/LucidDreamingFAQ2.html.

28. Mandell, "Toward a Psychobiology."

29. Anderson, "Ibogaine therapy."

30. Erowid Experience Vaults.

31. Devereux and Devereux, *Lucid Dreaming*.

32. Pickover, *Sex, Drugs, Einstein*, 9.

33. Ibid.

Chapter 6.
Exploring the Potential of Electronic Technologies

1. Hearne, *Dream Machine*, 90.

2. LaBerge and Levitan, "Validity established."

3. Hurd, "Lucid Dreaming Masks."

4. Gelhorn and Kiely, "Mystical states of consciousness."

5. Post, "Educational Frontiers of Training," 140.

6. Winter, "Personal Sleep Monitors."

7. Mordvintsev, Olah, and Tyka, "Inceptionism."

8. Ibid.

9. Horikawa et al., "Neural decoding."

10. Tong and Pratte, "Decoding patterns."

11. Oldis, "Can We Turn Our Dreams Into Watchable Movies?"

Chapter 7.
Communicating with Dream Characters,
Archetypes, Spirits, and Disembodied Entities

1. Jung, *Psychogenesis*.

2. Waggoner, "Learning the Depths," 203.

3. Jung, *Memories, Dreams*, 183.

4. Van Eeden, "Study of Dreams," 456.

5. Father X, quoted in Brooks and Vogelsong, *Conscious Exploration*, 24.

6. Domino, "Became Lucid."

7. Love, *Are You Dreaming?* 231.

8. Waggoner, *Lucid Dreaming*, 126–27.

9. Brooks and Vogelsong, *Conscious Exploration*, 76–77.

10. Ibid., 81.

11. LaBerge, *Lucid Dreaming: The Power of Being Awake*, 179.

12. Brooks and Vogelsong, *Conscious Exploration*, 242.

13. Hurd, "Doppelgänger."

14. Krippner and Faith, "Exotic dreams."

15. Chuang Chou, quoted in Soothill, *The Three Religions of China*, 75.

16. Hearne, *Dream Machine*, 55.

17. Zoe7, *Into the Void,* 43.

18. Waggoner, *Lucid Dreaming,* 47.

19. Barrett, "Dreaming as a Normal Model," 123.

20. Rosie D., "Aggressive alters."

21. Hallis, "The Death Interviews."

22. Gackenbach and Bosveld, *Control Your Dreams,* 168, 174; and Gackenbach, "Sex differences."

23. Ouspensky, *New Model,* 281–82.

24. LaBerge and Rheingold, *Exploring the World,* 135–36.

25. Garfield, *Creative Dreaming,* 169.

Chapter 8.
Dream Telepathy, Psychic Phenomena, Mutual Dreaming, and Shared Lucid Dreams

1. Radin, *Conscious Universe,* 22.

2. www.sheldrake.org/research/glossary.

3. Personal communication from psychologist Jean Millay.

4. "Psi-chedelic Science."

5. Gurney, Myers, and Podmore, *Phantasms of the Living.*

6. Krippner, Bogzaran, and de Carvalho, *Extraordinary Dreams,* 97.

7. Ibid., 101.

8. Persinger and Krippner, "Dream ESP Experiments and Geomagnetic Activity."

9. Krippner, "Pilot Study."

10. Sherwood and Roe, "Review."

11. Ibid.

12. C. Smith, "Can healthy, young adults uncover?"

13. Krippner, Bogzaran, and de Carvalho, *Extraordinary Dreams,* 1.

14. Ibid., 118.

15. Ibid., 107.

16. Garfield, *Creative Dreaming,* 18.

17. Radin, "Unconscious perception" and "Electrodermal presentiments."

18. Soon et al., "Unconscious determinants."

19. Laughlin, *Communing,* 216.

20. Krippner, Bogzaran, and de Carvalho, *Extraordinary Dreams,* 96.

21. McNamara, "Precognitive Dreams."

22. Hurd, *Big Dreams,* 24.

23. Sheldrake, *Sense of Being,* 242.

24. Hearne, *Dream Machine,* 105–6.

25. Fox, *Astral Projection*, 45–46.

26. Krippner, "A psychic dream?"

27. Krippner, Bogzaran, and de Carvalho, *Extraordinary Dreams*, 119.

28. Soik, www.linkedin.com/in/hunterleesoik.

29. Van de Castle, *Our Dreaming Mind*, 49.

30. Castaneda, *Art of Dreaming*.

31. Magallon, *Mutual Dreaming*.

32. Fox, *Astral Projection*, 47.

33. Poirier, "This Is Good," 113.

34. Kellogg, "Mutual lucid dream."

35. Shohet, *Dream Sharing*.

36. Krippner, Bogzaran, and de Carvalho, *Extraordinary Dreams*, 122–23.

37. Martone, "Scientists Discover."

38. Hamilton, "Twin Telepathy."

39. LaBerge, *Lucid Dreaming: The Power of Being Awake*, 251.

40. Kellogg, "Tails."

Chapter 9.
Out-of-Body Experiences,
Parallel Universes, and Alternate Dimensions

1. Laughlin, *Communing*, 69.

2. Ibid., 82.

3. Krippner, Bogzaran, and de Carvalho, *Extraordinary Dreams*, 107.

4. Nietzsche, *Human*.

5. Braithwaite et al., "Cognitive correlates."

6. Irwin, "Out of Body."

7. McCreery, "Schizotypy."

8. Monroe, *Far Journeys*, 265.

9. Monroe, "Wanted," 49.

10. Boyd, "Astral Projection 101."

11. Fox, *Astral Projection*, 40.

12. Brooks and Vogelsong, *Conscious Exploration*, 151–53.

13. Ibid., 39.

14. Ibid., 40.

15. Blackmore, "Theory of Lucid Dreams," 375–77.

16. Ibid. 384.

17. Blackmore, "Postal survey."

18. Green and McCreery, *Lucid Dreaming*, 52–64.

19. Green, *Out-of-the-Body.*

20. Levitan and LaBerge, "In the mind."

21. LaBerge, "Stuff of dreams."

22. Irwin, *Flight.*

23. Braithwaite et al., "Cognitive correlates."

24. Nicholls, *Navigating.*

25. Graff, *Tracks.*

26. McMoneagle and May, *Memoirs.*

27. Tart, "Psychophysiological study."

28. "Transmitting Thought."

29. Gackenbach and Bosveld, *Control Your Dreams,* 129.

30. Sartori, *Near-Death Experiences.*

31. Van Lommel et al., "Near-death experience."

32. Parnia et al., "AWARE."

33. Brown, *Frontiers,* 39.

34. Alexander, *Proof,* 46.

35. Ibid., 142.

36. Harris, *Waking Up,* 174–86.

37. Personal communication with neuroscientists Paul Goodwin and David E. Nichols.

38. Sheldrake, *Seven Experiments,* 262–63.

39. Mays and Mays, "Phantom limb 'touch'."

40. Brown, *Frontiers,* 203.

41. Fox, *Astral Projection,* 72–73.

42. Hurd, "Guarding."

43. Wolf, *Dreaming Universe.*

44. Kaku, *Parallel Worlds.*

45. "Reality Fishing," 71.

46. Bryanton, *Imagining the Tenth Dimension,* 3.

47. Wilson and Grant, "Man from Taured."

48. Laughlin, *Communing,* 45.

49. Erlacher et al., "Time for actions."

50. "Very, very long dreams."

51. "Can We Really Spend Years"; and "Time Dilation."

52. "Story of Narada."

Chapter 10.
Conscious Dreaming as a Path to Spiritual Awakening

1. Green and McCreery, *Lucid Dreaming,* 147.

2. LaBerge and Rheingold, *Exploring the World of Lucid Dreaming*, 10–11.

3. Green and McCreery, *Lucid Dreaming*, 145.

4. Grof, *When the Impossible Happens*.

5. "About Edgar Cayce's A.R.E."

6. Personal communication from Alison Ray, marketing and public information manager of A.R.E.

7. Krippner, Bogzaran, and de Carvalho, *Extraordinary Dreams*, 130.

8. Morley, *Dreams of Awakening*, 24.

9. Tarthang, *Openness*, 74.

10. Pollan, "Trip Treatment."

11. Waggoner, *Lucid Dreaming*, 97–106.

12. Evans-Wentz, *Tibetan Yoga*, 221–22.

13. Waggoner, "Learning the Depths," 193.

14. Kellogg, "Lucid Dream Information."

15. Morley, *Dreams of Awakening*, 246.

16. Young, "Buddhist Dream Experience," 18.

17. Laughlin, *Communing*, 159.

18. Green and McCreery, *Lucid Dreaming*, 101–2.

19. Ibid., 102.

20. Garfield, *Creative Dreaming*, 65.

21. Garfield, *Dream Messenger*.

22. Ibid., from the inside dust jacket of the book.

23. Ibid., 33.

24. Griffiths et al., "Psilocybin can occasion mystical-type experiences."

25. Bogzaran, "Experiencing the divine."

26. Bogzaran, "Images," 209–13.

27. Hurd, "Exploring the Void."

28. Zoe7, *Back from the Void*, 23.

29. Tarthang, *Openness*, 86.

30. Summarized by O'Flaherty in "Uses and misuses," 219–20.

31. Ibid., 220.

32. Stevens, *Private Myths*.

BIBLIOGRAPHY

"About Edgar Cayce's A.R.E." www.edgarcayce.org/are/edgarcayce.aspx?id=1036 [accessed Mar. 5, 2016].

Alexander, Eben. *Proof of Heaven: A Neurosurgeon's Journey into the Afterlife.* New York: Simon and Schuster, 2012.

Alleyne, Richard. "Black and White TV Generation Have Monochrome Dreams." *Telegraph,* October 17, 2008. www.telegraph.co.uk/news/science/science -news/3353504/Black-and-white-TV-generation-have-monochrome-dreams .html [accessed Feb. 16, 2016].

Anderson, Carl M. "Ibogaine therapy in chemical dependency and posttraumatic stress disorder: A hypothesis involving the fractal nature of fetal REM sleep and interhemispheric reintegration." *MAPS Bulletin* 8, no. 1 (1998): 5–14.

Antrobus, J. "The Neurocognition of Sleep Mentation: Rapid Eye Movements, Visual Imagery and Dreaming." In *Sleep and Cognition,* edited by Richard Bootzin, John F. Kihlstorm, and Daniel Schacter, 1–14. Washington, D.C.: American Psychological Association, 1990.

Aristotle. *Works of Aristotle Part 1.* Vol. 8. Edited by Robert M. Maynard. Chicago: Encyclopaedia Britannica, 1952.

Arnold-Foster, Mary. *Studies in Dreams.* London: Allen and Unwin, 1921. Repr. ed. Forgotten Books, 2015.

Baker, Jonathan. "Tradition and toxicity: Evidential cultures in the kava safety debate." *Social Studies of Science* 41, no. 3 (2011): 361–84.

Barasch, Marc Ian. *Healing Dreams: Exploring the Dreams That Can Transform Your Life.* New York: Riverhead, 2000.

Barker, Steven, Jimo Borjigin, Izabela Lomnicka, and Rick Strassman. "LC/MS/MS analysis of the endogenous dimethyltryptamine hallucinogens, their precursors, and major metabolites in rat pineal gland microdialysate." *Biomedical Chromatography* 27, no. 12 (2013): 1690–1700.

Barrett, Deirdre L. *The Committee of Sleep: How Artists, Scientists, and Athletes Use Their Dreams for Creative Problem Solving and How You Can Too*. Oneiroi Press, 2010.

———. "Dreaming as a Normal Model for Multiple Personality Disorder." In *Dissociation: Clinical and Theoretical Perspectives,* edited by Steven J. Lynn and Judith W. Rhue, 123–25. New York: The Guilford Press, 1994.

"Behavior of Split Brain Patients." otsr.virtualave.net/Hammond/Behavior_of _Split_Brain_Patients.doc [accessed Feb. 13, 2016].

Beyer, Stephan V. *Singing to the Plants: A Guide to Mestizo Shamanism in the Upper Amazon*. Albuquerque, N.M.: University of New Mexico Press, 2009.

Blackmore, Sue. "A postal survey of OBEs and other experiences." *Journal of the Society for Psychical Research* 52 (1984): 227–44.

———. "A Theory of Lucid Dreams and OBEs." In *Conscious Mind, Sleeping Brain: Perspectives on Lucid Dreaming,* edited by Jayne Gackenbach and Stephen LaBerge, 373–87. New York: Plenum, 1988.

Boerner, R. J., H. Sommer, W. Berger, U. Kuhn, U. Schmidt, and M. Mannel. "Kava-Kava extract LI 150 is as effective as Opipramol and Buspirone in Generalised Anxiety Disorder: An 8-week randomized, double-blind multi-centre clinical trial in 129 out-patients." *Phytomedicine* 10, suppl. 4 (2003): 38–49.

Bogzaran, Fariba. "Experiencing the divine in the lucid dream state." *Lucidity Letter* 9, no. 1 (1990).

———. "Images of the Lucid Mind: A Phenomenological Study of Lucid Dreaming and Modern Painting." Ph.D. dissertation, University of Michigan, 1996.

Bogzaran, Fariba, and Daniel Deslauriers. *Integral Dreaming: A Holistic Approach to Dreams* (SUNY Series in Dream Studies). Albany, N.Y.: State University of New York Press, 2012.

Bourguignon, Erika. "Dreams and Altered States of Consciousness in Anthropological Research." In *Psychological Anthropology* 2nd ed., edited by Francis L. K. Hsu, 403–34. Cambridge, Mass.: Schenkman, 1972.

Bourke, Patrick, and Hannah Shaw. "Spontaneous lucid dreaming frequency and waking insight." *Dreaming* 24, no. 2 (2014): 152–59.

Boyd, Ryan. "Astral Projection 101: DMT and Sleep Paralysis." *Spirit Science,* March 21, 2012. http://thespiritscience.net/2012/03/21/astral-projection-101-dmt -sleep-paralysis/ [accessed Mar. 3, 2016].

Braithwaite, J. J., D. Swanson, I. Apperly, E. Broglia, and J. Hulleman. "Cognitive correlates of the spontaneous out-of-body experience (OBE) in the psycho-logically normal population: Evidence for an increased role of temporal-lobe instability, body-distortion processing, and impairments in own-body transformations." *Cortex* 47, no. 7 (2011): 839–53.

Brooks, Janice E., and Jay Vogelsong. *The Conscious Exploration of Dreaming: Discovering How We Create and Control Our Dreams.* 1st Book Library, 2000.

Brown, David Jay. *Conversations on the Edge of the Apocalypse: Contemplating the Future with Noam Chomsky, George Carlin, Deepak Chopra, Rupert Sheldrake, and Others.* New York: St. Martin's Press, 2005.

———. *Frontiers of Psychedelic Consciousness: Conversations with Albert Hofmann, Stanislav Grof, Rick Strassman, Jeremy Narby, Simon Posford, and Others.* Rochester, Vt.: Park Street Press, 2015.

———. *Mavericks of Medicine: Conversations on the Frontiers of Medical Research.* Smart Publications, 2006.

———. *The New Science of Psychedelics: At the Nexus of Culture, Consciousness, and Spirituality.* Rochester, Vt.: Park St. Press, 2013.

———. *Psychedelic Drug Research: A Comprehensive Review.* Reality Sandwich/ Evolver Press, 2012.

Brown, David Jay, and Rebecca McClen Novick. *Mavericks of the Mind: Conversations for the New Millenium.* Crossing Press, 1993.

Bryanton, Rob. *Imagining the Tenth Dimension.* Victoria, British Columbia: Trafford Publishing, 2006.

Brylowski, Andrew, Lynne Levitan, and Stephen LaBerge. "H-reflex suppression and autonomic activation during lucid REM sleep: A case study." *Sleep* 12, no. 4 (1989): 374–78.

Bulkeley, Kelly, ed. *Dreams: A Reader on Religious, Cultural and Psychological Dimensions of Dreaming.* New York: Palgrave, 2001.

Campbell, Jean. *Group Dreaming: Dreams to the Tenth Power.* Norfolk, Va.: Wordminder Press, 2006.

"Can We Really Spend Years in a Lucid Dream?" www.dreamviews.com/attaining -lucidity/123728-can-we-really-spend-years-lucid-dream.html [accessed Mar. 5, 2016].

Carey, Benedict. "LSD Reconsidered for Therapy." *New York Times,* March 3, 2014.

Carhart-Harris, R. L., D. Erritzoe, T. Williams, J. M. Stone, L. J. Reed, A. Colasanti, R. J. Tyacke et al. "Neural correlates of the psychedelic state as determined by fMRI studies with psilocybin." *Proceedings of the National Academy of Sciences* 109, no. 6 (2012): 2138–43.

Casale, Pete. "Lucid." www.youtube.com/watch?v=gLRVfkNL2CA [accessed Feb. 17, 2016].

Castaneda, Carlos. *The Art of Dreaming.* New York: Harper Perennial, 1993.

————. *Journey to Ixtlan: The Lessons of Don Juan*. New York: Washington Square Press, 1991.

————. *A Separate Reality: Further Conversations with Don Juan*. New York: Washington Square Press, 1991.

————. *The Teachings of Don Juan: A Yaqui Way of Knowledge*. New York: Washington Square Press, 1985.

Catlow, B. J, S. Song, D. A. Paredes, C. L. Kirstein, and J. Sanchez-Ramos. "Effects of psilocybin on hippocampal neurogenesis and extinction of trace fear conditioning." *Experimental Brain Research* 228, no. 4 (2013): 481–91.

Cavanna, Roberto, and Emilio Servadio. Preface by Charles Tart. *ESP Experiments with LSD25 and Psilocybin*. 2nd ed. Parapsychological Monographs 5. New York: Parapsychology Foundation, 2010.

Coxhead, D. Hiller. *Dreams: Visions of the Night*. New York: Crossroad Publishing, 1982.

Damer, Bruce, and David Deamer. "Coupled phases and combinatorial selection in fluctuating hydrothermal pools: A scenario to guide experimental approaches to the origin of cellular life." *Life* 5, no. 1 (2015): 872–87.

Dane, Joe. "Non-REM lucid dreaming." *Lucidity Letter* 5, no. 1 (1986). http://library.macewan.ca/lucidity/issue%205.1/LL5_1_Dane.htm [accessed Feb. 16, 2016].

Daulerio, A. J. "Lucid Dreams Deferred: Jared Loughner's Extraordinary Email Madness." November, 9, 2012. http://gawker.com/5959006/lucid-dreams-deferred-jared-loughners-extraordinary-email-madness [accessed Feb. 22, 2016].

Davis, Erik. "Ayahuasca and James Cameron's *Avatar*." *MAPS Bulletin* 22, no. 1 (2012): 12–13.

Davis, Simon. "Being in a Coma Is Like One Long Lucid Dream." *Vice*, August 31, 2015. www.vice.com/read/being-in-a-coma-is-like-one-long-lucid-dream-511[accessed Feb. 19, 2016].

De Becker, Raymond. *The Understanding of Dreams and Their Influence on the History of Man*. New York: Hawthorn Books, 1968.

De Konick, Joseph, François Prévost, and Monique Lortie-Lussier. "Vertical inversion of the visual field and REM sleep mentation." *Journal of Sleep Research* 5, no. 1 (1995): 16–20.

Devereux, Paul, and Charla Devereux. *Lucid Dreaming: Accessing Your Inner Virtual Realities*. Daily Grail Publishing, 2011.

DMT: The Spirit Molecule, directed by Mitch Schultz. Burbank, Calif.: Warner Bros., 2010.

Dobkin de Rios, Marlene, and Oscar Janiger. *LSD, Spirituality, and the Creative*

Process: Based on the Groundbreaking Research of Oscar Janiger, MD. Rochester, Vt.: Park Street Press, 2002.

Dodet, P., M. Chavez, S. Lev-Semenescu, J. L. Golmard, and I. Amulf. "Lucid dreaming in Narcolepsy." *Sleep* 38, no. 3 (2015): 487–97.

Domhoff, G. William. "The Dreams of Men and Women: Patterns of Gender Similarity and Difference." University of California, Santa Cruz, 2005. http://dreamresearch.net/Library/domhoff_2005c.html [accessed Feb. 16, 2016].

———. "Senoi Dream Theory: Myth, Scientific Method, and the Dreamwork Movement." March 2003: www2.ucsc.edu/dreams/Library/senoi.html [accessed April 11, 2016].

Domino, Sir. "Became Lucid, and held a meeting with all my dream characters discussing THEIR reality . . . Anyone have a similar experience?" Reddit.com, October 2015. www.reddit.com/r/LucidDreaming/comments/3kscdl/became_lucid_and_held_a_meeting_with_all_my_dream [accessed Feb. 29, 2016].

Dresler, Martin, Stefan P. Koch, Renate Wehrle, Victor I. Spoormaker, Florian Holsboer, Axel Steiger, Philipp G. Sämann, Helmuth Obrig, and Michael Czisch. "Dreamed movement elicits activation in the sensorimotor cortex." *Current Biology* 21, no. 21 (2011): 1833–37.

Ebben, M., A. Lequerica, and A. Spielman. "Effects of pyridoxine on dreaming: A preliminary study." *Perceptual and Motor Skills* 94, no. 1 (2002): 135–40.

Echenhofer, Frank. "The dynamics of healing and creativity during ayahuasca shamanic journeys." Presentation at the annual conference of the Society for the Anthropology of Consciousness, Berkeley, Calif., March 20, 2010.

Edelman, Gerald, and Giulio Tononi. *A Universe of Consciousness: How Matter Becomes Imagination.* New York: Basic Books, 2000.

Edelstein, J., and Stephen LaBerge. "The best time for lucid dreaming: Naps, mishaps, and recaps." *NightLight* 4, no. 4 (1992): 4–9.

Ehrenreich, Barbara. *Blood Rites: Origins and History of the Passions of War.* New York: Hold Paperbacks, 1998.

Ehrlich, Ben. "Read the Lost Dream Journal of the Man Who Discovered Neurons." *Nautilus,* August 20, 2015. http://nautil.us/issue/27/dark-matter/read-the-lost-dream-journal-of-the-man-who-discovered-neurons [accessed Mar. 7, 2016].

Ekirch, A. Roger. *At Day's Close: Night in Times Past.* New York: W. W. Norton, 2005.

Epel, Naomi, ed. *Writers Dreaming.* New York: Vintage Books, 1994.

Erlacher, Daniel, Melanie Schadlich, Tadas Stumbrys, and Michael Schredl. "Time for actions in lucid dreams: Effects of task modality, length, and complexity." *Frontiers in Psychology* 16 (2014). http://journal.frontiersin.org/Journal/10.3389/fpsyg.2013.01013/full [accessed Mar. 5, 2016].

Erlacher, Daniel, and Michael Schredl. "Applied research practicing a motor task in a lucid dream enhances subsequent performance: A pilot study." *Sport Psychologist* 24, no. 2 (2010): 157–67.

———, "Cardiovascular responses to dreamed physical exercise during REM lucid dreaming." *Dreaming* 18, no. 2 (2008): 112–21.

———, Tsuneo Watanabe, Jun Yamana, and Florian Gantzert. "The incidence of lucid dreaming within a Japanese university student sample." *International Journal of Dream Research* 1, no. 2 (2008): 39–43.

Erowid Experience Vaults. www.erowid.org/experiences/exp.php?ID=37057Erowid [accessed Mar. 10, 2016].

Evans-Wentz, Walter Yeeling. *Tibetan Yoga and Secret Doctrines; or, Seven books of wisdom of the great path, according to the late Lāma Kazi Dawa-Samdup's English rendering; arranged and edited with introductions and annotations to serve as a commentary.* London: Oxford University Press, H. Milford, 1935.

Fadiman, James. *The Psychedelic Explorer's Guide: Safe, Therapeutic, and Sacred Journeys.* Rochester, Vt.: Park Street Press, 2011.

Faraday, Ann. *The Dream Game.* New York: Harper and Row, 1974.

———. *Dr. Ann Faraday's Dream Power.* Repr. ed. New York: Berkeley Books, 1997.

Father X. "Reflections on 20 years of 'conscious' sleep experiences." *Lucidity Letter* 9, no. 2 (1990): 53–57.

Filevich, Elisa, Martin Dresler, Timothy R. Brick, and Simone Kühn. "Metacognitive mechanisms underlying lucid dreaming." *Journal of Neuroscience* 35, no. 3 (2015): 1082–88.

Fischer, C., J. Gross, and J. Zuch. "Cycle of penile erection synchronous with dreaming (REM) sleep." *Archives of General Psychology* 12 (1965): 29–45.

Fox, Oliver. *Astral Projection: A Record of Out-of-Body Experiences.* New York: University Books, 1962.

Freemon, F. R. "The effect of chronically administered delta-9-tetrahydrocannabinol upon polygraphically monitored sleep of normal volunteers." *Drug and Alcohol Dependence* 10, no. 4 (1982): 345–53.

Freemon, Frank R., and Murtadha S. H. Al-Marashi. "Long-term changes in the sleep of normal volunteers administered multiple doses of delta-9-tetrahydro-cannabinol." *Drug and Alcohol Dependence* 2, no. 1 (1977): 39–43.

Freud, Sigmund. *The Interpretation of Dreams.* Translated by James Strachey. New York: Basic Books, 1955.

Gackenbach, Jayne. "Sex differences in lucid dreaming frequency: A second look." *Lucidity Letter* 4, no. 1 (1985): 127.

———. "Video game play and lucid dreams: Implications for the development of consciousness." *Dreaming* 16, no. 2 (2006): 96–110.

Gackenbach, Jayne, and Jane Bosveld. *Control Your Dream*. New York: Harper Perennial, 1990.

Gackenbach, Jayne, Robert Cranson, and Charles Alexander. "Lucid dreaming, witnessing dreaming, dreaming, and the Transcendental Meditation technique: A developmental relationship." *Lucidity Letter* 5, no. 2 (1986): 34–40.

Gackenbach, Jayne and Harry T. Hunt. "A Deeper Inquiry into the Association between Lucid Dreams and Video Game Play." In *Lucid Dreaming: New Perspectives on Consciousness in Sleep*, vol. 1, edited by Ryan Hurd and Kelly Bulkeley, 231–53. Santa Barbara, Calif.: Praeger, 2014.

Gackenbach, Jayne, and Stephen LaBerge, eds. *Conscious Mind, Sleeping Brain: Perspectives on Lucid Dreaming*. New York: Plenum Press, 1988.

Garfield, Patricia. *Creative Dreaming: Plan and Control Your Dreams to Develop Creativity, Overcome Fears, Solve Problems, and Create a Better Self.* New York: Fireside, 1995.

———. *The Dream Messenger: How Dreams of the Departed Bring Healing Gifts.* New York: Simon and Schuster, 1997.

———. *The Healing Power of Dreams*. New York: Fireside, 1992.

Gelhorn, E., and W. F. Kiely. "Mystical states of consciousness: Neurophysiological and clinical aspects." *Journal of Nervous and Mental Diseases* 154 (1972): 399–405.

Gillis, Lucy. "Dream Trips: Dream Drugs as Metaphor." www.improverse.com/ed-articles/lucy_gillis_2001_april_lucidexchange.htm [accessed Feb. 15, 2016].

Gomez-Ramirez, Manuel, Beth A. Higgins, Jane A. Rycroft, Gail N. Owen, Jeanette Mahoney, Marina Shpaner, and John J. Foxe. "The deployment of intersensory selective attention." *Clinical Neuropharmacology* 30, no. 1 (2007): 25–38.

Graff, Dale E. *Tracks in the Psychic Wilderness: An Exploration of ESP, Remote Viewing, Precognitive Dreaming and Synchronicity*. Darby, Pa.: Diane Publishing, 1998.

Green, Celia. *Lucid Dreams*. Oxford, UK: Institute of Psychophysical Research, 1968.

———. *Out-of-the-Body Experiences*. New York: Ballantine, 1975.

Green, Celia, and Charles McCreery. *Lucid Dreaming: The Paradox of Consciousness during Sleep*. New York: Routledge, 1994.

Greenwood, P., D. H. Wilson, and M. S. Gazzaniga. "Dream report following commissurotomy." *Cortex* 13, no. 3 (1977): 311–16.

Griffiths, R., W. A. Richards, U. McCann, and R. Jesse. "Psilocybin can occasion mystical-type experiences having substantial and sustained personal meaning and spiritual significance." *Psychopharmacology* 187, no. 3 (2006): 268–83.

Grof, Stanislav. *When the Impossible Happens: Adventures in Non-Ordinary Reality*. Boulder, Co.: Sounds True, 2005.

Gurney, Edmund, Frederic W. H. Meyers, and Frank Podmore. *Phantasms of the Living.* Vol. 1. London: Trubner, 1886; online facsimile ed. Esalen CTR. www .esalen.org/ctr-archive/book-phantasms.html [accessed July 5, 2016].

Hall, Calvin S., and Robert L. Van de Castle. *Content Analysis of Dreams.* New York: Appleton-Century Crofts, 1966.

Hallis, Howard. "The Death Interviews: A Talk with Robert Anton Wilson and Timothy Leary." *Ben Is Dead Magazine* 1994 ("The Death Issue"). www .howardhallis.com/bis/deathinterviews [accessed Mar. 1, 2016].

Hamilton, Cathy. "Twin Telepathy: Sibling Bonds Sometimes Exceed What Researchers Can Explain." *Lawrence Journal-World,* December 6, 2009.

Harris, Sam. *Waking Up: A Guide to Spirituality without Religion.* New York: Simon and Shuster, 2014.

Hart, Hornel. *The Enigma of Survival: The Case For and Against an After Life.* London: C. C. Thomas, 1959.

Hartman, David, and Diane Zimberoff. "REM and non-REM dreams: Dreaming without a dreamer." *Journal of Heart Centered Therapies* 15, no. 2 (2012): 27–52.

Hartmann, Ernest. "Why Do We Dream?" *Scientific American,* July 10, 2006. www .scientificamerican.com/article/why-do-we-dream [accessed Feb. 26, 2016].

Hearne, Keith. *The Dream Machine: Lucid Dreams and How to Control Them.* Aquarian Press, 1990.

———. "Insight into Lucid Dreams." *Nursing Mirror* 150, no. 1 (1980): 2–22.

Hobson, A., and U. Voss. "A mind to go out of: Reflections on primary and secondary consciousness." *Conscious and Cognition* 20 (2011): 993–97.

Hobson, J. Allan. *The Dreaming Brain: How the Brain Creates Both the Sense and the Nonsense of Dreams.* New York: Basic Books, 1989.

———. "REM sleep and dreaming: towards a theory of proto-consciousness." *Nature Reviews: Neuroscience* 10, no. 11 (2009): 803–14.

Hobson, J. Allan, and R. McCarley. "The brain is a dream state generator: An activation-synthesis hypothesis of the dream process." *American Journal of Psychiatry* 134 (1977): 1335–48.

Holzinger, Brigitte. "Lucid Dreaming in Psychotherapy." In *Lucid Dreaming: New Perspectives on Consciousness in Sleep,* vol. 1, edited by Ryan Hurd and Kelly Bulkeley, 37–62. Santa Barbara, Calif.: Praeger, 2014.

Horikawa, T., M. Tamaki, Y. Miyawaki, and Y. Kamitani. "Neural decoding of visual imagery during sleep." *Science* 340, no. 6132 (2013): 639–42.

Hoyle, Ben. "Science Wakes Up to People's Increasing Ability to Manipulate Their Own Dreams." *Australian Times,* October 18, 2010.

Hunt, Harry T. "Some relations between the cognitive psychology of dreams and dream phenomenology." *Journal of Mind and Behavior* 7, nos. 2–3 (1986): 213–28.

Hurd, Ryan. *Big Dreams: Psi, Lucid Dreaming and Borderlands of Consciousness (Dream Like a Boss Book 2)*. Dream Studies Press, 2015.

———. "The Doppelgänger: Facing the Otherworldly Mirror." Dream Studies Portal. http://dreamstudies.org/2011/11/09/doppelganger-spirit-double-theories [accessed Mar. 1, 2016]

———. *Dream Like A Boss: Sleep Better, Dream More and Wake Up to What Matters Most*. Dream Studies Press, 2014.

———. "Exploring the Void in Lucid Dreaming." Dream Studies Portal. http://dreamstudies.org/2010/05/13/exploring-the-void-in-lucid-dreaming [accessed Mar. 6, 2016].

———. "Guarding the Threshold: The Use of Amulets and Liminal Objects for Sleep Paralysis Night-mares." http://dreamstudies.org/2012/11/30/guarding-the-threshold-the-use-of-amulets-and-liminal-objects-for-sleep-paralysis-night-mares [accessed Mar. 4, 2016].

———. "Initial Findings about Galantamine's Effect on Lucid Dreaming Qualities." July 16, 2015. http://dreamstudies.org/2015/07/16/initial-findings-about-galantamines-effect-on-lucid-dreaming-qualities [accessed Feb. 27, 2016].

———. "Lucid Dreaming Masks: Reviewing the Next Generation." Dream Studies Portal. http://dreamstudies.org/2012/07/06/lucid-dreaming-masks-reviewing-the-next-generation [accessed Feb. 29, 2016].

———. "Lucid Dreaming as Shamanic Consciousness." Reality Sandwich, 2011. http://realitysandwich.com/57338/lucid_dreaming_shamanic_consciousness/#/_edn7 [accessed Mar. 7, 2016].

———. "Unearthing the Paleolithic Mind in Lucid Dreams." In *Lucid Dreaming: New Perspectives on Consciousness in Sleep,* vol. 1, edited by Ryan Hurd and Kelly Bulkeley, 277–324. Santa Barbara, Calif.: Praeger, 2014.

Hurd, Ryan, and Kelly Bulkeley, eds. *Lucid Dreaming: New Perspectives on Consciousness in Sleep.* 2 vols. Santa Barbara, Calif.: Praeger, 2014.

Irwin, Harvey J. *Flight of Mind: A Psychological Study of the Out-of-Body Experience.* Metuchen, N.J.: Scarecrow Press, 1986.

———. "Out of Body Experiences and Dream Lucidity." In *Conscious Mind, Sleeping Brain: Perspectives on Lucid Dreaming,* edited by Jayne Gackenbach and Stephen LaBerge, 353–71. New York: Plenum, 1988.

James1982, "What's the deal with hands and lucid dreaming?" July 22, 2011. www.abovetopsecret.com/forum/thread731498/pg1.

Johnson, Clare R. "Magic, Meditation, and the Void: Creative Dimensions of Lucid Dreaming." In *Lucid Dreaming: New Perspectives on Consciousness in Sleep,* vol. 2, edited by Ryan Hurd and Kelly Bulkeley, 45–71. Santa Barbara, Calif.: Praeger, 2014.

Jung, Carl Gustav. *Dreams*. (From volumes 4, 8, 12, and 16 of *The Collected Works of C. G. Jung*). Jung Extract Series. Foreword by Sonu Shamdasani. Translated by R. F. C. Hull. Princeton University Press, 2010.

———. *Memories, Dreams, Reflections*. Edited by Aniela Jaffe Jung. New York: Pantheon Books, 1963.

———. *The Psychogenesis of Mental Disease*. Vol. 3 of *The Collected Works of C. G. Jung*. Princeton, N.J.: Princeton University Press, 1960.

Kaku, Michio. *Parallel Worlds: A Journey through Creation, Higher Dimensions, and the Future of the Cosmos*. New York: Anchor, 2005.

Karacan, I., C. A. Moore, M. Hirshkowitz, S. Sahmay, E. M. Narter, Y. Tokat, and L. Tuncel. "Uterine activity during sleep." *Sleep* 9, no. 3 (1986): 393–98.

Kärkkäinen, J., T. Forsström, J. Tornaeus, K. Wähälä, P. Kiuru, A. Honkanen, U.-H. Stenman, U. Turpeinen, and A. Hesso. "Potentially hallucinogenic 5-hydroxytryptamine receptor ligands bufotenine and dimethyltryptamine in blood and tissues." *Scandinavian Journal of Clinical and Laboratory Investigation* 65, no. 3 (2005): 189–99.

Kasatkin, Vasily N. *Theory of Dreams*. Leningrad: Meditsina, 1967. http://bigbasepd .tk/catalog-013/a-theory-of-dreams.pdf [accessed Feb. 18, 2016].

Kaufman, Rachel. "Dreams Make You Smarter, More Creative, Studies Suggest." *National Geographic,* August 13, 2010.

Kay, A. S. "Psychedelics and Lucid Dreaming: Doorways in the Mind." http:// library.macewan.ca/lucidity/Issue7_1/LL7_1_Kay.htm.

Kellogg, Edward W. "Lucid Dream Healing Experiences: Firsthand Accounts." Paper presented at the Association for the Study of Dreams (ASD) Conference, Santa Cruz, Calif., July 6–10, 1999.

———. "The Lucid Dream Information Technique." *Lucid Dream Exchange,* December 2004. www.improverse.com/ed-articles/ed_kellogg_2005_sep_lde _challenge_dec04.htm [accessed Mar. 6, 2016].

———. "Mutual lucid dream event." *Dream Time* 14, no. 2 (1997): 32–34.

———. "A Personal Experience in Lucid Dream Healing." *Lucidity Letter* 8, no. 1 (1989): 6–7.

———. "Tails of the Astral Plane." Paper presented at the International Association for the Study of Dreaming 11th PsiberDreaming Conference, Sept. 23–Oct. 7, 2012. http://asdreams.org/telepathy/kellogg_articles/ KelloggPDC2012TOTAP.pdf [accessed Mar. 3, 2016].

Kharitidi, Olga. *The Master of Lucid Dreams*. Charlottesville, Va.: Hampton Roads Publishing, 2001.

Krippner, Stanley. "A Pilot Study in Dream Telepathy with the Grateful Dead." http://stanleykrippner.weebly.com/a-pilot-study-in-dream-telepathy-with-the -grateful-dead.html [accessed Mar. 1, 2016].

——. "A psychic dream? Be careful who you tell." *Dream Network* 14, no. 3 (1995): 35–36.

——. "The psychology of shamans and shamanism." *Dreamtime* 21, no. 1 (2004): 10–12.

Krippner, Stanley, Fariba Bogzaran, and André Percia de Carvalho. *Extraordinary Dreams and How to Work with Them* (SUNY Series in Dream Studies). Albany, N.Y.: State University of New York Press, 2002.

Krippner, Stanley, and L. Faith. "Exotic dreams: A cross-cultural survey." *Dreaming* 11 (2001): 73–82.

Labate, Beatriz Caiuby, and Clancy Cavnar, eds. *Ayahuasca Shamanism in the Amazon and Beyond.* New York: Oxford University Press, 2014.

LaBerge, Stephen. *Lucid Dreaming: A Concise Guide to Awakening in Your Dreams and in Your Life.* Boulder, Co.: Sounds True, 2004, 2009.

——. *Lucid Dreaming: The Power of Being Awake and Aware in Your Dreams.* New York: Ballantine, 1986.

——. "Lucid Dreaming: Psychophysical Studies of Consciousness during REM Sleep." In *Sleep and Cognition,* edited by Richard R. Bootzen, John F. Kihlstrom, and Daniel L. Schacter, 109–26. Washington, D.C.: American Psychological Association, 1990.

——. "Lucid Dreaming in Western Literature." In *Conscious Mind, Sleeping Brain: Perspectives on Lucid Dreaming,* edited by Jayne Gackenbach and Stephen LaBerge, 11–25. New York: Plenum, 1988.

——. "The stuff of dreams." *Anthropology of Consciousness* 5, no. 3 (1994): 28–30.

LaBerge, Stephen, and W. C. Dement. "Lateralization of alpha activity for dreamed singing and counting during REM sleep." *Psychophysiology* 19 (1982b): 331–32.

LaBerge, Stephen, W. Greenleaf, and B. Kedzierski. "Physiological responses to dreamed sexual activity during REM sleep." *Psychophysiology* 19 (1983): 454–55.

LaBerge, Stephen, and Lynne Levitan. Substances That Enhance Recall and Lucidity during Dreaming. United States Patent Application 10/604138, June 27, 2003.

——, "Validity established of DreamLight cues for eliciting lucid dreaming." *Dreaming* 5, no. 3 (1995). www.asdreams.org/journal/articles/laberge5-3.htm [accessed Feb. 29, 2016].

LaBerge, Stephen, L. E. Nagel, W. C. Dement, and V. P. Zarcone. "Lucid dreaming verified by volitional communication during REM sleep." *Perceptual and Motor Skills* 52 (1981): 727–32.

LaBerge, Stephen, Leslie Phillips, and Lynne Levitan. "An Hour of Wakefulness before Morning Naps Makes Lucidity More Likely." *NightLight* 6, no. 3 (1994): www .lucidity.com/NL63.RU.Naps.html [accessed Mar. 17, 2016].

LaBerge, Stephen, and Harold Rheingold. *Exploring the World of Lucid Dreaming.* New York: Random House, 1990.

La Marca, K., and Stephen LaBerge. "Pre-sleep treatment with galantamine increases the likelihood of lucid dreaming." Poster session, June 25, 2012, at the annual conference of the International Association for the Study of Dreams, Berkeley, Calif.

Lang, Andrew. *The Book of Dreams and Ghosts.* Amazon Digital Services, 2011.

Lanza, Robert, and Bob Berman. *Biocentrism: How Life and Consciousness are the Keys to Understanding the True Nature of the Universe.* Dallas, Tx.: BenBella Books, 2009.

Laughlin, Charles D. *Communing with Gods: Consciousness, Culture and the Dreaming Brain.* Brisbane, Australia: Daily Grail Publishing, 2011.

Lehrer, Jonah. "Does Marijuana Make You Stupid?" *Wired,* August 2012. www .wired.com/2011/08/does-marijuana-make-you-stupid [accessed Feb. 26, 2016].

Lehrl, S. "Clinical efficacy of kava extract WS 1490 in sleep disturbances associated with anxiety disorders. Results of a multicenter, randomized, placebo-controlled, double-blind clinical trial." *Journal of Affective Disorders* 78, no. 2 (2004): 101–10.

Levitan, Lynne. "Sleep on the right, as a lion doth . . ." *NightLight* 3, no. 3 (1991): 4.

Levitan, Lynne, and Stephen LaBerge. "In the mind and out-of-body." *NightLight* 3, no. 2 (1991): 1–4, 9.

Levitan, Lynne, Stephen LaBerge, Jeanette Edelstein, and Jennifer Dole. "The look and feel and sound of one hand dreaming." *NightLight* 4, no. 3 (1992): 4–8.

Lilly, John C. *Programming and Metaprogramming the Human Biocomputer: Theory and Experiments.* 2nd ed. New York: Three Rivers/Julian Press, 1987.

Love, Daniel. *Are You Dreaming? Exploring Lucid Dreams: A Comprehensive Guide.* Enchanted Loom Publishing, 2013.

Lucas, Dustyn. Online portfolio. http://decovermag.com/artistes/dustyn-lucas [accessed Feb. 17, 2016].

Lutz, Antoine, Lawrence Greishar, Nancy B. Rawlings, Matthieu Ricar, and Richard J. Davidson. "Long-term meditators self-induce high-amplitude gamma synchrony during mental practice." *Proceedings of the National Academy Science* 101, no. 46 (2004): 16369–73.

Madrigal, Alexis C. "The Dark Side of the Placebo Effect." *Atlantic,* Sept. 14, 2011.

Magallon, Linda Lane. *Mutual Dreaming: When Two or More People Share the Same Dream.* New York: Pocket Books, 1997.

Magaña, Sergio. *The Toltec Secret: Dreaming Practices of the Ancient Mexicans.* New York: Hay House, 2014.

Malcolm, Norman. *Dreaming: Studies in Philosophical Psychology.* London: Routledge and Kegan Paul, 1976.

Mandell, Arnold J. "Toward a Psychobiology of Transcendence: God in the Brain." In *The Psychobiology of Consciousness,* edited by Julian M. Davidson and Richard J. Davidson, 379–464. New York: Plenum, 1980.

Martone, Robert. "Scientists Discover Children's Cells Living in Mother's Brains." *Scientific American,* December 2012. www.scientificamerican.com/article/ scientists-discover-childrens-cells-living-in-mothers-brain [accessed Mar. 3, 2016].

Masako, T., J. W. Bang, T. Watanabe, and Y. Sasaki. "Night Watch in One Brain Hemisphere during Sleep Associated with the First-Night Effect in Humans." *Current Biology* 16, no. 9 (2016): 1190–94.

Maury, Louis Ferdinand Alfred. *Le sommeil et les reves. Études psychologiques sur ces phénomènes et les divers états qui s'y rattachent, suivies de recherches sur le développement de l'instinct et de l'intelligence dans leurs rapports avec le phénomène du sommeil.* Paris: Didier et Cie, 1861. Available at https://play.google .com/store/books.

Mayagoitia L., Jose-Luis Diaz, and Carlos M. Contreras. "Study on *Calea zacatechichi* (Dream Herb)." *Journal of Ethnopharmacology* 18 (1986): 229–43.

Mays, Robert, and Suzanne Mays. "Phantom limb 'touch' suggests that a 'mind-limb' extends beyond the physical body." Paper presented at Toward a Science of Consciousness Conference, Tucson, Arizona, 2008. http://selfconsciousmind .com/phantomlimbresearch [accessed Mar. 4, 2016].

McCormick, L., T. Nielsen, M. Ptito, F. Hassainia, A. Ptito, J. G. Villemure, C. Vera, and J. McNamara, P., J. Clark, and E. Hartman. "Handedness and dream content." *Dreaming* 8, no. 1 (1998): 15–22.

McCreery, Charles. "Schizotypy and Out-of-Body Experiences." Unpublished Oxford University Ph.D. thesis, 1993, quoted in Celia Green and Charles McCreery, *Lucid Dreaming: The Paradox of Consciousness during Sleep.* New York: Routledge, 1994.

McKenna, Terence. "Trialogue: Cannabis." Psychedelic Salon.com Podcast 124. https://archive.org/details/PsychedelicSalon121-122-trialogue-1991 [accessed April 11, 2016].

McMoneagle, Joseph, and Edwin C. May. *Memoirs of a Psychic Spy: The Remarkable Life of U.S. Government Remote Viewer 001.* Charlottesville, Va.: Hampton Roads Publishing Co., 2006.

McNamara, Patrick. *Nightmares: The Science and Solution of those Frightening Visions during Sleep.* Westport, Conn.: Praeger, 2008.

———. "Precognitive Dreams." *Psychology Today,* July 30, 2011. www.psychologytoday
.com/blog/dream-catcher/201107/precognitive-dreams [accessed Mar. 3, 2016].

Mithoefer, M. C., M. T. Wagner, A. T. Mithoefer, L. Jerome, and R. Doblin. "The safety and efficacy of ±3,4-methylenedioxymethamphetamine-assisted psychotherapy in subjects with chronic, treatment-resistant posttraumatic stress disorder: The first randomized controlled pilot study." *Journal of Psychopharmacology* 25, no. 6 (2011): 852.

Moers-Messmer, Harold von. "Traume mit der gleichzeitigen erkenntnis des traumzustandes" [Dreams with concurrent knowledge of the dream state]. *Archives fur Psycologie* 102 (1938): 291–318.

Monroe, Robert. *Far Journeys.* New York: Broadway Books, 2001.

———. *Journeys Out of the Body.* New York: Broadway Books, 1992.

———. "Wanted: New Mapmakers of the Mind." *Lucidity Letter* 4, no. 2 (1985): 47–53.

Montplaisir, J. "REM sleep dream mentation in right hemispherectomized patients." *Neuropsychologia* 35, no. 5 (1997): 695–701.

Moorcroft, William H. *Understanding Sleep and Dreaming.* New York: Springer, 2013.

Mordvintsev, Alexander, Christopher Olah, and Mike Tyka. "Inceptionism: Going Deeper into Neural Networks." June 17, 2015. http://googleresearch.blogspot .co.uk/2015/06/inceptionism-going-deeper-into-neural.html [accessed Feb. 29, 2016].

Morin, Roc. "What People around the World Dream About." *Atlantic,* May 14, 2015.

Morley, Charlie. *Dreams of Awakening: Lucid Dreaming and Mindfulness of Dream and Sleep.* New York: Hay House, 2013.

Moss, Robert. *Active Dreaming: Journeying Beyond Self-Limitation to a Life of Wild Freedom.* Novato, Calif.: New World Library, 2011.

———. *Conscious Dreaming: A Spiritual Path for Everyday Life.* New York: Three Rivers Press, 1996.

———. *Dreamgates: Exploring the Worlds of Soul, Imagination, and Life beyond Death.* Novato, Calif.: New World Library, 2010.

———. *Dreaming the Soul Back Home: Shamanic Dreaming and Becoming Whole.* Novato, Calif.: New World Library, 2012.

———. *The Secret History of Dreaming.* Novato, Calif.: New World Library, 2010.

Murray, Robin M., M. C. H. Oon, R. Rodnight, J. L. T. Birley, and A. Smith. "Increased excretion of dimethyltryptamine and certain features of psychosis: A possible association." *Archives of General Psychiatry* 36, no. 6 (1979): 644–49.

Nicholls, Graham. *Navigating the Out-Of-Body Experience: Radical New Techniques.* Woodbury, Minn.: Llewellyn Worldwide, 2012.

Nielsen, Tore A. "Mentation during Sleep: The NREM/REM Distinction." In

Handbook of Behavioral State Control, edited by Ralph Lydic and Helen A. Baghdoyan, 101–28. Boca Raton, Fla.: CRC Press, 1999.

Nielsen, Tore A., and Philippe Stenstrom. "What are the memory sources of dreaming?" *Nature* 437, no. 27 (2005): 1286–89.

Nielsen, Tore A., Tomoka Takeuchi, Sebastien Saucier, Jessica Lara-Carrasco, Elizaveta Solomonova1, and Emilie Martel. "Partial REM-sleep deprivation increases the dream-like quality of mentation from REM sleep and sleep onset." *Sleep* 28, no. 9 (2005): 1083–89.

Nietzsche, Friedrich. *Human, All-Too-Human.* Prometheus Books, 2009.

Novick, Rebecca McClen, and David Jay Brown. *Voices from the Edge: Conversations with Jerry Garcia, Ram Dass, Annie Sprinkle, Matthew Fox, Jaron Lanier, and Others.* Brainchild Productions, 2013.

O'Flaherty, Wendy Doniger. "The uses and misuses of other people's myths." *Journal of the American Academy of Religion* 54 (1986): 219–39.

Oldis, D. "Can We Turn Our Dreams Into Watchable Movies?" *The Huffington Post,* February 4, 2016. www.huffingtonpost.com/dreamscloud/can-we-turn -our-dreams-in_b_9152612.html [accessed April 11, 2016].

Oneironaut: Explorer of the Dream World. https://vimeo.com/3971434.

Ouspensky, Peter D. *A New Model of the Universe.* Alfred A. Knopf, 1967.

———. *On the Study of Dreams and Hypnotism.* Kessinger, 2010.

Pace-Schott, Edward F. *Sleep and Dreaming: Scientific Advances and Reconsiderations.* Cambridge, UK: Cambridge University Press, 2003.

Padgett, Jason. *Struck by Genius: How a Brain Injury Made Me a Mathematical Marvel.* New York: Houghton Mifflin Harcourt, 2014.

Page, Larry. Transcript of 2009 commencement address to the University of Michigan. http://googlepress.blogspot.com/2009/05/larry-pages-university-of -michigan.html.

Palhano-Fontes, F., K. C. Andrade, L. F. Tofoli, A. C. Santos, J. A. Crippa, J. E. Hallak, S. Ribeiro, and D. B. de Araujo. "The psychedelic state induced by ayahuasca modulates the activity and connectivity of the default mode network." *PLoS One* 10, no. 2 (2015): doi:10.1371/journal.pone.0118143.

"Parkinson Disease." *New York Times,* Health Guide, July 30, 2014. www.nytimes .com/health/guides/disease/parkinsons-disease/levadopa-(l-dopa).html [accessed Feb. 26, 2016].

Parnia, Sam, K. Spearpoint, G. de Vos, P. Fenwick, D. Goldberg, J. Yang, J. Zhu et al. "AWARE—AWAreness during REsuscitation—A prospective study." *Resuscitation* 85, no. 12 (2014): 1799–805.

Parnia, Sam, and Josh Young. *Erasing Death: The Science That Is Rewriting the Boundaries between Life and Death.* New York: HarperOne, 2014.

Persinger, M. A., and S. Krippner. "Dream ESP Experiments and Geomagnetic Activity." *Journal of Psychical Research* 83 (1989): 101–15.

Pert, Candace B. *Molecules of Emotion: The Science behind Mind-Body Medicine.* New York: Touchstone, 1999.

Peters, Larry G., and D. Price-Williams. "Towards an experiential analysis of shamanism." *American Ethnologist* 7 (1980): 397–418.

Petri, Giovanni, Paul Expert, F. Turkheimer, Robin Carhart-Harris, David Nutt, Peter J. Hellyer, and Francesco Vaccarino. "Homological scaffolds of brain functional networks." *Journal of the Royal Society Interface* 11, no. 101 (2014). doi:10.1098/rsif.2014.0873.

Pickover, Clifford A. *Sex, Drugs, Einstein, and Elves: Sushi, Psychedelics, Parallel Universes and the Quest for Transcendence.* Smart Publications, 2005.

Pilcher, Helen. "Dreamless woman remains healthy: Stroke study suggests humans can live without dreams." *Nature,* Sept. 10, 2004. doi:10.1038/news040906-16.

Poirier, Sylvie. "'This Is Good Country. We Are Good Dreamers': Dreams and Dreaming in the Australian Western Desert." In *Dream Travelers: Sleep Experiences in the Western Pacific,* edited by Roger Ivar Lohmann, 107–26. New York: Palgrave, 2003.

Pollan, Michael. "The Trip Treatment." *New Yorker,* February 9, 2015.

Post, Tim. "Educational Frontiers of Training Lucid Dreamers." In *Lucid Dreaming: New Perspectives on Consciousness in Sleep,* vol. 1, edited by Ryan Hurd and Kelly Bulkeley, 127–44. Santa Barbara, Calif.: Praeger, 2014.

"Psi-chedelic Science: An Approach to Understanding Exceptional Human Experience." www.maps.org/news-letters/v21n1/v21n1-59to60.pdf [accessed Mar. 1, 2016].

Radin, Dean. *The Conscious Universe: The Scientific Truth of Psychic Phenomena.* New York: HarperOne, 2009.

———. "Electrodermal presentiments of future emotions." *Journal of Scientific Exploration* 18, no. 2 (2004): 253–73.

———. "Unconscious perception of future emotions: An experiment in presentiment." *Journal of Scientific Exploration* 11, no. 2 (1997): 163–80.

Ragno, Kristin. "Why skullcap is one of my all-time favourite medicinal plants." http://kristenragno.com/why-skullcap-is-one-of-my-all-time-favourite-medicinal-plants/ [accessed April 1, 2016].

"Reality Fishing." In *Salvia Divinorum and Salvinorin A: The Best of the Entheogen Review 1992–2000,* 2nd ed., ER Monograph Series no. 2, edited by David Aardvark. The Entheogen Review, 2005.

Reed, Henry R. "Learning to remember dreams." *Journal of Humanistic Psychology* 13 (1973): 33–48.

Regalado, Antonio. "The Thought Experiment: A Brain-Controlled Robotic Arm." *MIT Technology Review*, June 17, 2014. www.technologyreview.com/featuredstory/528141/the-thought-experiment [accessed Feb. 29, 2016].

Reiss, Diana. *The Dolphin in the Mirror: Exploring Dolphin Minds and Saving Dolphin Lives*. New York: Houghton Mifflin Harcourt, 2011.

Revonsuo, A. The reinterpretation of dreams: An evolutionary hypothesis of the function of dreaming." *Behavioral and Brain Sciences* 23, no. 6 (2000): 877–901; discussion 904–1121.

Richardson, Hayley. "Psychedelic Drugs 'Safe as Riding a Bike or Playing Soccer.'" *Newsweek*, April 1, 2015.

Riley, A. "Bees learn while they sleep and that means they might dream." BBC, June 25, 2016. http://www.bbc.com/earth/story/20160621-do-bees-dream [accessed July 6, 2016].

RosieD. "Aggressive alters and dream visitors." PsychForums, May 5, 2011. www.psychforums.com/dissociative-identity/topic63764.html [accessed Mar. 1, 2016].

Rupprecht, C. S. "Our unacknowledged ancestors: Dream theorists of antiquity, the Middle Ages, and the Renaissance." *Psychiatric Journal of the University of Ottawa* 15, no. 2 (1990): 117–22.

Rycroft, Charles. *The Innocence of Dreams*. New York: Pantheon, 1979.

Saint-Denys, Marquis d'Hervey. *Dreams and How to Guide Them*. Translated by Nicholas Fry. Edited by Morton Schatzman. London: Duckworth, 1982.

———. *Les rêves et les moyens de les diriger; observations pratiques*. Paris: Amyot, 1867. English translation available online at https://openlibrary.org.

Sampson, Harold. "Psychological effects of deprivation of dreaming sleep." *Journal of Nervous and Mental Diseases* 143, no. 4 (1966): 305–17.

Sartori, Penny. *The Near-Death Experiences of Hospitalized Intensive Care Patients: A Five-Year Clinical Study*. Lewiston, N.Y.: Edwin Mellen Press, 2008.

Schredl, Michael. "Creativity and dream recall." *Journal of Creative Behavior* 29, no. 1 (1995): 16–24.

———. "Questionaire and diaries as research instruments in dream research: Methodological issues." *Dreaming* 12 (2002): 17–26.

Schredl, Michael, and Daniel Erlacher. "Frequency of lucid dreaming in a representative German sample." *Perceptual and Motor Skills* 112, no. 1 (2011): 104–8.

"Scientists Measure Dream Content for the First Time: Dreams Activate the Brain in a Similar Way to Real Actions." *Science Daily*, Oct. 28, 2011. www.sciencedaily.com/releases/2011/10/111028113626.htm [accessed Feb. 19, 2016].

Serafetinides, E. A., J. T. Shurley, and R. E. Brooks. "Electroencephalogram of the pilot whale, *Globicephala scammoni*, in wakefulness and sleep: Lateralization aspects." *International Journal of Psychobiology* 2 (1972): 129–35.

Servillo, L., A. Giovane, M. L. Balestrieri, R. Casale, D. Cautela, and D. Castaldo. "Citrus genus plants contain N-methylated tryptamine derivatives and their 5-hydroxylated forms." *Journal of Agricultural and Food Chemistry* 61, no. 21 (2013): 5156–62.

Servillo, Luigi, Alfonso Giovane, Maria Luisa Balestrieri, Domenico Cautela, and Domenico Castaldo. "N-Methylated tryptamine derivatives in Citrus genus plants: Identification of N,N,N-trimethyltryptamine in bergamot." *Journal of Agricultural and Food Chemistry* 60, no. 37 (2012): 9512–18.

Shanon, Benny. *The Antipodes of the Mind: Charting the Phenomenology of the Ayahuasca Experience.* Oxford, UK: Oxford University Press, 2002.

Sheldrake, Rupert. *The Sense of Being Stared At: And Other Aspects of the Extended Mind.* New York: Arrow, 2004.

———. *Seven Experiments That Could Change the World.* Rochester, Vt.: Park Street Press, 2002.

Sherwood, Simon J., and Christopher A. Roe. "A review of dream ESP studies conducted since the Maimonides dream ESP programme." *Journal of Consciousness Studies* 10, nos. 6–7 (2003): 85–109.

Shirley, Ralph. *The Mystery of the Human Double: The Case for Astral Projection.* University Books, 1965.

Shohet, Robin. *Dream Sharing.* Turnstone Press, 1985.

Shroomery. www.shroomery.org/forums/showflat.php/Number/5427986.

Shulgin, Alexander, and Ann Shulgin. "DMT Is Everywhere." In *TIHKAL: The Continuation,* 247–85. Berkeley, Calif.: Transform Press, 1997.

Smith, Carlyle. "Can healthy, young adults uncover personal details of unknown target individuals in their dreams?" *Explore: The Journal of Science and Healing* 9, no. 1 (2013): 17–25.

Smith, Robert C. "Do dreams reflect a biological state?" *Journal of Nervous and Mental Disease* 175, no. 4 (1987): 201–7.

———. "Traumatic dreams as an early warning of health problems." In *Dreamtime and Dreamwork: Decoding the Language of the Night,* edited by Stanley Krippner, 226–27. Los Angeles, Calif.: Jeremy Tarcher, 1990.

Soik, Hunter Lee. Linkedin profile: www.linkedin.com/in/hunterleesoik [accessed Mar. 2, 2016].

Solms, Mark. "Dreaming and REM sleep are controlled by different brain mechanisms." *Behavioral and Brain Science* 23 (2000): 843–50.

Soon, Chun Siong, Marcel Brass, Hans-Jochen Heinze, and John-Dylan Haynes. "Unconscious determinants of free decisions in the human brain." *Nature Neuroscience* 11 (2008): 543–45.

Soothill, William Edward. *The Three Religions of China: Lectures Delivered at Oxford*. New York, London, and Toronto: Hodder and Stoughton, 1913.

Sparrow, Gregory Scott. *Lucid Dreaming: Dawning of the Clear Light*. A.R.E. Press, 1982.

Springer, Sally P., and Georg Deutsch. *Left Brain, Right Brain: Perspectives From Cognitive Neuroscience*. New York: W. H. Freeman and Co., 2001.

Stevens, Anthony. *Private Myths: Dreams and Dreaming*. Cambridge, Mass.: Harvard University Press, 1996.

Stevenson, Robert Louis. "A Chapter on Dreams." In *Across the Plains: With Other Memories and Essays*, 206–30. London: Chatto and Windus, 1892.

St. John, Graham. *Mystery School in Hyperspace: A Cultural History of DMT*. Berkeley, Calif.: Evolver Editions, 2015.

"Story of Narada." http://dropyourhat.blogspot.it/2013/03/the-story-of-narada .html [accessed Mar. 5, 2016].

Strassman, Rick. *DMT, The Spirit Molecule: A Doctor's Revolutionary Research into the Biology of Near-Death and Mystical Experiences*. Rochester, Vt.: Park Street Press, 2001.

Stumbrys, Tadas, and Daniel Erlacher. "Lucid dreaming during NREM sleep: Two case reports." *International Journal of Dream Research* 5, no. 2 (2012): 151–55.

———. "The Science of Lucid Dream Induction." In *Lucid Dreaming: New Perspectives on Consciousness in Sleep*, vol. 1, edited by Ryan Hurd and Kelly Bulkeley, 77–102. Santa Barbara, Calif.: Praeger, 2014.

Szpakowska, Kasia. "Through the Looking Glass: Dreams in Ancient Egypt." In *Dreams: A Reader on Religious, Cultural and Psychological Dimensions of Dreaming*, edited by Kelly Bulkeley, 29–44. New York: Palgrave MacMillan, 2001.

Tagliazucchi, E., R. Carhart-Harris, R. Leech, D. Nutt, and D. R. Chialvo. "Enhanced repertoire of brain dynamical states during the psychedelic experience." *Human Brain Mapping* 35, no. 11 (2014): 5442–56.

Taitz, Isaac Y. "Clinical Applications of Lucid Dreaming Therapy." In *Lucid Dreaming: New Perspectives on Consciousness in Sleep*, vol. 1, edited by Ryan Hurd and Kelly Bulkeley, 167–92. Santa Barbara, Calif.: Praeger, 2014.

Tart, Charles T. *The End of Materialism: How Evidence of the Paranormal Is Bridging Science and Spirit*. Oakland, Calif.: New Harbinger, 2009.

———. "The High Dream: A New State of Consciousness." In *Altered States of Consciousness*, edited by Charles Tart, 169-174. New York: John Wiley and Sons/Anchor, 1969.

———. "A psychophysiological study of out-of-the-body experiences in a selected subject." *Journal of the American Society for Psychical Research* 62, no. 1 (1968): 3–27.

———. "Towards the experimental control of dreaming: A review of the literature." *Psychological Bulletin* 64, no. 2 (1965): 88.

Tarthang Tulku. *Openness Mind: Self-knowledge and Inner Peace through Meditation.* Berkeley, Calif.: Dharma Publishing, 1978.

"Time Dilation in Lucid and Non-Lucid Dreams." http://mortalmist.com/forum/index.php?PHPSESSID=6bpi2ut1d2muso0ovdg8c3p9h0&topic=6105.0;wap2 [accessed Mar. 5, 2016].

Tong, F., and M. S. Pratte. "Decoding patterns of human brain activity." *Annual Review of Psychology* 63 (2012): 483–509.

Torda, Clara. "Contribution to serotonin theory of dreaming (LSD infusion)." *New York State Journal of Medicine* 68 (1968): 1135–38.

"Transmitting Thought: A Documentary on the Famous Maimonides Dream Telepathy Experiments." *Daily Grail,* June 2015. http://dailygrail.com/mind -mysteries/2015/6/transmitting-thought-documentary-the-famous-maimonides -dream-telepathy-experim [accessed Mar. 4, 2016].

Tuccillo, Dylan, Jared Zeizel, and Thomas Peisel. *A Field Guide to Lucid Dreaming: Mastering the Art of Oneironautics.* New York: Workman Publishing Company, 2013.

Ullman, Montague, Stanley Krippner, and Alan Vaughan. *Dream Telepathy: Experiments in Nocturnal Extrasensory Perception.* Charlottesville, Va.: Hampton Roads Publishing, 2001.

Valli, Katja, Thea Strandholm, Lauri Sillanmäki, and Antti Revonsuo. "Dreams are more negative than real life: Implications for the function of dreaming." *Cognition and Emotion* 22, no. 5 (2008): 833–61.

Van de Castle, Robert L. *Our Dreaming Mind.* New York: Ballantine Books, 1995.

Van der Helm, Els, and Matthew P. Walker. "Sleep and emotional memory processing." *Sleep Medicine Clinics* 6, no. 1 (2011): 31–43.

Van Eeden, Frederik. "A Study of Dreams." *Proceedings of the Society of Psychical Research* 26 (1913): 431–61.

Van Lommel, Pim. *Consciousness Beyond Life: The Science of the Near-Death Experience.* Repr. ed. New York: HarperOne, 2011.

Van Lommel, Pim, Ruud Van Wees, Vincent Myers, and Ingrid Elfferich. "Near-death experience in survivors of cardiac arrest: A prospective study in the Netherlands." *Lancet* 358, no. 9298 (2001): 2039–45.

"Very, very long dreams." Lucidpedia forum. www.lucidipedia.com/forum .php?section=viewtopic&t=4147 [accessed Mar. 5, 2016].

Voss, Ursula, Romain Holzmann, J. Allan Hobson, Walter Paulus, Judith Koppehele-Gossel, Ansgar Klimke, and Michael A Nitsche. "Induction of self awareness in dreams through frontal low current stimulation of gamma activity." *Nature Neuroscience* 17 (2014): 810–12.

Voss, Ursula, Romain Holzmann, Inka Tuin, J. Allan Hobson. "Lucid dreaming: A state of consciousness with features of both waking and non-lucid dreaming." *Sleep* 32, no. 9 (2009): 1191–200.

Waggoner, Robert. "Learning the Depths of Lucid Dreaming." In *Lucid Dreaming: New Perspectives on Consciousness in Sleep,* vol. 1, edited by Ryan Hurd and Kelly Bulkeley, 193–212. Santa Barbara, Calif.: Praeger, 2014.

———. "A Look at Lucid Dreams and Healing." www.improverse.com/ed-articles/ robert_waggoner_2003_apr_lde_healing.htm [accessed Feb. 19, 2016].

———. *Lucid Dreaming: Gateway to the Inner Self.* Needham, Mass.: Moment Point Press, 2009.

Waggoner, Robert, and Caroline McCready. *Lucid Dreaming, Plain and Simple: Tips and Techniques for Insight, Creativity, and Personal Growth.* San Francisco, Calif.: Conari Press, 2015.

Wagner, U., S. Gais, H. Heider, R. Verleger, and J. Born. "Sleep inspires insight." *Nature* 427, no. 6972 (2004): 352–55.

Wallace, B. Alan, and Brian Hodel. *Dreaming Yourself Awake: Lucid Dreaming and Tibetan Dream Yoga for Insight and Transformation.* Boston, Mass.: Shambhala, 2012.

Wallace, Robert Keith. "Physiological effects of Transcendental Meditation." *Science* 167, no. 3926 (1970): 1751–54.

Wang, Shirley S. "The Benefits of Lucid Dreaming: Researchers Decipher Clues from Those with Greater Awareness, Control of Behavior in Dreams." *Wall Street Journal,* August 12, 2014.

Wangyal, Tenzin. *The Tibetan Yogas of Dream and Sleep.* Edited by Mark Dahlby. Ithaca, N.Y.: Snow Lion, 1998.

Wehr, T. A. "In short photoperiods, human sleep is biphasic." *Journal of Sleep Research* 1, no. 2 (1992): 103–7.

What Are Dreams? Inside the Sleeping Brain. BBC/PBS documentary, 2009.

Wilson, Colin, and John Grant, eds. "The Man from Taured." In *The Directory of Possibilities,* 86. New York: Smithmark Publishing, 1982.

Winkelman, Michael J. *Shamanism: A Biopsychosocial Paradigm of Consciousness and Healing.* Santa Barbara, Calif.: Praeger, 2010.

Winter, Christopher. "Personal Sleep Monitors: Do They Work?" *Huffington Post,* Nov. 2, 2014.

Wolf, Fred Alan. *The Dreaming Universe: A Mind-Expanding Journey into the Realm Where Psyche and Physics Meet.* New York: Touchstone, 1994.

Young, Serinity. "Buddhist Dream Experience: The Role of Interpretation, Ritual and Gender." In *Dreams: A Reader on Religious, Cultural and Psychological Dimensions of Dreaming,* edited by Kelly Bulkeley, 9–28. New York: Palgrave MacMillan, 2001.

"Your Brain on Magic Mushrooms Is Actually Similar to Dreaming, Brain Scan Study Shows." *Huffington Post,* Sept. 5, 2014.

Yuschak, Thomas. *Advanced Lucid Dreaming: The Power of Supplements.* Lulu Enterprises, 2006.

Zappaterra, Mauro, Jim Lysander, Sanjog Pangarkat. "Chronic pain resolution after a lucid dream: A case for neural plasticity?" *Medical Hypotheses* 82, no. 3 (2014): 28–90.

Zimmerman, J., J. Stoyva, and D. Metcalf. "Distorted visual field feedback and augmented REM sleep." *Psychophysiology* 27 (1970): 298–303.

Zoe7. *Back from the Void.* Z Media, 2005.

———. *Into the Void: Exploring Consciousness, Hyperspace and Beyond Using Brain Technology, Psychedelics and Altered-Mind States.* Zon Worldwide Media, 2001.

ONLINE RESOURCES

The International Association for the Study of Dreams (IASD) is "a non-profit, international, multidisciplinary organization dedicated to the pure and applied investigation of dreams and dreaming," and they hold regular conferences:

www.asdreams.org

LDE (Lucid Dreaming Experience), "an independently published quarterly e-zine dedicated to educating and inspiring lucid dreamers everywhere," edited by Robert Waggoner:

www.dreaminglucid.com

The Lucidity Institute, founded by Stephen LaBerge, published a lucid-dream journal called *NightLight* from 1989 to 1995. The issues are archived online, and the institute has been offering intensive training workshops for over twenty years:

www.lucidity.com

Lucidipedia has an active lucid dream forum and offers courses and tutorials in lucid dreaming:

www.lucidipedia.com

The Monroe Institute conducts research into, and offers programs and CDs for developing, OBEs and other altered states of awareness:

www.monroeinstitute.org

Spirit Watch archives the research and writings of Jayne Gackenbach:

www.spiritwatch.ca

Great selections of quality dream enhancing herbs and herbal tinctures:
www.dreamcatcherbotanicals.com
www.iamshaman.com

The REM-Dreamer is available from
www.remdreamer.com

Dream Studies Portal, edited by Ryan Hurd, has great information about lucid dreaming:
www.dreamstudies.org

World of Lucid Dreaming is devoted to articles, essays, and reviews about lucid dreaming:
www.world-of-lucid-dreaming.com

Intelclinic's NeuroOn:
https://neuroon.com

Shadow, app for world's largest dream database:
www.discovershadow.com

iWink's Aurora:
https://iwinks.org

The Lucid Talisman, designed by dream researcher Ryan Hurd and Lee Adams, to help remind us of when we're awake and when we're dreaming:
https://dreamstudies.com/shop/exclusives lucid-dreaming-talisman/

To see some wonderful lucid-dream-inspired paintings, check out artist Dustyn Lucas's website:
http://dustynlucas.com

Clare Johnson's website about creativity and lucid dreaming:
www.DeepLucidDreaming.com

To participate in Lucid Dreaming Day—an annual celebration started by Daniel Love—see:
www.luciddreamingday.com

INDEX

Page numbers in *italics* indicate illustrations.

ABOUT THE AUTHOR

(Photo by Keana Parker,
www.keanaparker.com)

David Jay Brown is the author of *The New Science of Psychedelics: At the Nexus of Culture, Consciousness, and Spirituality*. He is the coauthor of five best-selling volumes of interviews with leading-edge thinkers: *Mavericks of the Mind*, *Voices from the Edge*, *Conversations on the Edge of the Apocalypse*, *Mavericks of Medicine*, and *Frontiers of Psychedelic Consciousness*. Brown is also the author of two science-fiction novels, *Brainchild* and *Virus*, and is the coauthor of the health science book *Detox with Oral Chelation*. He holds a master's degree in psychobiology from New

York University and was responsible for the California-based research in two of British biologist Rupert Sheldrake's books on unexplained phenomena in science, *Dogs That Know When Their Owners Are Coming Home* and *The Sense of Being Stared At*. His work has appeared in a number of magazines, including *Wired, Discover,* and *Scientific American,* and he was the senior editor of the special edition *MAPS Bulletin* (Multidisciplinary Association for Psychedelic Studies) from 2007 to 2012. In 2011, 2012, and 2013, Brown was voted "Best Writer" in the annual *Good Times* and *Santa Cruz Weekly*'s "Best of Santa Cruz" polls, and his news stories have been picked up by the *Huffington Post* and *CBS News*. To find out more about his work see:

www.mavericksofthemind.com